CW00793638

KILLING STRANGERS

Killing Strangers

How Political Violence Became Modern

T. K. WILSON

OXFORD
UNIVERSITY PRESS

OXFORD
UNIVERSITY PRESS

Great Clarendon Street, Oxford, OX2 6DP,
United Kingdom

Oxford University Press is a department of the University of Oxford.
It furthers the University's objective of excellence in research, scholarship,
and education by publishing worldwide. Oxford is a registered trade mark of
Oxford University Press in the UK and in certain other countries

First Edition published in 2020

Impression: 1

Published in the United States of America by Oxford University Press
198 Madison Avenue, New York, NY 10016, United States of America

British Library Cataloguing in Publication Data
Data available

Library of Congress Control Number: 2020930789

ISBN 978–0–19–886350–2

Printed and bound by
CPI Group (UK) Ltd, Croydon, CR0 4YY

To my father, one of the better things to come out of the 1930s
(W.H. Auden's 'low dishonest decade')
and
To my mother (Blitz Baby, 1940)

Preface

Some go in for counting beads
More go in for chasing women
The scholar sits at home and reads:
Give me the glass with porter brimming![1]

I never was much good at maths (or, indeed, seduction). Reading, it is true, has been more of a personal strength (or obsession). But either way, it is certainly now high time for a drink and a chance to reflect. Writing a book is an inevitably educational experience. One learns through a few notorious lapses that self-indulgence does not notably improve self-awareness ('I'm *not* stressed: I'm focused!'). As a pet project, the book so monstrously petted, inevitably becomes a monstrous pet. Weekends and evenings disappear mechanically down its ravenous maw. Even a short book represents a long haul.

So my thanks, first and foremost, to family for waiting with such patience until *Killing Strangers* was finally skewered and dispatched. To my children—to Anna, Jonny, and Rozie—I am sorry for all of my frequent absences, both mental and physical. To Anna—thank you for your help in compiling an ever-shifting bibliography: here you made the great mistake of proving yourself genuinely useful for the future. Jonny and Rozie: I'm sorry that I followed few (any?) of your suggestions as to what this book should really be about. But to all three of my children what matters is this: you are my emotional foundation in this world, and a healthy reminder of how little this book really matters.

To my beloved Denise, all my own words of thanks are tawdry and trite. So I'll plunder some from Friedrich Schiller instead:

Wer ein holdes Weib errungen
Mische seinen Jubel ein!

Which means (roughly):

Whoever has 'won' a lovely wife
He, too, should join in the general jubilation![2]

And I do. Every single day. You have taught me how to live.

My own parents, Tony and Tina Wilson, launched me on this path many years ago in what I now realize was a highly supportive academic environment and succeeding in making intellectual curiosity seem normal and foundational. To them

[1] Clancy Brothers and Tommy Makem, 'Water is alright in Tay': https://genius.com/Clancy-brothers-water-is-alright-in-tay-lyrics

[2] 'Whoever has won a lovely woman/He, too, should join in the rejoicing!' See: https://archive.schillerinstitute.com/transl/schiller_poem/ode_to_joy.pdf

this book is dedicated as a token of appreciation. I hope they will forgive my advertising their ages in it.

Like the Victorian imperialist of whom it was said that his 'knowledge of foreign relations must have been acquired in a music hall' (but without his values), I have been somewhat surprised by my own official apotheosis as an expert in International Relations.[3] I suspect many of my academic colleagues have been, too. And yet these colleagues have welcomed this stray refugee from a history department with nothing but warmth and encouragement since 2011. I deeply appreciate that. Especial thanks are due to Ryan Beasley, Roddy Brett, Caron Gentry, Tony Lang, and Gabriella Slomp for all their personal and professional encouragement down the years. We at St Andrews still miss the untimely loss of Alex Danchev, Nick Rengger, and Mark Currie; as so many further afield doubtless do as well.

More specifically, this book firmly belongs to the Centre for the Study of Terrorism and Political Violence (CSTPV): the oldest such research centre in Europe (founded in 1994) and, I dare to think, still the finest. Somehow I have found myself its Director in 2016. The support of colleagues in this new role has been deeply humbling. My gratitude thus goes to: Diego Muro, Peter Lehr, Bernhard Blumenau, Gilbert Ramsay, Nick Brooke, Kieran McConaghy, and Javier Argomaniz. Everything would have ground to a shuddering halt long ago without the administrative support of Julie Middleton and Kim Cartwright, needless to say. And Gillian Brunton alone knows all she does for the Centre: the lead engineer in the CSTPV Engine Room. We would not get far without her.

None of this would have been possible without the sterling back-up and mentoring given to me down long years by Richard English. His support and mentoring have never flagged, ever since he bought me lunch as a postgraduate student at Queen's University Belfast back in 2001 (and then gave me a job at St Andrews ten years later). He has taught me more than he knows: and I trust he will recognize his influence in some of what follows. Others who seem to have believed in me and from whom I have learnt infinite amounts are: Alvin Jackson, Caoimhe Nic Dháibhéid, Ian McBride, Senia Pašeta, and Roy Foster. In scale, my intellectual debts to Marc Mulholland err towards truly aristocratic excess: I humbly and gratefully acknowledge them here.

Across the Atlantic, Bruce Hoffman at Georgetown has been a huge support and encouragement down long years. I deeply value that friendship. At a crucial juncture, Audrey Cronin thoughtfully hand-delivered a copy of her *Power to the People* to St Andrews—allowing me early sight of a superb study that overlaps with (but I hope does not entirely pre-empt) my own. When I first met Martha Crenshaw c. 2012 she generously expressed an interest in my research on the deep background of political violence. She has had a very long wait to see what I might produce: but I hope this book may still be of some interest to her. Likewise, Max Abrahms has consistently been a heavyweight cheerleader and supporter for CSTPV.

[3] M. Bentley, *Lord Salisbury's World: Conservative Environments in Late Victorian Britain* (Cambridge, 2001).

For all such kindnesses, both formal and informal, I offer sincere thanks. A scholar is truly lucky to have such friends. All have planted many good ideas in my mind. All my errors I harvested without assistance.

Students have also taught me far more than they can possibly realize. I am particularly grateful to Dan Keenan for all support. Librarians and archivists, the Engineering Corps of the Army of Knowledge, were invariably helpful at every turn. We could not advance far without the foundations they lay down. For grace under pressure, therefore, I especially wish to thank the staffs of: St Andrews Library, the British Library, the Bodleian Library, and the National Archives in London. Someone has to fetch the books and files from the stacks.

Someone, too, has to produce the books in the first place. I am indebted to my editor at Oxford University Press, Cathryn Steele both for her general enthusiasm for this project and for her tolerance of its erratic process of generation. I apologize for alternating prolonged silences with occasional slab avalanches of text. As an avowed technophobe who can barely wire a plug, I am grateful to the extraordinarily generous Roger Davies for explaining the long history of explosives to me so patiently. Like so many other researchers, I feel privileged to be able to raid the unique treasure house of information that is the Global Terrorism Database. Long may it thrive.

All work and no play have certainly taken their toll. During the course of writing this book, I once made the mistake of outlining the plot of Stanley Kubrick's classic 1980 horror film *The Shining* to my (then) ten-year-old son, Jonny. I explained in basic outline that the Jack Nicholson character, so-to-speak, 'loses it a bit' after holing up in an out-of-season mountain hotel to write his masterpiece. Weekend disappearances to work on this manuscript were, thereafter, inevitably punctuated by regular telephone calls to ask: 'Daddy, have you gone crazy yet?'

No doubt my own kith and kin have their own answers ready to that particular query.

Readers and reviewers, I dare to hope, may have others.

Contents

List of Figures

A Note on Nomenclature and Geographical Parameters

Definitional dragons such as 'terrorism', 'violence', and 'modernity' must all wait their turn for attempted slaying (however messily). Here I simply wish to note that I interpret the phenomenon of the 'coup' rather narrowly—as an armed putsch, rather than in the broader sense of the state breaking its own constitution to override a parliament.

This is a book primarily about North America and Europe. For convenience, I refer to this trans-Atlantic zone by its traditionalist label; 'The West'. Since these regions comprise the historic heartlands of what is now often called the 'Global North', I sometimes use that term as well (but do not include Japan by it).

It is worth noting that my analytical treatment of 'Europe' is also somewhat fluid. Between 1945 and 1990, for instance, the experience of Soviet-dominated Europe rather fades from view. Besides sporadic doomed uprisings, political violence here overwhelmingly consisted of hijackings to facilitate escape to the West. So in practice my area of focus remains firmly on North America and (Western) Europe; although in an interconnected world of decontextualized borrowings, it occasionally makes sense to glance further afield as well.

Introduction

> All these things belong to the Dark Ages.
>
> – David Cameron, British Prime Minister on the 'Islamic State'[1]

> Standing aghast is an unrewarding posture for anyone trying to pay close attention to the thread of history.
>
> – Franklin L. Ford.[2]

At the heart of this book lies a simple ambition—to explore how forms of political violence have changed over time. Literatures on political violence spread ever larger: new mountain ranges of specialist studies are pushed up every year. The early twenty-first century has turned out to be a Golden Age for studying that very nineteenth-century notion, the 'propaganda of the deed'. And yet it remains a defensible general observation that most scholars involved in this burgeoning field remain far more interested in propaganda than in deeds.

By contrast, this is a book emphatically about 'deeds': or, more precisely, violent actions. Its starting premise is that the changing forms of political violence are well worth studying in detail and in their own right. Rather than treat them merely as incidental phenomena, it seeks to make acts (rather than ideas or ideologies) the central focus of study. It is most interested in 'how' questions: how have acts of political violence changed over time? How have they evolved in conjunction with other forces? And if 'why' questions are entertained, they are deliberately of a 'second order' variety: why does *this* type of violence occur, and not *that*? These may seem small questions. But they cast long shadows. Although a fuller exploration must necessarily wait until later, it is perhaps worth sketching three of the most imposing implications that stem from them here.

First, no general assessment of contemporary political violence in the twenty-first century can avoid some engagement with questions of how far its quality and quantity is truly distinctive—in (at the very least, implicit) comparison with previous ages. And here it seems hard to avoid attempting some analysis of changing patterns of action. General databases of terrorist incidents are indeed enormously helpful here. But very few stretch back more than fifty years; and, by their very nature, they bleach events of context. Arguably, the most interesting big questions—such as whether Western societies underwent a general 'brutalization' pro-

[1] *Daily Telegraph*, 27 September 2014.

[2] Franklin L. Ford, quoted in: R. Lewin, *Hitler's Mistakes* (London, 1984), p. 2.

cess after the First World War; or whether a distinctively 'New Terrorism' arose in the late twentieth century—can only be assessed meaningfully both with close regard to what actually happened, but also against longer term contextual backdrops. Attractively gnostic pronouncements ('terrorism is as old as human civilisation...and as new as this morning's headlines') do not really help us much here.[3]

Secondly, only a relatively fine-grained survey of changing patterns of action can hope to capture something of the relationship between contemporary political violence and modernity. This project is all the more necessary since too often contemporary violence is simply interpreted as representing some profound *failure* of modernization: a medievalism mercurially equipped with machine guns. This is a widespread popular assumption. But it is also one that commands some scholarly support as well. 'Wherever modernization touches societies', writes Michael Mazarr 'it leaves instability and disaffection in its wake'. Hence violence is essentially a symptom of incomplete or unsuccessful transition to modernity.[4] More optimistically, and heavily influenced by the work of Norbert Elias on changing manners, Steven Pinker sees modernity as a broad 'escalator of reason' that sweeps away the 'futility of cycles of violence'.[5] What such approaches have in common is a basic indifference to understanding how violence actually 'works': and the sheer complexity of the relationships between violent acts and both changing technology and changing attitudes.[6]

Finally, and as a related point, a study of actual violent incidents against changing contexts might shed some light on what is one of the most puzzling features of so much contemporary political violence—its stunning impersonality. Acts of 'universal malice'—to borrow the phrasing of the English common law—often seem particularly baffling.[7] But it is precisely here that longer-term historical perspectives prove their value. Seen as a recurrent phenomenon, the bomb at the airport departure gate clearly does *not* belong to the same world of intimate killing that characterizes the pre-modern feud, the vendetta, or the duel. A central assumption of this book is that different types of society will tend to facilitate different types of atrocity. Like broadly parallel (but apolitical) phenomena such as serial or spree killing, the airport bomb belongs to the *Gesellschaft* (a society of impersonal transactions), and not the *Gemeinschaft* (a society shaped primarily by face-to-face relationships). Its victims just happen, as the saying goes, to 'be in the wrong place at the wrong time'. How killing became 'unchained' from inter-personal relationships, then, forms a major running theme of this book.

So a close-up focus on acts of political violence potentially opens up some surprisingly broad vistas of historical enquiry. Yet before they can be surveyed even impressionistically, some dense conceptual undergrowth in the foreground needs

[3] R. Law, *Terrorism: A History* (Cambridge, 2009), p. 1.

[4] M. Mazarr, *Unmodern Men in the Modern World* (Cambridge, 2007), p. 2.

[5] S. Pinker, *The Better Angels of Our Nature* (London, 2011, 2012), p. xxv.

[6] Pinker does not engage at all with the work of Zygmunt Bauman, Eric Hobsbawm, Michael Mann, or Siniša Malešević. Neither does Mazarr.

[7] L. Fairfield (ed.), *The Trial of Peter Barnes and Others: The I.R.A. Coventry Explosion of 1939* (London, 1953), p. 41.

to be cleared. Two impressively prickly thickets stand out above all at first glance: political violence and terrorism. Here my intention is to find a path forward that makes sense—one that allows an attempt to chart, however impressionistically, shifting patterns of violent actions through time and changing contexts. It is not to establish conceptual categories of unimpeachable purity. This is a messy story.

I

How should we study such violence most profitably? Keep the subject area tight, suggests Randall Collins in his study of confrontation: 'not violent individuals, but violent situations' should hold the limelight.[8] It is good advice. A focus on micro-actions involving, or at least threatening, the 'deliberate hurting of others' seems highly advisable.[9] Such tight focusing allows us to discard briskly classic notions such as Johann Galtung's 'structural violence' to describe the fate of those who—to lift a phrase from Bob Dylan—are 'bent out of shape by society's pliers'.[10] Social structures are indeed often deeply oppressive: but this level of analysis risks taking us away from any consideration of grassroots actions.

In general, the leading analysts of violence have tended to resist conceptual stretching and narrowed 'down the definition of violence to its physical dimension'.[11] Randall Collins is particularly forthright in his dismissal here of attempts to expand understandings of what constitutes violence further. '"Symbolic Violence"', he writes, 'is mere theoretical word play; to take it literally would be to grossly misunderstand the nature of real violence'.[12]

And yet the notion of 'symbolic violence' is not quite so easily dismissed: at least in modern societies that pride themselves upon the immaculate maintenance of public order. Here many threats are indeed clearly mainly or 'only' symbolic: but may still constitute a significant disruptive intervention in public life. A bomb at the Eiffel Tower is always newsworthy, even if it was designed to hurt no one. Arguably, we need to leave analytical room for such theatrics in any long-term account of the development of political violence. A parallel point might be made about sabotage. Still, even within this broader field of view, it is at the level of specific actions and threats that we must arguably focus if we are to capture the changing 'quality' of violence over time.

[8] R. Collins, *Violence: A Micro-Sociological Theory* (Princeton, 2008), p. 1.

[9] Popitz quoted in: D. Ellerbrock, 'Gun Violence and Control in Germany 1880–1911: Scandalizing Gun Violence and Changing Perceptions as Preconditions for Firearm Control' in W. Heitmeyer (et al., eds), *Control of Violence: Historical and International Perspectives on Violence in Modern Societies* (New York, 2011), p. 186.

[10] B. Dylan, *Writings and Drawings* (London, 1972, 1987), p. 287; J. Galtung, 'Violence, Peace, and Peace Research', *Journal of Peace Research*, 6 (3) 1969, pp. 170–1. For a usefully wide-ranging discussion: S. Carroll, 'Introduction' in S. Carroll (ed.), *Cultures of Violence: Interpersonal Violence in Historical Perspective* (Basingstoke, 2007), pp. 1–43.

[11] S. Kalyvas, *The Logic of Violence in Civil War* (Cambridge, 2006, 2008), p. 19.

[12] Collins, *Violence*, p. 25.

Keeping a deliberately broad understanding of what might constitute *political* violence also seems sensible. As a shorthand concept, political violence implies some kind of intervention in the exercise of public power from the margins (that is, the state's own violence is rarely described as 'political'). Broadly, I work within the parameters of this general understanding. Yet even here dilemmas remain. One of the old (but still rare) attempts 'to relate assassination to broader social, economic, or political factors' reached the noticeably open-ended conclusion 'only a fraction of political figures who are assassinated are killed for motives that are purely political'.[13] It is a useful reminder that the intentions of those who commit violence are often mixed, or opaque: perhaps even to themselves. Conversely, there is plenty of evidence that the publicity that violence can bring itself represents a form of influence and hence 'power', however fleeting, to truly 'marginal people' or 'killer nerds'.[14] Here Elliot Leyton has offered a powerful account of serial killers as representing a rare but 'logical extension of many of the central themes in their culture—of worldly ambition, of success and failure, and of manly avenging violence'.[15]

Where, then, should one draw the line? Perhaps there are no entirely satisfactory answers here for a study focused on acts rather than intentions. I shall keep the main focus of analysis firmly on acts conventionally understood as 'political': that is, where violence was generally perceived as serving some wider public cause. Yet I shall endeavour to leave room to acknowledge the often close 'family resemblances' and close cultural ties between distinctly modern types of violence that are too often segregated analytically into quite separate categories. After all, the spree killing and the marauding terrorist attack are essentially the same atrocity by different names.

A focus on acts in historical context also avoids the arid definitionalism that has characterized so much analytical discussion of terrorism. Defining a concept like terrorism tightly, and then reverse-engineering a genealogy to suit seems an unpromising way to write a social history of political violence. Despite claims to the contrary, key concepts are anything but 'relatively timeless'.[16] They do not stand outside their time and place. But this is not to say that attempts at definition are entirely useless: it is simply to stress that their value for the historian may be suggestive, rather than proscriptive. Arguably, the chief value of Alex Schmid's monumental definitional labours is their unconsciously modernist assumption of a widespread abstraction of social relations. According to Schmid, terrorism is

> ... an anxiety-inspiring method of repeated violent action employed by (semi-) clandestine individual, group or state actors, for idiosyncratic, criminal, or political reasons, whereby—in contrast to assassination—the direct targets of violence are not the main targets. The immediate human victims of violence are generally chosen ran-

[13] M. C. Havens, C. Leiden, and K. M. Schmitt, *The Politics of Assassination* (Englewood Cliffs, NJ, 1970), pp. 6, 149.

[14] J. Bowyer Bell, *Assassin* (New Brunswick, 1979, 2005), p. 73; A. Goldman, *The Lives of John Lennon* (New York, 1988), p. 669.

[15] E. Leyton, *Hunting Humans* (London, 2001), p. 10.

[16] B. J. Lutz, 'Historical Approaches to Terrorism' in E. Chenoweth (et al., eds), *The Oxford Handbook of Terrorism* (Oxford, 2019), p. 194.

> domly (targets of opportunity) or selectively (representative or symbolic targets) from a target population, and serve as message generators.[17]

Such a usefully provocative definition begs enough questions to keep conferences of historians busy for years. How did such a distinctively indirect type of violence emerge? And under what sort of historical conditions, and in what sort of societies, does a type of violence flourish in which the 'direct targets... are not the main targets'?

These are questions that can all be usefully kept in mind throughout this book. I do not attempt to define exactly where the phenomenon of terrorism begins and ends. Such a shape-shifting term—that has evolved from its common eighteenth- and nineteenth-century usage as implying 'the intimidation of the forces of reaction' into a standard designation for a broad swathe of non-governmental violence—clearly needs to be handled with more analytical care than my broad historical narrative is able to offer.[18] But I do broadly refer to 'terroristic' acts in the Schmidian sense of actions that seem geared to a widespread broadcasting in which individual victims serve as mere 'message generators'. In these cases, the main point remains that these 'particular victims are interchangeable'. They carry semiotic or exchange value only. They are meat cashed in for mass publicity.[19]

In general, this shift towards depersonalized killing remains one of the least explained features of the broader transformation of Western societies into late modernity. This study attempts to make some sense of this evolving quality of public cruelty with reference to wider forces along the lines rather impressionistically sketched by Ze'ev Iviansky way back in 1977. Such 'individual terror' was, Iviansky asserted, 'one of the manifestations of the modern age of violence, a symptom and expression of the great changes taking place in the spheres of social stratification, government, technology, ideology and revolutionary activity'.[20] Yet this approach begs fresh questions in its turn about what parameters should be placed upon the search for origins. How far back should we look? And where?

II

On the morning of 11 November 1918, the German machine gunners near Mons fired off their ammunition up until the stroke of 11 o'clock. Then they rose, bowed, turned, and walked away from the war.[21] Even in defeat there could hardly have

[17] A. P. Schmid, 'The Definition of Terrorism' in A. P. Schmid (ed.), *The Routledge Handbook of Terrorism Research* (Abingdon, 2011, 2013), p. 61.

[18] I owe this felicitous phrasing to Marc Mulholland.

[19] L. Richardson, *What Terrorists Want: Understanding the Terrorist Threat* (London, 2006), p. 22.

[20] Z. Iviansky, 'Individual Terror: Concept and Typology', *Journal of Contemporary History*, 12 (1), 1977, p. 44.

[21] H. Hagenlücke, 'Germany and the Armistice' in H. Cecil and P. H. Liddle (eds), *At the Eleventh Hour: Reflections, Hopes and Anxieties at the Closing of the Great War, 1918* (Barnsley, 1998), p. 37; J. E. Persico, *11th Month, 11th Day, 11th Hour: Armistice Day 1918: World War One and Its Violent Climax* (London, 2004), p. 353.

been a more impressive demonstration of the modern state's ability to turn on, and off, titanic quantities of destruction at will. Just a few weeks later, in a celebrated lecture, the great sociologist Max Weber was to elevate precisely this ability to the status of a definition: a state, he argued, was an entity that claims a monopoly of legitimate violence within a defined territory.[22] And yet as Weber knew only too well as the German Revolution bubbled away in the background, that monopoly was never total: and the 'illegitimate' violence committed by those who do not wear uniforms is never banished totally, or at least not so for long. Even the most stable state will face such 'residual' violence in the shape of acute political unrest from time to time.

A full century on from the guns falling silent upon the Western Front (but opening up on the streets of Berlin) seems an appropriate moment to reflect upon *western* traditions of violence. Deliberately this study concentrates upon those strong states that were globally dominant from the late eighteenth to the opening of the twenty-first century: those of Europe and America—the core of what is now often termed 'the Global North'. Dynamically capitalist and militarily overbearing, this mere handful of societies upended established orders across the globe. Yet at the same time profound social transformations *within* the Global North themselves proved conducive to the emergence of new constellations of violence.

Of course, such changes were never simply self-generating: nor hermetically sealed. It could hardly be otherwise during an age when European powers were so aggressively seeking to incorporate much of the globe into their own economic systems and formal empires. Despite asymmetries of power and influence, a-contextual borrowings of violent tactics and technologies were almost inevitable under such conditions. And they flowed in all directions. Russia has long conventionally been seen as a sort of 'terrorism laboratory' after 1878: the action templates of *Narodnya Volya* ('the People's Will')—in particular, its early and enthusiastic adoption of dynamite—were soon revered and copied much further west.[23] At the same time Indian nationalists were also not slow to exploit new western technologies of destruction against British dominance.[24] And yet there still seems some merit in re-focusing analytical attention back upon western societies as incubators of

[22] H.H. Gerth and C. Wright Mills (eds), *From Max Weber: Essays in Sociology* (London, 1948, 1977), p. 78.

[23] The literature on the Narodnya Volna and its successors is vast. See: A. Anemone (ed.), *Just Assassins: The Culture of Terrorism in Russia* (Evanston, ILs, 2010); L. Clutterbuck, 'The Progenitors of Terrorism: Russian Revolutionaries or Extreme Irish Republicans?', *Terrorism and Political Violence*, 16 (1) Spring 2004; A. Geifman, *Thou Shalt Kill: Revolutionary Terrorism in Russia, 1894–1917* (Princeton, 1993); A. Geifman, *Death Orders: The Vanguard of Modern Terrorism in Revolutionary Russia* (Santa Barbara, 2010); L. Hartnett, 'The Making of a Revolutionary Icon: Vera Nikolaevna Figner and the People's Will in the Wake of the Assassination of Tsar Alexandr II', *Canadian Slavonic Papers*, 43 (2/3) June-September 2001; S. K. Morrissey, 'The "Apparel of Innocence": Toward a Moral Economy of Terrorism in Late Imperial Russia', *The Journal of Modern History*, 84 (3) September 2012; N. M. Naimark, 'Terrorism and the Fall of Imperial Russia', *Terrorism and Political Violence*, 2 (2) Summer 1990; D. Offord, *The Russian Revolutionary Movement in the 1880s* (Cambridge, 1986).

[24] D. Ghosh, *Gentlemanly Terrorists: Political Violence and the Colonial State in India, 1919–1947* (Cambridge, 2017), pp. 1–9.

western political violence. Even during the high noon of late nineteenth-century globalization, for instance, dynamite bombing remained overwhelmingly a western phenomenon.[25]

'When historians describe that whole network of changes that transformed Europe and the wider world from predominantly agrarian or small-town communities, governed by ancient religious and a customary tradition-bound culture, to a largely urban, industrial, secular society', writes Richard Overy, 'they use the term "modernisation"'.[26] Of course, the shorthand term is a rough-and-ready one only; and globally such processes are far more open-ended and contingent than once thought. But, if used carefully, the terms 'modernity' and 'modernization' still retain some analytical utility since they can 'capture a singular condition or process that societies experience, albeit in their own peculiar ways'.[27] Among other key changes in these emerging 'societies of strangers' was the increasing abstraction of many human relations. Indeed, 'the mobility and anonymity of modern society are very marked features of it'.[28]

Violence is not immune from such profound changes. Indeed, it represents a key site of human interaction to observe such changes in action: as Albert Camus noted in 1946 'just as we love one another by telephone and work not on matters but machines, we kill and are killed nowadays by proxy. What is gained in cleanliness is lost in understanding.'[29] This book is written from the conviction that, if studied carefully, the detail of such violence may indeed illuminate a wide social landscape: and tell western moderns something about themselves. But as Camus noted, this is not easy to do.

It is not easy to do for—at least—two very good reasons. First, there is what might be termed the dazzling cleanliness of 'modernity's faith in its own distance from violence'.[30] Western civilization often appears to be built upon a social conquest of violence. Such views were already commonplace in the later nineteenth century. Ironically, the man who did more than any other individual to give modern political violence its distinctive cast—Alfred Nobel, the 'Lord of Dynamite'—prophesied that progress would banish weapons.[31] Especially in post-1968 European societies, *all* violence came to be seen as 'the antithesis of civilisation'.[32]

The second good reason why modern violence is hard to study in social context, is the degree of dominance of the modern western state both over, and through, society. What was distinctive about the European state that emerged in the course of the nineteenth century was its tentacular reach: its 'pedantically systematic, inhuman, and impersonal bureaucratic practice' (in the appalled judgement of the

[25] See the stark pattern thrown up by this map: A. K. Cronin, *Power to the People: How Open Technological Innovation is Arming Tomorrow's Terrorists* (Oxford, 2020), p. 86.

[26] R. J. Overy, *The Interwar Crisis, 1919–39* (London, 1994, 1995). p. 24.

[27] J. Vernon, *Distant Strangers: How Britain Became Modern* (Berkeley, 2014), p. xii.

[28] Gellner, *Nationalism*, p. 28.

[29] J. Lèvi-Valensi (ed.), *Camus at Combat* (Princeton, 2007), p. 260.

[30] S. Neitzel and H. Welzer, *Soldaten: On Fighting, Killing and Dying* (London, 2011, 2012), p. 343.

[31] E. Bergengren, *Alfred Nobel* (London, 1962), p. 196.

[32] Neitzel and Welzer, *Soldaten*, p. 50.

leading anarchist of the day, Mikhail Bakunin).[33] Although such states privileged respect for the private sphere, they squashed public challenges with firmness.[34] Less dramatically, the expectations of governments were becoming harder and harder to ignore in daily life. Almost all levels of society seemed thoroughly penetrated through the unceasing activity of its police, functionaries, and bureaucrats. When needed, such regimes seemed to be everywhere. 'All is clockwork, all is order', observed Mark Twain wonderingly of France in 1867.[35] And yet the twentieth century was to transfer such governmental interventionism remorselessly to the USA as well.

Against such imposing state facades of dominance, anti-state violence can often seem a rather paltry and episodic subject. The disjuncture with pre-modern societies—and their often distant governments—is a sharp one: and it has been mirrored by a pronounced academic gap. Indeed, the general shift from occasional mass violence (of, say, the *charivari* shaming ceremony, or the spectacle lynching) towards more serial 'terroristic' violence (of often tiny and clandestine groups of ideologues) remains strikingly unexplored.[36]

Yet the way ahead is not entirely trackless. In practice, violent outrages tend to settle into semi-fixed and semi-predictable constellations—although there is always some, usually limited, room for adaption and innovation. Here we can very usefully borrow one of social movement theory's more accessible notions—that of the 'repertoire of action'. In the words of Charles Tilly, 'the word repertoire identifies a limited set of routines that are learned, shared, and acted out through a relatively deliberate process of choice'.[37]

A further advantage of a concentration on such repertoires of violence is that it has the advantage of sensitizing us to the structuring role of (semi-submerged) social *assumptions* rather than explicitly-stated political *ideologies*. Ideologies matter greatly, of course: indeed, and a rich vein of scholarship has had some success in explaining terrorist targeting primarily with reference to them.[38] But even the most hardcore ideologues have to navigate specific social contexts that will modify their room for manoeuvre significantly since 'ideas alone do not move history: to have an impact, they must have a socio-political base in society. Ideas, in short, must be actualized'.[39] In sum, the approach of Charles Tilly (and many other imitators) is a useful reminder of the dividends that morphology—the study of pattern—can yield.

[33] M. Bakunin, *Statism and Anarchy* (Cambridge, 1990), p. 105. The immediate context of the passage is a discussion of Germany.

[34] M. Mulholland, *Bourgeois Liberty and the Politics of Fear: From Absolutism to Neo-Conservatism* (Oxford, 2012), pp. 80–112.

[35] M. Twain, *The Innocents* (New York, 1869, 1966), p. 80.

[36] For a rare exception: E. Hobsbawm, *Bandits* (London, 1969, 2001), pp. 185–99.

[37] C. Tilly quoted in: M. Traugott, *The Insurgent Barricade* (Berkeley, 2010) footnote 34, p. 323. See also: B. Hoffman, 'Terrorist targeting: tactics, trends, and potentialities', *Terrorism and Political Violence*, 5 (2), 1993.

[38] C. J. M. Drake, *Terrorists' Target Selection* (Basingstoke, 1998), pp. 23, 25; A. Dolnik, *Understanding Terrorist Innovation* (London, 2007), p. 4.

[39] J. M. Diehl, *Paramilitary Politics in Weimar Germany* (Indiana, 1977), p. ix.

Such approaches informed classic studies of older forms of proto-political violence such as social banditry: also, incidentally, a typically small group phenomenon. Coincidentally or not, the classic size of the rural bandit gang very much mirrors that of both the nneteenth-century revolutionary conspiracy and the twentieth-century terrorist movement: a cell of about five or six members.[40] Given the research difficulties involved, the analytical richness of the historians' studies that examined 'Small Violence' 'from below' is impressive indeed. Despite uniformly hostile evidence in the state archives, the efforts of those who sought to oppose, or rival, the authority of the emergent modern state has been insightfully explored. Fifty years ago the renowned historian of the French Revolution, Richard Cobb, feared that

> ... the deserter, the mutineer, the primitive rebel, the rural bandit, the market rioter, the urban criminal, the pickpocket, and the village prophet have been taken in as honoured, pampered members of Senior Common Rooms.[41]

Rioting and banditry have both spawned rich literatures by European historians who seek to understand such action within its local context; and to rescue, as far as is now possible, the perspectives of those who acted this way, and what they actually did.[42] Popular shaming ceremonies tinged with at least the threat of violence—the so-called 'rough music' or *charivari* rituals—have also been diligently examined for what they tell us of the local societies that still felt that the administration of 'justice' and punishment was their business.[43] American historians, for their part, have finally begun to engage seriously with rough music's much rougher cousin: the practice of lynching.[44] All of these practices might reasonably be viewed as forms of political, or proto-political, violence.

40 J. H. Billington, *Fire in the Minds of Men: Origins of the Revolutionary Faith* (Abingdon, 1980, 2017), pp. 110 [Ireland, Italy, and Poland in early nineteenth century], 136 [France, early nineteenth century], 180–1 [Blanquists]; G. Bradley (with B. Feeney), *Insider: Gerry Bradley's Life in the IRA* (Dublin, 2009, 2011), p. 161 [Provisional IRA squads of four to six men]; R. Clutterbuck, *Guerrillas and Terrorists* (Ohio, 1977, 1980), p. 13 ['half a dozen men and women']; R. Gildea, *Fighters in the Shadows* (London, 2015, 2016), p. 92 [groups of three or four]; W. Laqueur, *Terrorism* (London, 1977, 1980), pp. 108, 263 [urban terrorists operate in units of between three and ten]; E. Rosenhaft, *Beating the Fascists? The German Communists and Political Violence, 1929–1933* (Cambridge, 1983), p. 103 [Communist cells of five].

41 R.C. Cobb, *The Police and the People: French Popular Protest 1789–1820* (Oxford, 1970), p. 3.

42 For rioting: E. Hobsbawm and G. Rudé, *Captain Swing* (London, 1969, 1993); G. Rudé, *The Crowd in the French Revolution* (Oxford, 1972); G. Rudé, *The Crowd in History: A Study of Popular Disturbances in France and England, 1730–1848* (London, 1995); E. P. Thompson, *The Making of the English Working Class* (London, 1963, 1991); E. P. Thompson, 'The Moral Economy of the English Crowd in the Eighteenth Century', *Past and Present*, 50 (1), pp. 76–136 (1971); C. Tilly, L. Tilly, and R. Tilly, *The Rebellious Century 1830–1930* (Harvard, 1975). For banditry: A. Blok, *Honour and Violence* (Cambridge, 2001), esp. Chapter 1, 'Social Banditry Reconsidered'; M. Broers, *Napoleon's Other War: Bandits, Rebels and their Pursuers in the Age of Revolutions* (Oxford, 2010); Hobsbawm, *Bandits*.

43 E. P. Thompson, 'Rough Music Reconsidered', *Folklore*, 103 (I), 1992; E. Weber, *Peasants into Frenchmen: The Modernization of Rural France, 1870–1914* (Stanford, 1976), pp. 399–406.

44 J. Allen (et al.), *Without Sanctuary: Lynching Photography in America* (Sante Fe, 2000); A. S. Buckser, 'Lynching as Ritual in the American South', *Berkeley Journal of Sociology*, 37, 1992, pp. 11–28; P. Dray, *At the Hands of Persons Unknown: the Lynching of Black America* (New York, 2002, 2003); W. Fitzhugh Brundage, *Lynching in the New South: Georgia and Virginia, 1880–1930* (Chicago,

Violence, then, one might almost say, has never been so in research fashion as during the past fifty years since the excitements of 1968. But there are limits. Studies are overwhelmingly of popular violence in agrarian societies: or, at least, of societies still only lightly touched by industrialization. Striking by their absence are serious attempts to write general or thematic histories of public violence in the West since the late eighteenth century: conventionally taken as the watershed of its political modernity. The airport bomber and drive-by shooter have not been welcomed in to join the motley crew in Richard Cobb's already overcrowded Senior Common Room. It is as if the generalist historian of little violence has been defeated by the transition to modernity itself. We have good accounts of individual movements, but not synthetic accounts grounded in wider contexts. We lack a social history in one of the arenas where perhaps we need it most.

However, if we move beyond the historical profession, it is true that more recent patterns of atrocity have been better charted here by social scientists than their more distant ancestors. Global diffusion of suicide bombing from the late twentieth century has been particularly well studied.[45] Longer genealogies, though, appear much less clear. The 1960s technocratic fashion for counting has bequeathed an invaluable legacy of 'event databases' tracing political violence globally over the past half-century or so.[46] Whatever the a-contextual classification dilemmas that always lurk in the foundation of such compilation exercises, these can help to identify both general trends and sharp break points (such as the early 1970s impact of airport security measures on aircraft hijackings). Some notable attempts have also been made to trace the longer genealogies of both the car bomb and aircraft hijacking.[47] Yet these studies remain very much the praiseworthy exceptions. Before the mid-twentieth century (at the most optimistic assessment) we remain very largely in the dark. It is particularly here that this book hopes to spread a little light, however diffuse.

1993); W. Fitzhugh Brundage (ed.), *Under Sentence of Death: Lynching in the South* (London, 1997); M. J. Pfeifer, *Rough Justice: Lynching and American Society 1874–1947* (Chicago, 2004); S. E. Tolnay and E. M. Beck, *A Festival of Violence: An Analysis of Southern Lynchings, 1882–1930* (Chicago, 1993).

[45] M. Bloom, *Dying to Kill: The Allure of Suicide Terror* (New York, 2005); D. Gambetta (ed.), *Making Sense of Suicide Missions* (Oxford, 2005, 2012); I. Overton, *The Price of Paradise: How the Suicide Bomber Shaped the Modern Age* (London, 2019); R. Pape, *Dying to Win: The Strategic Logic of Suicide Terrorism* (New York, 2005); A. Pedhazur (ed.), *Root Causes of Suicide Terrorism: The Globalization of Martyrdom* (London, 2006); R. Singh, *Hamas and Suicide Terrorism: Multi-Causal and Multi-level Approaches* (London, 2011); R. Singh, 'Suicide Terrorism' in E. Chenoweth, R. English, A. Gofas, and S. Kalyvas (eds), *The Oxford Handbook of Terrorism* (Oxford, 2019), pp. 429–44.

[46] See: N.G. Bowie and A. P. Schmid, 'Databases in Terrorism' in A. P. Schmid (ed.), *The Routledge Handbook of Terrorism Research* (Abingdon, 2011, 2013), pp. 294–340.

[47] M. Davis, *Buda's Wagon: A Brief History of the Car Bomb* (London, 2007); R. T. Holden, 'Contagiousness of Aircraft Hijacking', *American Journal of Sociology*, 91 (4) Jan., 1986, pp. 874–904; P. Baum, *Violence in the Skies: A History of Aircraft Hijacking and Bombing* (Chichester, 2016); D. Gero, *Flights of Terror: Aerial Hijack and Sabotage since 1930* (Sparkford, 1997); D. Phillips, *Skyjack: The Story of Air Piracy* (London, 1973); Y. Veilleux-Lepage, *How Terror Evolves: The Emergence and Spread of Terrorist Technique* (Lanham, 2020).

III

How, then, should such a wide-ranging and ambitious historical exploration be structured? Some judicious balance between breadth and depth needs to be struck. A loose overall structure therefore deliberately allows some room for a survey of the major social forces operating over two centuries and across two continents that have shaped the evolution of political violence. It therefore takes the form of two main parts.

Part One opens by taking as its subject: the State. More than any other constraint, it was the development of an interventionist state of enormous coercive bureaucratic capacity that relentlessly squeezed political violence into highly innovative—that is, recognizably modern—forms. This development provided the key pressure—or 'push factor'—that moulded action into distinctive, and often unprecedented, patterns.

Beginning with the conventional watershed of western modernity—the twin American and French revolutions of the late eighteenth century, Chapter One traces how burgeoning state power transformed the prospects of violent dissidence. By the later nineteenth century recognizably modern states had arisen that were essentially impervious to overthrow from below, except in truly exceptional circumstances such as a defeat in a major war. This was true on both sides of the Atlantic—although the USA always exhibited a far greater social tolerance for violence that was not genuinely system-threatening: and remained until at least the 1930s very lightly policed. Chapter Two takes up the story from 1939 to the present day. Chapter Three takes space to survey this long trajectory of state power projection more thematically. This chapter ends with some reflection on the Western state in the early twenty-first century: a strikingly open-ended moment where the exponentially accelerating volume of information and capital flows seems—to some analysts—to threaten state capacity to manage public order as efficiently as before.[48]

Part Two reverses polarity. Rather than surveying how political violence has been moulded by the power of the state, it examines how both social and technological changes have opened up new possibilities. It concentrates on 'pull factors': the forces that have facilitated new experiments in destruction and atrocity. In 1893—at about the time anarchist bombs were starting to explode across Paris—Emile Durkheim published his classic study, *The Division of Labour in Society*. Here Durkheim argued that human societies were evolving 'from those based on "mechanical solidarity" (solidarity based on likeness of ancestry, religion, and collective sentiments) to those based on "organic solidarity" (solidarity based on difference and interdependence).'[49] In this broadly Durkheimian spirit, Part Two relates changing patterns of violent action to the changing structure of society itself. Structure will not dictate individual behaviour, of course: maverick agency is

[48] M. Castells, *End of Millenium*, Vol. III (Chichester, 1998, 2010).

[49] A. L. Haynor, 'Classical Sociological Theory' in K. O. Korgen, *The Cambridge Handbook of Sociology*, Vol. 1 *Core Areas in Sociology and the Development of the Discipline* (Cambridge 2017), p. 102.

always possible. But even here it is certainly likely to help mould options in certain directions rather than others.

Chapter Four traces the background to the broad 'democratization' of assassination. A threat once targeted only at the very apex of society has evolved into something much more diffuse, inchoate, and ubiquitous. In a parallel process, the spread of hostage-taking is also considered. Against a backdrop of revolutions in communication, and the emergence of mass audiences, it notes the relentlessly downward diffusion of political killing.

Chapter Five has a deliberately narrow focus. It simply examines the actual means of destruction: and how these have been employed. Thus it surveys the evolution of contemporary atrocity through its tools—the advent of miniaturized high explosives in the later nineteenth century; and the evolution of firearms. As cultural anthropologists note, there is an 'agency of things'. Certain technologies allow, and indeed encourage, some types of innovative behaviour over others.[50] And yet any such historical account must also acknowledge enduring continuities as well: not least, the stubborn persistence of low-technology weapons such as knives.

Chapter Six surveys wider changes that have allowed new types of attack to emerge: the opportunities provided by mobility. It pays particular reference to the twentieth century's transport revolutions of automobiles and airplanes. Tactics of forced immobilism—sabotage—are also considered under this broad rubric. Although in origin primarily a rebel technique pioneered from below, sabotage has tended to be developed most effectively with state support. Unsurprisingly, it is states that understand best how to disrupt other states.

A conclusion stands back from the detail to survey the historical road travelled. Deliberately its tone is tentative rather than definitive. To offer any general account of the historical development of our current predicaments is a daunting task. But then no amount of familiarity with contemporary realities should blind us to their intrinsic strangeness, either.

IV

In a typically lucid discussion first published in 1981 entitled 'The Causes of Terrorism', Martha Crenshaw set out a general protocol that is still useful for any analytical dissection of political violence:

> To develop a framework for the analysis of likely settings for terrorism, we must establish conceptual distinctions among different types of factors. First, a significant difference exists between 'preconditions,' factors that set the stage for terrorism over the long run, and 'precipitants,' specific events that immediately precede the occurrence of terrorism. Second, a further classification divides preconditions into enabling or permissive factors, which provide opportunities for terrorism to happen, and situations that directly inspire and motivate terrorist campaigns. Precipitants are similar to the direct causes of terrorism.[51]

[50] P. Lehr, *Counter-Terrorism Technologies: A Critical Assessment* (Cham, Switzerland, 2019), p. 9.

[51] M. Crenshaw, 'The Causes of Terrorism' in M. Crenshaw, *Explaining Terrorism: Causes, Processes and Consequences* (Abingdon, 2011), p. 36.

In Crenshawian terms, this is a book that pays significant attention to the general 'preconditions' for political violence. Deliberately, then, this is book that lingers precisely in the places where other analysts hurry forward to get into action. Rather than treat social background as low-grade research ore to be dug through at speed, it treats it as foreground. It is written in the conviction that political violence always has a social hinterland: and that understanding that hinterland must be a vital part of any general analysis of the whole phenomenon. Moreover, this is even more the case when, as so often in the contemporary world, that violence seems most characterized by its preeminent quality of 'blood-stained inanity'.[52] However understandable, such deep bewilderment should spur us on to better, and more searching, attempts at analysis. 'Rather than defining violence *a priori* as senseless and irrational', argues Anton Blok powerfully 'we should consider it as a changing form of interaction and communication, as a historically developed cultural form of meaningful action.'[53]

And it is precisely here, in the truly wrenching transitions that modernity has wrought, that a historical study of political violence through its actions has perhaps most to offer. How exactly violence has evolved in that great transition from societies 'of proximity and reciprocal surveillance' (and that are ruled by 'the law of shame') into our own world of instant and 'universal comparison' (so mercilessly governed by its mass flows and surges of decontextualized information) demands an attempt at a fine-grained approach.[54] And yet applying a quasi-anthropological gaze to contemporary violence through a 'thick description' of local context often seems hardest precisely because the forces of modernity have blown apart the isolation of hermetically-sealed local context so spectacularly from the old days when—to borrow a traditional phrase—France remained obstinately 'sixteen days wide and twenty-two days long'.[55] By contrast, we moderns stand stupefied before a much narrower global landscape. Here the canvas is impossibly crowded: the sheer complexity of its unceasing movements, the relentlessness of its image flows, the capriciousness of its mass attention fads—the whole eludes our understanding.

Once again longer-term historical perspectives can offer some degree of illumination to this new landscape. If nothing else, such perspectives confront us with the jarringly unfamiliar assumptions of the past. Such contrasts can, perhaps, in turn invite us to fresh introspection about ourselves, making helpfully strange to us again our own times and our own predicaments.

A letter that survives from southern France in the turbulent mid-1790s makes the point with some economy. 'You can grasp that we could not be the enemies of people we don't know', a harassed government official in the Rhone Valley wrote simply to his superiors in Nîmes. He was trying to clear his village of involvement in a series of murders: and clearly thought such social distance a clinching point in

[52] J. Conrad, *The Secret Agent* (London, 1907, 2007), p. 249 (Author's Note from 1920).

[53] Blok, *Honour and Violence*, p. 104.

[54] R. Muchembled (transl. J. Birrell), *A History of Violence* (Cambridge, 2012), p. 26 (on 'reciprocal surveillance' and the 'law of shame'); Z. Bauman, *Liquid Modernity* (Cambridge, 2000, 2012), p. 5 ('universal comparison').

[55] Quoted in: C. Tindall, *Célestine: Voices from a French Village* (London, 1995, 1996), p. 10.

his favour.[56] In this world, one had to know first in order to hate. Enemies were still made, and not begotten. As its historian has explained: 'victims and killers very often knew each other; the refrain of man of those arrested was "I did it to revenge my father/brother/uncle/cousin". This was in keeping with tradition'.[57]

Although communications with the outside world were indeed due to multiply exponentially just a few decades later, it seems safe to conclude that for most people in late eighteenth-century southern France—and far beyond—the social world remained one of very partial and limited horizons.[58] In short, the great sundering of organic relationships between time and space that lies at the heart of modernity was still largely unknown: and the coming impact of its resulting turbulences remained quite unsuspected.[59] Enemies were still made through the frictions of local intimacy, and not by the pronouncements of deracinated category. Relatively speaking, the modern mystery of 'abstract hatred' was still little known.[60]

Of course, there could be exceptions. We should beware a caricature of this world as dominated by utter parochialism and quite immune to the appeal of any mass ideology.[61] Global shockwaves caused by the American Revolution alone demonstrate the opposite: indeed, a conviction of rebel solidarity 'radicalized' James Aitken—'the first modern terrorist' to his biographer—to launch his solo four-month campaign of arson against Royal Navy dockyards across southern England in the autumn of 1776.[62] And it is also worth stressing, to glance back more broadly, that the anonymous and largely apolitical violence of unknown strangers has a very long history. Roving beggars always evoked intense hostility in the rural communities Eugen Weber studied.[63] With very good reason, peasants traditionally hated soldiers; just as merchants traditionally despised bandits and pirates.[64]

But a social world in which such threats *occasionally* intruded is a very different social world to one in which they are fully expected. Back in 2017 when drafting

[56] C. Lucas, 'Themes in Southern Violence' in G. Lewis and C. Lucas (eds.), *Beyond the Terror* (1983) pp. 168–9.

[57] MBroers, *Napoleon's Other War: Bandits, Rebels and their Pursuers*, p. 37.

[58] For the classic account: Weber, *Peasants into Frenchmen*, Part I, 'The Way Things Were'.

[59] Bauman, *Liquid Modernity*, p. 8.

[60] The phrase belongs to the poem by W. B. Yeats: 'The Blood and the Moon' in D. Albright (ed.), *W.B. Yeats: The Poems* (London, 1990, 2001), p. 288.

[61] For instance, see the diary entry for 5 October 1803 in: J. Ayers (ed.), *Paupers and Pig Killers: The Diary of William Holland, A Somerset Parson, 1799–1818* (Gloucester, 1984), p. 91: 'Mr and Miss Keats could not come to dinner having had a serious Rumpus among the servants. That tribe of beings are much altered of late years, no subordination among them. The Glorious Effects of the French Revolution'.

[62] J. Warner, *John the Painter: The First Modern Terrorist* (London, 2004). By contrast national prejudice seems more fluidly conceived in the British diaries of the generation before the French and American Revolutions: F. Pottle (ed.), *Boswell's London Journal 1762–3* (London, 1950, 1966); T. Smollet *Travels Through France and Italy* (Oxford, 1979, 1992); T. Turner, *The Diary of a Georgian Shopkeeper* (Oxford, 1925, 1979).

[63] Weber, *Peasants into Frenchmen*, p.44. But for a counter-example from 1870 of anonymous peasant violence—the killing of a nobleman—see: A. Corbin, *The Village of Cannibals: Rage and Murder in France, 1870* (Harvard, 1992).

[64] M.S. Anderson, *War and Society in Europe of the Old Regime, 1618–1789* (1988, 1998), pp. 67–8; Weber, *Peasants into Frenchmen*, pp. 295, 435.

of this book began, the news was awash with the details of the latest horror committed by violentIslamists . Thirteen had been killed in a van attack in Barcelona, and then five militants shot dead by counter-terrorist police in nearby Cambrils.[65] By the time this book appears, other atrocities will have intervened to overlay it. That is both tragic—and utterly predictable.[66] That is the way it goes. Deep down we expect no different. And that is why such atrocities must be repeated if our attention is to be re-engaged. Deep down we expect that, too.

So I deliberately ask in this book—with calculated naivety, but I think also with some good reason—the very simplest of questions. How on earth did we get here?

[65] BBC News, 20 August 2017.

[66] They did. 'Spectaculars' since have included: the Christchurch mosque attacks, New Zealand (15 March 2019) and Sri Lanka (21 April 2019).

PART I

THE STATE

INTRODUCTORY REMARKS

If modernity makes sense as an analytical category, then studying *modern* political violence necessarily dictates some brief exploration of contrasts with *pre-modern* violence as well. And this is not easy. A basic starting point in the late eighteenth century cannot avoid some degree of arbitrariness, of course: but the challenges lie deeper than this. Even if attention is restricted to Europe over the preceding millennium the picture remains quite bewilderingly complex. By their very nature empires tend both to rise and fall. So, too, do their abilities to control public violence.

How, then, can we begin to generalize about pre-modern violence in any meaningful way? As far as we can gauge, levels of pre-modern violence were not always or necessarily astronomically high. Indeed, 'some parts of thirteenth-century England experienced levels of violence little different from those found in much of the west today'. And yet, adds Warren Brown in his seminal study of medieval violence, 'what is certain . . . is that medieval societies were *differently* violent'.[1] Certainly, they seem to have been entirely unsurprised by (more-or-less) calibrated uses of violence by elites to settle their power struggles over, and through, the bodies of their social inferiors. Indeed, this was expected behaviour.

To read the memoirs of Philippe de Commynes, diplomatic counsellor to Louis XI, King of France (1461–83), is therefore to plunge into an interminable round of armed bickerings over dynastic status and property.[2] Such confrontations 'had the structure and logic of lawsuits in which violence was considered to be a legitimate mechanism of conflict resolution'.[3] Violence was thus central—but limited. It was something to be avoided or deployed (but not, as such, deplored). In practice, such violence could often simply be worked around by everyone else. Even at the height of the 'Wars of the Roses' (1460–61) it is clear that life in England went on:

[1] W. Brown, *Violence in Medieval Europe* (Harlow, 2011), p. 5. Emphasis in original.

[2] P. de Commynes (transl. M. Jones), *Memoirs: the Reign of Louis XI 1461–1483* (Harmondsworth, 1972).

[3] V. Swaroop Sharma, 'War, Conflict and the State Reconsidered' in L. Bo Kaspersen and J. Strandsbjerg (eds), *Does War Make States? Investigations of Charles Tilly's Historical Sociology* (Cambridge, 2017), p. 194.

'the civil war takes its place beside the floods of November 1460 as a temporary obstacle to the conduct of business'.[4] It is hard to avoid the impression that Europeans of the fifteenth century must have been far more skilled than their twenty-first century descendants in gauging what outbreaks of violence were, and were not, truly threatening to their lives and livelihoods.

Such realities did not change quickly. War and peace long remained highly relative, and not antonymic, conditions. Indeed, 'armed conflict in early 17th century Europe…ramified into every aspect of life and was able to do this because it was in many ways badly defined, because the boundary between peace and war was still fuzzy'.[5] So, too, were boundaries between foreign and civil wars. External wars almost inevitably sparked tax rebellions closer to home: between 1635 and 1660 there were 282 of these in France alone.[6]

Wars, then, were not yet 'total' in the monstrous twentieth-century sense of that term.[7] Nor—a closely related point—were state monopolies of violence. 'Even in peacetime', writes Peter Wilson 'most people carried a knife or club if they went out after dark or any distance from home'.[8] And yet the destruction of war often ran into social limits and attempts at negotiation: even during highly extreme situations such as the sack of Magdeburg in 1631.[9] Wilson makes the important point that truly indiscriminate violence often followed the breakdown of negotiation: 'this might explain the frequent reference to foreign perpetrators since they could not make their demands understood to the local population'.[10] Conversely, 'the comparative absence of atrocities during the first English Civil War was due to the fact that both sides spoke the same language'.[11] Hence face-to-face encounters—and their failure—continued to structure the course of violence in very immediate ways.

Several features stand out here. First, impersonal killing in this world was essentially the by-product of cultural collisions: between rival armies, or—as the brutal scenes of murder painted by the Dutch artist David Vinckeboons in the 1620s testify—between soldiers and peasants.[12] Otherwise, though, sudden and premediated random killings seem a rare feature of this most troubled period. Only, perhaps, in the decimations inflicted on the Hapsburg regiments after their disappointing performances at Lützen (1632) and Leipzig (1642) do we glimpse a pure

[4] K. B. McFarlane, *England in the Fifteenth Century: Collected Essays* (London, 1981), p. 242.

[5] M. S. Anderson, *War and Society in Europe of the Old Regime, 1618–1789* (Stroud, 1988, 1998), p. 16.

[6] W. Doyle, 'Introduction' in W. Doyle (ed.), *Old Regime France 1648–1788* (Oxford, 2001), p. 1.

[7] For a useful discussion of the concept of 'total war' and its limitations, see: R. Chickering, 'Introduction to Part II' in R. Chickering (et al., eds), *The Cambridge History of War*, Vol. IV, *War and the Modern World* (Cambridge, 2012), pp. 184–9.

[8] P. H. Wilson, *Europe's Tragedy: A New History of the Thirty Years War* (London, 2009, 2010), p. 841.

[9] H. Medick and P. Selwyn, 'Historical Event and Contemporary Experience: the Capture and Destruction of Magdeburg in 1631', *History Workshop Journal*, No. 52 (Autumn, 2001), pp. 23–48.

[10] Wilson, *Europe's Tragedy*, p. 834.

[11] C. Carlton, 'The Impact of the Fighting' in J. Morrill (ed.), *The Impact of the English Civil War* (London, 1991), p. 19.

[12] G. Parker and A. Parker, *European Soldiers 1550–1650* (Cambridge, 1977), p. 31.

arbitrary interchangeability to victim selection.[13] And such instances were clearly a special case: a product of brutal military cultures that were increasingly a law unto themselves.

Indeed, it is a striking feature of the early modern period that military and civilian worlds were slowly, but inexorably, separating out. By the eighteenth century 'in Western Europe armies were becoming more than ever before separate and distinct societies enclosed within larger civilian ones'.[14] Moreover, in an opposite process, civilian society was itself becoming disarmed: by 1730 noblemen in London had stopped carrying swords in public.[15] By the mid-1760s rules against openly carrying pistols and daggers were being enforced at Nice.[16] Over time this bifurcation of military and civilian spheres opened up new space for distinctively new traditions of political violence to emerge.

Thirdly, 'the distinction between "internal" and "external" politics, once quite unclear, became sharp and fateful'.[17] Put differently, the state was emerging as the premier political unit: an arena in which power was contested within increasingly well-defined boundaries. At the tail end of the eighteenth century the French Revolution made the scale of change brutally manifest: 'among other things, polite travelers were shocked to discover that they could no longer go freely to countries with which their own was at war'.[18]

Behind all of these processes lay the extraordinary rise of the coercive power of the modern western state. 'War made the state, and the state made war' claimed Charles Tilly back in 1975.[19] Be that as it may, the rise of the modern western state had been a slow process. Certainly, it had been well underway before the twin American and French revolutions of the late eighteenth century. But that rise accelerated exponentially thereafter. That further acceleration (along with its spreading ramifications) forms the basic subject of Chapters One and Two.

[13] Anderson, *War and Society in Europe of the Old Regime*, pp. 64–5.

[14] Anderson, *War and Society in Europe of the Old Regime*, p. 173.

[15] R. Muchembled, *A History of Violence* (Cambridge, 2012), p. 220.

[16] T. Smollett, *Travels through France and Italy* (Oxford, 1979, 1981), p. 168 [Letter XX, 22 October 1764].

[17] C. Tilly, *Coercion, Capital, and European States AD 990–1992* (Malden, 1990, 1992), p. 70.

[18] W. Doyle, *The Oxford History of the French Revolution* (Oxford, 1989, 1991), p. 391.

[19] Quoted in: L. Bo Kaspersen, J. Strandsbjerg, and B. Teschke, 'Introduction' in L. Bo Kaspersen and J. Strandsbjerg (eds) *Does War Make States? Investigations of Charles Tilly's Historical Sociology* (Cambridge, 2017), p. 1. For the record, this volume gathers specific critiques of aspects of the Tilly thesis. I do not enter in these debates here.

1

The Modern State and the Society of Hyper-Order to 1939

All modern revolutions have ended in a reinforcement of the power of the State.

– Albert Camus[1]

If everyday one eats and drinks, travels safely to one's pleasures, without being run over in the streets, drowned in the Seine, suffocated in the theatres, not poisoned by the wine merchants, rescued in case of accidents; if lunatics do not run wild, abandoned babies find wet nurses, scandals within families are held in check and are hidden from the public, we owe all this to the Prefecture of Police.

– Duchamp, 1872[2]

For the past 200 years the defining feature of most domestic contests between Western governments and armed opponents has tended to be their lopsided asymmetry. We shall understand very little about the dynamics of recent political violence if we do not recognize this reality squarely from the outset. Rebel ideology is indeed often a worthwhile object of study in its own right. But the study of rebel ideas—however innately fascinating to intellectuals—only takes us a certain distance in explaining why the limited violence that *does* occur, tends to take certain forms (but not others). It also has little to say about why there has not been far *more* anti-state violence.

From the standpoint of historical sociology, the more interesting questions lie elsewhere. Since the later nineteenth century a recurrent phenomenon of Western societies has been hopeless micro-insurrections mounted against stable societies: the armed utopianism of the violently delusional, the wars of the 'six against sixty million' (to borrow Heinrich Böll's characterization of the Red Army Faction in West Germany).[3] Time and again, it is only society's dreamers and deranged who have dared to mount any kind of sustained violent challenge to the state. Indeed, in the early twenty-first century 'armed struggle' is for those who believe—against all evidence—that God will favour the small battalions.

[1] A. Camus, *The Fastidious Assassins* (London, 1951, 2008), p. 72.

[2] Quoted in: M. Anderson, *In Thrall to Political Change: Police and Gendarmerie in France* (Oxford, 2011), p. 245.

[3] S. Aust, *The Baader Meinhof Complex* (London, 2008), p. 119.

Such forces of the fringe cannot muster *any* big battalions, of course: even when they are 'assisted' by the inevitable admixtures of pro-state spies and *agents provocateurs*. Typically, their violence either emerges on the very edge of much larger social movements: or from within the pressure-cooker environments of tiny 'underground' cells. But either way such violence tends to be an essentially liminal phenomenon. And such restricted organizational forms in their turn inevitably impose their own strict operational constraints.

By contrast, the coercive potential of the modern state is titanic: as Max Weber recognized a century ago, the state seeks to 'monopolize' violence.[4] At a minimum—the American template—the state seeks to 'out-bid' the violence of any challenger so decisively that macro-stability is preserved (even if it also proves expedient in practice to tolerate significant levels of inter-personal and ghettoized bloodshed). At a maximum—the Western European model in good times—the state professes a sort of totalitarian neo-pacifism (even if this means radically reclassifying residual violence as 'merely' inter-personal or criminal). All 'monopolies of violence' contain some degree of sleight of hand. But that does not mean they are shams. On the contrary, since 1865 the bulk of serious disorder in Western countries has been the direct result of defeat in war with external powers: a remarkable record.

Such successful monopolies of violence have not simply been a question of states marshalling and centralizing superior means of destruction against all domestic challengers. They have also reflected an ability to coerce invisibly. Indeed, the hallmark of successful coercion is that it is no longer recognized as coercion at all by wider society. Actual violence—inevitably called 'force'—must be used very sparingly, if at all.

As has been recognized, the true core of the modern state's extraordinary power as it has evolved in the West is thus not overwhelming force as such, but the infrastructural capacity that lies behind it.[5] Or to put it more precisely, the overwhelming force comes *from* the infrastructural capacity. Bureaucracy and coercion must both be examined, because they belong together.[6] Here knowledge is indeed the true crucible of power. Such states 'embrace' (*erfassen*) their citizens: and the lives of the latter are 'fixed' in the official records as flies in amber.[7] All control—and assistance—ultimately depends upon access to the files: a dictatorship of the secretariat.

The key point is that such states leave literally nowhere safe to hide.[8] Everywhere is eventually—if perhaps intermittently—registered, inspected, taxed, or otherwise monitored. 'Modern man is strapped down by a network of rules and regulations' wrote the neo-Luddite Theodore Kaczynski in *The Unabomber Manifesto*. His own

[4] H. H. Gerth and C. Wright Mills (eds), *From Max Weber: Essays in Sociology* (London, 1948, 1977), p. 78.

[5] M. Mann, 'The Autonomous Power of the State: its Origins, Mechanisms and Results', *European Journal of Sociology*, 25 (2) 1984, pp. 185–213.

[6] For a useful introductory discussion: S. Malešević, *The Sociology of War and Peace* (Cambridge, 2010), pp. 5–7.

[7] J. C. Torpey, *The Invention of the Passport: Surveillance, Citizenship and the State* (Cambridge, 2000, 2018), p. 14. Torpey's translation.

[8] R. Postgate, *How to Make a Revolution* (Yardley, 1934, 2018), p. 147.

experience of clandestinity was telling enough here. Kaczynski had holed up in a self-built log cabin in the Western Montana wilderness. He was meticulous in removing every last fingerprint from every mail bomb that he dispatched. Over seventeen years, his bombs succeeded in killing three people, and injuring twenty-three.[9] But even this 'Scarlet Pimpernel of Mailbombers' could not evade the visits of the census taker.[10]

Overall, the result of this infrastructural evolution of the Western state is that its citizens have increasingly lived under regimes of hyper-regulation: a 'cumulative bureaucratisation of coercion'.[11] Micro-rules permeate, and structure, their daily lives to a degree that would have confounded their ancestors. Any serious social study of contemporary political violence must therefore recognize that public life is an arena of intense scrutiny in which the governed are intensely regulated and monitored by their own governments.

But the reverse is also increasingly true: governments are increasingly scrutinized by their own citizenry: and, it seems, with increasing scepticism. This first half of the book in its first two chapters devotes most of its attention to tracing the effects of the state's long-term growth of infrastructural capacity: and what that has meant for trajectories of political violence from the late eighteenth century up until the later twentieth century. In practice, I deal in most detail with the period from the late nineteenth to the later twentieth century since I believe it is here that we tend to lack integrated accounts of how violence has been constricted by the burgeoning power of the modern state. Yet my third chapter deliberately reserves some space to consideration of whether the information revolution of recent decades—the rise of the so-called 'network society' of the early twenty-first century—has helped reverse this slow process of 'squeezing out' insurrectionist violence from society: and whether the blood-dimmed tide of violence that states cannot hope to control is rising inexorably once more. Any serious survey of the contemporary scene must contend with debates as to whether state power, and its ability to face down violent challenges, is ebbing once more.[12]

I

How did the rise of the infrastructural state come about? It certainly has deep roots; and is the outcome of a long period of historical development that can only be traced here in outline. Europe led the way here. Its modern political cosmos was born in the massive 'Big Bang' moment at the end of the eighteenth century that

[9] D. R. Liddick, *Eco-Terrorism: Radical Environmental and Animal Liberation Movements* (Westport, 2006), p. 103.

[10] Green Anarchist (ed.), *'Industrial Society and Its Future': The Unabomber Manifesto* (Camberley, 1995), p. 27; R. Graysmith, *Unabomber: A Desire to Kill* (New York, 1997, 1998), pp. 20, 24.

[11] Malešević, *The Sociology of War and Violence*, pp. 5–7.

[12] S. Strange, *The Retreat of the State: The Diffusion of Power in the World Economy* (Cambridge, 1996, 1998); M. Mann, *The Sources of Social Power*, Volume 4: *Globalizations, 1945–2011* (Cambridge, 2013), p. 419.

we call the French Revolution. From 1789 France became the 'kettle of magicians' (to borrow the description of Edmund Burke, an appalled observer).[13] Out of it bubbled key developments that have helped shape the development of the modern state: war, nationalism, class-based politics, and the emergence of 'the people' as a political actor in its own right. And, in response over the coming years and decades, the French state introduced the census, mass conscription, and the gendarmerie.[14] We can glimpse the sharply declining space for rebel manoeuvre in the evolving plans of the Vendée leadership to remove the dictator, Napoleon Bonaparte. Bandit tactics to lure him to favourably remote terrain and then ambush his coach were eventually discarded in favour of radical innovation. A massive bomb hidden in a cart narrowly failed to kill him on his way to the opera on Christmas Eve 1800: arguably, the first vehicle bomb of its kind.[15] Results were certainly spectacular, if politically ineffectual. Casualty figures were uncertain in the chaotic aftermath, but perhaps seven or eight were dead, and scores more badly maimed.[16] All in all, 'Paris had been hit by a new kind of atrocity and no one knew quite how to react.'[17]

A stunning growth in governmental power and capacity for control was the chief legacy of the wars that wracked Europe between 1792 and 1815: beyond the Napoleonic myth, 'another heritage survived throughout Europe, greyer, but stronger than the heroic legend, hated and admired: the modern state'.[18] Although little noticed, one direct consequence of this enhanced state capacity for repression was the early extinction in Western Europe of 'the deadly ethnic riot'—a massive and sudden episode of civilian-on-civilian violence, structured by targeting that runs along perceived communal lines.[19] Unlike America, this tradition was here burnt out by the close of the eighteenth century—the last examples occurring in London (1780) and at Nîmes (1791). Death tolls ran into the hundreds in both cases.[20]

Contrary to conservative and aristocratic fears, then, the industrial revolution led not to anarchy but to far stronger governments. State power happily piggy-backed on these headlong advances in transport and communication since they allowed it to concentrate overwhelming force where, and when, needed. Repression, in turn, became far more finessed. 'The bloody scuffle in St Peter's Field at Manchester which was contemptuously named 'Peterloo' took place in 1819; but there were no Peterloos in the railway era'.[21] By 1844, instead of taking seventeen days to march from London to Manchester, 1,000 troops could arrive within nine

[13] E. Burke, *Reflections on the Revolution in France* (Harmondsworth, 1790, 1969), p. 194.

[14] M. Broers, *Napoleon's Other War* (Witney, 2010), pp. 194–5; E. Hobsbawm, *On the Edge of the New Century* (New York, 2000), pp. 32–3.

[15] J. North, *Killing Napoleon: The Plot to Blow up Bonaparte* (Stroud, 2019), pp. 147–55.

[16] North, *Killing Napoleon*, p. 153. [17] North, *Killing Napoleon*, p. 154.

[18] M. Broers, *Europe under Napoleon 1799–1815* (London, 1996), p. 274.

[19] D. L. Horowitz, *The Deadly Ethnic Riot* (Berkeley, 2001).

[20] C. Hibbert, *King Mob: The Story of Lord George Gordon and the Riots of 1780* (London, 1959); W. Doyle, *The Oxford History of the French Revolution* (Oxford, 1989, 1991), p. 138.

[21] The battle of Waterloo had taken place just four years earlier. M. Robbins, *The Railway Age* (Harmondsworth, 1962, 1970), p. 141.

hours, still fresh.[22] Similarly, the first reaction of the beleaguered French government in June 1848 was to give 'orders to all the regiments posted along the railways to converge on Paris'.[23] By the 1860s, London, Berlin, and Vienna were literally wide open for business. All had destroyed their city walls and toll-gates.[24]

This not to say that governments were never challenged, or never in danger of losing control. In 1848, indeed, thrones had tottered all over Europe. But it is to stress that until the late 1870s or so, European states had tended to be fortunate in the nature of the militancy that they faced. For the most part, they were able to fight challengers openly in the field—or, rather, in the streets and plazas of their capital cities. The fall of the Bastille in 1789 had bequeathed revolutionaries a template for popular action that they followed faithfully all the way down to 1871. It delivered some short-term triumphs—notably between 1830 and 1848 when the emergence of the barricade tradition in Paris substantially boosted insurgent strength against governmental power. Their significance was—to borrow from Trotsky's much later analysis—essentially 'moral'.[25] Repeated barricades provided formidable obstacle courses for the forces of counter-revolution: and if military forces were slowed down long enough their discipline might be successfully subverted by appeals to fraternity. As late as 1991 this is exactly how they were used by insurgents to defeat the Moscow coup.[26]

In the mid-nineteenth century, though, balances of power were shifting decisively to governments' advantage. Based upon colonial tactics developed in Algeria, the French army produced the first manual on 'urban warfare' in 1847.[27] Over the coming decades, technological change smiled more and more upon the big battalions. Not only could the forces of the state manoeuvre and concentrate more effectively than ever before, but they increasingly out-gunned insurgents who had little answer to the firepower of rifles and breech-loading cannon.[28] Finally, Baron Haussmann's rebuilding of central Paris showed how urban insurrection might be largely 'designed out' by massive boulevards whose wide vistas appealed to shoppers and tourists (but also to artillery officers).[29]

[22] E. Royle, *Revolutionary Britannia? Reflections on the Threat of Revolution in Britain, 1789–1848* (Manchester, 2000), p. 185.

[23] E. Hazan, *A History of the Barricade* (London, 2013, 2015), p. 92.

[24] H. Liang, *The Rise of the Modern Police and the European State System From Metternich to the Second World War* (Cambridge, 1992, 2002), p. 27; J. Robert, 'Paris, London and Berlin on the eve of the war' in J. Winter and J. Robert (eds), *Capital Cities at War: Paris, London, Berlin 1914–1919* (Cambridge, 2007).

[25] L. Trotsky, *1905* (Harmondsworth, 1971, 1973), pp. 411–12.

[26] As so often, I owe this astute point to Marc Mulholland. See: *Guardian*, 20 August 1991 ('Everyone's a loser in army's undisciplined takeover'); *The Times*, 20 August 1991 ('Crowds look for answers on streets of confusion').

[27] S. Graham, 'Cities as Strategic Sites: Place Annihilation and Urban Geopolitics' in S. Graham (ed.), *Cities, War and Terrorism: Towards an Urban Geopolitics* (Malden, 2004), p. 36.

[28] For the consequences, see: Hazan, *A History of the Barricade*, pp. 85, 92–6. See also: M. Mulholland, *The Murderer of Warren Street* (London, 2018), p. 181.

[29] S. Graham, 'Cities as Strategic Sites: Place Annihilation and Urban Geopolitics' in Graham (ed.), *Cities, War and Terrorism*, p. 36.

As confrontations became explicitly militarized, outcomes after early 1848 were thus increasingly one-sided.[30] Artillery won.[31] Counter-revolutionary forces had the great luxury of fighting military engagements on essentially their own terms so long as they did not disperse their strength. To give just one example: in the French street fighting of June 1848 between 1,700 and 3,000 insurgents were killed.[32] 'At the sound of the grapeshot, which, from minute to minute, tears the air, the whole population trembles; every woman ask herself if this is the blow which has taken from her a husband, a son, a friend' a contemporary noted.[33] Blood poured down the drains of Paris ('like so many Orinocos').[34]

Right across Europe, indeed, the counter-revolution waded through blood to victory. Johann Strauss's 'Radetzky March' is a rather uplifting musical composition. The episode it commemorates was not:

> While the Italian revolutionaries were losing popular sympathy in the countryside, General Radetzky's remaining forces were mounting a vigorous campaign of terror there. On learning, in mid-April, that insurgent forces were stationed in the village of Montebello in Venetia, Radetzky sent a detachment of soldiers to drive out the insurgents, burn the village and murder every man, woman and child in it.[35]

That atrocities were central to the triumph of the Counter-Revolution in 1848–9 has therefore tended to be subsumed into the military campaigns to suppress the revolutions. State terror was obscured by battle-smoke. But as that smoke cleared, it revealed the emergence of enhanced regimes of police control. The new state intimidation could afford to be more discreet because it had become more pervasive. This was rule, no longer by demonstrative atrocity but by system: of spies, informers, identity checks, press seizures, and quiet deportations of unwanted foreigners.[36] Even if embryonic by the standards of later surveillance regimes, the reach and grasp of the state's bureaucracy was proliferating fast. For Karl Marx, indeed, this 'enormous bureaucratic and military organization' had become an 'appalling parasitic growth, which enmeshes the body of French society like a net and chokes all its pores'.[37]

Comprehensive defeat of revolutionary movements right across Europe certainly stimulated fresh thinking amongst their sympathizers. As early as 1853, the failed Prussian bureaucrat Karl Heinzen published 'Murder and Liberty': a call to

30 M. Traugott, *The Insurgent Barricade* (Berkeley, 2010), pp. 178–224.

31 J. Sperber, *The European Revolutions, 1848–1851* (Cambridge, 1994), p. 217.

32 A. J. Mayer, The *Furies: Violence and Terror in the French and Russian Revolutions* (Princeton, 2000, 2002), p. 108.

33 Quoted in: Mulholland, *The Murderer of Warren Street*, p. 91.

34 Baudelaire, quote in: Hazan, *A History of the Barricade*, p. 96.

35 Sperber, *The European Revolutions*, p. 207. My general discussion here is based both upon my earlier work and discussions with Marc Mulholland: T. K. Wilson, 'State Terrorism: An Historical Overview' in G. Duncan (et al., eds), *State Terrorism and Human Rights: International Responses Since the End of the Cold War* (Abingdon, 2013), pp. 19–20.

36 D. Blackbourn, *The Fontana History of Germany 1780–1918: The Long Nineteenth Century* (London, 1997), pp. 230–1.

37 Quoted in: J. H. Kautsky, 'Centralization in the Marxist and in the Leninist Tradition', *Communist and Post-Communist Studies*, 30 (4) 1997, pp. 388–9.

harness scientific destruction in the cause of both tyrannicide and mass murder ('the path to humanity leads over the summit of barbarism').[38] Yet it enjoyed little short-term resonance. In an equally innovative (and equally ineffectual) development, the Italian nationalist Carlo Pisacane—who has been described as 'the first ideological hijacker of the modern era'—led the armed takeover of the postal steamer *Cagliari* on 25 June 1857.[39] But this adventure also proved to be a tactical dead end. Notably, he made no attempt to exploit the ships' passengers as hostages. More suggestive for the future was the flirtation of the London Central Committee of the Communist League with targeting 'hated individuals or public buildings associated with hated memories'.[40]

All in all the post-1848 development of resilient forms of socialist and nationalist insurrectionary underground movements across Europe represented the maturing of much earlier templates such as the Carbonari that had emerged in Naples as early as 1807.[41] What was new now was both the reach and tactical sophistication of the emergent movements. A particularly influential model here was that of Auguste Blanqui who had pioneered attempts to free the French masses in both 1839 and 1848.[42] Blanquism evolved into a disciplined elitist conspiracy: always lurking to exploit the revolutionary opportunities that periodic mass unrest would—supposedly—generate.[43]

Increasingly, revolutionary cadres linked up: a far-flung, even transnational, 'network of networks' emerged. It was essentially composed of small rebel nodes, each of which took the classic 'cellular' form of a small number of highly dedicated activists. Indeed, its hallmark was that '19th century novelty, the professional revolutionary...working for the overthrow of the established order, in season and out'.[44] If the general political weather often remained obstinately unrevolutionary for these 'dangerous dreamers of the absolute', the tempo of circulation of both their ideas and their tactics could still be impressive enough.[45] In 1858, the Italian nationalist Felice Orsini used a new type of fulminate mercury grenade to attempt to assassinate the French Emperor Napoleon III on his way to the opera in Paris. The device had been designed by an Austro-Hungarian artillery officer; was manufactured in Birmingham, England: a version later turned up in Arkansas.[46]

[38] D. Bessner and M. Stauch, 'Karl Heinzen and the Intellectual Origins of Modern Terror', *Terrorism and Political Violence*, 22 (2), April–June 2010, p. 163.

[39] J. H. Billington, *Fires in the Minds of Men: Origins of the Revolutionary Faith* (London, 1980, 2017), p. 331.

[40] Quoted in: Billington, *Fires in the Minds of Men*, p. 284.

[41] W. Laqueur, *Terrorism* (London, 1977, 1980), pp. 37–9.

[42] R. Gildea, *Barricades and Borders: Europe 1800–1914* (Oxford, 1987, 2003), pp. 78, 92, 223; Mulholland, *The Murderer of Warren Street*, pp. 72–4.

[43] R. Postgate, *How To Make A Revolution* (Yardley, 1934, 2018), pp. 112–13.

[44] M. Mulholland, 'Inventing the Working Class', *Dublin Review of Books* (June 2013).

[45] Karl Marx quoted in: A. Schmid (ed.), *Routledge Handbook of Terrorism Studies* (London, 2011, 2013), p. 85.

[46] R. Davies, 'The Felix Orsini Bomb' (30 December, 2012). Available at: http://www.standingwellback.com/ See also: M. Pinfari, 'The Orsini Attentat and Terrorist Assassinations', *Terrorism and Political Violence*, 21 (4) (October–December 2009), p. 583.

Since mass rebellion was becoming rarer, so too was blatant state repression—although there were spectacular exceptions both in the suppression of Confederacy during the American Civil War (1861–5) and the extinguishing of that social laboratory, the Paris Commune (1871).[47] As the leading historian of post-war Reconstruction in the USA has commented, 'in their unprecedented expansion of federal power and their effort to impose organization upon a decentralized economy and fragmented polity, these measures reflected what might be called the birth of the modern American state'. By the war's end, the federal bureaucracy (of 53,000 employees) 'was the largest employer in the nation'.[48] Even if much of the United States remained remarkably lightly policed and administered by European standards, this still represented a step-jump in the capacity of central government.

Across both the Old and the New Worlds, then, overall trends were becoming clear enough. Growing power of governance in major states was reflected by the growing infrequency of their internal crises. Before 1850, in Europe, revolutionary situations ignited wars. After 1850, wars ignited revolutionary situations. Certainly, that was the clear pattern following defeats for France (1870–1), Russia (1905–6) and, on a more localized scale in Catalonia, for Spain as well (1909). Elsewhere it was becoming impossible for urban insurrections to achieve even the most fleeting success—as the repetitive trajectory of failure in Dublin (1867), Bologna (1874), and Milan (1898) demonstrated rather unambiguously.[49] By 1895 even Friedrich Engels had come to recognize 'that in an age of railways and modern military technology revolutionary enthusiasts could not hope to succeed on the barricades.'[50]

Nor was he alone: just two years earlier the future leader of the Bavarian Republic of 1918–19, Kurt Eisner, had reached the same conclusion that 'alley revolutions are a means of earlier times... today at best still appropriate in Russia'.[51] By the later nineteenth century, then, the major states of western Europe and north America looked all but impregnable to any 'traditional' challenges from below. It was this realization—just as much as the appearance of dynamite—that helped foster the radical innovation of the 1880s: the urban bombing campaign. Campaigns of violent protest against the state had been largely driven deep underground. By the early years of the twentieth century, it was clear that a general tendency had emerged 'for the old ferocity to be replaced by cunning'.[52]

Put more precisely, bombs now 'became the favourite device of revolutionaries, though not Marxist ones, and not for genuinely insurrectionary purposes'.[53] This

[47] Mayer, *Furies*, p. 109.

[48] E. Foner, *Reconstruction: America's Unfinished Revolution 1863–1877* (New York, 1988, 2014), pp. 23, 364–5.

[49] For Dublin: P. Bew, *The Politics of Enmity 1789–2006* (Oxford, 2007), pp. 259–61; S. Takagamli, 'The Fenian Rising in Dublin 1867', *Irish Historical Studies*, 39 (15) May 1995. For Bologna: G. Woodcock, *Anarchism* (London, 1963, 1975), pp. 169–70. For Milan: C. Tilly, L. Tilly, and R. Tilly, *The Rebellious Century 1830–1930* (Harvard, 1975), p. 153.

[50] R. J. Goldstein, *Political Repression in 19th Century Europe* (London, 1983), p. 348.

[51] Quoted in: A. Mitchell, *Revolution in Bavaria, 1918–1919: the Eisner Regime and the Soviet Republic* (Princeton, 1965), p. 42.

[52] G. Sorel, *Reflections on Violence* (Cambridge, 1999, 2012), p. 187.

[53] E. J. Hobsbawm, *Revolutionaries*, (London, 1973, 1977), pp. 226–7.

was a highly disturbing development since, in the words of the *New York Tribune* in 1884, 'a few years ago all expression of dominant physical force was monopolised by governments'.[54] Now whole populations were awakening to the novel reality that bombers moved amongst them. A sharp-eyed Beatrix Potter—not yet famous as the author of Peter Rabbit—noticed a new sense of unease amongst Londoners in 1884 ('the least thing causes an alarm').[55] Within ten years Parisians were showing many of the same symptoms. 'The nervous tension in Paris was at this time very great' wrote one eye-witness of this period (March 1892–June 1894): 'a trifling mishap' such as the accidental collapse of scenery at a theatre, or a tram throwing out sparks, caused stampedes.[56] Yet this was the same city that not long before (January 1871) had shown quite exemplary fortitude under a much more lethal Prussian bombardment.[57]

With their repeated series of (often pre-timed) explosions aimed at amplifying public panic, this phenomenon was indeed something genuinely new and disturbing.[58] Sustained and transnational campaigns primarily targeted leading industrial centres and communication nodes: London was hit first by teams of Irish American bombers (1881–7), then more loosely organized anarchist campaigns appeared to threaten in Chicago (1885–6), as well as taking more definite and sustained form in both Barcelona (1893–6) and Paris (1893–4).[59] Their legacy is the modern security state they inspired with its insistent bias towards protecting key metropolitan infrastructure: in both the United Kingdom and France 'political police forces' were consolidated in these years, and specialist legislation pioneered.[60] By 1900 all major cities in the industrialized world had specialist bomb disposal units with paraphernalia whose basic outlines remain recognizable even today: strict handling procedures, armoured vehicles, and x-ray machines.[61]

However, these dynamite campaigns were the exception to more general trends. European governments had otherwise largely squeezed private violence out of most of society, or at least to the margins of bourgeois consciousness (which

[54] Quoted in: S. Kenna, *War in the Shadows: the Irish-American Fenians Who Bombed Victorian Britain* (Sallins, 2014), p. 155.

[55] L. Linder (ed.), *The Journal of Beatrix Potter: from 1881 to 1897* (London, 1966), p. 69.

[56] E. A. Vizetelly, *The Anarchists: Their Faith and Their Record Including Sidelights on the Royal and Other Personages Who Have Been Assassinated* (London, 1911), pp. 163–4.

[57] For comparison, 111 were killed in 1871 but 'only' nine between 1892 and 1894. See: M. Kranzberg, *The Siege of Paris 1870–1871: A Political and Social History* (Ithaca, 1950), p. 133; G. Woodcock, *Anarchism* (Harmondsworth, 1963, 1975), p. 287.

[58] N. Whelehan, *The Dynamiters: Irish Nationalism and Political Violence in the Wider World, 1867–1900* (Cambridge, 2012), pp. 1, 80.

[59] K.R.M. Short, *The Dynamite War: Irish American Bombers in Victorian Britain* (Dublin, 1979); P. Avrich, *The Haymarket Tragedy* (Princeton, 1984), pp. 168, 206; J. Merriman, *The Dynamite Club; How a Bombing in Fin-de-Siècle Paris Ignited the Age of Modern Terror* (London, 2009); R. Hughes, *Barcelona* (London, 1992, 1996), pp. 418–22.

[60] Anderson, *In Thrall*, p. 76. Also: R. Bach Jensen, *The Battle Against Anarchist Terrorism: An International History, 1878–1934* (Cambridge, 2014), pp. 203–14; B. Porter, *The Origins of the Vigilant State: the London Metropolitan Police Special Branch Before the First World War* (London, 1987).

[61] R. Davies, 'IED Response Operations 1880–1910' (23 September 2014); '1894 Bomb Disposal Techniques' (29 July 2016); 'Victorian Era Bomb Basket' (30 September 2015). Available at: http://www.standingwellback.com/ For Barcelona: M. Davis, *Buda's Wagon: A Brief History of the Car Bomb* (London, 2007), p. 14.

amounted to much the same thing). To achieve this degree of public order was simply unprecedented.[62] As Eric Hobsbawm notes, 'in the nineteenth century, the ability of the majority of states to prevent the inhabitants from going around armed, is truly remarkable. One of the few exceptions was the United States, which chose not to do so, although it could have. In Canada, for example, it was carried out'.[63]

American exceptionalism in the management of public violence repays close examination. Here 'the availability of personal handguns after the Civil War, in particular, helped prop up the notion that the private individual could, indeed, act as a repository of violence in a manner that was previously impossible'.[64] The security of a hegemonic federal government that was quite immune from any threat of foreign invasion was found quite compatible with an indulgent toleration of more local horrors since here public security became more than ever 'at some level, a private matter'.[65] And so long as the local brutality of strikebreaking, or lynching, remained screened from the larger polity, there could be business as usual.[66]

This re-established complacency in the wake of the Civil War of 1861–5 is rather striking. In many ways, that conflict had been the direct ancestor of the 'total wars' of the twentieth century: a grinding contest of attrition in which victory went to the side that could mobilize the most resources the longest to the most devastating effect. By the end, indeed, 'much of the Southern landscape, from forest to farms to cities, was in ruins. Nearly half the livestock in the South was killed, and two-thirds of all farm machinery destroyed.'[67] And yet if the course of the Civil War foreshadowed total war, and if its verdict in denying the secession bid of the Confederacy was correspondingly decisive, its social outcome was much less so. Despite the formal abolition of slavery, indeed, it remained strikingly tentative and open-ended in the years immediately following the Confederacy's collapse in the spring of 1865. A decade of faltering attempts at social engineering by Republican administrations in Washington followed before Reconstruction petered out.[68] By 1875–6, indeed, all the basic foundations of a resurgent racial caste system had been put in place.

Between 1881 and 1915 further legal elaboration at the state and local level followed to build an authentically American apartheid: the so-called 'Jim Crow' system.[69] Out of the ruins of the ex-Confederacy arose white supremacy once more: 'the white tribe was back in the saddle'.[70] Racist supremacy had been snatched

[62] Hobsbawm, *On the Edge*, p. 33. [63] Hobsbawm, *On the Edge*, p. 33.

[64] J. Obert, *The Six-Shooter State* (Cambridge, 2018), p. 259.

[65] Obert, *The Six-Shooter State*, p. 260.

[66] For the classic analysis: R. Hofstadter, 'Reflections on Violence in the United States' in R. Hofstadter and M. Wallace (eds), *American Violence: A Documentary History* (New York, 1971), pp. 3–43.

[67] R. Blakeslee Gilpin, 'American Racial Terrorism' in Randall D. Law (ed.), *The Routledge History of Terrorism* (Abingdon, 2015), p. 146.

[68] For an accessible short introduction, rich on detail and atmosphere: M. Fellman, *In the Name of God and Country: Reconsidering Terrorism in American History* (New Haven, 2010), Chapter 3, pp. 97–142.

[69] R. Cook, *Sweet Land of Liberty? The African-American Struggle for Civil Rights in the Twentieth Century* (London, 1998), p. 23.

[70] Fellman, *In the Name of God and Country*, p. 142.

from the jaws of overwhelming military defeat. It was to last for nearly another full century: 'as late as 1945, thirty states retained constitutional or legal bans on inter-racial marriage and many of these had recently extended or tightened their rules'.[71]

How was this achieved? A partial answer is: through terror. Loosely-organized, but systematic, supremacist vigilantism outbid the coercive power and political stamina of the federal government in Washington. At first, such efforts to intimidate blacks and their white allies from voting had a partially submerged quality to evade prosecution of individuals by federal authorities: that, after all, was the point of night rides and Ku Klux Klan hoods. But confidence quickly built. Vigilantes proved strikingly successful as social engineers: 'mutilated carcasses hanging from trees, lying in the middle of city streets, or dotting country roads served as emblems and warnings of the fundamental meaning of white power'.[72] Such displays, like the parades and torchlight processions that flourished with them, served as 'ocular proofs of our power' (to borrow the description of one enthusiastic participant).[73]

As has been well recognized, overt white supremacy was built upon a structure of intimidatory violence that was repetitively-patterned and geographically far-ranging. Violence might take very many forms, of course, lethal and non-lethal. But its sheer scale was clearly impressive, as were its racial and geographical emphases. A snapshot estimate: between 1880 and 1930, 3,943 persons were victims of lynching in the USA. Most were male. Of these 3,943, no less than 3,220 were Afro-American.[74] By another broadly convergent estimate, 88 per cent of lynchings took place in the eleven states of the ex-Confederacy.[75] One survey of lynchings between 1895 and 1905 has found 97 per cent of victims were male and that 79 per cent were Afro-Americans.[76] In summary: for decades a broad potential for vigilantism upheld a system of racial control whose effects were sweeping and general right across the South, not least because it worked as an adjunct to the court system. So-called 'lynch law' did not strive to replace the forces of law and order. Rather, it strove to enhance their effectiveness as a buttress of white supremacy.

Lynching was thus a key component in a total system of the social regulation of race relations: an 'industry' as activist opponents were calling it by 1916.[77] But it also represented a chain or series of intensively *local* dramas. Just to give one example: in 1913 a black man named General Boyd was lynched in Walton County, Georgia, supposedly for entering a white woman's bedroom while she slept. The news took four days to travel outside the borders of the county.[78] This was a local spectacle primarily for local consumption. Sites of individual lynchings

[71] N. Ferguson, *The War of the World: History's Age of Hatred* (London, 2006, 2007), p. 273.

[72] M. Fellman, *In the Name of God and Country*, p. 117.

[73] Quoted in: Fellman, *In the Name of God and Country*, p. 130.

[74] D. F. Krugler, *1919: The Year of Racial Violence: How African Americans Fought Back* (Cambridge, 2015), p. 9.

[75] Cook, *Sweet Land of Liberty?*, p. 27.

[76] A. S. Buckser, 'Lynching as Ritual in the American South', *Berkeley Journal of Sociology*, 37, The Politics of Identity and Difference (1992), p. 14.

[77] See: 'The Waco Horror', *Crisis*, July 1916. Available here: https://credo.library.umass.edu/view/pageturn/mums312-b163-i124/#page/1/mode/1up

[78] L. Wexler, *Fire in a Canebrake: the Last Mass Lynching in America* (New York, 2003), p. 75.

might, indeed, remain local landmarks for decades afterwards.[79] One study of ten southern counties in the 1890–1919 period suggests that the actual occurrence of a lynching significantly *reduced* the possibility of further lynchings happening in that locale for a long while afterwards. An obvious inference is that local Afro-Americans went out of their way in the aftermath to avoid any behaviour that might remotely be construed as provocative or transgressive to whites: a single lynching served as a mechanism of neighbourhood dominance, in effect.[80]

Strikingly, the sporadic nature of lynchings also meant that 'most participants had little or no first-hand experience on which to pattern their activity'.[81] And yet they tended to do very much the same kind of thing, replicating 'a remarkably constant framework in most turn-of-the-century lynchings'.[82] Of course, there was much room for improvisation and local variation. But much more remarkable are the centripetal convergences in procedure. If there were no hard and fast 'rules', there were certainly some clear-cut conventions. Nurses in 1919, for instance, objected not to the lynching of one of their patients, but that the act had disrupted the smooth running of their hospital.[83] In their firmly held opinion, there was a time and place for such acts.

But where and when? 'In a broad sense', remarks Andrew Buckser in his useful attempt to sketch an archetype, 'a lynching began as soon as a crime was discovered.'[84] Crimes might be of variegated types: murder was the most common accusation, sparking 30–50 per cent of the lynchings in the sample he studied. Rape was by far the most notorious trigger: and, indeed, many contemporary commentators such as President Theodore Roosevelt seem automatically to have assumed that lynching was primarily about the policing of Afro-American desire for white women.[85] Theft might also be deemed sufficient provocation. And yet other direct catalysts for lynchings appear more deeply located in the murky and shifting world of inter-communal perceptions—imputed sleights or gestures of defiance from Afro-Americans. Some lynchings came from practically nowhere: at least for those on the receiving end.

Discovery of crimes inspired lynching posses—groups of men led by prominent local figures. A race often ensued with the official forces of law enforcement to apprehend a likely suspect (or suspects). Relations between vigilantes and law enforcement officials were often deeply ambiguous, ranging from the openly cooperative to the mutually hostile. In Buckser's considered judgement, the forces of law and order generally 'objected less to the killing of the prisoner than to the breach of legal procedure'.[86]

79 Wexler, *Fire in a Canebrake*, pp. 23, 43.

80 S. E. Tolnay, G. Deane, and E.M. Beck, 'Vicarious Violence: Spatial Effects on Southern Lynchings, 1890–1919', *American Journal of Sociology*, 102 (3) November 1996, p. 788–815.

81 Buckser, 'Lynching as Ritual in the American South', p. 14.

82 Buckser, 'Lynching as Ritual in the American South', p. 14.

83 Krugler, *1919*, p. 280.

84 Buckser, 'Lynching as Ritual in the American South', p. 15.

85 W. L. Ziglar, 'The Decline of Lynching in America', *International Social Science Review*, 63 (1) Winter 1988, pp.18–20.

86 Buckser, 'Lynching as Ritual in the American South', p. 17.

Here, however, the posse had protocol of their own to follow. The suspect was often taken to the victim of the crime, or their family, for positive identification: conversely, torture might be used to obtain a confession. Either way, 'the attempted proof of guilt through one of these means seems to have occurred in almost all lynchings'.[87] Other procedures were, apparently, more contingent. Some sort of proclamation might or might not then be made in advance of the actual killing: by which time, indeed, crowds might already have gathered in their hundreds. Women might, or might not, leave together just before the climax of the lynching rite.

Killing was usually accomplished by hanging or shooting; or, indeed, both.[88] Mutilation and torture often accompanied these acts. Suspension of the body allowed maximum crowd participation—either to join in the desecration of the corpse, or at least to pose beside it afterwards. Bodies were usually left hanging, or at least tied. Burning at the stake was another variant: again the body was always left prominently. Eventually, municipal authorities would step back into the process to clean up in a physical, though, not a legalistic sense: indeed, 'legal punishment was extremely rare' for those who had participated in lynchings. Buckser concludes that 'for the whites, lynchings were community recreation as well as community retribution, and they formed the basis of local stories for years afterwards'.[89]

What are we to make of this tradition? Although peaking in an age of emergent mass literacy, urbanization, and photography, lynching clearly derives from a genre of older, rural traditions of communal self-policing imported from Europe. Traditional divisions of labour predominated—lynching was men's work, predictably enough: but, as seen, women could often be spectators. And children might be explicitly encouraged to attend as a rite of passage.[90] Lynching was folk theatre with active audience participation: 'a form of collective violence'.[91]

Most obviously, it was also, in the eyes of its enthusiasts and practitioners, rough justice: with the emphasis more upon the *justice* than the roughness of method. Strikingly, its dramatic forms were essentially antiphonal to those of the official law: they parodied, but also paralleled, the procedures of law and order. Like the less lethal English 'rough music' or the French *charivari*, lynching 'belongs to a mode of life in which some part of the law belongs still to the community and is theirs to enforce'.[92] 'Lynch law' was, for its supporters, a moral law that enforced collectively-held values.

Display was thus particularly central to the full-blown lynching ritual: 'the spectacle lynching', as it has been aptly been termed.[93] Punishments fitted supposed crimes in ways that were emotionally satisfying—crime victims and their families might be allowed the first blows; rapists were castrated, and so on. Perhaps 15,000

[87] Buckser, 'Lynching as Ritual in the American South', p. 17.

[88] Buckser, 'Lynching as Ritual in the American South', pp. 17–18.

[89] Buckser, 'Lynching as Ritual in the American South', pp. 18–19.

[90] J. Allen (et al.), *Without Sanctuary: Lynching Photography in America* (Sante Fe, Twin Palms, 2000), plates 33, 38, 54, 57.

[91] Wexler, *Fire in a Canebrake*, p. 126.

[92] E. P. Thompson, 'Rough Music Reconsidered', *Folklore*, 103 (1) 1992, p. 20.

[93] R. M. Miller, 'Lynching in America: Some Context and a Few Comments', *Pennsylvania History: A Journal of Mid-Atlantic Studies*, 72 (3) Summer 2005, pp. 275–91.

people were present at Waco, Texas, when the suspected 17-year-old rapist Jesse Washington was castrated and very slowly burnt to death over an open fire on 15 May 1916.[94] Such a size of audience for the lynching performance was undoubtedly exceptional: certainly, the death of Washington garnered an unusual amount of outside interest (and, indeed, condemnation). But lynchings were, typically, memorable local spectacles that drew crowds; and crowds, by the very fact of their very presence, radiated back collective approval.

Of course, we do not know what every last member of any crowd may actually have been privately thinking. Witnesses often claimed, at least long afterwards, to have been entirely sickened.[95] Perhaps some were. But many look jubilant and self-satisfied: generally photographs tend to show grinning crowds posing beside mutilated corpses. Indeed, the very size of the crowds and their manner of dress (i.e. a fair smattering of suits and straw boaters) suggests substantial 'respectable' support for such action.[96] Lynching 'was a socially accepted, or at least well-known, event given tacit approval or even support by the leaders of society': that is, of course, white society.[97] Brisk trading in lynching souvenirs points in the same direction. Fragments of the hangman's rope were especially prized; but so, on occasion, were actual body parts of the dismembered victim.[98] W. E. B. Du Bois once saw the knucklebones of a lynching victim displayed at an Atlanta grocery store.[99] But in general such mementos seem to have served more private purposes. Above all, they were primarily kept for the luck they were thought to bring.[100] Why else keep a severed penis?

All in all, then, it seems hard to avoid the conclusion that self-righteousness was the magnetic force that drew in, sustained, and energized the lynching crowd. In their eyes, their own violence was anything but random. While lynching certainly upheld a general racial caste system across the old Confederacy, for its perpetrators it also represented appropriately local justice. Lynchers often seem to have had rather specific and localized target audiences in mind for the message they wished to broadcast.[101] In practice, the American south remained a place apart.

II

To return to the big picture: in general, it is rather curious how little this overall growth and deepening of state control in the late nineteenth century was appreciated

[94] The 17-year-old was supposed to have raped, and murdered, a white woman. He was found guilty in court before being lynched outside. See: P. Dray, *At the Hands of Persons Unknown: The Lynching of Black America* (New York, 2002, 2003), pp. 215–19; 'The Waco Horror', *Crisis*, July 1916.

[95] M. F. Greene, *The Temple Bombing* (London, 1996), p. 87.

[96] J. Allen (et al.), *Without Sanctuary*, plates 2, 5, 7, 15, 17, 20, 24, 31, 33, 34, 35, 38, 41, 55, 56, 57, 79.

[97] Ziglar, 'The Decline of Lynching in America', p. 15.

[98] L. Wexler, *Fire in a Canebrake*, p. 73.

[99] Wexler, *Fire in a Canebrake*, p. 73.

[100] A. S. Buckser, 'Lynching as Ritual in the American South', *Berkeley Journal of Sociology*, Vol. 37, The Politics of Identity and Difference (1992), p. 23.

[101] L. Wexler, *Fire in a Canebrake*, p. 95.

by some of the most incisive minds of the age: even in Europe where such tendencies were most pronounced. While Engels continued rather hopefully to prophesy a future 'withering away' of the state (*er stirbt ab*) and Gustav Le Bon worried over the capacity of authorities to control mob disorder, the modern state marched on from strength to strength.[102]

A surer guide to the coercive capacities of the modern state was to be found in the behaviour of its opponents. Revolutionary refugees in London were notably highly-strung: they preferred renting downstairs front rooms (for ease of escape), and invariably walked down the middle of the road (to avoid any policemen lurking in doorways). Writing to his family back in Latvia on New Year's Day 1911, Fritz Svaars was rightly pessimistic about his chances of dodging the official dragnet that was out for him ('The whole of London is buried in police'). Hours later he perished in the inferno of the Sidney Street Siege.[103]

When they chose, western states were now able to project their power with a greater degree of evenness over their entire national territory. The litmus test here was the eradication of banditry. And this transformation was no small matter.[104] Bandits may have lived on the margins, observes Michael Broers, 'but they were also very much part of their communities. They had to be, for behind every small band of extroverts stood a vast network of blacksmiths, horse traders, gunsmiths, innkeepers, "fences" and often whole communities, bound by ties of blood in every sense'.[105] They were deeply rooted in some specific, if remote, community: and bound in turn by both its rhythms, and its horizons. The season of the great fairs was their preferred 'killing times'; and even their most famous number were barely known during their lifetimes further from 20 miles from their own stamping grounds.[106]

As early as 1847, a Moroccan emissary to France had already been impressed by the 'complete security' for travellers.[107] By the 1870s, banditry survived in the major states only in special pockets. Germany's Wild East, the industrial boom region of Upper Silesia that was sandwiched between the poorly-policed borders with both Russian and Austrian Poland, was briefly the happy hunting crowds of the bandit chief, Karol Pistulka before his traditional demise (through the inevitable betrayal by a false lover). By American standards, Pistulka's three-year long (1873–5) bandit career was not especially long. But these things are relative, and locally it was clearly startling and celebrated enough to generate legends of hidden treasure and children's hide-and-seek games in some profusion.[108] His more

[102] S. F. Bloom, 'The "Withering Away" of the State', *Journal of the History of Ideas*, 7 (1) Jan. 1946, p. 116; J. Van Ginneken, *Crowds, Psychology and Politics, 1871–1899* (Cambridge, 1992), pp. 130–87.

[103] D. Rumbelow, *The Houndsditch Murders and the Siege of Sidney Street* (London, 1973, 1990), pp. 52, 55, 57–8, 137–40, 210.

[104] A. Blok, *Honour and Violence* (Cambridge, 2001), esp. Chapter 1, 'Social Banditry Reconsidered'; Broers, *Napoleon's Other War*; E. J. Hobsbawm, *Bandits* (London, 1969, 2001).

[105] Broers, *Napoleon's Other War*, p. 15.

[106] Broers, *Napoleon's Other War*, pp. 8–11; Hobsbawm, *Bandits*, pp. 34–45.

[107] S. G. Miller (ed. and transl.), *Disorientating Encounters. Travels of a Moroccan Scholar in France in 1845–1846* (Oxford, 1992), p. 95.

[108] S. Karski, 'Das Deutsche Kattowitz von 1865 bis 1922' in H. Kostorz and S. Karski (eds), *Kattowitz: seine Geschichte under Gegenwart* (Dülmen, 1985), p. 58. Also: www.zbojnickiszlak.pl: entry on Karol Pistulka.

famous American counterpart, Jesse James, pioneered hold-ups along the new railroads that were opening up the West during a prolonged (if rather intermittent) spree that lasted from 1873 to 1881. Like Pistulka, a supposed Robin Hoodism was part of a carefully cultivated public image.[109] Both were essentially transitional figures: with a foot in both the 'traditional' world of banditry, and the modern realm of celebrity: Pistulka indeed was later apotheosized as a waxwork in 'Castans Panopticum' tourist attraction on Berlin's chief boulevard, Unter den Linden.[110]

By the century's end, across both Europe and America, the traditional bandits really survived only in the very remotest and very poorest of regions.[111] And even here they were turning themselves into media personalities:

> As the twentieth century began, the celebrated bandit Giuseppe Musolino held Aspromonte the rugged hills of Southern Calabria in thrall. Modernized enough to give interviews to eager jounalists even while the police were hunting him, Musolino ignited much moralizing from urban Italians and visiting foreigners about the 'traditional backwardness' and 'bloodthirstiness' of his region.[112]

Yet such reputations had their own attractions: indeed, The Earl of Richmond seems to have treated hunting bandits in the Etruscan hills a picturesque diversion during his 1896 visit to the region.[113] For better or for worse, this was a world that was shrinking fast.

We should not exaggerate such transformations Everywhere peasantries declined slowly in both absolute and relative numbers: and where terrain remained remote and inaccessible, communities remained semi-isolated and the state an inevitably rather distant presence. When war was announced throughout rural France in 1914 it was done in the same manner as in the time of Napoleon a century before—the drummer boy walking from farm to farm, announcing his dire tidings.[114] In many districts the peasants were puzzled by the sudden ringing of the church bells—since it was surely obvious during such fine weather that no storm was on its way.[115] And in the Piedmontese hills of northern Italy, the peasant conscripts were every bit as clueless as their Russian counterparts as to whom they were being sent to fight against and where, and why:

> When their men were drafted and taken away, the women accepted that once more they were to fight against 'Austria', but they did not understand where that country was, comprehending merely that their men must spend many days in a train or on

[109] T. J. Stiles, *Jesse James: Last Rebel of the Civil War* (London, 1993, 2007), pp. 242, 267–8, 302, 355, 369, 375.

[110] www.zbojnickiszlak.pl: entry on Karol Pistulka.

[111] Even the sub-prefect of Bastia, Corsica, thought banditry had been vanquished by 1896: E. Weber, *Peasants into Frenchmen: The Modernization of Rural France, 1870–1914* (Stanford, 1976), p. 55.

[112] R. J. B. Bosworth, *Mussolini's Italy: Life under the Fascist Dictatorship, 1915–1945* (London, 2005, 2006), p. 41.

[113] A. M. W. Stirling (ed.), *The Richmond Papers* (London, 1926), p. 404.

[114] G. Tindall, *Célestine: Voices From a French Village* (London, 1995, 1996), pp. 207–8.

[115] E. Weber, *Peasants into Frenchmen*, p. 43.

foot to get there. Peasants had neither reason nor opportunity to master the finer points of international diplomacy or ideological debate.[116]

But if peasants were not interested in the war, the war was to prove only too interested in them. No one, and no corner, was to remain quite immune from the shockwaves caused by the coming catastrophe of European civilization.

III

It is hard at a century's distance to grasp the sheer depth of dislocation and disorientation the Great War wrought to the nineteenth-century bourgeois society of hyper-order and financial stability. 'Reared in an age of security, Hitler's generation experienced the collapse of the Wilhelminian Empire as an unprecedented disruption of its social bonds', writes J. P. Stern of Germany: but (to admittedly varying degrees) his comment holds true more widely as well.[117] From the very top came a cascade of crowns: eight kings and five emperors fell during the reign of King George V of England (1910–36).[118] Everywhere from the Russian steppe to southern Ireland aristocracies were in full retreat, if not in actual and headlong rout. A crazy paving of new borders spread inexorably across Central and Eastern Europe.

All across these vanquished and vanished ex-empires people now got by however they could. In this looking-glass world, age and experience were bankrupt.[119] Hunger ruled supreme. By 1923, indeed, even the German Finance Ministry was paying its staff partially in potatoes.[120] Values can change very fast under such circumstances. Adam Ferguson captures well the moral maelstrom that took hold:

> In war, boots; in flight, a place in a boat or a seat on a lorry may be the most vital thing in the world, more desirable than untold millions. In hyperinflation, a kilo of potatoes was worth, to some, more than the family silver; a side of pork more than a grand piano. A prostitute in the family was better than an infant corpse; theft was preferable to starvation; warmth was finer than honour, clothing more essential than democracy, food more needed than freedom.[121]

What patterns of political violence can we see in this chaos? Admittedly, the general picture is a highly complex, and shifting one. But some basic general parameters can still be offered upfront. First, and unsurprisingly, state authority appeared most compromised in the defeated powers (or, more accurately, their successor states).[122]

116 Bosworth, *Mussolini's Italy*, p. 57; O. Figes, *A People's Tragedy: The Russian Revolution 1891–1924* (London, 1996, 1997), pp. 257–8.

117 J. P. Stern, *Hitler: the Führer and the People* (Glasgow, 1975), pp. 16–17.

118 C. L. Mowat, Introduction in C. L. Mowat (ed.), *The New Cambridge Modern History* (Cambridge, 1960, 1968, 1988), Vol. 12, p. 6.

119 Stern, *Hitler*, p. 21; S. Haffner, *Defying Hitler* (London, 2002, 2003), p. 51.

120 A. Ferguson, *When Money Dies: The Nightmare of the Weimar Hyperinflation* (London, 1975, 2010), p. 205.

121 Ferguson, *When Money Dies*, p. 256.

122 R. Gerwarth, *The Vanquished: Why the First World War Failed to End, 1917–1923* (London, 2016, 2017), pp. 12–13.

Secondly, even here, the retreat of governmental authority was sharp, but not final. The experience of 'total war' had enmeshed government bureaucracies ever deeper into the workings of the economy and society. Since governments were now meant to have pro-active policies to manage the economy, and spread burdens fairly, failure here could easily be presented as elite betrayal.[123] Crises of governance were thus felt sharply in the 1918–23 period; and again with the onset of the Great Depression. But the governmental revolution of the war years could not be unlearnt: and, indeed, continued under its own momentum, boosting yet further 'that burgeoning "infrastructural" power to "grasp" individuals that distinguishes modern states from their predecessors'.[124]

An immediate, if indirect, consequence of this governmental revolution was the sudden prominence that the coup now assumed at the heart of European politics. As its leading student has neatly summarized it, this technique uses parts of the state to seize the controlling levers over the rest: 'a coup consists of the infiltration of a small but critical segment of the state apparatus, which is then used to displace the government from its control of the remainder'.[125] This was new. Outside of Spain there had been no coups in western Europe for decades. But now attempts came thick and fast: and the new states of eastern Europe here proved just as vulnerable as their traditionally weaker southern counterparts.[126]

By contrast, Germany had effectively seen off a long run of coup attempts by late 1923.[127] A combination of determined bureaucratic non-cooperation and strike paralysis demonstrated that often 'a coup can be defeated by any sign of organized resistance, which immediately reveals the weaknesses of the bid for power, and may also give time for the rest of the armed and civilian apparatus to decide that there is no cause to change sides'.[128] In essence, a successful coup relies upon violence being plausibly threatened, but not actually used. And here the merest hint of hesitation was freighted with risk. 'Strangely scrupulous', the Kapp putschists of 1920 ran into early trouble when the leader entrusted with the vital task of forcing open the banks to pay their own troops 'replied that a German officer could not appear in the guise of a safe-cracker. The money was never released'.[129] In addition, they simply had no effective answer to the electricity being turned off.[130]

More 'traditional' attempts at mass insurrection along the lines of the previous century were even less successful. Here the judgement of Count Harry Kessler on

123 R. J. Overy, *The Inter-War Crisis 1919–1939* (London, 1994), p. 17.

124 Torpey, *The Invention of the Passport*, p. 149.

125 E. N. Luttwak, *Coup d'État: A Practical Handbook* (Harvard, 1968, 2016), pp. 4, 12.

126 C. Malaparte (transl. J. Bertrand), *Technique du Coup d'Etat* (Paris, 1931).

127 Kapp Putsch (12–17 March 1920); Buchruckser Putsch (1 October 1923), Hitler Putsch (8–9 November 1923). See: J. M. Diehl, *Paramilitary Politics in Weimar Germany* (Indiana, 1977), pp. 67–74, 140–1, 150. Also: R. G. L. Waite, *Vanguard of Nazism: The Free Corps Movement in Postwar Germany 1918–1923* (New York, 1952, 1969), pp. 140–67, 248–59.

128 E. J. Hobsbawm, *Revolutionaries* (London, 1973, 1977), p. 196.

129 B. Wasserstein, *The Secret Lives of Trebitsch Lincoln* (London, 1988, 1989), p. 182.

130 Malaparte, *Technique du Coup d'État*, p. 154.

the Spartacist disturbances in Berlin in January 1919 was harsh, but hardly unfair: 'shooting is the workers' least effective weapon, amateurish and out-of-date, revolution in a romantic wrapper'.[131] It was also, to a perhaps surprising degree, simply absorbed into daily life. Again and again memoirs confirm that even prolonged gun battles had—by the febrile public safety standards of the early twenty-first century—remarkably little effect on the public behaviour of a major city such as Berlin which like 'an elephant stabbed with a penknife shakes itself and strides on as if nothing had happened'.[132] Dancing was far too valued a social distraction to be interrupted by the unwanted percussion of shooting in the background.[133] Crises were instead gauged by whether the trams kept running or not: a much more reliable indicator of serious trouble.[134]

Ambitious attempts at leftist or nationalist urban insurrections in fact simply involved a re-run of the same old nineteenth-century experiments; and with exactly the same results. Artillery won decisively all over again. As George Orwell recognized ruefully, its possession represented 'the determining factor in street warfare'.[135] The Austrian Defence Ministry reached the same conclusion, noting with some satisfaction that 'sections of the population which are hostile but have remained on the sidelines feel intimidated by gun fire that can be heard from far away'.[136] Repeatedly, the barricades succumbed to the inexorable bludgeoning of the heavy guns: first in Dublin (1916), and then in Berlin (in January and March 1919), Florence (1921), Dublin again (1922), Vienna (1934), and finally, Barcelona (1937).[137] Even shaky regimes such as the German Republic (in 1919) or the Irish Free State (in 1922) could win on these kinds of terms.

And yet the inter-war years saw street politics acquire a wholly new prominence as a primary arena for the contestation of power. Although strangely forgotten, 1919–20 was, indeed, the age of the great crowd massacre.[138] Against leftist and ethnic enemies, the machine-gun was used indiscriminately: 19 were killed at Königshütte, Upper Silesia (3 January 1919); 22 at Kadaň, Czechoslovakia; 34 in Berlin (March 1919); 42 in Berlin again (13 January 1920); and 14 in Dublin

131 H. Kessler, *Diaries of a Cosmopolitan, 1918–1937* (London, 1961, 1971), p. 61.

132 H. Kessler, *Diaries of a Cosmopolitan*, pp. 59–60.

133 F. Glombowski, *Frontiers of Terror: the Fate of Schlageter and His Comrades* (London, 1934); Kessler, *Diaries of a Cosmopolitan*, p. 59.

134 S. Haffner, *Defying Hitler*, p. 35; Kessler, *Diaries of a Cosmopolitan*, pp. 10–11, 56, 61, 79.

135 G. Orwell, *Homage to Catalonia* (London, 1938, 1989), p. 115.

136 Quoted in: Liang, *The Rise of the Modern Police and the European State System*, p. 279 (Vienna).

137 M. Jones, *Founding Weimar: Violence and the German Revolution of 1918–1919* (Cambridge, 2016), pp. 183 (January 1919) 210, 231, 253–4, 264 (March 1919); A. Richie, *Faust's Metropolis: A History of Berlin* (London, 1999), p. 306; G. Botz, 'Political Violence, its Forms and Strategies in the First Austrian Republic' in J. Mommsen and G. Hirschfeld (eds), *Social Protest, Violence and Terror in 19th and 20th Century Europe* (London, 1982), p. 302 (Vienna); C. Townshend, *Easter 1916: The Irish Rebellion* (London, 2005, 2006), pp. 255–6 (Dublin, 1916); C. Townshend, *The Republic: the Fight for Irish Independence, 1918–1923* (London, 2013, 2014), pp. 407–10 (Dublin, 1922).

138 Although they explicitly exclude 'situations of insurrection, revolution, or civil war' it still seems striking that this period does not figure in this brief overview discussion: J. House and N. MacMaster, *Paris 1961: Algerians, State Terror, and Memory* (Oxford, 2006, 2009), pp. 1–2, note 1.

(14 November 1920).[139] And these were only the set-piece atrocities. Perhaps as many as 1200 were killed in the suppression of the general strike of March 1919 in Germany.[140] Perhaps 100 were slaughtered in a semi-official pogrom of black sharecroppers in Phillips County, Arkansas in October of the same year.[141]

The key point here is that such suppression was never used against right-wing crowds and demonstrations. Both Italian fascists and Nazi stormtroopers pioneered thuggish strategies focused upon the 'conquest of the streets' precisely because their leaders realized early on that they would not face this kind of police or military response.[142] As has been pointed out, the Nazis

> did not intend to conquer the state by direct paramilitary power, since they knew they could never take on the Germany army. Nazi violence had three other goals: actually to solidify their own comradeship, emotionally 'toughened by battle,' to intimidate their opponents, and to demonstrate that the 'Marxist threat' could be overcome by their own disciplined paramilitarism. Nazi propaganda and the biased press then transmitted this claim to millions who had never directly witnessed the violence.[143]

Borderlands played a key role here as laboratories of confrontation. The hallmark of micro-confrontation in many such regions was their social intimacy—since national choices were new and populations often ambivalent, these conflicts often took the form of 'wars amongst neighbours' rather than between well-defined rival communal blocs. The distinctive fighting unit was the young male gang. Thus Upper Silesia had its Polish *bojówki* (fighting squads) and German *Stosstruppler* (raiding units); just as Teschen Silesia next door boasted its rival movements of 'Czech rowdies' and 'Polish roughs'; and Carinthia had its Slovene *Sokols* (Falcons) and Austrian *'Prügelbanden'* (roving thugs).[144] On occasion, such hostilities escalated into terror rampages—hit-and-run bombings or pot shots taken at rival meetings.[145] But they retained an essentially amateur and improvised quality.

Borderlands also bred more sustained proxy wars which in turn sucked in and sustained mass paramilitary formations. The Baltic states led the way here in 1918–19; later the chaotic aftermath of the Upper Silesian plebiscite of 1921

[139] For Berlin: *Volkswille*, 4, 5, 10 January 1919; E. J. Gumbel, *Vier Jahre politischer Mord* (Berlin, 1922), p. 82; *Western Mail*, 15 January 1920 (42 dead in Berlin). For Czechoslovakia: M. W. Campbell, 'The Making of the "March Fallen": March 4, 1919 and the subversive potential of occupation', *Central European History*, 39 (1) March 2006, p. 1. For Bloody Sunday in Dublin: Townshend, *The Republic*, pp. 201–2. For comparison: the *official* death toll of the massacre that British forces committed at Amritsar, India, on 13 April 1919 was 379: R. Cavendish, 'The Amritsar Massacre', *History Today*, 59 (4) April 2009.

[140] Jones, *Founding Weimar*, p. 5.

[141] Krugler, *1919, The Year of Racial Violence*, p. 180.

[142] Bosworth, *Mussolini's Italy*, p. 131; D. Siemens, *Stormtroopers: A New History of Hitler's Brownshirts* (New Haven, 2017), p. 39.

[143] M. Mann, *Fascists* (Cambridge, 2004, 2006), pp. 174–5.

[144] S. Wambaugh, *Plebiscites Since the World War: With a Collection of Official Documents* (Washington, 1933), Vol. 1, p. 157, 195–6. Also: T. K. Wilson, *Frontiers of Violence: Conflict and Violence in Ulster and Upper Silesia, 1918–1922* (Oxford, 2010), pp. 113, 141, 143, 145, 184.

[145] B. Karch, *Nation and Loyalty in a German-Polish Borderland: Upper Silesia, 1848–1960* (Cambridge, 2018), p. 124 [August 1920]; P. Chmiel, 'Zur Nationalitätenfrage in Ostoberschlesien im Spiegel der "Kattowitzer Zeitung" under des "Oberschlesischen Kuriers"', *Oberschlesisches Jahrbuch*, 2, 1986, pp. 58–86 [1925 attacks].

loomed large as a magnet for both disaffected veterans and teenage thrill-seekers.[146] A key feature of the post-war period in Europe (and, indeed, the USA as well) was this pronounced turn towards paramilitarism, that is 'military or quasi-military organizations and practices that either expanded or replaced the activities or conventional military formations'.[147] The consequences of such developments were felt very far from the front lines of 1914–18. Even race riots in the USA (1919), or sectarian violence in Belfast (1920–2), became notably more lethal as military skills came home to roost.[148] Even the streets of 1920s Harlem had their parades of Universal African Legionnaires with shouldered rifles.[149]

As has been astutely pointed out with particular reference to the European experience, 'what was distinct about these new movements was that they appeared *after* a century in which national armies had become the norm and modern police formations, penal codes and prions had helped to firmly establish a largely unchallenged monopoly of force in the hands of the state.'[150] Ironically, Max Weber's diagnosis of the monopoly of violence came at the moment of its (partial) dissolution: from strict monopoly to a loosely licensed deployment of overwhelming intimidation on the state's behalf.[151]

IV

And yet we should not become too blinded by novelty. Where defeat in war brought on a semi-paralysis of governance, much older patterns of violence could reassert themselves with quite bewildering speed. By July 1919 roaming bands of armed men near Dresden were said to have rendered conditions 'reminiscent of the period after the Thirty Years War'.[152] Further east, Upper Silesia had briefly found a new bandit hero in the darkly charismatic figure of Erich Hajok—and even though he was dead by the summer of 1919, his fellow bandits still carried his photograph in late 1920.[153] Banditry, indeed, here was to endure as a persistent problem until after the partition of the region in the summer of 1922.[154]

At a more general level, as some sort of provisional European social order did finally emerge from the cataclysm of the Great War 1914–18, the backwash of

[146] Waite, *Vanguard of Nazism*, pp. 227–32.

[147] R. Gerwarth and J. Horne (eds), *War in Peace* (Cambridge, 2012, 2013), p. 2; Krugler, *1919, The Year of Racial Violence*, pp. 6–7, 70.

[148] Krugler, *1919, The Year of Racial Violence*, pp. 30–1, 50–8, 115–17, 129, 160; Wilson, *Frontiers of Violence*, pp. 37, 178–80.

[149] B. Burrough, *Days of Rage: America's Radical Underground, the FBI, and the Forgotten Age of Revolutionary Violence* (New York, 2015, 2016), p. 29.

[150] Gerwarth and Horne, *War in Peace*, p. 2.

[151] Gerwarth and Horne, *War in Peace*, p. 2.

[152] Quoted in: R. Bessel, *Germany after the First World War* (Oxford, 1993, 2002), p. 243.

[153] F Glombowski, *Frontiers of Terror*, pp. 27–9 [the death of Hajok]; R. Vogel, *Deutsche Presse und Propaganda des Abstimmungskampfes in Oberschlesien* (Beuthen, 1931), p. 61; *Kattowitzer Zeitung*, 14 December 1920.

[154] For banditry in Upper Silesia in this period: *Der Oberschlesische Arbeiterfreund*, 7 November 1918, 23 January, 11 February, 1 March, 1919; *Kattowitzer Zeitung*, 17 July 1919; *Polak*, 27 January 1920; *Die Oberschlesische Grenzzeitung*, 3 May 1922.

popular violence that accompanied this transition clearly bore many traces of older worlds and values. Even before the war was over, rationing and food shortages led inexorably to the re-appearance of the European food riot in which rioting crowds attempted to impose 'fair prices' and a 'moral economy' that they recognized as just.[155] Furthermore—although it has been given relatively little sustained attention by historians—it is worth noting that the temporary retreat of state authority that followed the European revolutions of 1917–19 was accompanied by the dramatic resurgence of traditions of rural protest that had seemed before the war to be in retreat before the remorseless pressure of gendarmeries and constabularies.

As a catch-all term, we might group many of these disturbances under the loose label of *charivari* or, to use an equivalent old English term, 'rough music'. These intensely choreographed repertories of action had their own local colorations of course: but more striking are the transnational regularities in behaviour that stretch right across Europe (and, indeed, the USA).[156] First: rough music was as, the name suggests, both very loud and very public. However spuriously, it sought to embody and demonstrate the (supposedly unified) will of a local community and belonged 'to a mode of life in which some part of the law belongs still to the community and is theirs to enforce'.[157] It was 'noisy disorder' to 'bring about a just order'.[158] Secondly, such semi-violent demonstrations were highly targeted and discriminate. Individuals were singled out and humiliated for their supposed personal transgressions of communal norms. Thirdly, the impact of rough music relied upon a dramatic reversal of status hierarchies that all recognized and understood. At the heart of rough music stood the parade—of victims on a cart, or perhaps backwards on a rail or donkey—but always to make individual shame as public as possible. Desecrations of personal dignity and social standing, rather than the actual taking of life, was the hallmark of such parades: although of course they remained infused with the threat of violence and coercion.

Rather than the sharp emergence of any distinctly 'modern' class violence, the militant industrial protest that now erupted across Central and Eastern Europe bore the stamp of these venerable traditions. In the industrial heartlands of Upper Silesia, for instance, Spartacist protest was notably rustic in idiom. To give an illustrative example that must stand for many: at Gotthardtschacht in Upper Silesia, the general manager was paraded through the colliery village on 28 December 1918, was forced to raise his hat to the haulers and younger miners, and then eat

[155] S. Goebel, 'Cities' in J. Winter (ed.), *Cambridge History of The First World War* (Cambridge, 2014), Vol. II, pp. 364–68. For rioting: E. Hobsbawm and G. Rudé, *Captain Swing* (London, 1969, 1993); G. Rudé, *The Crowd in the French Revolution* (Oxford, 1972); G. Rudé, *The Crowd in History: A Study of Popular Disturbances in France and England, 1730–1848* (London, 1995); E. P. Thompson, *The Making of the English Working Class* (London, 1963, 1991); E. P. Thompson, 'The Moral Economy of the English Crowd in the Eighteenth Century', *Past and Present*, 50 (1), pp. 76–136 (1971); Tilly (et al.), *The Rebellious Century 1830–1930*.

[156] EWeber, *Peasants into Frenchmen*, pp. 399–406; RHofstadter and Wallace, *American Violence*, pp. 76–9 ['Terrorism Against Loyalists, 1774–1775'].

[157] Thompson, 'Rough Music Reconsidered', p. 20.

[158] I. Favretto, 'Rough Music and Factory Protest in Post-1945 Italy', *Past and Present*, 228(1) August 2015, p. 247.

up a whole turnip, stalk and all. This notorious 'fahren mit Karren' which one might loosely translate as the 'wheelbarrow parade', usually ended ignominiously in a pond or on a manure heap.[159] Exactly similar scenes of status reversal were also a regular feature of revolutionary turmoil right across the industrial regions of Russia.[160] We should not forget just how recent an experience industrialization still was for many Europeans in the early twentieth century.

Nor, however, were such borrowings the exclusive preserve of the Left. 'Repertoires' of violent actions have often proven surprisingly resilient: even when appropriated by relatively small numbers of political militants to impose their will more widely. Public shaming of women, for instance, through forced hair-cutting seems both an age-old and ubiquitous tactic by which men have repeatedly sought to control female behaviour. Very often this involved no more than the 'small politics' of the aggressive localized policing of sexual honour: but its suitability for wider political appropriation is obvious.[161] The diverse military occupations, official and unofficial, that both accompanied, and followed, the Great War offered rich opportunities for nationalists to punish women they deemed inappropriately intimate terms with foreign soldiers.[162] Closely convergent examples can be drawn freely from right across Europe: and from regions as diverse and remote from each other as the industrial Upper Silesia or Ruhr basins or rural Ireland.[163]

Rough music was, in essence, intense drama suited for the small stages of villages and sleepy market towns. Still, it moulded the emerging tactics of fascist movements significantly: the public humiliation of opponents through parades and derogatory placards accompanied all fascist take-overs.[164] One of the notorious signature cruelties of Italian fascism, indeed, was the forced administration of castor oil, the highly laxative 'golden nector of nausea'. Effects were dramatic and highly public: 'forced to drink it, helplessly soiling themselves, victims were sickened and grossly humiliated'.[165] Such was the international renown of Italian fascism that such tactics were, for a brief while, in vogue amongst groups as diverse as Nazi Stormtroopers, Spanish Blackshirts, the French *Camelots du Roi* ['Street-Hawkers of the King']

[159] T. Jędruszak and Z. Kolankowski (eds), *Żrodła do dziejów powstań Śląskich* (3 vols, Wrocław, 1963–1974), Vol. 2, p. 381.

[160] O. Figes, *A People's Tragedy*, p. 115; W. G. Rosenberg, 'Paramilitary Violence in Russia's Civil Wars 1918–1920' in R. Gerwarth and A. Horne (eds), *War in Peace: Paramilitary Violence in Europe after the Great War* (Oxford, 2012), p. 28. V. Serge (transl. P. Sedgwick and G. Paizis), *Memoirs of a Revolutionary* (New York, 1951, 2012), p. 97; H. Kuromiya, *Freedom and Terror in the Donbas: A Ukrainian-Russian Borderland, 1870s–1990s* (Cambridge, 1998), pp. 81, 83.

[161] P. Wilson, *Women in 20th Century Italy* (London, 2010), p. 9. For much earlier examples from the French Revolution in May 1792: S. Loomis, *Paris in the Terror* (Harmondsworth, 1964, 1970), pp. 64–5.

[162] Wilson, *Frontiers of Violence*, pp. 114–15.

[163] Wilson, *Frontiers of Violence*, pp. 114–15; F. Biały, *Niemieckie Ochotnicze formacje zbrojne na Śląsku, 1918–1923* (Katowice, 1976), pp. 138–9. *Impartial Reporter*, 9 February 1922.

[164] Siemens, *Stormtroopers*, p. 126; R. Ruruep (ed.), *Berlin 1945* (Arenhoevel, 1995), p. 94 [Munich lawyer paraded through streets, March 1933].

[165] L. Hughes-Hallett, *The Pike: Gabriele D'Annunzio. Poet, Seducer and Preacher of War* (London, 2013), p. 524.

and even the Belfast IRA.[166] But even here such apparently innovative tactics remained, to some extent, mere adaptions of much older repertoires. In Europe, then, the small town market square still remained a key political arena: and the peasantries, though slowly shrinking, key political audiences. For all its vaunting pretensions to radical transformation, fascist violence reflected the inertia of these continuing realities.

By contrast, though, these were years which saw a marked change in the USA. While the Jim Crow caste system of the southern states remained firmly intact, one of its main cultural props disappeared. After 1920, what might loosely be termed 'spectacle lynchings'—a sort of lethal American version of rough music ceremonies—went into very sharp decline. Although the issue is clouded by disputes over exactly what types of racist killing should be classified as genuine 'lynchings' a general trajectory is clear enough: 'the incidence of lynching declined after its peak in 1892, though it continued to claim roughly twenty-five black victims a year through the 1920s, and roughly ten black victims a year though the 1930s'.[167] Already at low ebb by the eve of the Second World War, such exhibition killing was to decline still further in its aftermath.[168]

The reasons for this decline were many and varied—clearly the moral force of lobbying campaigns should not be downplayed. Nor should the role of wider socio-economic transformations that were gradually breaking down the cultural isolation of the South. The verdict of the Baltimore journalist H. L. Mencken was that lynching simply supplied a need for entertainment elsewhere met by 'the merry-go-round, the theatre, the symphony orchestra, and other diversions common to large communities'. Condescending as this claim was, it did at least reflect the insight that certain types of violence 'belong' inexorably to certain types of society: and change with them.[169] As contemporaries noted in the 1930s, gala atrocities with their (sometimes huge) crowds and elaborate rituals were giving way to 'underground lynching': clandestine small-group killings protected by codes of silence.[170] With hindsight it seems a rather significant shift. According to a 1937 Gallup poll, 65 per cent of all Southerners supported legislation that would have made lynching a federal crime.[171]

A key driver behind this shift was an enhanced, if still uneven, general desire on the part of US law enforcement agencies to assert the prerogatives of their states against freelance vigilantes. According to one estimate by the Commission on

[166] M. R. Ebner, *Ordinary Violence in Mussolini's Italy* (Cambridge, 2011), pp. 8–9, 32; L. Rees, *The Nazis: A Warning from History* (London, 1997, 1998), p. 71; E. Weber, *Action Française: Royalism and Reaction in Twentieth-Century France* (Stanford, 1962), p. 142; M. Richards, *After the Civil War: Making Memory and Remaking Spain since 1936* (Cambridge, 2013), p. 61; P. Brendon, *The Dark Valley: A Panorama of the 1930s* (London, 2000), p. 317; T. P. Coogan, *The IRA* (London, 1970, 1971), p. 228.

[167] L. Wexler, *Fire in a Canebrake*, p. 205.

[168] L. Wexler, *Fire in a Canebrake*, p. 76.

[169] Quoted in A. L. Wood, *Lynching and Spectacle: Witnessing Racial Violence in America, 1890–1940* (Chapel Hill, NC, 2009), p. 5.

[170] Dray, *At the Hands of Persons Unknown*, pp. 382–3.

[171] S. E. Tolnay and E. M. Beck, *A Festival of Violence: An Analysis of Southern Lynchings, 1882–1930* (Urbana and Chicago, 1995), p. 203.

Interracial Cooperation (CIC), in the decade before 1920 only 39 per cent of attempted lynchings were prevented. This proportion rose to 77 per cent in the 1920s; and indeed reached 84 per cent in the 1930s.[172] Radio-dispatched state patrols assisted greatly here.[173]

In 1926 Governor W. J. Fields of Kentucky had shown what could be done with a serious political will to face down the threat of lynch mobs. To protect the trial of Ed Harris, a black farmhand accused of murdering his employer's family, Fields 'ordered to the Fayette County courthouse no fewer than eight infantry companies, four troops of mounted cavalry, two machine-gun squads with thirty machine guns, three .37-millimeter guns, and for good measure, a tank battalion'.[174] Thus was the inherent majesty of the law protected. Due process was not, however, necessarily better justice: from start to finish, the Fayette courthouse took just 16 minutes to condemn Harris to death.[175]

Such formidable re-fortification of the law represented a significant assertion of American statism: and paved the way for the mass incarceration of young black males that remains such a prominent structural feature of race relations in the USA of the early twenty-first century. Lynching, was, to some extent, merely replaced by a judicial slaughter of blacks: 'executions by states, in fact, increased tenfold as popular violence declined, although the total number never again reached 1890 levels'.[176] We might also note in passing that the deployment of military and police in labour disputes led to notably high death tolls: 13 in the national cotton strikes (1934), 15 in the Little Steel Strike (1937), and 10 during the Republic Steel Strike (also 1937).[177]

What is notable here, though, is how closely the incidence of unofficial American public executions tracked those of *official* public executions. Both spectacles declined. The last *public* hanging in the USA indeed took place in 1936.[178] But France, too, staged its final public guillotining in 1939.[179] Everywhere the official executioner was retreating firmly behind the prison walls.

State killing was thus undergoing a general process of becoming both increasingly centralized, and increasingly hidden. Dictatorships experimented enthusiastically in such comfortable darkness: and to mixed international reaction. Only the outbreak of war in 1939 prevented Sir Norman Kendal, head of Britain's Scotland Yard, from taking up a German invitation to tour Dachau in order to study these innovative new policing methods in action.[180] As the very name implies, the 'concentration camp' itself suggests a deliberate removal of the damned from wider society. Clerks were the high priests of this underworld; and the tyranny of their

172 Tolnay and Beck, *A Festival of Violence*, p. 203.
173 Tolnay and Beck, *A Festival of Violence*, p. 203.
174 Dray, *At the Hands of Persons Unknown*, p. 274.
175 Dray, *At the Hands of Persons Unknown*, p. 275.
176 T. Laqueur, 'Festival of Punishment', *London Review of Books*, 22 (19), 5 October, 2000, p. 19.
177 Hofstadter, 'Reflections', p. 19.
178 *Associated Press*, 8 December 2011 ('After 75 years, last public hanging haunts City').
179 D. King, *Death in the City of Light* (London, 2011, 2012), pp. 323–4.
180 M. Mazower, *Dark Continent: Europe's Twentieth Century* (London, 1999), p. 100.

files condemned, or spared, according to classificatory whim.[181] All in all, 'the dozen years of existence of the "Thousand-year Reich" would generate a proliferation of censuses, statistical investigations, registers of foreigners, identity cards, and residence lists that ultimately constituted the administrative foundations for the deportations to Auschwitz and the other death camps'.[182]

At the same time, it is important to note the renewed moves during the 1930s to re-assert the state's control over *private* violence in society as well. Laws on the sale and possession of handguns were tightened up at the very end of the Weimar Republic.[183] Duelling was eventually outlawed by the Nazi regime (although its paladins had once celebrated it as a social institution that 'strengthens personal courage, self-control and will power').[184] As Hitler himself observed, honour was no longer 'the privilege of a caste'.[185] To the German state alone was now due the privilege of disposing of human life: and that in ever increasing quantities. One can always go faster in atrocity, since the 'gears move faster and faster', as the ex-French Premier Léon Blum recognized unflinchingly in 1942.[186]

V

> When the crash came the man who could control the streets would win.
>
> – Oswald Mosley[187]

'From the vantage point of the late 20th century' writes Martin Miller 'the years between the world wars appear but an interlude in the evolution of terrorism, a deceptive calm before the emergence of an even more ferocious period of political violence reaching further around the globe and deeper into the lives of ordinary civilians.'[188] Sidestepping the vexed question of the exact understanding of terrorism at stake here, this general contention remains an intriguing one. It is certainly not true that these decades were entirely barren of innovation. A brand new development was the appearance of the lone serial bomber waging a high-profile but deeply private war against an entire urban society. Both 'the Hell Judge' of Paris and George Metesky, the 'Mad Bomber' of New York, first appeared in the 1930s.[189] But it is true that one of the lesser noticed corollaries of the mass paramilitary turn does seem to have been a concomitant general retreat from the small-group

[181] Z. Bauman, *Modernity and the Holocaust* (Cambridge, 1991, 2006), pp. 102–6.

[182] Torpey, *The Invention of the Passport*, pp. 163–4.

[183] H. H. Liang, *The Berlin Police Force in the Weimar Republic* (Berkeley, 1970), pp. 110–11.

[184] Nazi commissioner for the Prussian Ministry of Justice, Herr Kerrl quoted in: R. Hopton, *Pistols at Dawn: A History of Duelling* (London, 2007), pp. 377–8.

[185] H. Trevor-Roper (ed.), *Hitler's Table Talk 1941–1944* (Oxford, 1988), p. 227.

[186] M. Mazower, *Hitler's Empire: Nazi Rule in Occupied Europe* (London, 2008, 2009), pp. 9–10.

[187] Quoted in: Brendon, *The Dark Valley*, p. 170.

[188] M. A. Miller, 'The Intellectual Origins of Modern Terrorism in Europe' in M. Crenshaw (ed.), *Terrorism in Context* (University Park, Pennsylvania, 1995) p. 57.

[189] *The Yorkshire Evening Post*, 22 June 1934; M. M. Greenburg, *The Mad Bomber of New York* (New York, 2011).

conspiratorial politics of armed struggle on *both* the far-left and the far-right.[190] Such a shift demands more analytical attention—and qualification—than it customarily receives.

The decline of anarchist terror in particular is a more mysterious, and unexpected, development than is often recognized. Indeed, a late upsurge in 1918–23 here eclipsed anything seen for nearly two decades.[191] Anarchist assassinations claimed the lives of the rightist activist Marius Plateau in France (22 January 1923) and the Czechoslovak Finance Minister, Alois Rašín (died 18 February 1923).[192] The French Premier Georges Clemenceau was shot and wounded during the Paris Peace Conference (1919).[193] Bombers struck in both Milan (October 1920) and Turin (May 1921). A spectacularly botched assassination attempt at the Diana Theatre in Milan killed twenty-one (23rd March, 1921).[194] In the USA, the Galleanist faction waged both a sophisticated mail bomb offensive and a sustained campaign of mass casualty bombings that killed up to sxity-seven people, most of them in the truly spectacular Wall Street atrocity of September 1920.[195] As Richard Bach Jensen notes, 'these two series of bombings were the most widespread coordinated attacks in anarchist history'.[196] Moreover, the slow-burning controversy over the fates of the Italian American anarchists Sacco and Vanzetti that lasted from 1920 to 1927 galvanized very considerable international support (and even some sympathetic rioting, mail bombs as well as an explosion at the 28th Street Subway Station in New York that injured twelve).[197] The American journalist Elliot Paul captured the response to the news of their eventual execution in one Parisian café:

> A hush fell over the company when Monsieur Henri, who had gone to the corner to telephone, returned with incredulous sorrow on his face, looked apologetically at me and dropped his eyes'
>
> 'They have killed those men?' asked Noël, in his deep bass voice, almost a whisper.

[190] This period, writes Rik Coolsaet, remains 'overlooked in almost all terrorism research': R. Coolsaet, 'Anticipating the Post-Daesh Landscape', Egmont Paper 97, 2017, p. 12.

[191] T. Jones, 'Anarchist Terrorism in the United States' in Randall D. Law (ed.), *The Routledge History of Terrorism* (Abingdon, 2015), pp. 130–42.

[192] Piers Brendon, *The Dark Valley: A Panorama of the 1930s* (London, 2000), pp. 14–15; J. Rothschild, *East Central Europe between the Two World Wars* (Seattle and London, 1974, 1990), pp. 106–7.

[193] Gerwarth, *The Vanquished*, p. 154.

[194] R. Bach Jensen, 'Anarchist Terrorism in Europe/World' in R. Law (ed.), *The Routledge History of Terrorism* (Abingdon, 2015), p. 123 [misdated here to 1923]; *New York Times*, 25 March 1921.

[195] B. Gage, *The Day Wall Street Exploded: A Story of America in Its First Age of Terror* (Oxford, 2009, 2010), pp. 31–6.

[196] Bach Jensen, *The Battle Against Anarchist Terrorism*, pp. 359–60.

[197] For the 1921 protests in Paris (including bomb throwing and rioting), see: *Northern Whig*, 22 October 1921; *Irish News*, 24 October 1921. For the 1927 bombing in New York: B. Whalen and J. Whalen, *The NYPD's First Fifty Years* (Lincoln, Nebraska, 2014), p. 141. For international reaction: Gage, *The Day Wall Street Exploded*, pp. 219–20; Bach Jensen, *The Battle Against Anarchist Terrorism*, pp. 359–60; J. Gardiner, *The Thirties: An Intimate History of Britain* (London, 2011), p. 719; R. Graves and A. Hodge, *The Long Weekend: A Social History of Great Britain, 1918–1939* (London, 1940, 1950), p. 167.

Monsieur Henri's head inclined itself a little more. The women gasped.

'That was ignoble,' said Madame Berthe Dossot.[198]

And yet during these years, as both inspiration and example, the Russian Revolution was changing the face of leftist violence. Anarchist templates of small group or individualistic action faded dramatically. Rather than some natural law of slowly fading forty-year long generational cycles, it was this that surely, if partially, accounts for the sharp falling off in anarchist attacks in the years immediately after the Russian Revolution—although official deportations by both France and the USA surely helped to deplete key cadres.[199] This 'revolution in identification' hit anarchist movements hard. In short, the protectionist states that emerged from the aftermath of the world war proved distinctly inhospitable arenas for anarchist terror.[200]

Communist movements were much blamed for post-war terror: although it has to be acknowledged that this often merely reflected the biases and lack of curiosity of investigators.[201] For its part, the German Communist Party remained too wedded to the ideal of mass action and the general strike to make any determined transition to underground action on a small-group template. In 1932, with street battles raging with the Nazis, elements in the Berlin leadership pressed hard for a turn to 'individual terror', but were roundly rebuffed by their leadership for 'adventurist fooling around with explosives'.[202] They were even less well placed to resist when the Nazi dictatorship consolidated its grip on power during the following spring. Years earlier, the Italian Communist Party had made a similar deliberate decision to reject a strategy of armed struggle by small groups, although the idea of using bombings to 'consolidate' a general strike lingered rather longer.[203]

Only in Bulgaria did the Communists show any real conspiratorial flair. Here, though, their ambitions were of Guy Fawksian dimensions: they attempted to decapitate an entire government. First, they assassinated Constantin Georgieff, a senior parliamentarian: then they mined his funeral held at the Sveta Nédélia Cathedral on 16 April 1925. Realizing that the crypt and ground floor would be searched thoroughly beforehand, they deliberately struck from above, planning to bring the roof down on the congregation. The results were indeed truly spectacular—with a predictably enormous casualty toll (160 fatalities in a mid-range estimate). The key figures of the regime were, however, fortuitously protected by 'an iron stay connecting two pillars. Most of those standing immediately behind them

198 E. Paul, *The Last Time I Saw Paris* (London, 1942, 2011), pp. 119–20.

199 D. Rapoport, 'The Four Waves of Rebel Terror and September 11' in C. W. Kegley (ed.), *The New Global Terrorism: Characteristics, Causes, Controls* (New Jersey, 2003), pp. 36–7; VSerge, *Memoirs of a Revolutionary*, pp. 77–8.

200 Torpey, *The Invention of the Passport*, pp. 145, 149.

201 Bach Jensen, *The Battle Against Anarchist Terrorism*, p. 360.

202 E. Rosenhaft, 'The KPD in the Weimar Republic and the Problem of Terror during the "Third Period", 1929–33', in W. J. Mommsen and G. Hirschfeld (eds), *Social Protest, Violence and Terror in 19th and 20th Century Europe* (London, 1982), pp. 347–50.

203 P. Edwards, *More Work! Less Pay! Rebellion and Repression in Italy, 1972–7* (Manchester, 2009), p. 32.

were killed.'[204] By this 'singular chance, the Government and the royal family were unscathed'.[205] Repression predictably followed hot and hard: and there were to be no more grandiose Communist experiments in elite decapitation.[206]

On the far-right, there was a rough symmetry in the move towards the politics of mass mobilization that Italian fascism pioneered. There were some notable, if brief, exceptions. In the early years of the Weimar Republic the failure of coup strategies after the Kapp Putsch of March 1920 led to more elaborate plotting in the shape of the Organization Consul. This shadowy, but well-connected, outfit pulled off a string of assassinations that culminated in the killing of the Foreign Minister, Walter Rathenau, on 24 June 1922.[207] Their intentions seem to have been structured by classic strategies of provocation—the left would be lured into a general uprising which could, in turn, be crushed leading to a military dictatorship of the right. But the resulting manhunt that followed the Rathenau assassination finished the organization: and revealed the extent to which it had survived up until this point through high-placed indulgence rather than by its own intrinsic resilience.[208] In these years allied occupations in Upper Silesia, the Saar, and the Ruhr also invited more guerilla-style underground campaigns of sabotage and train bombings.[209]

Strikingly, though, it was precisely such conspiratorial politics that Adolf Hitler had quite explicitly rejected by 1926. A key passage in *Mein Kampf* is worth quoting at length for its ominous prescience:

> Only very small groups, by years of sifting, can assume the character of real secret organisations. But the very smallness of such organisations would remove their value for the National Socialist movement. *What we needed and still need were and are not a hundred or two hundred reckless conspirators, but a hundred thousand and a second hundred thousand fighters for our philosophy of life. We should not work in secret conventicles, but in mighty mass demonstrations, and it is not by dagger and poison or pistol that the road can be cleared for the movement, but by the conquest of the streets. We must teach the Marxists that the future master of the streets is National Socialism, just as it will some day be the master of the state.*[210]

Even less welcome to the leaders of the big battalions was the 'assistance' of lone assassins, however congenial their ideological motivation. Since both communists and fascists believed in building mass movements, the actions of mavericks were often not especially welcome. On 21 October 1916, Friedrich Adler (the secretary

[204] British Ambassador's report quoted in: A. D. Harvey, 'The Attempt to Assassinate the Bulgarian Cabinet, 16 April 1925', *Terrorism and Political Violence*, 4 (1) Spring 1992, pp. 100–8.

[205] V. Serge, *Memoirs of a Revolutionary*, p. 209.

[206] Gerwarth, *The Vanquished* p. 152.

[207] M. Sabrow, *Der Rathenaumord: Rekonstruktion einer Verschwörung gegen die Republik von Weimar* (Oldenbourg, 1994), pp. 86–8.

[208] M. Sabrow, *Der Rathenaumord*, pp. 8–9, 119–21, 155.

[209] *Exeter and Plymouth Gazette*, 2 July 1923 [9 Belgian soldiers dead in train bombing at Duisburg]; *Western Daily Press*, 4 July 1923 [time-fuse bombs found in tunnel near Mayence]. See also: P. Ackerman and C. Kruegler, *Strategies of Nonviolent Conflict: the Dynamics of People Power in the Twentieth Century* (Westport, 1994), Chapter 4, 'The Ruhrkampf: Regional Defence against Occupation, 1923', pp. 128–31.

[210] A. Hitler (transl. R. Manheim), *Mein Kampf* (London, 1969, 1992), p. 494. Emphasis in original.

of the Austrian social democrats) shot dead Count Stürgkh (the Austrian prime minister) as a protest against the war. Adler's action attracted widespread sympathy on the left.[211] But Trotsky was withering about such self-indulgent 'opportunism' while Lenin 'merely wondered why a man in his position had not taken the less dramatic but more effective step of circulating the party activists with an anti-war appeal.'[212] On the right, Count Anton Arco-Valley, the proto-fascist killer of Kurt Eisner was arrested by the Nazis as soon as they took power in 1933.[213]

'By and large', concludes Walter Laqueur, there was 'comparatively little terror, for this was the age of mass parties on both the right and the left'.[214] This summary seems a little bald. The Weimar Republic in particular was not spared some classically 'terroristic' bombing attacks, albeit still mostly fairly amateur in execution. In early March 1921, a Communist faction in Saxony bombed the town hall in Falkenstein: and then court buildings in Dresden, Freiberg, and Leipzig.[215] From the right, a campaign of minor bombings targeted eight public buildings over a two-month period in 1929.[216] A series of limited bombings also occurred across the Palatinate from the summer of 1931 into the spring of 1932; and a brief (but far more intense) 'terror campaign' was launched from 6 to 9 August 1932 by the Nazi stormtroopers or *Sturm Abteilung* (SA) across eastern German cities.[217] Shooting incidents also featured: such as on 23 November 1930 when fifteen SA men shot up a workers' club at Eden Palast, Charlottenburg in Berlin.[218] In general, though, Laqueur is correct to the extent that these rampages were very much a *secondary* feature of this Brownshirt terror. Indeed, one is left with an impression of a rather disorganized terror, largely spontaneous: and using whatever hand-grenades and handguns happened to be to hand.

Such reckless attacks seem to have received little encouragement from above, even when they were not explicitly disowned.[219] 'The "street," as Goebbels saw it, was the decisive place in which policy was made.'[220] Here the important thing for the Nazi leadership was *not* to attack the state head on; nor to rely on such dramatic means of destabilization (such as bombing) that the state could not afford to ignore. The assumption that the 'streets are for traffic' commented one observer in 1927 'appears to have become obsolete under postwar conditions and the repeated

[211] J. Braunthal, *In Search of the Millennium* (London, 1945), pp. 188–98. I am indebted to Marc Mulholland for this information.

[212] L. Trotsky, 'Terrorism and Communism: A Reply to Karl Kautsky' (1920), Chapter 9 [on opportunism]. Available here: https://www.marxists.org/archive/trotsky/1920/terrcomm/; For Lenin's pragmatism, see: Hobsbawm, *Revolutionaries*, p. 214, note 4.

[213] And again in 1944: F. Reck-Malleczewen, *Diary of a Man in Despair* (London, 2000, 2001), pp. 226, 248 (note 64). Mitchell, *Revolution in Bavaria, 1918–1919*, p. 272.

[214] W. Laqueur, *The Age of Terrorism* (London, 1987), p. 20.

[215] M. Hoelz, *Vom 'Weissen Kreuz' zur roten Fahne: Jugend-, Kampf- und Zuchthauserlebnisse* (Berlin, 1929, 2019), pp. 125–30.

[216] *Larne Times*, 7 September 1929 [Reichstag bomb with mention of other bombings]. Also, for a slightly later hoax: *Hartlepool Northern Daily Mail*, 1 April 1930 [fake bomb at Berlin Town Hall].

[217] Siemens, *Stormtroopers*, pp. xv, 51; R. Bessel, *Political Violence and the Rise of Nazism: The Stormtroopers in Eastern Germany1925–1934* (Yale, 1984), pp. 88–91.

[218] Liang, *The Berlin Police Force in the Weimar Republic*, p. 110.

[219] D. Siemens, *Stormtroopers*, pp. 51–2.

[220] Laqueur, *Terrorism*, p. 93.

parades of political demonstrations. It now often appears as if the sole purpose of the streets is to provide a suitable field for the sport of political demonstrations.'[221] July 1932 saw 400 street battles in Berlin alone.[222] Yet once a Nazi dictatorship had been established and consolidated in 1933–34, Hitler was able to retire what has always been a rather carefully calibrated brand of thuggishness.

The one exception to this trend was the Kristallnacht state pogrom of 1938: and it was no accident that it was never repeated (despite Hitler's blessing). It was too embarrassing. Both domestic and international reaction was almost universally condemnatory. Onlookers were outraged at the sight of children throwing cobblestones through the windows of private property.[223] Even elite Nazis were opposed: twenty-eight out of a sample of forty-one expressed strong disapproval in a contemporary study.[224] Secret police reports in Milan similarly recorded that people reacted to the news 'with horror complaining that the Germans were proving as "barbarous" as were the "reds" who sacked churches in Spain'.[225] As the *Chicago Tribune* commented acidly, such wild scenes of disorder broadcast all the wrong wider messages:

> If it is the policy of the German state to eliminate Jews from business, the government is presumed to have the means to accomplish it in legal forms and by its own agencies. To turn the task over to unrestrained private fury is the negation of civilized political responsibility.[226]

Like Italian Fascism, the public glory of the Nazi regime in its heyday was its truly spectacular use of set-piece mass demonstrations of hyper-order: the 'oceanic crowds' that tamely lapped the Berlin Olympics of 1936 and the Nuremberg rallies.[227] 'We were not afraid of a strong state—on the contrary, we demanded it' recalled Klaus Mehnert, comparing the late 1960s with his own interwar student days.[228]

For these regimes, then, violent destabilization instead became the export tactic of choice. This, too, was new. What today would be termed 'state sponsored terrorism' was essentially invented in Europe in the mid-1930s (rather than being, as so often implied, a by-product of Cold War).[229] As so often, Italian fascism blazed a trail that Nazism later followed. Italian fascist sponsorship of the bombing campaigns of its proxies in the Croatian *Ustashe* ('insurgents': against Yugoslavia from 1931 onwards) and of the *Comité Secret d'Action Révolutionnaire* (CSAR) better known by their nickname of the *Cagoulards* ('Hooded Men': against the French Popular Front government, 1937–8) tended to be more arms-length affairs than

[221] Diehl, *Paramilitary Politics in Weimar Germany*, p. 197.
[222] Richie, *Faust's Metropolis*, pp. 400–1.
[223] A. Read and D. Fisher, *Berlin: The Biography of a City* (London, 1994), p. 217.
[224] M. Mann, *The Dark Side of Democracy: Explaining Ethnic Cleansing* (Cambridge, 2005), p. 194.
[225] Bosworth, *Mussolini's Italy*, p. 420.
[226] Quoted in: A. Cockburn, *Corruptions of Empire* (London, 1987, 1989), pp. 312–13.
[227] Bosworth, *Mussolini's Italy*, p. 11; D. Hart-Davis, *Hitler's Olympics: The 1936 Games* (London, 1986), pp. 137–8.
[228] K. Mehnert, *The Twilight of the Young: the Radical Movement of the 1960s* (London, 1976), pp. 372–75.
[229] D. Byman, *Deadly connections: States that Sponsor Terrorism* (Cambridge, 2005), pp. 1–2; Rapoport, 'The Four Waves of Rebel Terror and September 11', p. 48.

the broadly parallel phenomenon of Nazi Germany using cellular armed groups across neighbouring countries, most prominently in Austria (1933–34) and Poland (1939).[230]

Still, several broad observations can be offered here. First, at least in the eyes of their ultimate sponsors, these were essentially speculative and opportunistic expeditions—their aim being, in the words of an Austrian Nazi planning document from 1931, 'to increase the emotional turbulence until conditions are ripe for "everything" '.[231] Tactics were accordingly opportunistic (if still occasionally spectacular). Their highlights (if they may be called that) were the successful assassinations of two European premiers—King Alexander I of Yugoslavia (1934) and Chancellor Dollfuss of Austria (1934)—and a rash of unsuccessful coup attempts or plans that signally failed to deliver instant regime change in Lithuania, Memel, and Austria.[232] Secondly, these bombing campaigns were inexorably drawn towards international transport nodes and routes. A key signature tactic here was the bombing of international train services, including the prestigious Orient Express.[233] As early as 1931, the Yugoslav authorities had been forced to make international travellers disembark at their frontier and re-board a new train, rather than allow through traffic.[234] Thirdly, the means of destruction made available to these bombers from state arsenals were truly enormous: resources that the contemporary IRA or Irgun could only have dreamt about in their wildest fantasies.[235] In the Paris area alone, the police seized 'nearly 250 machine-guns and automatic weapons, 300–400 army and hunting rifles; about 300,000 cartridges; and over 7,000 grenades'.[236] Indeed, when the French authorities raided a Cagoulard hideout at Villejuif, Paris in 1938 they uncovered a single cache of at least 3,000 grenades: their careless handling of it then promptly caused an explosion which blew four-

[230] J. Rothschild, *East Central Europe between the Two World Wars* (Seattle and London, 1974, 1990), pp. 245–6; P. Bourdrel, *La Cagoule* (Paris, 1970), p. 65; D. L. L. Parry 'Counter Revolution in Conspiracy, 1935–37' in N. Atkin and F. Tallett (eds), *The Right in France: From Revolution to Le Pen* (London, 2003), pp. 161–82.

[231] Linz secret conference, 6 December 1932, quoted in: Botz, 'Political Violence, its Forms and Strategies in the First Austrian Republic', p. 321.

[232] R. Seton-Watson, 'King Alexander I's Assassination: Its Background and Effects', *International Affairs*, 14 (1), Jan–Feb 1935, pp. 20–42; World Committee for the Victims of German Fascism, *Das Braune Netz: wie Hiters Agenten im Auslande arbeiten und den Krieg vorbereiten* (Paris, 1935), pp. 183, 268.

[233] G. Chaliand and A. Blin, *The History of Terrorism: From Antiquity to Al-Qaeda* (Berkeley, 2007), p. 191 (Orient Express). For details on Yugoslav train bombings see: *Daily Herald*, 6 January 1931; *Dundee Courier*, 4 August 1931; *Leeds Mercury*, 23 January 1934; *Larne Times*, 27 January 1934; *The Scotsman*, 6 June 1934. For Austria: *The Scotsman*, 11 June 1934; *Yorkshire Post and Leeds Intelligencer*, 11 June 1934; *The Scotsman*, 15 June 1934; Anonymous (transl. J. Messinger), *The Death of Dollfuss: An Official History of the Revolt of July, 1934, in Austria* (London, 1935), pp. 35–6, 85.

[234] *Dundee Courier*, 4 August 1931.

[235] Anonymous, *The Death of Dollfus*, pp. 85, 87 [110 hand grenades, 120 stick bombs etc]. Also: Boudrel, *La Cagoule*, p. 103; Laqueur, *Terrorism*, p. 142. See the photo of a rather meagre-looking IRA arms dump in A. Parkinson, *Belfast's Unholy War: The Troubles of the 1920s* (Dublin, 2004), between pp. 160–1. G. K. Brunelle and A. Finley-Croswhite, *Murder in the Métro: Laetitia Toureaux and the Cagoule in 1930s France* (Baton Rouge, 2010), pp. 123–32.

[236] Parry 'Counter Revolution in Conspiracy, 1935–37', p. 162. See also: Laqueur, *Terrorism*, p. 142; Bourdrel, *La Cagoule*, p. 304.

teen policemen to bits.[237] And when the Polish authorities arrested the Nazi agent Rudolf Wilsch at Huta Laura, Polish Silesia, they found no fewer than seventy-two pistols in his flat.[238] Such groups often seem to have had more arms than they could ever have been able to use.

Being shrouded in official deniability, these campaigns remain inevitably rather shadowy escapades. They were the direct ancestors of many later twentieth-century similar state-sponsored and transnational horrors is clear enough, even if they have been almost entirely ignored by historians and scholars of terrorism.[239] Even if only fleetingly, they could cause genuine alarm. Official security was tightened notably across capital cities and major international transport routes.[240] According to one press report from 19 November 1937, 'guards at strategic points in Paris have been strengthened, and orders have been given that strangers entering Government buildings who do not stop after being called upon twice to do so are to be shot'.[241] 'Paris itself, inclined a few days ago to scoff at the Cagoulards story, is now frankly nervous' confirmed the *Aberdeen Journal* just a few days later.[242] English tourists cancelled their bookings to Paris in droves.[243] If all this seems to presage an eerily similar atmosphere across European and American cities forty years later, we should also be careful to recognize the limits to the 1930s campaigns. Such campaigns killed relatively few civilians: and it seems quite deliberately so. As with street fighting, their sponsors here proved themselves adept at calibrating violence with half an eye to wider audiences that they did not wish to alienate irrevocably.[244] State-sponsored terror as practised by fascist regimes showed some finesse and restraint (although it was always more ambitious than the Soviet speciality of long-distance assassination of exiles).[245] In any case, all such campaigns were overshadowed by the prospect of renewed world war that hung so heavily over these years ('Everyday life is as it were impregnated by this general fear').[246]

But definite precedents had indeed now been established: and with them a distinctly ominous new chapter in international relations opened. An obscure atrocity in southern Poland on the night of 28 August 1939 pointed the way to this darker future. At 23.38 hours that night a suitcase bomb planted by a Nazi agent devastated the main buildings at Tarnów railway station. Twenty-two people died in the

[237] R. Davies, 'Explosion at C-IED Lab, Paris, 1938' (16 July 2015). Available at: http://www.standingwellback.com/See also: Bourdrel, *La Cagoule*, pp. 266–7.

[238] K. M. Pospieszalski, 'The Bomb Attack at Tarnów and Other Nazi Provocations Before and After the Outbreak of the 1939 War. Did Hitler Want the German Minority to Suffer Losses?', *Polish Western Affairs*, 2, 1986, p. 254.

[239] To his credit, Laqueur does include a brief discussion: Laqueur, *The Age of Terrorism*, p. 20.

[240] D. Footman, *Balkan Holiday* (London, 1935), p. 284.

[241] *Dundee Evening Telegraph*, 19 November 1937.

[242] *Aberdeen Journal*, 22 November 1937. [243] Bourdrel, *La Cagoule*, p. 294.

[244] J. J. Sadkovich, 'Terrorism in Croatia, 1929–1934', *East European Quarterly*, XXII, 1, March 1988, pp. 61, 75, note 27.

[245] J. Bowyer Bell, *Assassin: Theory and Practice of Political Violence* (New Jersey, 1979, 2005), pp. 112–15, 143–7 (attempts to kill Trotsky); F. L. Ford, *Political Murder: From Tyrannicide to Terrorism* (Harvard, 1985), pp. 269–70. Also: *Irish News*, 26 May 1938 (Ukrainian nationalist killed with time bomb in Rotterdam).

[246] Green, quoted in: E. Weber, *The Hollow Years: France in the 1930s* (London, 1995), p. 243.

rubble; perhaps another thirty-five were injured.[247] In quieter times, such carnage might well have captured and held the headlines for a few days. But not now. On 1 September 1939 another total collapse of European civilization threatened as the Nazis invaded Poland. And Tarnów was relentlessly swallowed up in its turn by unimaginably larger, and longer, horrors.

[247] Pospieszalski, 'The Bomb Attack at Tarnów and Other Nazi Provocations, p. 241.

2

The Modern State and the Society of Hyper-Order from 1939

As the peak of organized killing in human history, the Second World War remains strikingly unintegrated into more general accounts of political violence 'from below'. Even distinguished historians of fascism such as Walter Laqueur or Michael Burleigh have tended to glide over the Second World War in their survey accounts of the historical development of terrorism.[1] Other overview accounts and essay collections in broadly the same tradition have similarly skirted the Second World War almost entirely.[2] Armed struggle against Nazi occupation has hardly gone unstudied, of course. But it has tended to be seen as an autonomous subject in its own right: as Resistance.

Naturally, and unsurprisingly, Nazi propagandists were unrestrained in labelling Resistance fighters as terrorists. Scholars have been notably reluctant to follow them in this categorization. The key question, though, is whether this makes sense analytically. In a rare explicit discussion of the wider issues, Caoimhe Nic Dháibhéid usefully draws out what is at stake here:

> much of the energy of the vibrant underground resistance press was devoted to asserting that the real terrorists were the German occupiers and the detested collaborationist regime. In the aftermath of the war, and with the scale of Nazi state terror across Europe becoming clear, these assertions gained a justifiable currency; but the value-driven separation of the categories of terrorism and resistance has arguably obscured a cold-eyed assessment of the strategy and tactics of the resistance groups, particularly in operations directed against compatriot collaborators.[3]

For their part, Heinz-Gerhard Haupt and Klaus Weinhauer argue a little opaquely that 'resistance to Nazism and to the policies of the Third Reich as an occupying

[1] W. Laqueur, *Terrorism* (London, 1977, 1980); M. Burleigh, *Blood and Rage: A Cultural History of Terrorism* (London, 2008, 2009). But see also: M. Burleigh, *The Third Reich: A New History* (London, 2000), pp. 665–728 (chapter on resistance in Germany, 1933–1945).

[2] Thus the Second World War is almost entirely neglected in: D. Rapoport, 'The Four Waves of Rebel Terrorism'; M. Carr, *The Infernal Machine: A History of Terrorism* (New York, 2006, 2007), pp. 63–5 (a brief discussion of the French resistance only); R. D. Law, *Terrorism: A History* (2009), p. 175; R. D. Law (ed.), *The Routledge History of Terrorism* (Abingdon, 2015).

[3] C. Nic Dháibhéid, *Terrorist Histories: Individuals and Political Violence Since the 19th Century* (London, 2017, 2018), p. 73.

power drew large numbers of Europeans into acts of violence which, though they were not terroristic in origin, often became in effect terroristic in character'.[4]

To unpick these issues, it is worth establishing some basic distinctions. The first is conceptual. Most obviously (and crucially) Resistance struggles in Europe between 1939 and 1945 were part of a much larger struggle. Their intensity rose and fell on the deeper tides of that conflict. Where military defeat on the battlefield had been crushing, Resistance 'from below' was usually negligible. That was the experience of both France (*c.*1940–2) and Germany (1945–6).[5] In the final analysis, 'the Resistance could have become a separate war, but it did not'.[6]

The second distinction is geographical. Resistance in Western Europe was a fundamentally different phenomenon to across much of the rest of the continent. The reasons for this were manifold—but, in brief, Nazi ideology (which planned and waged a racial war against Slavs and Jews in the east), population density and terrain all mattered greatly: 'Such was the topography of vast swathes of eastern Europe—extensive, often underdeveloped rural areas encompassing thick forests, copious swamps or extensive mountain ranges—that resistance there assumed the specific character of guerilla warfare far more than it did in flatter, more urbanized western Europe.'[7]

The third distinction is infrastructural. By 1940 Western Europe had a tradition of strong governance dating back 150 years to the French Revolution. Nazi conquest inherited these sophisticated working state bureaucracies, battered perhaps, but still essentially in working order. This mattered on several levels. Most obviously, it eased the Nazi task of resource extraction. But it also eased the challenge of control: especially in the early years of the Occupation. Especially when the future seemed an inevitable Nazi victory, armed resistance attracted only a fringe of utopians. Even for blatantly collaborationist regimes, 'state magic'—the automatic deference that society instils towards officialdom—faded rather slowly.[8] And for their part, state agencies worked hard to maintain that claim to loyalty: and with it, their own monopoly of violence. Without any sense of inconsistency, therefore, the Préfecture of Police in Paris could *both* round up 12,884 Jews for the gas chambers *and* spare no resources to track down a serial killer preying on (predominantly Jewish) fugitives trying to escape the official round-ups.[9] A genocidal order extended no tolerance to rival free-lancers.

[4] H. Haupt and K. Weinhauer, 'Terrorism and the State' in D. Bloxham and R. Gerwarth (eds), *Political Violence in Twentieth-Century Europe* (Cambridge, 2011), p. 193.

[5] For minor 'Werewolf' activity, see: *The People*, 9 September 1945; *Dundee Evening Telegraph*, 8 February 1946.

[6] P. Calvocoressi and G. Wint, *Total War: Causes and Courses of the Second World War* (Harmondsworth, 1972, 1974), p. 279.

[7] B. Shepherd and J. Pattinson, 'Introduction' in B. Shepherd and J. Pattinson (eds.), *War in a Twilight World: Partisan and Anti-Partisan Warfare in Eastern Europe, 1939–45* (Basingstoke, 2010), p. 2.

[8] Bourdeiu, quoted in: M. Miller, 'Ordinary Terrorism in Historical Perspective', *Journal for the Study of Radicalism*, 2 (1) Spring 2008, p. 135.

[9] Who apparently even used his own homemade gas chamber: D. King, *Death in the City of Light* (London, 2011, 2012), pp. 335–42; L. Sante, *The Other Paris: An Illustrated Journey Through A City's Poor and Bohemian Past* (London, 2015), p. 85 (round up of 12,884 Jews, July 1942).

All of these factors structured the first armed resistance groups that emerged in the cities of Western Europe in profound ways. As a sociological phenomenon, they shared features of their predecessors in the earlier Blanquist tradition of the clandestine underground. But they operated in far less congenial circumstances even than those true believers had done in that nineteenth-century heyday of global free movement. By contrast, the mid-twentieth-century state with its elaborate and pervasive regimes of identity inspection was a daunting adversary merely to evade, let alone confront: 'it was not lost on occupied and terrorized populations that the systems of identification and registration were vital to the implementation of the Nazis' designs for mastery of Europe and its racial purification.'[10] Inevitably, counter-bureaucracies emerged: a veritable cottage industry spewing out false identities and forged aliases. Such work, though, naturally 'demanded the utmost in patience, endurance and sheer drudgery'.[11] Whatever else they were, or became, all Resistance struggles in the tightly-governed territories of Western Europe were inevitably wars of paper: each police checkpoint its own ordeal.[12]

Under such circumstances, to begin a shooting war from a standing start was not easy. Albert Ouzoulias later recalled of this crucial period of initial escalation in France in mid-1941 that

> it was not easy to progress from underground leafleting, organizing strikes and even cutting cables and sabotage to guerrilla actions. You have to imagine what it was like for an 18-year-old—or indeed for anyone—to go into a Paris street one evening and wait alone for a Nazi officer or solider and execute him.[13]

It can be no accident, then, that those who moved first were very often the very young. Indeed, what impresses about early resistance actions is thus their sheer recklessness. The *Bataillons de la Jeunesse* of the French Communist Party (that began an assassination campaign against German officers in 1941) or the White Rose group in Munich (in 1942–3)—which, to be accurate, engaged in public anti-Nazi propaganda, although its members do seem to have been considering armed escalation—simply leapt in the dark.[14]

Beginnings might indeed be reckless; but any sustained campaigns of armed resistance could not afford to be. All modern insurgencies are primarily struggles over the control of key information: and the quickest way to stop knowledge spreading is to impose social isolation. Thus in France, 'careless talk had enabled the Gestapo and the Vichy Police to penetrate the organization [of the Communist Party]. To counteract this the *Franc-Tireurs et Partisans* had been split up into small hermetically sealed cells'.[15] Such corpuscular units were meant to operate in 'small

[10] J. C. Torpey, *The Invention of the Passport: Surveillance, Citizenship and the State* (Cambridge, 2000, 2018), p. 176.

[11] R. Hanser, *A Noble Treason* (New York, 1979), p. 211.

[12] B. Marshall, *The White Rabbit* (London, 1952, 1954), pp. 35–6; T. Bower, *Klaus Barbie: Butcher of Lyons* (London, 1984, 1987), p. 110; M. R. D. Foot, *Resistance* (London, 1976, 1978), pp. 95–8.

[13] Quoted in: R. Gildea, *Fighters in the Shadows: A New History of the French Resistance* (London, 2015, 2016), p. 88.

[14] M. Cobb, *The Resistance: The French Fight Against the Nazis* (London, 2009), pp. 76–7.

[15] Marshall, *The White Rabbit*, p. 41.

groups of three or four who would attack the Germans and then slip away, like "blobs of mercury"'.[16]

Exactly the same pattern emerged among the *Gruppi di Azione Patriottica* (GAPS) across the cities of northern Italy from the autumn of 1943:

> Another feature appears in the testimonies regarding the Gappists: the tense and obsessive sense of loneliness that hung over this combatant, who was generally compelled to live in absolute and often solitary clandestinity.... There are pages in the memoirs of a Bologna Gappist which well convey the atmosphere that was born when one had to spend days on end shut up in a tiny apartment: 'Another three days went by, three interminable days of solitude and hunger. We would spend them listless and inert, looking out of the windows, leafing through the few remaining books, hunting down lice and cursing fate'.[17]

Such fighters effectively became their own jailers.[18]

Resistance groups of this type inevitably fought a rather limited war in terms of the very restricted destructive capabilities that they actually commanded. In terms of evaluating their place within longer trajectories of political violence, the key question remains: did they also do so by design? Was this a self-limiting struggle, or just a materially feeble one? How 'indiscriminate' was such violence?

We need here to draw a basic analytical distinction between distinct, though related, armed struggles that Resistance movements waged. Most obviously, there was the direct fight against Nazi Occupation forces. Such efforts were hardly without their own moral dilemmas, of course—how far should one risk provoking disproportionate retaliation on local civilian populations? And how far should one go to avoid any 'collateral' damage amongst civilians? Severe miscalculations clearly did happen: the derailing of a Dijon-bound train on 7 October 1943, for instance, led to a collision with the oncoming Paris express that killed thirty-one.[19] Such risks are inherent to all guerilla struggles: and do not change the foundational reality that German occupation forces remained the primary target. In this context, alienating wider populations was highly counter-productive: 'when a train was carrying French civilians the idea was to keep casualties down; we did not want to give the Resistance a bad name'.[20]

Resistance movements also waged armed struggle against regimes of collaboration that supported Nazi occupation as well. Of course, Resistance here involved opposing collaborationist governments and their bureaucracies. But collaboration was a more diffuse social phenomenon than this. Some degree of popular support, or at least acquiescence, was a necessary condition for business as usual under the Occupation. Populations negotiated the moral dilemmas of micro-complicity on a daily basis; and any decline in the efficacy of oppression was likely to bring these

[16] Gildea, *Fighters in the Shadows*, p. 92.

[17] C. Pavone, *A Civil War: A History of the Italian Resistance* (London, 2013, 2014), p. 598.

[18] Pavone, *A Civil War*, p. 599.

[19] L. Broch, *Ordinary Workers, Vichy and the Holocaust: French Railwaymen and the Second World War* (Cambridge, 2016), p. 158.

[20] M. Buckmaster, *They Fought Alone* (London, 1958, 2014), p. 135.

long-suppressed frustrations sharply to the surface. Spectres of civil war thus waxed as Nazi power visibly waned.

Unlike the Balkans, however, these civil wars remained semi-submerged: and consequently, semi-restrained. Since control of the state machinery remained the prize in contention, decapitation strategies were in vogue. Pro-fascist elites, functionaries, administrators, and activists remained the main targets of the Resistance: their militias and death squads in turn tried to pick off key Resistance activists. Such tit-for-tat cycles of assassination were frequently characterized by their toxic intimacy: curiously personal struggles in the midst of total war.

Amongst the Italian Communist formations, Claudio Pavone notes an obsessive tendency towards list-making of legitimate targets, commenting in a crucial insight that 'a meticulous list like this distances itself from the merely symbolic violence that strikes a human being, depersonalizing him, only insofar as it sees incarnated in him something that transcends him'.[21] If this was 'terrorism', in terms of nineteenth-century templates it resembled the approach of the Russian People's Will, rather than the anarchist excursions into mass slaughter of civilians.

Such list-making invites deeper reflection on the statist pretensions of Resistance movements 'Born as outlaws instinctively we tended to re-enter the law', as one Italian anti-fascist observed.[22] However chaotic their operational realities, an obsessive pseudo-legalism remains amongst the most striking characteristics of the Second World War resistance movements.[23] Deep desire for protocol surfaced in the most unlikely of circumstances. As a 16-year-old hitman for the Polish Home Army, Stefan Dąmbski seems to have been meticulous in reading the death sentence to those he shot as traitors—even when they were old school mates, and the execution place was their own favourite clearing in the woods.[24] Even Benito Mussolini received the pronouncement of 'a few words very quickly' before being machine-gunned at the Villa Belmonte.[25]

As Resistance counter-states struggled to be born within the magic caul of their own proceduralism, the balance of infrastructural power began to slide. Occupation regimes degenerated into gangster predation rackets whose 'underworld *was* the State'.[26] It is notable that from late 1943 fascist death squads first began to proliferate in earnest: the *Silbertanne* hit-squad in the Netherlands, *Service Spécial de Sécurité* and *Mouvement National anti-Terrorist* in France as well as the *Banda Koch* in the Salò Republic, to name but a handful.[27] Although a liminal phenomenon,

21 Pavone, *A Civil War*, p. 593. 22 Pavone, *A Civil War*, p. 149.

23 For France: G. Millar, *Maquis* (London, 1945, 1957), pp. 244.

24 S. Dąmbski, *Egzekutor* (Warsaw, 2010), pp. 13–14.

25 C. Hibbert, *Benito Mussolini* (Harmondsworth, 1962, 1965), pp. 367–8.

26 Bower, *Klaus Barbie*, pp. 62–3 [Emphasis in original].

27 D. Littlejohn, *The Patriotic Traitors: A History of Collaboration in German Occupied Europe 1940/1945* (London, 1972), pp. 45 (Rinnan Gang, Norway), 77 (*Peter-Gruppen*, Denmark), 118–19 (*Silbertanne*, Holland), 177 (*Rex* and *Vlaamsch National Verbond* offshoots, Belgium), 260, 359 n. 58 (*Service Spécial de Sécurité*; *Groupes d'action*, France); *The Independent*, 21 December 2013 [obituary of Heinrich Boere, *Silbertanne* gunman]; Bower, *Klaus Barbie*, pp. 62–3 (*Mouvement National anti-Terrorist*); Pavone, *A Civil War*, p. 350. R. Aron, *Histoire de L'Épuration* (Paris, 1967), pp. 452–5.

this breeding of corpuscular terror groups was a sure early sign of fascism's decay.[28] Conquest of the streets was giving way to a defence of the shadows: exactly the strategy that had been rejected by Hitler in *Mein Kampf*.

Much of this killing was the work of small groups. But as both fascist militias and Resistance units assumed genuinely mass dimensions, the potential spiral of vengeance widened dramatically. George Millar captures well what this could involve in his account of the detention of two members of the fascist *Milice* near Besançon, eastern France, in 1944:

> Soon the woman was digging too. It was horrible.... At last I saw the man standing on the edge of his grave. A long shudder ran through him, and he ran for it. He was shot with a burst of five from a Sten gun that caught him across the small of the back. He died instantly.
>
> It was probably the most horrible sight of my life. I did not know where to look, what to do. I felt subhuman. The woman was on her knees, begging Paincheau for her life. She got up and clutched at his coat. Paincheau made a sign, and one of the maquisards behind her blew away the back of her head. It was disgusting and shaming; it was nearly unbearable. I borrowed one of Paincheau's motor-cycles, and rode hell for leather to Vielley, not caring if there were Germans to stop me.[29]

Since pro-fascist militias had been mass formations there was ample scope for their defeat to open the way to wide massacre. But mostly it did not. Chaos came late: and was short-lived. The state vacuum that opened up across much of Western Europe in 1944–5 had not lasted long. Still, its appearance had been a dramatic enough moment while it lasted. Everyone had glimpsed the chasm beneath public order. It is to the detail of this transition that we must now turn.

I

Basic contrasts with 1914–18 are here clear enough. This time around the war had been one of much wider manoeuvre and conquest: or, conversely, of occupation and resistance. The consequences were even more dramatic than in 1918 as well. State authorities had been demolished far more sweepingly and widely than in the Great War: and when the discredited Occupation or collaborationist governments did finally collapse in 1944–45, their fall looked gratifyingly total. As a result, one of the side effects of this war of movement was to rehabilitate the nineteenth-century leftist ideal of popular self-liberation through urban insurrection, 'the science of insurrection [that] had been passed down between the generations'.[30]

[28] M. Anderson, *In Thrall to Political Change: Police and Gendarmerie in France* (Oxford, 2011), p. 106.

[29] Millar, *Maquis*, pp. 215–16.

[30] Tollet, quoted in: Gildea, *Fighters in the Shadows*, p. 399. Oddly, Michel plays down the importance of nineteenth-century precedents: H. Michel, *The Shadow War: Resistance in Europe, 1939–45* (London, 1970, 1972), p. 318.

Timing here was everything. Dignity demanded autonomous attempts at open revolt be made while enemy strength was ebbing, but not yet gone. Judging that was a fine art: but one that Resistance movements managed to gauge with repeated success: in Naples first (1943), but then later in Paris (1944), and the northern Italian cities of Turin, Milan, and Genoa (April 1945).[31] In Turin, the partisan leader Ada Gobetti had rather expected the long-awaited rising as an 1848-esque moment 'of fiery, glorious feats'. But, as ever, it was the trams ceasing to run that was the first real sign of a shift in public authority.[32] Even if inevitably downplayed in collective memory afterwards, the proximity of Allied conventional forces within striking distance was the foundational condition for success in all these cases: and it was this that saved the risings in Florence (August 1944) and Prague (May 1945) from collapse.[33] Where such assistance was not at hand (or withheld), mere heroism was quite insufficient and the outcome predictably disastrous: as the fate of the 63-day long Warsaw Rising of August 1944 demonstrated so unequivocally.[34] But that the barricade tradition survived across Europe until well into the second half of the twentieth century owed much to this mid-century run of success: and the inevitable legends that arose from it. In May 1968, the commander of the insurrection against the Nazis in the Latin Quarter of Paris walked through the district 'touched and moved to see that young men who had not been born in 1944 had built several of their barricades in the same places as then'.[35]

Where successful, the immediate aftermath of such insurrections possessed a disorientating, if intoxicating, delirium. The memoir of Marguerite Duras captures well this dream world of liberation. By 21 August 1944 in Paris there had been no police on the streets for nearly a week: and hence no enforcement of traffic regulations. She describes driving a captured member of the militia named Ter to a makeshift prison where he was almost certain to be executed:

> A frenzy of disobedience, an intoxicating freedom, has taken hold of the people. Ter is fascinated by the speed of the cars, the number of cars, the guns protruding from their doors, glinting in the sun. 'Let's make all we can of it,' D. suddenly says, 'there are still no police, that kind of thing happens only once in a century.... Ter turned toward D., who kept the revolver trained on him. And he laughed. 'True enough, that.'[36]

And yet this 'anarchy' was also strikingly neo-traditionalist: suffused with a kind of savage joy derived from inherited iconographies of shaming and purification. Once more 'the spirit of carnival and charivari were abroad', just as in 1918–23.[37]

[31] M. Mazower, *Hitler's Empire: Nazi Rule in Occupied Europe* (London, 2008, 2009), pp. 507–8, 510: T. Behan, *The Italian Resistance: Fascists, Guerrillas and Allies* (London 2009), pp. 93–106.

[32] A. Gobetti (transl. J. Alano), *Partisan Diary: A Woman's Life in the Italian Resistance* (Oxford, 1956, 2014), p. 332.

[33] Behan, *The Italian Resistance*, pp. 88–92 [Florence]; K. Lowe, *Savage Continent: Europe in the Aftermath of World War II* (London, 2012, 2013), pp. 126–8 [Prague].

[34] N. Davies, *God's Playground: A History of Poland*, Vol. II: *1795 to the Present* (Oxford, 1981), p. 475.

[35] E. J. Hobsbawm, *Revolutionaries* (London, 1973, 1977), p. 233.

[36] Quoted in: R. Burton, *Blood in the City: Violence and Revelation in Paris, 1789–1945* (Ithaca, 2001), p. 236.

[37] Burton, *Blood in the City*, p. 237.

Once more there was the same patriarchal obsession with punishing errant female sexuality that had 'transgressed' supposedly inviolate national or political boundaries: the same very public mock-parading, the same hair shearing.[38] If these female victims usually escaped with their lives, the impact of this 'social death' could nevertheless be profound. And lasting. One recluse discovered in the Auvergne as late as 1983 had been just one such victim.[39]

What was different here from the relatively isolated scenes of 1918–23 was their sheer extent and prominence: this exuberant explosion of 'rough music' was a continent-wide phenomenon.[40] And it included such high-profile dramas as the ritual display and elaborate humiliation of Mussolini's corpse, along with his mistress, Clara Petacci, in the Piazzale Loreto in Milan. By all accounts, the mood of the crowd was entirely jubilant as they surveyed these grotesquely 'upended puppets' ('Well, I never, what nice little legs Petacci had').[41] The Duce's final appearance before 'his' people thus assumed a distinctly hybrid form, somewhere between a 'posthumous lynching' and the full theatre of a public execution. As such, it constituted the appropriately tawdry apotheosis of Italian fascism.[42]

II

In defeat, the Nazi Propaganda Minister Josef Goebbels sought consolation amidst such epic destruction. It had, he exulted, freed Europe from 'bourgeois restraint'.[43] An Italian witness put it rather less positively: 'everywhere the war has spread a facile cruelty, an unthinking, dull cruelty which is the worst secretion of man'.[44] As we have seen, a general notion of cultural 'brutalization' has been reached for to help explain the condition of Europe after 1918.[45] Strangely, though, it has not tended to be applied to the aftermath of the Second World War: even though the devastation in 1945 was clearly so much more general: '2,000 days of war [that] had cost the lives of 500 Europeans every hour'.[46] And the Soviet advances in particular ended in a veritable pandemic of rape: in Berlin alone, over 90,000 women

[38] For Italy: V. Mussolini, *Mussolini* (London, 1973, 1975), p. 111. For France: D. Boyd, *Voices from the Dark Years: The Truth About Occupied France 1940–1945* (Stroud, 2007), pp. 253–9; Cobb, *The Resistance*, pp. 280–1; J. Jackson, *France: The Dark Years 1940–1944* (Oxford, 2001, 2003), pp. 580–3; I. Ousby, *Occupation: The Ordeal of France 1940–1944* (London, 1997, 1999), p. 306. For Holland: J. C. Kennedy, *A Concise History of the Netherlands* (Cambridge, 2017), p. 381.

[39] H. R. Lottman, *The People's Anger: Justice and Revenge in Post-Liberation France* (London, 1986), p. 68.

[40] A. Warring, 'Intimate and Sexual Relations' in R. Gildea, O. Wieviorka, and A. Warring (eds), *Surviving Hitler and Mussolini: Daily Life in Occupied Europe* (Oxford, 2006), p. 88.

[41] Pavone, *A Civil War*, pp. 611–12.

[42] Hibbert, *Benito Mussolini*, pp. 365, 371.

[43] J. P. Stern, *Hitler: The Führer and the People* (Glasgow, 1975), p. 34.

[44] Giaime Pintor, quoted in: Pavone, *A Civil War*, p. 498.

[45] G. L. Mosse, *Fallen Soldiers: Reshaping the Memory of the World Wars* (Oxford, 1990, 1991), pp. 159–81.

[46] B. J. Elliott, *Western Europe After Hitler* (London, 1984), p. 1.

and girls sought medical assistance.[47] Across much of central Europe liberation took the form of a war against anyone female.

Of course, it is important to stress here that the physical destruction had been distinctly uneven. In the East it was of a quite different order: even hardened Red Cross personnel struggled to describe the state of Belorussia with its 9,000 destroyed villages.[48] Still, realities further west were dystopian enough. Domestic murder rates in Germany were running at about three times the pre-war rate.[49] In Hamburg, it took until March 1946 to break up the 'displaced persons' robber bands operating out of the suburb of Wentorf.[50] Although hardly classic outlaw territory, even rural Belgium developed a bandit problem.[51] All in all, the *New York Times* had concluded in March 1945 that much of Europe was 'in a condition which no American can hope to understand'.[52] With good reason, in time 1945 would come to be remembered by Europeans as a 'year zero' or, in the German equivalent, 'the hour of nothingness'.[53]

The 'wild' purges of Liberation could be dramatic enough while they lasted: May 1945 saw thirty-five bomb attacks against former collaborators on the Côtes du Nord alone.[54] But they also tended to burn themselves out relatively swiftly. As Mark Mazower notes, 'the random and brutal nature of such killings served in the long run to help discredit the whole idea of punishing collaborators at all; but in the short run they raised the spectre of outright civil war and prompted resistance movements to intervene and assert their own authority'[55] Overall, the privatization of vengeance was reigned in to a rather remarkable degree.[56]

It could hardly be expected that total peace would instantly follow on from total war, of course. As the burgeoning Cold War took hold, Communist movements in Western Europe feared, and with good reason, that they would be edged out of post-war settlements. Keeping back some guns 'just in case' therefore seemed to many a sensible insurance policy.[57] 'Blessed be the hidden weapons!' as the Communist party leader Togliatti put it in the Italian parliament on 14 July 1948. With hindsight, it was an unfortunate choice of words: as he left, he was shot by a right-wing student, in turn sparking moves towards insurrection.[58] For a brief moment, Italy teetered on the edge of outright civil war once more: the barricades

[47] A. Read and D. Fisher, *The Fall of Berlin* (London, 1992, 1993), p. 440; Anonymous, *A Woman in Berlin* (London, 1954, 2011).

[48] Mazower, *Hitler's Empire*, p. 156.

[49] A. Kramer, '"Law Abiding Germans"? Social Disintegration, Crime and the Re-imposition of Order in Postwar Western Germany, 1945–1949' in R. Evans (ed.), *The German Underworld: Deviation and Outcasts in German History* (Abingdon, 1988), p. 247.

[50] Kramer, '"Law Abiding Germans"?', p. 255.

[51] M. Conway, *The Sorrows of Belgium: Liberation and Political Reconstruction, 1944–1947* (Oxford, 2012), p. 311.

[52] Lowe, *Savage Continent*, p. xiv.

[53] G. Trampe (ed.), *Die Stunde Null: Erinnerungen an Kriegsende und Neuanfang* (Stuttgart, 1995).

[54] J. Julian, *France: The Dark Years, 1940–1944* (Oxford, 2001), p. 584.

[55] M. Mazower, *Dark Continent: Europe's Twentieth Century* (London, 1998, 1999), pp. 233–4.

[56] P. Cooke, *The Legacy of the Italian Resistance* (Basingstoke, 2011), p. 154.

[57] Behan, *The Italian Resistance*, p. 136; *Yorkshire Post and Leeds Intelligencer*, 3 April 1948 [communist arms haul found].

[58] Behan, *The Italian Resistance*, p. 128.

rose in both Genoa and Milan in July 1948.[59] As sniping battles broke out across Genoa, the fate of Italian democracy hung in the balance.[60]

In the end, the Italian Christian Democrats successfully 'restored' order with their usual robustness: according to one estimate, sixty-four demonstrators were killed by police between 1948 and 1952. No fewer than 92,169 Communist party members were arrested between 1948 and 1950.[61] In retrospect, it seems remarkable that the partisan war of 1943–45 did not re-ignite more fully. But the foundations of future conflicts had certainly been laid down. For its part, the fascist right, defeated but not obliterated, had also kept some access to arms. Minor bombing campaigns provided off-stage percussion to Italian politics. Fascism had degenerated from the squadrist tactics of its early 1920s heyday to the clandestine bombinggang. But a tradition had survived altered, but not fundamentally, sundered. This was a highly ominous precedent for the future.[62]

By 1950, though, most Western European governments were firmly consolidated in power, just as their predecessors had been exactly one hundred years before. Left-wing resistance movements 'had been outflanked and found themselves helpless before "the continuity of the State"'.[63] In general what impresses here, though, is the clarity of the cultural dividing line between war and peace. As the Italian communist leader Roberto Battaglia advised succinctly in the war's closing stages: 'we must do the purging now, since after the Liberation we'll no longer be able to do it, because in war you shoot, but once the war's over you don't shoot anymore'.[64] Indeed, the most audacious revenge was highly covert: at Nuremburg and Dachau in April 1946, a cell of Jewish avengers succeeded in poisoning 2,283 SS prisoners with arsenic.[65] Even in this group, however, there was a striking reluctance to target German civilians: and their strategy of advertising the enormity of the Holocaust through revenge attacks soon fizzled.[66]

Against the backdrop of the Liberation 'carnival', we therefore need to acknowledge a widespread desire to re-impose the 'rule of rules'. As one SOE (Special Operations Executive) agent recalled, 'I had a lieutenant who came up to me and said: "I've got 300 German prisoners. What do the international conventions say about how much food and exercise they are entitled to every day?"'[67] Likewise, the Resistance leader Jean Garcin—who had shot his fair share of collaborators while

[59] Behan, *The Italian Resistance*, pp. 131–4; Mazower, *Dark Continent*, p. 251.

[60] Behan, *The Italian Resistance*, p. 131.

[61] Behan, *The Italian Resistance*, p. 136.

[62] *Gloucester Citizen*, 29 October 1946 [anniversary of the 'March on Roee'—bomb left outside the Chamber of Deputies]; *Derby Daily Telegraph*, 25 January 1947 [three fascist leaflet bombs in Rome]; *Gloucester Citizen*, 22 March 1950 [district offices of the Christian Democrat Party and Communist Party bombed]; *Dundee Courier*, 17 November 1950 [headquarters of the Italian Republican Party and Italian Socialist Party bombed]; *Aberdeen Evening Express*, 27 October 1955 [Communist Party office in Rome bombed].

[63] Mazower, *Dark Continent*, p. 237.

[64] Pavone, *A Civil War*, p. 607.

[65] Z. W. Mankowitz, *Life Between Memory and Hope: The Survivors of the Holocaust in Occupied Germany* (Cambridge, 2002), p. 238.

[66] Mankowitz, *Life Between Memory and Hope*, pp. 236–7. Also: J. Freedland, 'Revenge', *Guardian*, 26 July 2008.

[67] Quoted in: Mazower, *Dark Continent*, p. 234.

hostilities lasted—faced down an angry crowd outside the jail at Avignon to insist that all prisoners not detained by a proper judicial warrant be released.[68]

III

Background trends also assisted this wider reconsolidation, and renewed assertion, of state authority. An era of big government was emerging on both sides of the Atlantic. State bureaucracies grew luxuriantly. Such infrastructural power was often slow to galvanize and was clumsy. But it could be relentless once set in motion. Both the crime empires of Al Capone (1931) and the Second Ku Klux Klan (1944) were eventually shut down through federal government prosecutions for income tax evasion.[69] Slowly, falteringly, a national American police service emerged in the FBI: Edgar Hoover's 'college boys', although notoriously cack-handed in gun fights, slowly closed down the mid-west bank robbers in 1933–4. More than any other event, the hunt for John Dillinger 'would validate the Roosevelt administration's push for a national law-enforcement authority and enshrine the Bureau as an American institution'.[70]

A popular demand for more, and more effective, governance after the truly nightmare years that had been lost to the Great Depression and the Second World War was a marked feature of these post-war years. In the USA the number of civilian employees of the federal government had reached the unprecedented peak at 830,000 by 1938—but it was to climb to 2.9 million by 1945.[71]

Especially in Europe, but to some extent in the USA as well, the rise of the interventionist state was therefore the dominant political trend of the decades after 1945. Welfare inexorably followed warfare: overall, indeed, 'the twentieth century multiplied the occasions when it became essential for governments to govern'.[72] Stability was prized above all in this post-apocalyptic world: and even rowdy youth movements such as the American Greasers, English Teddy Boys, or West German *Halbstarken* caused genuine alarm. Martin Luther King's famous comment in his *Letter from Birmingham Jail* that the 'white moderate... is more devoted to "order" than to justice' was a well-aimed barb.[73]

Indeed, one of the most striking features of this post-1945 world is how far a (relatively) little political violence now went in grabbing headlines and wider attention. 'This was not a war of numbers' comments Bruce Hoffman simply in his study of the Irgun's campaign against British rule in Palestine: 'the butcher's bill was remarkably modest compared with the horrific standards of terrorism today.

[68] Nic Dháibhéid, *Terrorist Histories*, p. 87.

[69] J. S. Bowman, *The Cambridge Dictionary of American Biography* (Cambridge, 1995), p. 115; Laqueur, *Terrorism*, p. 21.

[70] B. Burrough, *Public Enemies: America's Greatest Crime Wave and the Birth of the FBI, 1933–34* (New York, 2004, 2005), p. 247.

[71] M. Mann, *The Sources of Social Power*, Vol. 4, *Globalizations, 1945–2011* (Cambridge, 2013), p. 38.

[72] E. Hobsbawm, *Age of Extremes: The Short Twentieth Century 1914–1991* (London, 1994, 1996) p. 140.

[73] M. L. King Jnr, *Why We Can't Wait* (New York, 1963, 1964), p. 84.

Between 1945 and August 1947, a total of 141 British soldiers and police and 40 terrorists died, including those executed or who committed suicide while awaiting execution. Civilian fatalities during the same period were also remarkably low.'[74] Indeed, this was a time when one stand-out major attack such as the bombing of the King David Hotel in Jerusalem in 1946 could become a cultural reference point for an entire British generation: a shared benchmark by which to measure individual experience.[75] Much later indeed—in 1973—one contributor to an anthology of sexual fantasies even dated a youthful real-life experience by it ('the Sunday papers carried news of a hotel being bombed in Jerusalem, and this was in the summer of 1946').[76]

Needless to say, these were inhospitable general conditions for the kind of mass paramilitarism that had flourished after 1918 to revive. But they were also not hospitable conditions in general for the development of long-running insurrectionist campaigns. The twin bombings of the Imperial Chemicals Industries building in Glasgow in 1943–4 were rather opportunistic affairs conducted by Scottish nationalist teenagers (with all too easy access to a generous cache of Home Guard hand-grenades).[77] A resurgent IRA threat to England in 1939–40 had been similarly finished off by enhanced wartime security measures: the promise of Nazi assistance never seems to have added up to anything very substantial here.[78] In fact, any taint of collaboration with the Third Reich was likely to be a toxic asset in the post-1945 world. Before the war Breton nationalists had staged repeated, if minor, bombings against symbolic targets of French state authority.[79] In its aftermath, they went notably quiet: the *Front de Libération de Bretagne* only appeared in 1968.[80] Not until 1973, indeed, did campaigns of nuisance explosions again revive in Britany.[81]

[74] B. Hoffman, *Anonymous Soldiers: The Struggle for Israel, 1917–1947* (New York, 2015) pp. 482–3.

[75] See also: D. Leitch, 'Explosion at the King David Hotel' in M. Sissons and P. French (eds), *Age of Austerity, 1945–1951* (Harmondsworth, 1963, 1964), p. 61. Also: Hoffman, *Anonymous Soldiers*, p. 306.

[76] N. Friday, *My Secret Garden: Women's Sexual Fantasies* (London, 1973, 1991), p. 156.

[77] The Imperial Chemical Industries (ICI) building in Glasgow was bombed by the *Fianna na h'Alba* ('Warriors of Scotland') on 24 December 1943 and again 7 January 1944. For reports: *Evening Despatch*, 31 December 1943; *Daily Record*, 1 January 1944; *Aberdeen Press and Journal*, 4 January 1944; *Dundee Courier*, 5 January, 1 February 1944; *Derby Daily Telegraph*, 8 January 1944; *Scotsman*, 5, 10 January 1944; *Dundee Evening Telegraph*, 31 December 1943, 13 January 1944; *Birmingham Mail*, 31 January 1944. I am deeply grateful to Nick Brooke for first bringing these incidents to my attention.

[78] T. P. Coogan, *The I.R.A.* (London, 1970, 1971), p. 169; R. English, *Armed Struggle: The History of the IRA* (London, 2003, 2004), pp. 60–5.

[79] *Leeds Mercury*, 8 August 1933 [bomb hurled from car at Hotel de Ville, Rennes]; *Nottingham Journal*, 19 December 1938 [monument blown up]; *Dundee Evening Telegraph*, 27 February 1939 [bomb in the cellar of the Prefecture, Quimper Finisterre].

[80] Littlejohn, *The Patriotic Traitors: A History of Collaboration in German Occupied Europe 1940/1945* (London, 1972), pp. 208, 261–2; J. O. Engene, *Terrorism in Western Europe: Explaining the Trends Since 1950* (Cheltenham, 2004), p. 124.

[81] Anderson, *In Thrall to Political Change*, p. 193 [six 'outrages' between May and December 1973].

Given that the post-war order saw so few boundary changes in Western Europe, it was striking that armed separatist movements were notable by their relative absence in the years immediately after 1945. In so far as the Resistance had bequeathed any practical templates for action here, they were technocratic ones. Between the early 1950s and late 1960s, when relatively minor campaigns by armed secessionist groups began to appear in Wales, Scotland, and South Tyrol, they primarily took the form of wars against infrastructure: all were obsessive pylon-topplers.[82] Republican efforts against Franco's Spain, re-kindled by the Resistance struggle in southern France, were to take much the same form, although with a greater predilection for railways and military targets.[83]

State-sponsored terror campaigns that had been such a marked feature of the late 1930s were now distinctly out of fashion. But other transnational threats now bubbled up from below. Diasporas showed their true potential as long distance convectors of sustained instability. Long-range 'overspill' thus emerged as a largely new, but direct, threat to European stability. With the exception of the militant fringe of Irish America, this had been a rather limited phenomenon before for European powers. But now contested territories such as Palestine began to function as off-shore laboratories for sustained experiments in atrocity.

Here the Irgun's experiments in transnational bombing were alarming: an ominous revival of a pattern of long-range tightly-organized campaigns last seen over fifty years before in the campaign of the Irish-American dynamiters.[84] On 31 October 1946 a Irgun team efficiently sheared off the façade of the British Embassy in Rome with suitcase bombs.[85] London was put on high alert shortly after in response to threats—the Irgun were early adopters of the telephone hoax warning ('Clear Buckingham Palace'!).[86] The Colonial Office in Whitehall was bombed on 18 April 1947.[87] Mail bombs for notable hate figures of the Irgun, including the anti-semitic General Barker, continued to arrive into the following year.[88] Months after the London bombings the British authorities were still worrying about an Anglophobic alliance of the Irgun with the militant Scottish nationalists of *Fianna na h'Alba* ('Warriors of Scotland') who had conducted the Glasgow bombings.[89] And there were other ominous, because more substantial, dangers that pointed towards the future as well: that Europe could become a proxy theatre for the neighbouring wars and quarrels of the Middle East. An unexploded bomb found in the

[82] For Scottish campaign: *Yorkshire Post and Leeds Intelligencer*, 18 November 1953; *Yorkshire Evening Post*, 25 November 1953; *The Berwick Advertiser*, 26 November 1953; *Berwickshire News and General Advertiser*, 1 December 1953. Also: N. Brooke, *Terrorism and Nationalism in the United Kingdom: The Absence of Noise* (London, 2018), pp. 19, 30. For Wales: Brooke, *Terrorism and Nationalism*, pp. 46–7, 53. For South Tyrol: A. E. Alcock, 'Terrorism in South Tyrol' in P. Janke (ed.), *Terrorism and Democracy* (London, 1991, 1992), pp. 8, 11–12 (1956 and 1961 campaigns respectively).

[83] *Nottingham Journal*, 26 July 1946 (dynamite charge found on railway bridge near Madrid); *Gloucestershire Echo*, 25 September 1946 (Military Governor's residence in Barcelona bombed).

[84] Hoffman, *Anonymous Soldiers*, pp. 338–40.

[85] *Derby Daily Telegraph*, 1 November 1946.

[86] *Palestine Post*, 31 January 1947.

[87] *Western Daily Press*, 17 April 1947.

[88] *Palestine Post*, 12 May 1948 (package bomb for General Barker, Surrey). Also: Hoffman, *Anonymous Soldiers*, p. 404–5.

[89] Hoffman, *Anonymous Soldiers*, pp. 1–15, 338–40; NA, KV3/439. 15/11/1947.

principal synagogue in Rome was 'believed to have been placed by anti-Jewish elements from the Middle East working with Italian Fascists'.[90] Such developments were, however, still aberrational. A quarter of a century later they would be a recurrent feature of European politics.

By contrast, the slow demise of French Algeria was far less easily contained: as a (supposedly) integral part of metropolitan France it acquired something of the status of Germany's 'bleeding' eastern frontier after 1918. A whiff of the Weimar disease of endemic instability thus long hung over France's Fourth Republic. And it bred many of the same symptoms—of democratic decay and the blatant indulgence of state massacres: of sanctioned torture, death squads, and recurrent coup threats. Indeed in 1961—a full 90 years after the horrors of the fall of the Paris Commune—the Prefecture of Police could turn the Seine into a bloodbath: and get clean away with it.[91] A central driver of instability was the appearance of sustained bombing campaigns: repetitious, indiscriminate, and deliberately sanguinary. Both the FLN and the rival OAS evolved here into truly efficient technicians of mass slaughter.[92]

American elites, for their part, still remained comfortably immune from the backwash of Middle Eastern turmoil. Congress was, however, briefly discomforted on 1 March 1954 by what the official record rather coyly described as 'a demonstration and the discharge of firearms' during a debate on Mexican Agricultural Workers: surprisingly this dramatic machine-gunning of the house by Puerto Rican nationalists succeeded in wounding just four Congressmen.[93] It seems to have been rather quickly forgotten. At the grassroots, though, domestic patterns of violence were undergoing more profound transformations. More individualistic types of violence were on the rise. Ominously for the future, there was 'an enormous glut of serial killers who grew up either during World War II or in the first fifteen baby boom years following the war'.[94] And these were also the years—1955–6–that George Metesky's solo bombing campaign in New York reached its height: sparking in turn 'the greatest manhunt in the history of the Police Department' in the words of Police Commissioner, Stephen Kennedy.[95]

Most obviously and immediately, however, these were also the years during which the rise of the civil rights movement sparked an era of 'massive resistance' by white supremacists. Yet at the sharpest end 'massive resistance' was anything but massive. Instead it was highly clandestine and cellular. The caste system was thus

90 *The Palestine Post*, 3 July 1947.

91 J. House and N. MacMaster, *Paris 1961: Algerians, State Terror, and Memory* (Oxford, 2006, 2009), pp. 161–79.

92 For a small sample of a large literature, see: M. Evans, *Algeria: France's Undeclared War* (Oxford, 2012, 2013); G. Fleury, *Histoire secrete de l'O.A.S.* (Paris, 2002); A. Horne, *A Savage War of Peace* (New York, 1977, 2006); M. Hutchinson, *Revolutionary Terrorism: The FLN in Algeria, 1954–1962* (Stanford, 1978).

93 United States of America Congressional Record, *Proceedings and Debates on the 83rd Congress*, 2nd Session, Vol. 100, Part 2, Feb. 8 1954 to March 8 1954 (Washington, 1954), p. 2434, Col. 1.

94 P. Vronsky, *Sons of Cain: A History of Serial Killers From the Stone Age to the Present* (New York, 2018), p. 310.

95 M. M. Greenburg, *The Mad Bomber of New York* (New York, 2011), between pp. 158 and 159.

defended not by spectacle lynchings, but by covert dynamite bombings: 588 in the 1960s alone.[96] The extent to which the federal state had managed to supplant the community as the violent enforcer of norms was reflected in the unease of many southern white racists not with the ultimate aims, but with the methods, of groups such as the Confederate Underground.

'Since racism could not be expressed overtly, it went covert' as Michael Mann puts it: and it seems racist violence had, to some degree, followed suit.[97] Nonetheless, it remained lethal enough: according to one estimate between 1954 and 1968, 'at least forty-four blacks and whites were murdered in pursuit of civil rights'.[98] Racism tended to structure white supremacist violence as a strategy of decapitation: with rabble-rousers and outsiders removed, the black masses would become satisfactorily docile once more. This was the old strategy of the 1870s reheated—intimidating blacks into not exercising their constitutional rights.[99] Key leaders, activists, and organizing centres such as community churches thus became the main targets of lethal violence, along with 'uppity blacks' who had moved into predominantly white lower middle-class neighbourhoods: a pattern long seen in the northern cities, but one which now spread to the south.[100] Unlike spectacle lynching, this was the violence of a decaying caste system, not an established one. Escalation into more indiscriminate terror remained a present danger: as the bombing of the 16th Street Baptist Church in Birmingham on 15 September 1963 demonstrated.[101]

Why was southern racist violence so furtive? Such a development is all the more remarkable given the entrenched hostility to de-segregation amongst southern governing elites and the coercive bureaucracies they had at their disposal. The set piece confrontations with Civil Rights marchers in Birmingham were only the most visible examples of this capacity for official repression by state governments. Death squads—along the classic lines of private-police partnerships that conduct 'murder with deniability'—also appeared in the wings of 'massive resistance': the notorious murders of three civil rights workers in the Mississippi delta in 1964 fitted this template exactly.[102] National Guardsmen entrusted with enforcing the desegregation of the University of Alabama were instead accused of a series of explosions there.[103]

[96] M. Miller, *Foundations of Modern Terrorism* (Cambridge, 2013), p. 227.

[97] Mann, *The Sources of Social Power*, Vol. 4, p. 81.

[98] S. J. Whitfield, *A Death in the Delta: The Story of Emmett Till* (New York, 1988), p. 101.

[99] C. Hewitt, *Understanding Terrorism in America: From the Klan to Al Qaeda* (London, 2003), p. 62.

[100] D. F. Krugler, *1919: The Year of Racial Violence: How African Americans Fought Back* (Cambridge, 2015), p. 9; *Birmingham Daily Post*, 6, 13 October 1958, 20 April 1960, 17 February 1964, 5 October 1964; *Lancashire Evening Post*, 10 January 1957; *Shields Daily News*, 10 September 1957; *Northern Daily Mail*, 28 April 1958; *Aberdeen Evening Express*, 10 February 1960; *Coventry Evening Telegraph*, 17 January 1962 and 25 September 1963; *Liverpool Daily Echo*, 25 September 1963; *Aberdeen Evening Express*, 30 September 1963, 24 September 1964.

[101] C. M. McKinstry (with Denise George), *While the World Watched: A Birmingham Bombing Survivor Comes of Age during the Civil Rights Movement* (Carol Stream, IL, 2011).

[102] B. B. Campbell, 'Death Squads: Definition, Problems and Historical Context' in B. B. Campbell and A. D. Brenner (eds), *Death Squads in Global Perspective: Murder with Deniability* (London, 2000, 2002), pp. 3–7. J. H. Skolnick, *The Politics of Protest* (New York, 1969), pp. 221–2.

[103] *Coventry Evening Telegraph*, 21 December 1963.

Given how entrenched racism was, the wonder was that there were not more such semi-official horrors.

Racist killing in the Civil Rights Era, then, was notably clandestine. In the rural areas of the Mississippi delta, for instance, the tradition of dumping corpses in local waterways was paramount. 'That was the custom, that was the procedure' notes the journalist Simeon Booker simply.[104] Hitch-hiking from Mobile to Montgomery in late 1959, John Griffin was assured casually, but plausibly, by a white truck driver that 'you can kill a nigger and toss him into that swamp and no one'll ever know what happened to him'.[105] This may, of course, have been just loose macho talk (although loose talk can, of course, be peculiarly illuminating precisely because it is uninhibited). But even as loose talk the threat seems somehow significant. During the search for the body of Emmet Till in the summer of 1955, the Tallahatchie River in Mississippi was similarly said to be full of missing Afro-Americans.[106] Such a method of disposing of bodies was too temptingly convenient to be in any way novel, of course: similar techniques were already standard in the late nineteenth century.[107] Rather, the point is that it seemed to have taken centre stage by the mid-twentieth century long after spectacle lynchings had slipped from view. Racist murder in 1910 could boast a cast of thousands; but by 1960 it had become a hidden act.

A major shift in patterns of American rioting was also underway after 1945. One-sided pogromic violence finally disappeared here as well, 150 years after it had disappeared from Western Europe. Donald Horowitz charts the shift well: 'the deadly riot receded and the violent protest demonstration by the former targets took its place during World War II. Detroit (1943) was the last major antiblack riot, and Harlem (1943) was the second major black violent protest demonstration. The violent protest demonstration is aimed at ethnic equality and, more to the point, does not require attitudes justifying killing in the way that deadly riots do.'[108] Indeed so—but official responses could nonetheless be ferocious enough. State forces were responsible for the most of the considerable death tolls at Watts, in 1965 (34 killed) and Detroit in 1967 (43 dead).[109] The Skolnik Report was particularly scathing about the latter case:

> Responsibility for riot control was divided between U.S. Army paratroopers on one side of town and a combination of Detroit police and the National Guard on the other. The Guard proved as untrained and unreliable as the police; and between the two, thousands of rounds of ammunition were expended and perhaps thirty persons were killed while disorder continued. Yet in paratrooper territory, only 201 rounds of

[104] Quoted in: H. Hampton and S. Fayer (eds), *Voices of Freedom: An Oral History of the Civil Rights Movement from the 1950s through the 1980s* (London, 1990, 1995), p. 7.

[105] J. Griffin, *Black Like Me* (Boston, 1961), p. 110.

[106] Whitfield, *A Death in the Delta*, p. 34.

[107] P. Dray, *At the Hands of Persons Unknown: The Lynching of Black America* (New York, 2002, 2003), p. 37.

[108] D. Horowitz, *Deadly Ethnic Riot* (Berkeley, 2001, 2002), p. 562.

[109] U.S. Riot Commission Report, *Report of the National Advisory Commission on Civil Disorders* (New York, 1968), pp. 38, 358.

ammunition were fired, mostly in the first several hours before stricter fire discipline was imposed, only one person was killed, and within a few hours quiet and order were restored in that part of the city. [110]

IV

> Fighting in the streets as a revolutionary technique—it is one of the few old-fashioned ideas still alive.
>
> – Richard Hofstadter, 1970[111]

> The urban guerrilla aims to destroy certain aspects of the state structure, and to destroy the myth of state omnipotence and invulnerability.
>
> – 'The Urban Guerrilla Concept', 1971[112]

Street-fighting was a defining feature of the turbulence of the late 1960s. The analytical challenge is how to explain such an abrupt—and apparently archaic—resurgence. Unflattering comparisons were widely drawn with the street violence of the interwar period. For the right-wing West German tabloid newspaper, *Bild*, the student protesters were a throwback to the paramilitary formations of four decades earlier. Similarly, the Marxist philosopher Theodor W. Adorno dismissed them as 'storm-troopers in jeans'.[113] Governor Rhodes of Ohio went further in both rhetoric and action. Considering the student protestors who burned down a training hut at Kent State university in May 1970 to be 'worse than the brownshirts' he fatally turned loose the trigger-happy National Guard on them.[114] To the renowned American historian Richard Hofstadter, though, it was 'the rising mystique of violence on the *left*' that was so disturbing, adding: 'some, no doubt, are reminded of the Paris Commune. Others will be reminded of the promises of Mussolini.'[115]

Such comparisons tended to be wildly over-drawn. American New Left activists had no theory of the street as a key arena for an orchestrated bid for power: it was merely their stage, not their parade-ground. Efficient technicians of refusnik publicity against the Vietnam War, they elevated the melee into a photo opportunity. They had no big battalions to hand: all in all, at most 600 activists took part in these chaotic rampages in Chicago in October 1969.[116] As a result, their spasmodic street-fighting tactics lacked basic stamina and could not be sustained—here the 'Days of Rage' were well-named. On the eve of confrontation, indeed,

[110] Skolnick, *The Politics of Protest*, p. 258.

[111] R. Hofstadter, 'Reflections on Violence in the United States' in R. Hofstadter and M. Wallace (eds), *American Violence: A Documentary History* (New York, 1970, 1971), p. 35.

[112] Quoted in: I. Sánchez-Cuenca, *The Historical Roots of Political Violence* (Cambridge, 2019), p. 35.

[113] D. Siemens, *Stormtroopers: A New History of Hitler's Brownshirts* (London, 2017), p. 327.

[114] R. Nixon, *The Memoirs of Richard Nixon* (London, 1978), p. 456.

[115] Hofstadter, 'Reflections on Violence in the United States', pp. 29–30. Emphasis added.

[116] J. Varon, *Bringing the War Home: The Weather Underground, The Red Army Faction, And Revolutionary Violence in the Sixties and Seventies* (London, 2004), p. 82.

Tom Hayden was struck by how the Weathermen milling around nervously 'in their battle dress of football and motorcycle helmets, heavy jackets and clubs, looked... "like a primitive, neophyte army"'.[117] To the Yippie leader, Abbie Hoffman, such adventurism was simply 'Gandhian violence for the element of purging guilt through moral witness'.[118] It certainly took the eye of faith to insist, as one Weatherman leader did, that 'just the fact that we are willing to fight the police is a political victory'.[119] Yet it also reflected an implicit recognition that they would not be massacred.

The events of May 1968 in Paris did indeed briefly look much more threatening to the established order. But this was not 1918, let alone 1848. In the damning verdict of one seasoned observer, revolutionary strategy often added up to little 'more than the pretence that behaving as though the barricades were up would somehow cause them to rise, by sympathetic magic'.[120] Even allowing for the frenzy of barricade-building that *did* take place in Paris, it seems that it was the instinct of street-theatre that dominated: 'no order was sent out, but perhaps at first from a feeling of exposure, perhaps, because, as they waited, the students had nothing better to do, barricades sprang up'.[121]

A couple of years later the London theatre critic, Kenneth Tynan, reflected back on the intense valorization of spontaneity amongst the student revolutionaries:

> Someone at the party says: 'Whatever happened to Danny Cohn-Bendit?' At once I am back in Clive Goodwin's flat, packed with every literary Leftist in London for the party he gave in the spring of '68 to celebrate Cohn-Bendit's flying visit to London. The barricades were up in Paris; everybody was talking about 'instant revolution'; and when Cohn-Bendit held a question-and-answer session with the guests, I made myself immediately unpopular by asking: 'What's your strategy? What is the next step the students will take?' C. B. said impatiently: 'The whole point of our revolution is that we do not follow plans. It is a spontaneous permanent revolution. We improvise. It is like jazz.' Everybody applauded and reproved my carping.'

Likewise, Tynan's follow-up question about the loyalty of the army was dismissed with equal hauteur ('the army is no problem. Many young officers agree with us').[122] And yet when the clouds of tear-gas finally cleared, it was not the student barricades that still stood intact. It was 'the unwithering state'.[123]

If the professional revolutionary had been a novelty of the nineteenth century, then the amateur revolutionary belonged just as distinctively to the later decades of the twentieth. In part this reflected an instinctive disdain for 'structure freaks'. Prototypically bourgeois values of efficiency and organization were not highly

[117] Varon, *Bringing the War Home*, p. 80.

[118] Quoted in: R. Jacobs, *The Way the Wind blew: a History of the Weather Underground* (New York, 1997), p. 70.

[119] M. Rudd, *Underground: My Life with SDS and the Weathermen* (New York, 2009, 2020), p. 178.

[120] Hobsbawm, *Age of Extremes*, p. 447.

[121] P. Seale and M. McConville, *French Revolution 1968* (Harmondsworth, 1968), p. 85.

[122] J. Lahr (ed.), *The Diaries of Kenneth Tynan* (London, 2001), pp. 73–4 [diary entry for 18 October 1971].

[123] D. Singer, *Prelude to Revolution: France in May 1968* (London, 1970), p. 349.

valued in preparing for the revolution.[124] But a wider cultural retreat from militarism seems also to have been a key precondition here: in the diagnosis of one Californian activist, 'the world needs less specialists in force and murder and more generalists in love'.[125] In the wake of imperial retreat and in the long shadows of nuclear confrontation, traditionalist warrior virtues had been increasingly held up to ridicule. And as has been insightfully noted, the hippies here constituted a strikingly effective anti-army: their deliberate 'inversion of military codes and conduct' helping to de-militarize Western societies profoundly.[126] During the 1970s, the mandatory salute in the Dutch military was abolished 'much to the unhappiness of the higher ranks'.[127]

Conversely, states were themselves becoming less overtly militaristic. Armies were increasingly being withdrawn from the streets. After the 1947–8 disorders, the French military was not deployed again against strikers.[128] And where possible, maintenance of public order was increasingly being left to police, and not to military, forces.

Massacres committed by official military or paramilitary forces—such as at Kent State university on 4 May 1970 (four dead) or in Derry on 30 January 1972 (fourteen dead, ultimately)—now became fully-fledged publicity disasters. Both of these incidents bore the hallmarks of the 'forward panic'—a massive and sudden release of aggression, after long period of tension beforehand.[129] At Kent State, indeed, 61 shots were fired within 13 seconds to kill 'just' four students, one of whom was walking towards class, and not part of the protest all.[130] Such wild firing is a recognized feature of confrontation on the battlefield. But against demonstrations, even with a fringe of stone-throwers, such utterly excessive violence increasingly seemed incomprehensible to large swathes of society. For President Nixon, indeed, 'those few days after Kent State were among the darkest of my presidency'.[131]

Public order policing, too, was learning restraint: or, at least, some basic discretion in the light of increased public scrutiny. After the end of the Algerian war, the policing of major demonstrations in Paris was transferred from the Prefecture of Police to the Gendarmerie and the *Compaignies républicaines de sécurité* (CRS): as a result, 'loss of life in demonstrations almost disappeared after 1962'.[132] At much the same time, the 80 cm long police baton was abandoned in favour of lighter and shorter models; a crucial change that probably saved lives since the CRS were

[124] J. Alpert, *Growing up Underground* (New York, 1981), pp. 188–9, 197, 199, 275; J. Bryan, *This Soldier Still at War* (New York, 1975), p. 7.

[125] Pat Tuli Kupferberg quoted in: Bryan, *This Soldier still at War*, p. 55.

[126] M. Mulholland, *Bourgeois Liberty and the Politics of Fear: From Absolutism to Neo-Conservatism* (Oxford, 2012), p. 243.

[127] Kennedy, *Concise History of the Netherlands*, p. 415.

[128] Anderson, *In Thrall to Political Change*, p. 93.

[129] M. McCleery, 'Randall Collins' forward panic pathway to violence and the 1972 Bloody Sunday killings in Northern Ireland', *The British Journal of Politics and International Relations*, 18 (4), 2016, pp. 966–80.

[130] R. Collins, *Violence: A Micro-Sociological Theory* (Princeton, 2008), p. 113.

[131] Nixon, *The Memoirs of Richard Nixon*, pp. 457.

[132] Anderson, *In Thrall to Political Change*, pp. 118, 386.

hardly gentle with their opponents when they cornered them.[133] And yet in the final analysis just three people died in France during the 1968 disturbances: a notable contrast with the wanton massacre of Algerians in 1961.

All this was part of a wider pattern of spreading restraint across Western Europe and the USA. To some extent, this was a longer-term partial trend of mutual de-escalation in street confrontations between police and publics. A key factor was the rise of what the *Unabomber Manifesto* later termed the 'masochistic tendency' that increasingly distinguished leftist protest tactics.[134] Since the 1930s there had been a growth in techniques of evasive confrontation, such as the sit-in, or sit-down protest: 'a tactical device that tended to avert rather than precipitate acts of outright violence'.[135] By the end of 1960, a hundred cities across the southern USA had witnessed 'sit-in protests in which 70,000 students had taken part'.[136] The guiding credo of the Freedom Riders in 1961 was unequivocal here: 'the thing you must remember to do when you get involved in one of these things is always to remain non-violent'.[137] And the more savvy southern police chiefs, such as Laurie Pritchett of Albany, learnt to keep beatings off camera.[138]

But shifts could also be more sudden as well. Above all, it was the advent of satellite television that proved strikingly effective in taming the state's thugs. Even the toughest police forces found they could be easily embarrassed.[139] As the Royal Ulster Constabulary learnt in Derry on 5 October 1968 a couple of minutes' worth of unflattering footage of their crowd dispersal techniques from just one television camera could help destabilize an entire society.[140] Years later, watching an anti-police riot in Portadown in 1985, the anthropologist Anthony Buckley was struck by the mutually restrained choreography of the entire encounter. This was, he thought, very much a confrontation that was choreographed between tacitly agreed rules and limits.[141] Similar mutually-limiting dynamics were noted in a minor riot between left-wing protestors and the police in Freiburg in 1980.[142]

[133] Anderson, *In Thrall to Political Change*, p. 383, no. 46. Also: D. Caute, *'68 The* Year of the Barricades (London, 1988), pp. 190–2.

[134] For the masochism of left-wing protest: Green Anarchist (ed.), *'Industrial Society and Its Future': The Unabomber Manifesto* (Camberley, 1995), p. 11. For 1930s sit-down strikes, see: S. Salerno, 'Introduction' in S. Salerno (ed.), *Direct Action and Sabotage: Three Classic IWW Pamphlets from the 1910s* (Oakland, 2014), p. 14 [USA]; P. Brendon, *The Dark Valley: A Panorama of the 1930s* (London, 2000), p. 498 [France]; R. Graves and A. Hodge, *The Long Weekend: A Social History of Great Britain 1918–1939* (London, 1940, 1950), pp. 332, 404–5 [UK].

[135] Hofstadter, 'Reflections on Violence in the United States', p. 37. For sit-ins connected to the Civil Rights struggle, see: R. Cook, *Sweet Land of Liberty? The African-American Struggle for Civil Rights in the Twentieth Century* (London, 1998), pp. 76, 113; B. J. Dierenfeld, *The Civil Rights Movement* (London, 2004), pp. 53, 60 [Greensboro].

[136] G. Lewis, *Massive Resistance: the White Response to the Civil Rights Movement* (London, 2006), p. 131.

[137] James Peck in: R. Hofstadter and M. Wallace (eds.), *American Violence: A Documentary History* (New York, 1970, 1971), p. 370.

[138] Dierenfeld, *The Civil Rights Movement*, p. 76.

[139] Caute, *'68 The Year of the Barricades*, pp. 277–8.

[140] G. Gillespie, *Years of Darkness: The Troubles Remembered* (Dublin, 2008), pp. 5–8.

[141] A. Buckley, 'Fighting and Fun: Spectators and Stone-Throwers in Ulster Riots'. Available at: http://www.anthonydbuckley.com/fighting-and-fun-stone-throwers-and-spectators-in-ulster-riots.html.

[142] J. C. Häberlen, *The Emotional Politics of the Alternative Left: West Germany, 1968–1984* (Cambridge, 2018), p. 255.

With its plethora of different law enforcement agencies, and well-armed citizenry, late twentieth century USA presents a more complex picture of public order policing. Policing of black ghettoes retained its traditionally sharp edge of operational brutality: so long as majority white populations showed little interest in what went on there, this was business as usual ('if we have to patrol the city in tanks, that's what we'll do. This is war').[143] But labour disputes had become notably less deadly.[144] Harder to deal with was the resurrection of paramilitarism represented by groups such as the Black Panthers: these were less interested in urban parading than their 1920s forebears, but infinitely better armed. On occasion, the FBI found itself concentrating overwhelming firepower to overcome local resistance, but all this under the unblinking gaze of the television cameras. Caught between the rival imperatives of intimidation and restraint, the result was the emergence of that distinctively American media phenomenon: the prolonged stand-off at a fortified compound that becomes a hybrid of armed pageantry and state blockade. The 70-day confrontation between federal law enforcement officials and 400 Native Americans at Wounded Knee, South Dakota (from 28 February 1973) furnished an early example.[145]

Against this general backdrop, the emergence of armed campaigns on the fringes of the American New Left from 1969 onwards seems all the more remarkable. The Weather Underground (and their imitators) were the (largely) antiseptic militarists of a (largely) anti-militarist counter-culture; technicians of armed propaganda who never developed any serious cult of the gun (unlike the Black Panthers); and, in general, attempted purveyors of 'responsible terrorism' (the accidental explosion at the Townhouse in New York on 6 March 1970 notwithstanding).[146] It was fitting that the bombing cell at the Townhouse had been in a rush when they self-detonated so spectacularly: they were trying to clear up before parents returned. Cathy Wilkerson, indeed, was frantically ironing sheets:

> A blast reverberated through the house and in place of the ironing board, a mountain of splintered wood and brick rose up all around me. Plaster dust and little bits of debris blew out from everywhere, instantly filling the air. Even as I tried desperately to process what was happening, I noted with resignation that this was one mess I was not going to be able to clean up.[147]

Even on the most extreme fringes of the American Left, the attitude to violence was essentially flirtatious (with the movie *Butch Cassidy and the Sundance Kid* almost required viewing).[148] The tide of minor bombings rose sharply: from 56

143 Edward J. Kiernan, head of the police union in New York, quoted in: B. Burrough, *Days of Rage: America's Radical Underground, the FBI and the Forgotten Age of Revolutionary Violence* (New York, 2015, 2016), p. 197.

144 Hofstadter, 'Reflections on Violence in the United States', p. 19.

145 Bryan, *This Soldier still at War*, pp. 109–11.

146 Burrough, *Days of Rage*, pp. 106–11, 122. Strictly speaking, 'The Weather Underground' is an anachronistic title—in its early months, the group was known as 'Weatherman'.

147 C. Wilkerson, *Flying Close to the Sun: My Life and Times as a Weatherman* (New York, 2007, 2011), p. 345.

148 For the popularity of this film amongst the American New Left, see: S. Stern, *With the Weathermen: the Personal Journey of a Revolutionary Woman* (Piscataway, NJ, 2007), p. 263; J. Lerner,

(in 1968) to 236 (in 1969) and 546 (by 1970).[149] In 1972 alone, according to one ex-FBI agent there were over 1,900 domestic bombings.[150] This intense infatuation with explosives was something of a mystery to activists themselves. In the strikingly impressionistic assessment of Jonathan Lerner, 'our idea of armed action was bombing, perhaps because bombs are spectacular, or perhaps that's what the Weather Underground was doing every now and then'.[151] To Andrew Kopkind, bombings drove a sense of generic crisis: and thus helped force 'real existential choice' on the privileged middle-classes.[152] And for Abbie Hoffman, in one of his less brilliant formulations, 'plastics' were simply 'the grooviest explosive available'. He clarified helpfully that they 'dramatically make your point and then some'.[153]

This was the crux of the matter. In this grammar of protest high explosive functioned as an obligatory exclamation mark. As the historian of the American New Left's adventures in violence has commented shrewdly, 'most bombings were followed by communiqués denouncing some aspect of the American condition; bombs basically functioned as exploding press releases'.[154] Even if often minor in effects, the sheer frequency of such explosions in the mid- to late-1970s does seem striking enough (Figure 2.1).

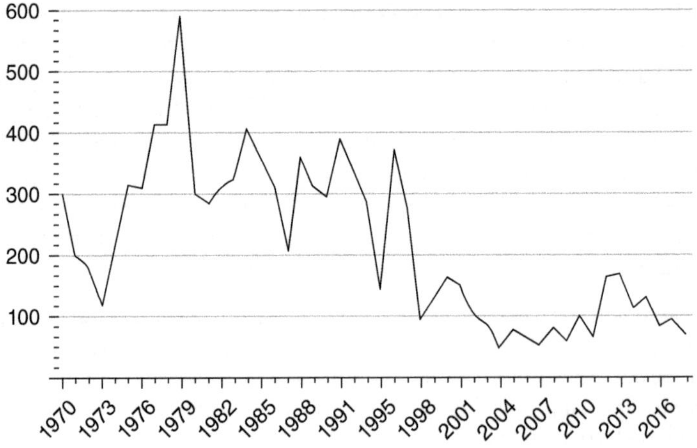

Figure 2.1. Attacks by explosives/bombs/dynamite in North America and Europe, 1970–2018

Source: The Global Terrorism Database.

Swords in the Hands of Children: Reflections of an American Revolutionary (New York, 2017), p. 149; Wilkerson, *Flying Close to the Sun*, p. 339; Rudd, *Underground*, p. 197; Burrough, *Days of Rage*, p. 83. For a parallel phenomenon in Britain: G. Carr, *The Angry Brigade: The Cause and the Case* (London, 1975), p. 67.

[149] Bryan, *This Soldier still at War*, p. 81.
[150] Burrough, *Days of Rage*, p. 5.
[151] Lerner, *Swords in the Hands of Children*, pp. 165–6.
[152] A. Kopkind, 'The Radical Bombers' in H. James (ed.) *Weatherman* (New York, 1970), pp. 501, 503.
[153] A. Hoffman, *Steal This Book* (New York, 1996, 2002), pp. 68, 177.
[154] Burrough, *Days of Rage*, p. 5.

Presumably, such pre-timed explosives appealed in part because they were not *directly* confrontational: after all, the bombers were middle-class youths for whom street-fighting had never come that naturally.[155] At least in the middle ranks, there does seem to have been an early flirtation with the idea of causing terror through bombings.[156] But only the Townhouse cell—who had been preparing a shrapnel bomb attack on an army dance—decisively embraced a strategy of mass casualty attacks (and this, apparently, without the slightest reflection about the likely consequences or reactions).[157]

After that self-inflicted disaster, the Weather Underground moved decisively away from such carnage-making. They also shrank as activists deserted in droves. A residual core evolved into proficient bombers of key buildings: most notoriously, the Capitol (1 March 1971) and the Pentagon (19 May 1972).[158] In effect, this armed struggle was evolving into a loose series of 'armed anecdotes' or 'explosive narrations'.[159] As if by design, the underground essentially devolved into the classic pattern of a loose network of a small number of tiny cells of perhaps five or six members: with all the pressure-cooker intensity that implies.[160] Indeed, the resilience of any kind of macro-network, however tenuous, was no mean logistical achievement.

It also survived some early—but near-disastrous—experiments in ritualized bullying (the notorious 'self-criticism sessions') and more-or-less mandatory promiscuity ('Everyone was fucking everyone else, in a wiggly, ugly pile, and yet during the day they could hardly stand to talk and look at each other, let alone touch each other in a nice, human way').[161] 'We didn't identify our organization as a cult, but I guess people in cults generally don't', comments Jonathan Lerner drily.[162] By 1975, even the last die-hards had accepted that the 'magical moment of insurrection' was not actually coming.[163]

What emerges most clearly, though, from the Weather Underground memoirs was the sheer unrelenting tedium of the underground struggle as it unfolded month after dreary month.[164] The antennae of the state seemed everywhere. Maintaining social invisibility under such conditions was all-consuming; and exhausting. Such outlaws became scrupulously law-abiding, taking particular care not to transgress speed limits (at the cost of intense personal frustration to some of their freer spirits).[165] Mobility was important to stay one step ahead of the law. But each and every change of address represented a major logistical challenge. In the

155 Jacobs, *The Way the Wind Blew*, p. 43.

156 Burrough, *Days of Rage*, p. 93; Lerner, *Swords in the Hands of Children*, pp. 27, 153.

157 Burrough, *Days of Rage*, pp. 102–4; Wilkerson, *Flying Close*, p. 350. Sánchez-Cuenca, *The Historical Roots of Political Violence*, pp. 203–4.

158 Burrough, *Days of Rage*, pp. 163, 231–2; Jacobs, *The Way the Wind Blew*, p. 142.

159 B. Ayers, *Fugitive Days: A Memoir* (Boston, 2001), pp. 256–7.

160 Burrough, *Days of Rage*, p. 128.

161 Stern, *With the Weathermen*, p. 197. See also: Burrough, *Days of Rage*, pp. 75–6.

162 Lerner, *Swords in the Hands of Children*, p. 82.

163 Prairie Fire Manifesto, quoted in: Jacobs, *The Way the Wind Blew*, p. 160.

164 Rudd, *Underground*, p. 199. Also: Burrough, *Days of Rage*, p. 137.

165 Alpert, *Growing Up Underground*, pp. 269–70; yers, *Fugitive Days*, p. 218.

wake of the Townhouse catastrophe, for instance, the New York collective at Cobble Hill decided to scatter: 'I remember it took a solid week to scrub every surface of that place, erasing every fingerprint', recalls Jonah Raskin, a frequent visitor. 'It was an unbelievable headache'.[166] Similar anecdotes of the crushing domestic mundanity of underground existence are legion across the international New Left. Dreaming of revolution, they were forced to focus on scrubbing the underside of toilet seats: a prime site, they had learnt, for fingerprint collection by police investigators.[167]

The rise of the violent New Left in Europe broadly paralleled its counterpart in the USA. This lurch towards leftist 'armed struggle' was a genuinely trans-Atlantic phenomenon: the first, indeed, since the fading of anarchist terror nearly fifty years before. In general, the peak of the drama came later: around 1977–8 in Western Europe (with the Schleyer/Moro kidnappings), at a time when the era of the 'urban guerilla' had very clearly long faded in both the USA and Canada.[168] In Europe, 1980 proved to be the most lethal year for such attacks.[169]

But this should not obscure the reality that the slide into terror was—initially—no less faltering in Europe than it had been in the USA. Flirtatious ambivalence ruled here as well: how else should one understand Rudi Dutschke's call for 'demonstrative and provocative counter-violence' against the violence that was constituent of the ruling system?[170] Dutschke's own practical contribution to such a project seems to have consisted of a rather furtive trundling of explosives around West Berlin in his son's pram.[171] Understandings of what constituted success were distinctly gnostic:

> What we are doing and what we want to show at the same time, is: that armed struggle can be carried out, that it is possible to pull actions off, where we can win, and not where the other side wins. And where it is, of course essential that they do not catch us, that is, so to speak, part of the success of the matter.[172]

Clearly, though, there was some widespread degree of fascination with violent strategies amongst European radical circles by 1970. Carlos Marighela's *Mini-Manual of the Urban Guerrilla* was the canonical text: and for those in a hurry to storm the future it held the immeasurable attraction of being short.[173] And yet thresholds to practical action remained stubbornly high: it was not at all intuitively

[166] Quoted in: Burrough, *Days of Rage*, p. 220.

[167] For American New Left groups, see: Ayers, *Fugitive Days*, p. 186; Burrough, *Days of Rage*, pp. 90, 510. For the West German Red Army Faction (and toilet seats): A. Dolnik, *Understanding Terrorist Innovation* (London, 2007), p. 169.

[168] D. Jenish, *The Making of the October Crisis: Canada's Long Nightmare of Terrorism at the Hands of the FLQ* (Toronto, 2018), pp. 285–6; Burrough, *Days of Rage*, p. 447.

[169] Engene, *Terrorism in Western Europe*, p. 62.

[170] I. Cornils, '"The Struggle Continues": Rudi Dutschke's Long March' in G. J. DeGroot (ed.), *Student Protest: The Sixties and After* (London, 1998), p. 111.

[171] Cornils, '"The Struggle Continues"', p. 106.

[172] Ulrike Meinhof, quoted in: E. Kolinsky, 'Terrorism in West Germany' in J. Lodge (ed.), *The Threat of Terrorism* (Brighton, 1988), p. 65.

[173] J. Becker, *Hitler's Children: the Story of the Baader-Meinhof Gang* (London, 1978), pp. 214–15; Varon, *Bringing the War Home*, pp. 71–2.

clear how fashionable *foco* ('revolutionary cells') theories of how to achieve social revolution could be adapted from Latin American conditions to the far richer societies of northern Europe with their well-resourced governments, and their all-enveloping bureaucracies of welfare (or surveillance). Geoff Eley in his discussion of leftist 'clandestine armed struggle, or terrorism as it became known' comments that

> Terrorism presupposed extremes of alienation, where people lost respect for the system. This went furthest in big cities with masses of younger people marginal to mainstream society—with higher educational qualifications yet displaced from career paths, partially employed, stylistically rebellious, and living and working in distinctive collective arrangements and quarters, often with bohemian or multicultural links, like the Hafenstrasse in Hamburg's St Pauli or Kreuzberg in West Berlin, with its 40,000 strong alternative scene, 40,000 Turks and 50,000 'normals' in 1989.[174]

Such areas were the European equivalents of the Haight-Ashbury district of San Francisco that had briefly spawned the Symbionese Liberation Army (SLA), rather mordantly described by Eric Hobsbawm as 'an otherwise negligible episode on the wilder fringes of Californian alienation':

> Traditional bandits were based on kin, neighbourhood and community. The Symbionese were unattached individuals by origin, none of whom had known or heard of each other until they met in the subcultural ghetto of the East Bay, as pebbles meet on a lowland sandbank, having been swept downstream along some complicated river-system.[175]

Strikingly, however, many of these dwarf armies of 6–10 active members were of exactly the same operating size as the traditional bandit gangs.[176] What was very different, though, was the vertiginous scale of ambition for tiny groups such as the SLA ('to unite all oppressed people into a fighting force and to destroy the system of the capitalist state and all its value systems'; adding for good measure the rallying slogan: 'Death to the fascist insect that preys upon the life of the people!').[177] Even in distinctly more idealistic times, this was not a message that was ever likely to resonate widely. In summary, 'the armed group becomes detached from society and engages in a purely bilateral war with the state, with very little participation of social movements'.[178] Left to their own momentum, the New Left's adventures in militarism gathered little intrinsic momentum. Neither revolution nor civil war were ever likely. 'Armed temptation' yielded arid fruit.[179]

[174] G. Eley, *Forging Democracy: A History of the Left in Europe, 1850–2000* (Oxford, 2002), p. 459.

[175] E. Hobsbawm, *Bandits* (London, 1969, 2001), pp. 190–1. Also: D. Boulton, *The Making of Tania Hearst* (London, 1975), p. 22.

[176] M. Broers, *Napoleon's Other War: Bandits, Rebels and their Pursuers in the Age of Revolutions* (Oxford, 2010), p. 15.

[177] J. Toobin, *American Heiress: The Kidnapping, Crimes and Trial of Patty Hearst* (London, 2016), pp. 32, 38, 68, 192.

[178] Sánchez-Cuenca, *The Historical Roots of Political Violence*, p. 58.

[179] Sánchez-Cuenca, *The Historical Roots of Political Violence*, p. 35.

Contextually, it is important to note that the self-consciously radical milieu that bred groups such as the SLA were distinctly liminal social bases from which to attempt such a frontal assault on society's key institutions. They could never serve as solid forward bases for political revolution. Counter-cultures built no counter-states. In the final analysis, 'the student urban guerillas were an armed vanguard in search of a revolutionary constituency'.[180]

Admittedly, this was not for want of trying. To focus just on the case of West Germany, it is striking that the first generation of the *Rote Armee Fraktion* (Red Army Faction) attempted to fight a limited struggle. They eschewed civilian targeting almost entirely: their one notable exception being the bombing of the Axel Springer building.[181] In the words of Ulrike Meinhof, 'terrorism operates amidst the fear of the masses. The city guerilla movement, on the other hand, carries fear to the machinery of the state'.[182] Such conceptual distinctions were self-serving, of course: but they also broadly reflected operational realities: 'the RAF's violence was not—as common denunciations of the group as fanatic, nihilistic, or sociopathic suggested—entirely without scruple or rationale'.[183]

Conceived as a contribution to the wider struggle against American imperialism raging in Vietnam, the RAF's bombing campaign of May 1972 concentrated primarily on security targets—the American military bases at Frankfurt and Heidelberg, the Augsburg police headquarters, the Criminal Investigations Headquarters in Munich and the office of a federal judge.[184] Indeed, such a list of the types of targets could have been borrowed wholesale from, say, the French Resistance of thirty years before. But the *Bundesrepublik* was not Vichy France: it could ride out such an assault with relative ease. The full-scale crisis of the 'German autumn' of 1977 lay still five years into the future.

In 1975 the Coordinator for Combatting Terrorism in the USA, Robert A. Fearey, observed: 'we've been very lucky in this country that international terrorism really hasn't reached us'.[185] Herein exactly lay the basic contrast with much of Western Europe. What elevated 'terrorism' (an increasingly standard label in public debate from this point) into a very major—if still intermittent—preoccupation of Western European governments during the 1970s was contagion. Spill-over from wider geo-political neighbourhoods elevated a series of largely disconnected, and containable, national crises into a general 'Age of Terror'.[186]

It bears emphasis that this new European Age of Terror that began in the early 1970s was *not* primarily a direct side-effect of a Cold War stand-off on the continent (which had itself become well established over the preceding two decades). Secret services fished in troubled waters, of course—as is their job. But they knew

[180] Carr, *The Infernal Machine*, p. 134.

[181] S. Aust, *The Baader Meinhof Complex* (London, 2008), p. 162.

[182] Aust, *The Baader Meinhof Complex*, p. 239. For a similar comment by Andreas Baader: p. 397.

[183] Varon, *Bringing the War Home*, p. 211.

[184] Aust, *The Baader Meinhof Complex*, pp. 159–63; B. Blumenau, *The United Nations and Terrorism* (London, 2014), pp. 19–20; Becker, *Hitler's Children*, pp. 277–78.

[185] Quoted in: W. P. Lineberry (ed.), *The Struggle Against Terrorism* (New York, 1977), p. 50.

[186] Y. Alexander, 'Age of Terror' in W. P. Lineberry (ed.), *The Struggle Against Terrorism* (New York, 1977), p. 5.

the limits. Superpower confrontation in Europe was so tense that it allowed little room for terroristic adventurism. The stakes were simply too high. Confident contemporary claims to the contrary have not aged well: the opening of the files post-1989 have revealed no huge and hidden terrorist 'basement' to the Cold War in Europe. Indeed, the emergent picture is one of mutual superpower restraint.[187]

With mayhem raging in Northern Ireland in 1972, the British Prime Minister Edward Heath was obliged to write to the US President Richard Nixon informing him of his intention, temporarily, to withdraw 20,000 troops from the British Army of the Rhine.[188] Yet the Soviets hardly meddled in Northern Ireland—beyond some rhetorical sympathy for the Official IRA.[189] Recurrent stories of Soviet snipers assisting the Provisional IRA revealed more about the imaginations of British tabloid journalists than about Moscow's intentions.[190] Likewise, the leading historian of the East German regime's relationship to the RAF has concluded that there was no official intention to use them in any serious attempt to destabilize West German society, commenting that these 'terrorists were no proxies in the Cold War: the GDR did not see them as another brigade actively involved in the conflict'.[191] Conversely, NATO was ultimately content to let anti-Soviet popular insurrections be crushed repeatedly: most notably in Berlin (1953), Poznań (1956), Budapest (1956), and Prague (1968). Otherwise, there was very little armed resistance against Soviet-backed regimes that could have been leveraged by the West: what 'terrorism' there was took the form of attempts at hijackings of those desperately attempting to escape to the West.[192]

Only in Italy did the CIA fuel unofficial terror more directly: from the *Gladio* network that they funded, re-emerged the neo-fascist 'strategy of tension' calculated to de-stabilize the country in preparation for a far-right take over. Express trains and major railway stations were again key targets (just as in the 1930s). But these bombing campaigns embraced mass casualty attacks—most notoriously in Milan (1969) and at Bologna Railway Station (1980)—in a way that was genuinely novel.[193] And in the Italian context, this neo-fascist *stragismo*—or slaughter tactics—was a long way from the fascist strutting and parading of the early 1920s.[194] It was distinctly impersonal in a way that administering castor oil had not been.

Violent conflict in Italy stayed close to the surface of public life, erupting sporadically in pustular fashion. Between 1969 and 1987, there were 14,591 attacks in

[187] J. L. Gaddis, *We Now Know: Rethinking Cold War History* (Oxford, 1997, 1998), p. 280; M. Wolf, *Memoirs of a Spymaster* (London, 1997, 1998), pp. 268, 275, 277–9.

[188] A. Craig, *Crisis of Confidence: Anglo-Irish Relations in the Early Troubles* (Dublin, 2010), p. 124; J. Bardon, *A History of Ulster* (Belfast, 1992, 1994), p. 698.

[189] B. Hanley and S. Millar, *The Lost Revolution: the Story of the Official IRA and the Workers' Party* (Dublin, 2009), pp. 141, 188, 196, 334.

[190] G. Styles, *Bombs Have No Pity: My War Against Terrorism* (London, 1975), pp. 75, 110.

[191] B. Blumenau, 'Unholy Alliance: The Connection between the East German Stasi and the Right-Wing Terrorist Odfried Hepp', *Studies in Conflict and Terrorism* (2018), p. 4.

[192] Blumenau, *The United Nations and Terrorism*, pp. 82, 168. See also: E. F. Mickolus (et al., eds), *International Terrorism in the 1980s: A Chronology of Events*, Vol. 2: *1984–1987* (Iowa City, 1989), pp. 618–19 [8 July 1987 hostage-taking at the Zlatni Pyasutsi tourist resort, Bulgaria].

[193] A. Jamieson, *The Heart Attacked: Terrorism and Conflict in the Italian State* (London, 1989), p. 21.

[194] Jamieson, *The Heart Attacked*), p. 21.

Italy that killed 419 and injured 1,182.[195] Politically, the extreme left saw the prospect of 'armed struggle' as an insurance against an anticipated coup from the right.[196] Socially, left-wing activism retained a broader social appeal than elsewhere in Western Europe: and even extreme groups such as the Red Brigades had a genuine foothold not only on university campuses but on factory floors as well. Until well into the 1970s strikes in the car factories of northern Italy were characterized by the persistence of 'rough music' traditions: 'as with charivari-like communitarian justice, the symbolic violence of Italy's factory workers did not punish randomly chosen symbolic targets, but focused on particularly unpopular "wrongdoers" within the factory'.[197]

However, it is important not to exaggerate Italian exceptionalism. Southern Europe in general remained in many ways a region apart. Its governments retained a distinctive fragility reminiscent of much of the rest of the continent earlier in the twentieth century. Right-wing dictatorships in Spain, Portugal, and Greece survived here into the mid-1970s. Coup attempts did not entirely die out until the early 1980s.[198] A distinct hint of fragility hung over Yugoslavia: and expressed itself in repeated bouts of constitutional engineering, each more elaborate than the last. The Communist regime could shrug off attempts by Croatian nationalist exiles to launch guerilla warfare inside their borders or to re-launch earlier Ustashe terror traditions of targeting international transport, but with the now fashionable emphasis on attacking the aviation industry.[199] More seriously, though, the Croatian Spring crisis of 1971 took on aspects of a full dress rehearsal for ethnic civil war: an ominous episode that historians of the post-1991 catastrophe have, curiously, entirely neglected.[200]

V

A key difference between America and Western Europe's domestic experience of terror in the 1970s remained the latter's vulnerability to overspill from the Middle East.[201] Of course, this was not in itself anything new: as Irgun's brief bombing campaigns in 1946–7 had demonstrated. But this became a far more serious threat in the 1970s for at least two main reasons. Both the quantity and quality of exported violence were transformed.

[195] Jamieson, *The Heart Attacked*, p. 19.

[196] P. Edwards, *More Work, Less Pay! Rebellion and Repression in Italy, 1972–1977* (Manchester, 2009), p. 15.

[197] I. Favretto, 'Rough Music and Factory Protest in Post-1945 Italy', *Past and Present*, 228 (1) August 2015, p. 215.

[198] P. Preston, *The Triumph of Democracy in Spain* (London, 1986), pp. 189–227.

[199] J. Bowyer Bell, *A Time of Terror: How Democratic Societies Respond to Revolutionary Violence* (New York, 1978), p. 17; P. Wilkinson, *Political Terrorism* (London, 1974), p. 150.

[200] A recent study focuses upon its international significance, rather than grassroots tensions: A. Batović, *The Croatian Spring: Nationalism, Repression and Foreign Policy under Tito* (London, 2017). For a glimpse of the grassroots tension at the time see: D. Doder, *The Yugoslavs* (New York, 1978, 1979), pp. 37–8.

[201] Varon, *Bringing the War Home*, 69.

At least three main reasons stand out here. First, and unlike the Irgun in 1946–47, the transnational arena became the *primary* theatre of operations for Palestinian militants.[202] Diplomatic neglect of the Palestinian quest for statehood was now to be punished creatively: 'the driving impulse was to shock the international community and shake its complacency regarding the plight of the Palestinians'.[203] And here the prior scattering of the Palestinian diaspora after 1948 had laid the foundations for a militant national movement that was inescapably transnational. Now that dispersed marginality was in turn leveraged as the basis for international attention-grabbing: in effect, the battlefield was deliberately, and radically, widened. From 1969 Israeli Embassies and the offices of the national airline, El Al, were being attacked across Europe.[204] In the cold-eyed assessment of George Habash, leader of the Popular Front for the Liberation of Palestine (PFLP) in 1970: 'We believe that to kill a Jew far away from the battleground has more effect than killing 100 of them in battle; it attracts more attention. And when we set fire to a store in London, those few flames are worth the burning down of two kibbutzim because we force people to ask what is going on'.[205] Thus a 'flying carpet revolution' succeeded in deliberately spreading mayhem far and wide: and eventually in provoking a spiral of Israeli counter-killings:

> Between September 1972 and July 1973, the capitals of Europe witnessed a string of reprisals and counter-reprisals. Arafat estimates that more than sixty of his people were killed or maimed in the ten-month shadow war. Israeli casualties were significantly fewer.[206]

Secondly, the early 1970s saw an adoption by several Arab regimes of the sort of 'state-sponsored terrorism' that European fascist regimes had pioneered forty years earlier. A strategy of proxy attacks offered the prospect to some states of advancing goals with a reduced—although as events were to show, hardly negligible—risk of provoking all-out conventional wars.[207] Small groups with state-backing may become far more lethal than those without: in turn fuelling fresh cycles of retribution.[208] Given the labyrinthine nature of Middle Eastern rivalries, such quarrels had the potential to feed off themselves almost endlessly: every Palestinian faction could always find its own state sponsor against its rivals. The shooting in London of the Jordanian ambassador by the Black September faction on 15 December 1971 merely set the pattern here.[209]

[202] B. Hoffman, *Inside Terrorism* (New York, 2006), pp. 63–80.

[203] Y. Sayigh, *Armed Struggle and the Search for State: The Palestinian National Movement, 1949–1993* (Oxford, 1997), p. 214.

[204] Y. Alexander and J. Sinai, *Terrorism: the PLO connection* (New York, 1989), p. 11.

[205] A. Merari and S. Elad, *The International Dimension of Palestinian Terrorism* (Abingdon, 1986, 2019), p. 19.

[206] B. Rubin, *Revolution Until Victory? The Politics and History of the PLO* (London, 1994), back of the dustjacket ['Flying carpet']: T. Walker and A. Gowers, *Arafat: The Biography* (London, 2003), p. 92.

[207] Given their subsequent loss of the Golan Heights in the 1967 war, the Syrian regime's support for PLO raids beforehand might be seen as a particularly poor investment: B. Morris, *Righteous Victims: A History of the Zionist–Arab Conflict, 1881–2001* (New York, 1999, 2001), p. 303.

[208] Byman, *Deadly Connections*, p. 53; A. Dolnik, *Understanding Terrorist Innovation*, p. 19.

[209] Y. Sayigh, *Armed Struggle*, p. 307.

Thirdly, and most significantly, the Israeli-Palestinian conflict post-1967 proved to be a particularly creative laboratory in atrocity. The general background here was a loosening of restraints in targeting civilians—both on the part of Palestinian bombers in Jerusalem; but also in Israeli reprisals.[210] And the key innovation here was the turn towards mass hostage taking as a tactic of coercive bargaining. According to one estimate in 1976, 'a total of twenty-nine hijackings have been staged by Palestinian and pro-Palestinian groups since 1968, plus three airport massacres'. Only eleven attempts had been foiled: and 201 people had been killed (as well as a further 213 injured).[211] Enhanced security of passengers eventually reigned in this 'hijacking carnival' but only at the cost of displacing the mayhem into airport massacres and bombings.[212] Secondly, and as a related tendency, there was a diffusion into set-piece 'barricade' situations, such as Embassy takeovers. The most spectacular publicity coup of all, naturally, was the storming of the Munich Olympics in 1972. Here the 20th Olympiad itself was turned into a televised Colosseum. It is worth noting that hostage-taking was not exclusively Middle Eastern. But it was the Palestinian adoption of this tactic that was to prove particularly fateful for admirers and allies. The result was a general rash of imitations across Europe: the second generation of the Red Army Faction's hostage-taking at the West German Embassy in Stockholm (24 April 1975) and the first South Moluccan train hijacking in the Netherlands (December 1975) being amongst the most notable exemplars. Mayhem was inexorably spreading into new arenas and new countries.[213]

Early enthusiasts for armed struggle on the New Left were often dismayed by this sudden advent of a 'flying circus of multinational terrorism'.[214] As 'Bommi' Baumann of the West German 2nd June movement put it of the 1978 hijackings: 'you can't take your life and place it above that of children and Majorca holidaymakers and say: *my* life is more valuable!'[215] As shrewd commentators recognized at the time, it was 'perhaps only in times of relative peace in the world' that such 'lesser episodes in violence' could monopolize attention. But that was cold comfort for governments increasingly forced by the tyranny of television news schedules to respond to crises on the hijackers', and not their own, schedule.[216] And as global theatre, the hostage drama was truly mesmeric.[217]

Since hostage-taking represented a form of coercive bargaining that governments initially found impossible to sideline, they took this emergent threat to both

[210] Morris, *Righteous Victims*, pp. 341–3, 363–74.

[211] T. Smith in W. P. Lineberry (ed.), *The Struggle Against Terrorism* (New York, 1977), p. 158.

[212] Quoted in: Y. Sayigh, *Armed Struggle*, p. 257.

[213] For South Moluccans: W. Mathewson, 'Incident in Holland' in W. P. Lineberry (ed.), *The Struggle Against Terrorism* (New York, 1977), pp. 62–8; *Birmingham Daily Post*, 25 April 1975 ('Deadline threat to hostages in guerrilla attack').

[214] Laqueur, *Terrorism*, p. 248.

[215] B. Hoffman, 'The Contrasting Ethical Foundations of Terrorism in the 1980s', *Terrorism and Political Violence*, 1, July 1989, pp. 363–4. Emphasis in original.

[216] Hoffman, *Inside Terrorism*, pp. 193–6.

[217] B. Jenkins, *International Terrorism: A New Kind of Warfare*, The Rand Paper Series, June 1974, pp. 4, 9.

their citizens and their own authority very seriously indeed. As Chancellor Schmidt put it, a government that could be blackmailed, was not a proper government.[218] As a result, the notable feature of these years was the growth across Europe of 'counter-terrorism special units... organized and trained like shock troops to neutralize (i.e. kill) terrorists rather than arrest them'.[219] In 1966, the first specialist firearms unit in the British police system was founded: by 1996, 89 per cent of the police departments serving large and medium cities had some kind of paramilitary unit.[220] The 1972 Munich debacle acted as a powerful catalyst for this kind of experimentation: both the West German G9 and its French equivalent, the GIGN (*Groupe d'intervention de la gendarmerie nationale*), were set up in its wake.[221] Israeli triumph at Entebbe in 1977 set a new standard.[222] In its wake, indeed, successful hostage rescue became a sort of 'yardstick for national virility'.[223]

Equally important in the longer term, though, was a general honing of the state's infrastructure to track and eliminate its sub-cultures of violent dissidents. Like the 1890s, indeed, the 1970s saw a veritable bureaucratic revolution in how Western states marshalled resources to face down what were usually tiny numbers of elusive opponents. In West Germany the Federal Criminal Office grew from 818 staff in 1965 to 3122 by 1978.[224] After the kidnapping of Hanns Martin Schleyer in 1977, the West German state similarly mobilized in earnest. Much the same pattern emerged the following year in Italy. After the kidnapping of the senior Christian Democrat politician, Aldo Moro, the Italian state deployed 16,000 Carabinieri, 18,000 police, 4,000 frontier guards and hundreds of army units to search for him. A total of 3.3 million cars were examined at 62,000 road blocks; and 35,000 houses searched.[225] None of these efforts saved either of these high-profile kidnapped victims as intended. But they did ensure these crises had a 'high noon' feel to them: the state rallied its resources in earnest, and its opponents found it impossible to repeat the challenge. In general, counter-terrorism budgets ballooned across the Western world in these years: 'by 1985 the United States was spending an estimated $4.2 billion per year and employing some 18,000 people on a range of anti-terrorist measures, from intelligence gathering and research to protection for diplomats and embassy officials abroad'.[226]

It is important to remember that most European anti-state terror 'campaigns', whether broadly leftist or nationalist in their origins, remained distinctly amateur

218 Blumenau, *The United Nations and Terrorism*, p. 76.

219 Anderson, *In Thrall to Political Change*, p. 196.

220 P. A. J. Waddington, 'Swatting Police Paramilitarism: A Comment on Kraska and Paulsen', *Policing and Society*, 9, 1999, pp. 126, 142.

221 Anderson, *In Thrall to Political Change*, p. 132.

222 Y. Ofer, *Operation Thunder: The Entebbe Raid. The Israelis' Own Story* (Harmondsworth, 1976); W. Stevenson, *90 Minutes at Entebbe* (New York, 1976).

223 J. Le Carré, 'Introduction' in The Observer, *Siege: Six Days at the Iranian Embassy* (London, 1980), p. 3.

224 G. Pridham, 'Terrorism and the State in West Germany during the 1970s: A Threat to Stability or a Case of Political Over-Reaction?' in J. Lodge (ed.), *Terrorism: A Challenge to the State* (Oxford, 1981), p. 48.

225 Carr, *The Infernal Machine*, p. 155.

226 Carr, *The Infernal Machine*, p. 206.

and transient. One survey of Western Europe between 1950 and 1995 found that 80.3 per cent (of 188) armed groups failed to stay active for more than two years; 55.1 per cent of all groups did not kill anyone.[227] In summary, in this period 'the majority of terrorist groups carry out few actions, kill few people or none at all, and disappear after a short time'.[228] Conversely, though, it is important to recognize that a small number of groups did show astonishing staying power. Sixteen stayed active for over a decade. Just nineteen high-lethality groups were 'responsible for the deaths of more than 90 per cent of the people killed by terrorist groups identified by name, which is close to 58 per cent of the total number of killings'.[229]

And yet from the late 1970s into the mid-1990s these 'high-lethality' groups were mostly themselves relentlessly ground down into the institutionalized purgatory of disbandment and ceasefires. Ultimately, they were contained and confined by superior state forces that boasted endless largesse for recruiting informers; tentacular bureaucracies to map whole target populations, and—increasingly—the computerized processing strength to digest the information captured ('a police service is as good as its archives').[230] By contrast, their most resilient enemies were boiled down into cells of hardened professionals who might continue, but could not escalate, their chosen armed struggles. Accounts of the lives of activists in Red Brigade cells hiding out in northern Italian cities (in the 1970s) read just like those of the Gappists (from the 1940s): with the same tedium, the same claustrophobia—although, it has to be conceded, a higher standard of material discontent (endless television; and complaints—from the southern Italian members—over the quality of the spaghetti). In the judgement of one thoroughly burnt-out activist:

> the preparation of an attack in the way we conduct our armed struggle, here and now in Italy, has much more in common with the approach of a scrupulous accountant than that of a guerilla fighter....I imagine that few wars or guerilla campaigns or armed uprisings, call it what you like, have required the level of drudge work, routine, or rat race that is so much a part of ours.[231]

Such malaise was, however, structural, not idiosyncratic. As convergent accounts from highly variant campaigns in this period agree: life in the underground overwhelmingly consisted of exactly this kind of 'drudge work'. And there was nothing specifically Italian about this inevitable outcome to such inescapably asymmetrical conflicts.

Loss of momentum, then, was the general fate of these armed struggles: they tended to evolve into socially detached duels of rival specialists. In Northern Ireland, where the British state faced a determined and tenacious Irish Republican insurgency from 1970 this process of containment was notably slow. But it was

[227] Engene, *Terrorism in Western Europe*, p. 73.
[228] Engene, *Terrorism in Western Europe*, p. 75.
[229] Engene, *Terrorism in Western Europe*, p. 73.
[230] Yves Bonnet, Director of the *Direction de la surveillance du territoire*, 1982–1985. Quoted in: Anderson, *In Thrall to Political Change*, p. 216.
[231] 'Giorgio', *Memoirs of an Italian Terrorist* (New York, 1981, 2003), pp. 156, 163–6. Admittedly, I take this memoir on trust as genuine.

also relatively sure (at least after the early chaotic months of the security forces' blundering repression). To read Gerry Bradley's memoir of his long career in the Provisional IRA is to chart this evolution as it played out in Belfast after 1969. An early underground army of hundreds conducting wildly spontaneous shooting attacks on the British army became, by the 1990s, 'a stripped-down core of twenty key operators now kitted out in boiler suits, ear plugs, and nose plugs' (to defeat the forensic teams).[232] The Northern Irish Secretary's boast at the end of 1977 that 'we are squeezing the terrorists like rolling up a toothpaste tube' may have been essentially macho posturing for the *Daily Express*: and highly premature at that.[233] But it was also not absolutely delusional. In this grinding contest of grossly unequal resources, the British state *would* ultimately contain the Provisionals' campaign to destabilize Northern Ireland: even if this holding operation on its own could deliver no political solutions.

Such attritional struggles, then, inevitably favoured the better resourced. States won decisively (again). In the USA from about 1985 a series of 'confrontations between state authority and the inhabitants of isolated compounds' taught far-right extremists the impossibility of withdrawing altogether from the government's surveillance.[234] A disastrous end to an armed stand-off at Waco in 1993 reinforced the lesson dramatically. As early as 1983 Louis Beam's advocacy of a so-called 'leaderless resistance' had started from a clear-eyed recognition of the federal state's impregnability ('the government will not doubt make today's oppressiveness look like grade school work compared to what they have planned in the future').[235] Strikingly, such strategic thinking resembled the 'anti-organizationists' of a full century earlier: it was a sort of 'anarchy of the right'.[236] And yet, with the notable exception of the Oklahoma City bombing of 1996, the true potential for such acephalous mayhem as yet remained largely unclear.[237]

At the other end of the political spectrum, domestic challengers withdrew as their once-clockwork expectations of victory—so tightly wound in 1968—slowly uncoiled. In general, the leftist movements faded rather more quickly than their nationalist counterparts: after all, they had smaller reservoirs of social support to draw upon. By 1995, concludes the student of long-term patterns in Western Europe, 'it is as if an age of terrorism draws towards its end'.[238]

[232] I. McBride, 'Provisional Truths' in S. Pašeta (ed.), *Uncertain Futures: Essays About the Irish Past for Roy Foster* (Oxford, 2016), p. 238.

[233] J. Bowyer Bell, *The Irish Troubles: A Generation of Violence 1967–1992* (Dublin, 1993, 1994), p. 531.

[234] J. Kaplan, 'Right Wing Violence in North America' in T. Bjørgo (ed.), *Terror from the Extreme Right* (London, 1995), pp. 80–1.

[235] L. Beam, 'Leaderless Resistance', *The Seditionist*, No. 12, February 1992, p. 1.

[236] N. Pernicone and F. M. Ottanelli, *Assassins Against the Old Order: Italian Anarchist violence in Fin De Siècle Europe* (Champaign, IL, 2018), p. 159.

[237] Hoffman, *Inside Terrorism*, pp. 101–18. D. Koehler, Right-Wing Terrorism: The 'National Socialist Underground' and the History of Terror From the Far-Right in Germany (Abingdon, 2017), pp. 114, 181; J. Kaplan, 'Leaderless Resistance', *Terrorism and Political Violence*, 9 (3), 1997, pp. 80–95.

[238] Engene, *Terrorism in Western Europe*, p. 171.

VI

At the dawn of the twenty-first century there was, therefore, very little indication that renewed terror threats would again soon come to preoccupy Western governments deeply, obsessively, and—as of the time of writing in 2019—apparently unendingly. In 1994, the special planning office at JFK airport was of the firm opinion that it was 'just impractical for Middle Eastern organizations to import terrorism here. It's too far away'.[239] By 2000, the FBI had assigned twice as many agents to drug enforcement duties as to counter-terrorism.[240] In the midst of this deep peace, almost nothing seemed more improbable than Manhattan being hit by the equivalent of a (medium-sized) Second World War bombing raid out of a perfectly azure sky.

And yet for those very few with eyes to see, the 1990s had already boasted its fair share of disturbing portents.[241] Just five years after Margaret Thatcher had described the Afghanistan Mujahideen as waging 'one of the most heroic resistance struggles known to history', a plot hatched on their guest fringe came close to toppling the south tower of the World Trade Center.[242] And the following year—1994—Islamist hijackers from Algeria also came close to pulling off a spectacular atrocity with a plan to fly an airliner into the Eiffel Tower.[243] What was distinctive about this kind of plotting was its vertiginous ambition: for there were relatively few precedents for such catastrophe so grandly conceived.[244] But this did not deter repeated attempts to pull off just such an epic of destruction. In that sense, something like 9/11 was waiting to happen.

By the mid-1990s, then, long-distance feedback loops were tightening between Western global hegemony and sub-cultures of Islamist resentment that bubbled up from, but which definitely no longer stayed confined to, the Middle East: 'European Muslims, and Muslims based in Europe, particularly in Germany, the UK, Spain and France, were critical in setting up the *al-Qaeda* infrastructure that prepared for 9/11'.[245] 'Overspill' and 'blowback' were now evolving into phenomena of truly global reach.[246] And the American-led invasions of Afghanistan (2001) and Iraq (2003) would, in their turn, create social and political consequences that would wash relentlessly back both on their own shores, and on Europe. Of 119 individuals convicted in Britain of Islamist terrorism offences between 1999 and 2009,

[239] Quoted in: K. James, *Heathrow Airport: An Illustrated History* (Stroud, 2016), p. 143.

[240] 9/11 Commission Report, p. 77.

[241] B. Hoffman, 'Terrorist targeting: Tactics, trends, and potentialities', *Terrorism and Political Violence*, 5 (2), 1993.

[242] M. Thatcher, 'Foreword' in S. Gall, *Afghanistan: Travels with the Mujahideen* (London, 1988, 1989), p. xiii. For World Trade Center attack: B. Hoffman, *Inside Terrorism*, pp. 89, 93, 99.

[243] P. Nesser, *Islamist Terrorism in Europe: A History* (London, 2015), pp. 67–83.

[244] The 1972 attack at the Munich Olympics is perhaps the nearest exemplar. But the latter's resonance was more due to its profanation of a near-sacred occasion: rather than to the intrinsic scale of the carnage, substantial though that turned out to be.

[245] M. Castells, *The Power of Identity*, Vol. II, *The Network Society* (Chichester, 1997, 2010), p. 119.

[246] Mann, *Sources of Social Power*, Vol. 4, p. 305.

69 per cent were of Pakistani descent, but born in the UK and holders of British passports. Of those caught attempting or plotting bombings *all* gave as their motivation a desire to oppose British foreign policy.[247] Similarly, albeit on a lesser scale, 'the rare cases of Muslim militants suspected of terrorist inclinations in America are usually poor African-Americans or Muslim immigrants'.[248]

Viewed against the longer history of the Western state as the guarantor of public order, this was a truly surreal opening to the twenty-first century. Governments were now thoroughly spooked by an Islamist global insurgency with only the most limited presence on their own doorsteps. Despite high birth rates, Muslims only comprised around 5 per cent of the population of Europe (by 2017), and a mere 1.1 per cent of the US population (by 2018).[249] Needless to say, the vast majority of these highly vulnerable populations held no appetite for provoking carnage; or for the inevitable wider Islamophobic hostility that such attempts would provoke. As Brian Jenkins wrote in 2010, 'the homegrown jihadist threat in America today consists of tiny conspiracies, lone gunmen, and one-off attacks'.[250] Al Qaeda could therefore only hope to rally the most miniscule fringe of these highly limited diasporas: factions drawn from fractions of fractions. Of all the hopeless revolutionary projects, this was surely the most hopeless.

Still, as far as tactics went, this shifting and evolving insurgency has been improvised but highly creative. The years after 2001 saw innovation after innovation in atrocity against civilians: the first suicide bombings and marauding firearms attacks in Europe, as well the adoption of vehicle attacks in crowded places. Complex as the attack patterns have been, they might usefully, if roughly, be analytically sorted into attempts at 'spectaculars' (involving elaborate conspiracies) and rather more spontaneous rampages (by isolated groups, or individuals).

Overall the pattern has been one of 'spasm terrorism'.[251] New communication technologies created alarmingly rhizoid possibilities: as early as 2001 it was noted that 'one manifestation of this networking is the proliferation of the amateur terrorist and the ad hoc terrorist group. Amateurs come together with the like-minded to conduct a terrorist attack and then disband'.[252] Such campaigns, however, have tended to lack staying power, and have generally been marked by relative

[247] Mann, *Sources of Social Power*, Vol. 4, p. 305.

[248] Castells, *The Power of Identity*, Vol. II, p. xxii.

[249] For Europe, see: B. Hackett, '5 Facts About the Muslim Population in Europe' (29 November 2017). Available at: https://www.pewresearch.org/fact-tank/2017/11/29/5-facts-about-the-muslim-population-in-europe/; For USA, see: B. Mohamed, 'New Estimates Show U.S. Muslim Population Continues to Grow' (3 January 2018). Available at: https://www.pewresearch.org/fact-tank/2018/01/03/new-estimates-show-u-s-muslim-population-continues-to-grow/

[250] B. Jenkins, 'Would-Be Warriors: Incidents of Jihadist Terrorist Radicalization in the United States Since September 11, 2001', Rand Occasional Paper, 2010, p. ix.

[251] P. Wilkinson, *Terrorism and the Liberal State* (London, 1977, 1979), pp. 139, 147.

[252] D. Tucker, 'What is New about the New Terrorism and How Dangerous is it?', *Terrorism and Political Violence*, 13 (3), 2001, p. 2.

technological primitivism (at least as compared to the Provisional IRA's bomb-making expertise in their heyday).[253]

Contemporary Islamist terrorism is also notably prodigal with its own talent. For all their variety, all three of the English attacks in the early summer of 2017 fully shared one common feature: that all five of the attackers went out, apparently, with a firm death wish and absolutely no intention of coming back. Even though only the Manchester attacker, Salman Abedi, actually blew himself up, it is hard to believe the other four attackers at Westminster and Borough Market did not expect to be gunned down—as they all promptly were.[254] Kamikaze tactics use up the most committed the quickest. They also have limited appeal—outside of truly desperate contexts such as prolonged military occupations.

And yet, in one form or other, and with shifting loyalties to differing groups, an Islamist insurgency has continued to reproduce itself across generations. It has established some vestigial presence in both the USA and Europe: and attracted recruits from Muslim diasporas as well as fresh converts. The latter, although numerically tiny, are very significantly over-represented amongst terror suspects: 35 per cent of 'European-born jihadis' were converts in the estimate of a 2006 survey.[255]

In the final analysis, the big picture remains disquieting. After all, it is well over 30 years since Osama Bin Laden first proclaimed his struggle: and still the 'the final chapter of Al Qaeda's long and bloody history has yet to be written'.[256] Bin Laden's model of international terror has distilled the most dystopian possibilities of globalization into a diffuse and general nightmare. In 2017 MI5 had 20,000 closed 'subjects of interest': that is, individuals they would like to know more about, but cannot justify prioritizing under current resource constraints.[257] Thirty years earlier, during the era of leftist terror, the equivalent size of the suspect category for the West German authorities would have been around 500.[258]

The pressure to make more resources available is, predictably, accordingly relentless. Security budgets and bureaucracies bulk and balloon alarmingly. As we approach the third decade of the twenty-first century, elephantiasis of the state's security organs seems to have become an enduring condition: a 'doom boom'.[259] There seems very little sign of any decisive end to the 'forever war' against Islamist

[253] A. Oppenheimer, *IRA: The Bombs and the Bullets: A History of Deadly Ingenuity* (Dublin, 2009, 2013), pp. 123–33.

[254] Pool Re Terrorism Research and Analysis Centre, 'Post-Incident Report: Three Attacks in three Months—Westminster, Manchester and London Bridge', 7 June 2017. For London Bridge attacks, see: *Guardian*, 5 June 2017; *Daily Mail*, 7 June 2017; *Daily Telegraph*, 7 June 2017. For Manchester: *The Times*, 24 June 2017.

[255] R. S. Leiken, *Europe's Angry Muslims: The Revolt of the Second Generation* (Oxford, 2012), pp. 233, 236.

[256] B. Hoffman, 'A First Draft of the History of America's Ongoing Wars on Terrorism', *Studies in Conflict and Terrorism* 38 (1) 2015, p. 82.

[257] *Guardian*, 19 June 2019 ('MI5 analysing former terror suspects to catch potential attackers').

[258] Kolinsky, 'Terrorism in West Germany', p. 68.

[259] J. Mueller *Overblown: How Politicians and the Terrorism Industry Inflate National Security Threats and Why We Believe Them* (New York, 2006), pp. 33–9; *The Mail on Sunday*, 2 June 2019 ('MI5 Spies Now Face Historic Assault').

terror: even with the crushing of the ISIS Caliphate in 2019. Such a strikingly open-ended moment is therefore as good a point as any to attempt a long-term survey of modern state capacity in the face of violent challenge: an audit of what a nineteenth-century British Prime Minister, William Gladstone, once termed 'the resources of civilization'.[260]

[260] The phrase comes from a speech on Irish political violence in October 1881: H. C. G. Matthew, *Gladstone, 1875–1898* (Oxford, 1995), p. 197.

3

The Resources of Civilization

In this chapter I examine the resilience of Western states and societies both against the long history of previous unrest, but with an eye to ongoing struggles as well. I turn from the welter of events to a survey of more general, and long-running, patterns. As already discussed, in both later nineteenth-century Europe and America a new kind of state emerged whose powers of coercion and social control were quite unprecedented. They were orderly to a degree that amazed contemporaries since 'violence recedes as power grows'.[1] Naturally, even these powerful states were never able to eliminate violence entirely. But at least as far as *public* challenges to state authority went, they were certainly able to recast it radically into distinctively late modern forms: chains of 'actions and reactions, which are oppositional but rarely equal'.[2] In effect, political violence was 'squeezed' into marginal and spasmodic expressions that (most) governments could manage (most) of the time without resorting to too blatant repression. And 'when securely institutionalized, coercion melts into the background of daily life, out of focus'.[3]

This chapter explores the consequences and form of this general remoulding: as well as its historic limits, its legacy, and its (apparent) recent decay. Indeed, across both the USA and Western Europe political and social turbulence currently seems to be running at its highest for a half century or so. If there have not been full-blown political revolutions, there have certainly been communication revolutions that look set to accelerate exponentially: and their (sometimes literally) explosive legacies are clearly not going to be easy to manage or contain even across immensely rich, powerful, and (relatively) well-resourced societies.[4] As we peer through a glass darkly into the looming decades left of the twenty-first century, any illumination from the past—however refracted or dim– seems worth the having.

I

> If you throw a stone, it's a crime. If a thousand stones are thrown, that's political.
>
> – Ulrike Meinhof[5]

[1] A. J. Mayer, The *Furies: Violence and Terror in the French and Russian Revolutions* (Princeton, 2000, 2002), p. 83.

[2] J. Lerner, *Swords in the Hands of Children: Reflections of an American Revolutionary* (New York, 2017), p. 2.

[3] Z. Bauman, *The Individualized Society* (Cambridge, 2001, 2005), p. 212.

[4] M. Castells, *The Information Age* (Chichester, 1996, 2010), Vol. 1, *The Rise of the Network Society*, pp. xvii–xliv (Preface of the 2010 edition).

[5] S. Aust, *The Baader Meinhof Complex* (London, 2008), p. 36.

From the nineteenth century onwards, the domestic prestige of Western states has rested upon their being able to guarantee a degree of public order so deeply embedded that it normally remains invisible. But crises can illuminate. June 1940 was one such moment. In Paris, people consoled themselves with *any* evidence of routine: 'how lovely it all looks with the Arc de Triomphe in the distance, and the fountains still playing in the gardens'.[6] Similarly, for another refugee, a 'sprinkler makes us think childish thoughts, it gives us confidence: "If things were that serious, they wouldn't think of watering the grass" '.[7] At such moments of social disintegration any evidence of continued order can seem disproportionately significant.

But the converse is also true. The paradox of such total order is its apparent fragility: any infraction can loom large.[8] One long-term side-effect of the growth of state power throughout the nineteenth century has therefore been the boosting of the social significance of (objectively rather minor transgressions) of public order. By the first half of the twentieth century, the street was emerging as a central arena for the contestation of power. As Diehl remarks, 'the idea that the streets were a political proving ground and that the winning of the streets was a primary political goal was widely propagated during the Weimar Republic, not only by the extremes such as the Nazis and the Communists but by others as well'.[9] In different ways, this contestation of the streets was a phenomenon that spanned quite different classes and causes. Certainly, that faithful prop of bourgeois status—the walking stick—was wielded with great enthusiasm in these troubled years.[10] By1925, indeed, municipal authorities in Berlin had banned the carrying of walking sticks in public altogether. Hamburg followed suit the next year.[11] But these years also saw the first emergence of the mass sit-down protest. When desperate unemployed workers blocked Oxford Street, the main consumption artery of central London, right at the height of the Christmas shopping season in 1938, local police were totally confounded ('Get up, you fellows, you're holding up the traffic').[12]

At the sharp edge, the emerging trajectory of window-breaking as a protest tactic illuminates these wider trends. As has been noted across diverse contexts, the act of breaking glass frequently has an 'electrifying' effect on crowds.[13] This is an age-old phenomenon: eighteenth- and nineteenth-century crowds were well aware of it. The period 1766–76, for instance, saw a peak of window-smashing by American students: much of it directed against unpopular tutors, but all of it

[6] A. Werth, *The Last Days of Paris* (London, 1940), p. 73.

[7] L. Werth, *33 Days* (London, 1992, 2015), p. 5.

[8] Z. Bauman, 'Soil, Blood and Identity', *The Sociological Review*, 1992, p. 687.

[9] J. M. Diehl, *Paramilitary Politics in Weimar Germany* (Indiana, 1977), p. 195.

[10] See photograph of a disturbance at Lubliniec/Lublinitz, Upper Silesia, 1920 in: F. Hawranek et al. (eds.), *Encyklopedia powstań Śląskich* (Opole, 1982), p. 577.

[11] Diehl, *Paramilitary Politics in Weimar Germany*, p. 194.

[12] R. Graves and A. Hodge, *The Long Weekend: A Social history of Great Britain, 1918–1939* (London, 1940, 1950), p. 404.

[13] B. Ayers, *Fugitive Days: A Memoir* (Boston, 2001), p. 170. See also: Kitty Maron, cited in: M. Arthur, *Lost Voices of the Edwardians* (London, 2006, 2007), p. 378; B. Buford, *Among the Thugs* (London, 1991, 1992), p. 205; T. Thomas, 'The Second Battle of Chicago 1969' in H. Jacobs (ed.), *Weatherman* (Berkeley, 1970), p. 201.

'cloaked in the rhetoric of liberty and revolution'.[14] In London, the March 1815 riots saw sustained bouts of window-breaking by opponents of the hated Corn Bill. But the Foreign Secretary, Lord Castlereagh ('perfectly calm and unconcerned') was observed 'quietly looking on while his windows were being broken by these ruffians'.[15] He thought 'the mob... not so dangerous as you think'.[16]

Such relaxed attitudes to the breaking of windows seemed to have lasted for much of the nineteenth century. Against the desperate economic backdrop of 1847 one window-smasher in Flanders declared that 'If I had ten francs, I would hire a lawyer to have my whole family jailed for half a year, so that they could leave prison fat and well-fed'.[17] During the 'cotton famine' caused by the American Civil War in 1863, a crowd at Stalybridge, Lancashire, smashed the windows of the members of a relief committee who had reduced their grants.[18] Similar scenes were witnessed during the 1868 strikes in France.[19] Breaking glass punctuated the bitter crisis of Irish nationalism in 1890–1: factions systematically targeted the residences of rival leaders. Even bishops were not immune.[20]

What is striking about these tactics is both how focused retribution was—it was after all the windows of individual domestic residences that were targeted—but also how socially acceptable. Such treatment was simply what one 'had to expect'.[21] As late as February 1878, indeed, William Gladstone had the windows of his house in Harley Street, London, broken by a pro-Tory crowd which he found 'not very sabbatical'.[22] In the long run, though, this element of popular protest repertories was doomed. By 1946 the British Prime Minister's residence, 10 Downing Street, had a permanent police guard to keep its windows intact.[23]

What had changed? As major cities grew to the point where they 'became simply too big to riot as a unit', tactics of window-breaking diffused and evolved: but also, perhaps, grew in impact.[24] Urban sprawl, class segregation, and improved policing all helped to put elite residences out of easy reach for working-class rioters. Unemployed demonstrators smashed the windows of Pall Mall clubs when returning from demonstrations in central London in February 1886; but the general tactic of taking grievances directly to the individuals held responsible was clearly in decline.[25] Nearly a century later the great English disturbances of 1981 took

[14] J. Angus Johnston, 'Student Activism in the United States Before 1960: An Overview' in G. J. DeGroot (ed.), *Student Protest: the Sixties and After* (New York, 1998), p. 13.

[15] Captain Gronow, quoted in: P. Johnson, *The Birth of the Modern: World Society, 1815–1830* (London, 1991, 1992), pp. 373–4.

[16] Captain Gronow, quoted in: Johnson, *The Birth of the Modern*, pp. 373–4.

[17] Quoted in: R. J. Goldstein, *Political Repression in 19th Century Europe* (London, 1983), p. 180.

[18] J. Stevenson, *Popular Disturbances in England, 1700–1870* (London, 1979), p. 293.

[19] C. Tilly, L. Tilly, and R. Tilly, *The Rebellious Century 1830–1930* (Harvard, 1975), p. 20.

[20] D. Lawlor, 'Political Priests: the Parnell Split in Meath', *History Ireland*, Issue 2 (March/April, 2010), Vol. 18. Available at: https://www.historyireland.com/18th-19th-century-history/political-priests-the-parnell-split-in-meath/

[21] In the words of one of those on the receiving end in 1815: Johnson, *The Birth of the Modern*, p. 373.

[22] H. C. G. Matthew, *Gladstone, 1875–1898* (Oxford, 1995), p. 38.

[23] G. Kelland, *Crime in London* (London, 1986, 1988), p. 22.

[24] E. Hobsbawm, *Revolutionaries* (London, 1977), p. 227.

[25] *Morning Post*, 10 February 1886.

intensely localized (though highly contagious) forms—as they were to do again in 2011. Here window-breaking simply functioned merely as a subsidiary tactic: to facilitate the looting of local shops.[26]

In the widespread French riots of autumn 2005, even this dynamic was muted since the disturbances often took place far from centres of conspicuous consumption. As one sociologist noted, 'youths didn't break shop windows because there were none to smash'.[27] Of € 200 millions' worth of damage, no less 80 per cent was caused to public property.[28] What drove the rioting appeared to be an intense spiral of mimetic rivalry:

> It became a contest of neighbourhoods, led by street gangs, each with a kind of local pride (*le nationalisme de quartier*), virtually the only pride remaining in these desolate zones. Who can set more fires, stone more officers, and attract more cameras? Each neighbourhood sought face time in a dismal and dire competition for recognition. And then the rivalry spread to quartiers in other French cities: Rouen, Lille, Lyon, Nice. But the rioting occurred exclusively in the ghettoes; there was no effort to attack the wealthier suburbs or the downtown. Local pride stayed home.[29]

Conversely, in city centre demonstrations breaking windows of business premises only slowly emerged as a classic signature tactic of escalation. As early as the 1830s, the first department stores with their huge shop-windows had emerged in Paris. Contemporaries were duly dazzled ('the great poem of displays sings its strophes of colour from the Madeleine to the Porte Saint-Denis').[30] Such theatres of consumption inevitably evolved into potential stages for violent displays as well. Destruction of shop windows in the West End of London during February 1886 greatly alarmed respectable opinion ('the aspect of the principal streets through which the mob passed was yesterday morning very nearly such as one might expect to find in a city which had just sustained a tolerably severe siege').[31] During the Boulanger crisis of 1888, the Paris Prefect of Police was criticized for not acting energetically enough against 'students who take too many liberties and think they have the right to cause scandals and to break shop windows'.[32] Plate-glass, in short, was becoming a sort of giant mirror of political stability (or its absence). As Rosa Luxemburg commented sarcastically in November 1918: if a window pane gets broken or a tyre bursts, people think 'the Spartacists are coming'.[33] By the first half of the twentieth

[26] L. Scarman, *The Scarman Report: The Brixton Disorders 10–12 April 1981* (London, 1981, 1982), pp. 53, 59; C. Bloom, *Riot City: Protest and Rebellion in the Capital* (Basingstoke, 2012), p. 79 [2011 London riots]. My wife Denise has clear memories of the sheer entertainment generated by the 1981 riots in Acton, West London. She was got out of bed aged 10 by her family 'to go and watch the riots'.

[27] BBC, 11 August 2011 (H. Astier, 'Do English Riots Parallel France?').

[28] R. S. Leiken, *Europe's Angry Muslims: the Revolt of the Second Generation* (Oxford, 2012), p. 37.

[29] Leiken, *Europe's Angry Muslims*, p. 40.

[30] Balzac, quoted in: E. Hobsbawm, *The Age of Revolution 1789–1848* (New York, 1962), p. 221.

[31] *Morning Post*, 10 February 1886.

[32] H. H. Liang, *The Rise of the Modern Police and the European State System from Metternich to the Second World War* (Cambridge, 1992, 2002), p. 144.

[33] Quoted in: M. Jones, *Founding Weimar: Violence and the German Revolution of 1918–1919* (Cambridge, 2016), pp. 96.

century, large amounts of broken glass in the streets of major cities was indeed a sure index of serious trouble: as the riots in Vienna (December 1921), Paris (1934), or the state pogrom of *Kristallnacht* (November 1938) demonstrated all too ominously.[34]

Amongst protest movements, the Suffragettes stand out both as early theorists, and practitioners, of window-smashing as a tactic of calculated protest. Long before Broken Windows Theory had been invented by sociologists, in February 1912, Emmeline Pankhurst was asserting that 'the argument of the broken window pane is the most valuable argument in modern politics'.[35] Suffragette window-breaking originated 'from below' as early in 1908: but was subsequently adopted, and blessed, by the leadership. Rather spuriously, it was claimed to stand fully in tradition of earlier protests.[36] It is indeed true that the houses of individual politicians were occasionally targeted in quasi-traditional manner. But more striking was the degree of tactical innovation. First, it was 'cold'—that is, it was planned, and not conducted under cover of a riot. Secondly, it could be highly organized—at its height being conducted in tightly synchronized relays: with fresh teams going into action at 15-minute intervals, well supplied with heavy flints.[37] Thirdly, the range of targets had widened radically: from private residences, to all major government buildings, post offices, and department stores.[38] (A few years later the IRA flirted with similar tactics, although with notably lesser stamina.)[39]

Suffragette innovation stands out here. Its origin in a women's movement seems suggestive: after all, shopping was one of the few public recreations available to bourgeois women in the early twentieth century. Yet, psychologically, the step was still a huge one—in effect, a leap into outlaw status. Suffragette memoirs speak of huge tension before a window-smashing operation, but also of its tremendous exuberance ('I'm doing it, I'm doing it!').[40] For Kitty Marion, simply, 'the sound of breaking glass filled the vicinity and electrified everybody'.[41] Over half a century later, both West German and American New Left activists described similar tensions, and reactions.[42] Susan Stern, for instance, vividly describes the ecstasies of

[34] A. Ferguson, *When Money Dies* (London, 1975, 2010), p. 59 [Vienna]; *The Times*, 2, 3, December 1921 [Vienna]; S. Neitzel and H. Welzer, *Soldaten: On Fighting, Killing and Dying* (London, 2011, 2012), p. 52; B. Jenkins and C. Millington, *France and Fascism: February 1934 and the Dynamics of Political Crisis* (Abingdon, 2015, 2016), p. 81.

[35] G. L. Kelling and J. Q. Wilson, 'Broken Windows: the Police and Neighbourhood Safety', *The Atlantic*, March 1982; G. Dangerfield, *The Strange Death of Liberal England* (New York, 1935, 1961), p. 170.

[36] E. Pankhurst, *Suffragette: My Own Story* (1914, 2016), p. 117.

[37] Pankhurst, *Suffragette*, pp. 197, 203; Dangerfield, *The Strange Death of Liberal England*, p. 171.

[38] D. Atkinson, *Rise up Women! The Remarkable Lives of the Suffragettes* (London, 2018), pp. 107, 150, 172–3, 182, 183, 208, 228, 230–1, 235, 270, 273, 288, 292, 294–8, 300, 303, 306, 308, 313, 318, 325, 327, 353, 367, 374, 407, 423, 439, 489.

[39] P. Hart, *The I.R.A. At War* (Oxford, 2003, 2005), pp. 158–9.

[40] B. Harrison, 'The Act of Militancy: Violence and the Suffragettes, 1904–1914' in M. Bentley and J. Stevenson (eds), *Peaceable Kingdom: Stability and Change in Modern Britain* (Oxford, 1982), pp. 71–2. See also: Arthur, *Lost Voices of Edwardians*, p. 378.

[41] Kitty Marion in: Arthur, *Lost Voices of the Edwardians*, p. 378.

[42] B. Baumann, *Wie alles anfing* (Berlin, 1991), p. 46.

transgression as she experienced them in anti-war protests in Chicago in August 1968:

> My arms were flung out in fists above my head and I pumped the air with them; I was boiling, singing, dancing, erupting with the spontaneous urge of freedom, of having the streets. Yes, I felt it, I knew it—crash—a gigantic rock hurled past my nose and a big bank window fell like billions of icicles.[43]

For none of these activists was there any *automatic* progression from smashing windows to the subsequent bombing campaigns that followed. But window smashing does seem to have constituted an important early threshold of escalation for those who did ultimately gravitate towards much more sustained, and much more serious, destruction.[44]

In short, the society of hyper-order which prioritizes the smooth flows of capitalist consumption above all else potentially magnifies the significance of window-breaking. By the early twentieth century the prominent anti-Suffragist A. V. Dicey claimed that every pane of glass broken would cost the cause of female suffrage ten votes.[45] Here the contrast with the paternalistic nonchalance of a hundred years before was stark. In October 1936, 200 pro-fascist youths rampaged down the Mile End Road in East London 'smashing Jewish shop windows and attacking anyone who might be thought to look Jewish': the British Union of Fascists were forced to disown them.[46]

More recently, there has been a systematic, but covert, fortification of conspicuous display. 'Massifs of plate glass and concrete' are not nearly as vulnerable as they may look.[47] Above all, the standard adoption of reinforced glass in the last decades of the twentieth century has apparently reduced both the incidence—and presumably the satisfactions—of window smashing.[48] As seen at Genoa (2001), or in the more recent 'yellow vest' protests across France (2018–19), it remains firmly part of the radical protest repertoire.[49] But since windows do not now disintegrate easily, it takes far more determination and effort than previously to achieve any discernible impact over a widespread area.[50] Glass walls turn the banks and restaurants of the rich into unbreakable goldfish bowls. The twenty-first century city of endlessly smiling consumption protects itself through its thousands of transparent exoskeletons. Its impregnability is no less real for being invisible.

[43] S. Stern, *With the Weathermen: the Personal Journey of a Revolutionary Woman* (Piscataway, NJ, 2007), p. 33.

[44] Ayers, *Fugitive Days*, p. 170. See also: Kitty Maron, cited in: Arthur, *Lost Voices of the Edwardians*, p. 378.

[45] T. K. Wilson, 'Why was women's suffrage so delayed?' (1993).

[46] N. Mosley, *Rules of the Game/Beyond the Pale: Memoirs of Sir Oswald Mosley and Family* (London, 1998), p. 379.

[47] Hobsbawm, *Revolutionaries*, p. 231.

[48] This supposition is drawn from a comparison of images of destruction on Google images. In Chicago 1968 plate glass has disintegrated into large shards. By the poll tax riots of March 1990 the windows of a McDonald's in London show the classic localized damage peculiar to safety glass.

[49] *Guardian*, 21 June 2001 ('Violence erupts again in Genoa').

[50] Bloomberg, 'Symbols of Luxury Smashed in Paris Yellow Vest Protests', 16 March 2019.

In any case, serious rioting is itself a declining skill. Overturning and burning cars may look dramatic enough on TV (or, latterly, social media)—but it is no substitute for the old technical skills of effective barricade-building that depended upon close-knit inner-city communities, respected local leadership, and some shared memory of how these things 'ought' to be done.[51] Such traditional resources simply no longer exist. Above all, the fact that all major national demonstrations (and hence potential riot situations) are invariably called for weekends is itself striking evidence of their tokenism. Even here, or especially here, the rhythm of the working week must remain sacrosanct. The threat of what Abraham Lincoln once called 'mobocracy' has been tamed: by the dawn of the twenty-first century 'few sober minds would sense in the plight of the contemporary poor and destitute a tangible threat of rebellion'.[52]

II

> If another Gunpowder Plot had been discovered half an hour before the lighting of the match, nobody would have been justified in saving the parliament until there had been half a score of boards, half a bushel of minutes, several sacks of unofficial memoranda, and a family vault of ungrammatical correspondence, on the part of the Circumlocution Office.
>
> – Charles Dickens, *Little Dorrit*, 1857[53]

If the capital cities of major western countries have become more-or-less immune to any serious prospect of massed insurrection, one might expect their authorities to remain relatively sanguine about any threats from 'the little platoons' of utopian radicals (however violent these may be).[54] And yet the very opposite is the case. Since the late nineteenth century, time and again, outbreaks of 'spasm terrorism' (to borrow Paul Wilkinson's phrase) have been met by a spasm of alarmism on the part of both governments and wider publics: the temporary, but also temporarily all-consuming, sense that this time the defences of civilization may not hold.[55] Such a phenomenon across late modern societies demands far more historical and sociological exploration than it customarily receives. What is doubly intriguing is that the phenomenon is essentially cyclical; but tends not to be recognized as such. Both official and social responses to outbreaks of terror tend to be 'frequently amnesiac'.[56] Each episode of the 'great fear' tends to be experienced as an entirely fresh nightmare.

[51] M. Mulholland, *The Murderer of Warren Street* (London, 2018), pp. 88–9; L. J. K. Setright, *Drive On! The Social History of the Motor Car* (London, 2002, 2004), p. 124.

[52] Bauman, *The Individualised Society*, p. 115.

[53] C. Dickens, *Little Dorrit* (London, 1857, 2003), p. 119.

[54] D. T. Rodgers, *Age of Fracture* (Harvard, 2011), p. 180.

[55] P. Wilkinson, *Terrorism and the Liberal State* (London, 1977, 1979), pp. 139, 147.

[56] R. English, *Terrorism: How to Respond* (Oxford, 2009), p. 57. For a similar observation: R. English, *Does Terrorism Work? A History* (Oxford, 2016), p. 18.

Explaining how this can be so takes us deep into a consideration of how the provision of public security actually works: and, with it, the public expectations that must be managed (at least under democratic conditions). 'Bureaucratic administration' in Max Weber's famous formulation may indeed mean 'fundamentally domination through knowledge': but bureaucracies are themselves also not easy to control.[57] As memorably satirized by Monty Python (in their 'Ministry of Silly Walks' sketch), 'it is a well-known rule of bureaucratic life that the instrument creates the function'.[58] Furthermore, 'all bureaucracies are to a certain degree utopian, in the sense that they propose an abstract ideal that real human beings can never live up to'.[59] 'Turf wars' thus emerge, not just because of the inevitable human rivalries—although these hardly help—but because all rival utopias are hard to mesh together harmoniously.[60] Hence the immense infrastructural power of the modern state can easily become its own worst enemy.

Moreover, all large bureaucracies are also potentially amnesiac: either because they are too large and cumbersome to use, or are poorly organized, or because they fail to capture operational experience in ways that are useful for posterity—or through some combination of these dysfunctionalities.[61] The botched upgrade that runs massively over budget, is finished late, and still fails to integrate previous systems of information management is, after all, the stuff of which public and private sector legends are made. But such challenges long predate computerization.

A good example of bad organization was the late nineteenth-century archive of the Paris Prefecture of Police that held registers of all condemnations of criminals in the country. Reconstituted from scratch after its destruction by fire in the Paris Commune, its utility remained highly 'limited because it was difficult to use; it contained over 8 million records in the 1890s, without an effective document retrieval system'.[62] An example of the files failing to keep pace with invaluable operational experience occurs in the memoirs of Bob Huntley, head of the Metropolitan Police's bomb squad during the Provisional IRA's 'Battle of London' in the early 1970s. From personal experience—he had been a young constable during the IRA's bombing campaign of 1939—Huntley decided to try to learn from the lessons of the past: 'We searched for their records at the Yard and found, to our astonishment, that nothing had been written down. Everything those men had learned was lost. It was an appalling waste.'[63] Under such conditions, information and experience are simply squandered.

[57] H. H. Gerth and C. Wright Mills (eds), *From Max Weber: Essays in Sociology* (London, 1948, 1977), p. 225.

[58] For Monty Python: https://www.youtube.com/watch?v=F3UGk9QhoIw. For the nature of bureaucracy: M. Castells, *End of Millennium*, Vol. III, *The Network Society*, (Chichester, 1998, 2010), p. 247.

[59] D. Graeber, *The Utopia of Rules* (London, 2015, 2016), pp. 26–7.

[60] K. McConaghy, *Terrorism and the State: Intra-State Dynamics and the Response to Non-State Political Violence* (London, 2017), pp. 5–9.

[61] L. Winner, 'Complexity and Human Understanding' in T. La Porte (ed.), *Organized Social Complexity: Challenge to Politics and Policy* (Princeton, 1975), p. 66.

[62] M. Anderson, *In Thrall to Political Change: Police and Gendarmerie in France* (Oxford, 2011), p. 254.

[63] B. Huntley (and H. Edgington), *Bomb Squad: My War Against the Terrorists* (London, 1977), p. 103.

Secondly, the state is hydra-headed. Multiple agencies have to be involved in the provision of public security: and all tend to guard their prerogatives jealously. France is—supposedly—a heavily centralized state: but its 'little war between the police and the Gendarmerie' is notorious.[64] Moreover, a much wider centrifugalism is institutionalized in France: a (non-comprehensive) list of its security agencies would have to include at a minimum the 'police, gendarmerie, prosecutor, Prefecture—with, in addition, three ministries responsible, four directorates general, a dozen specialized central directorates, almost 50 corps and special services'.[65] In 1984, the *Unité de coordination de la lute anti-terroriste* (UCLAT) was created as a counter-terrorist command to coordinate the efforts of police, gendarmerie, customs, and intelligence services. Yet UCLAT took fifteen years to begin to function effectively.[66]

Devolved administrations present even more complicated arenas. A shaming unfamiliarity of London with its own Northern Irish backyard was mercilessly exposed between 1969–71. The early Troubles presented a counter-insurgency shambles with the British Army, the Royal Ulster Constabulary (RUC), and the security agencies, MI5 and MI6, all tripping over themselves—and each other—to mount a coordinated response to a fast-deteriorating situation. 'All moved in isolation amid intensified bureaucratic mistrust', comments Bowyer Bell 'with the police and the army riding point: Their mistakes were visible'. Mass internment without trial in August 1971 derived directly from the highly partial vision of partial bureaucracies: 'the bottom line that was practical internment would depend upon RUC lists, and such lists, made no more inclusive by recent experience, were haphazard and specifically sectarian—not a single Protestant was thought subversive by the police'.[67]

Federal systems tend to be inevitably more complex still: with the USA boasting no fewer than 40,000 separate policing-related bodies: 'a vast complex of law enforcement agencies'.[68] Hence the long-term coordination challenges, and the possibility of inter-agency frictions, should not be under-estimated. Indeed, serious tensions between the Central Intelligence Agency (CIA) and the Federal Bureau of Investigations (FBI) form a running theme in the 9/11 Commission Report.[69] Such frictions are best seen as structural to the modern state: rather than the grand aggregation of all-too human petty rivalries.

What this means in practice can easily be imagined. In fast-moving and complex crises such as thrown up by international terrorist incidents, some confusion of institutional responses is highly likely. A 1979 briefing note preserved in the British national archives laments that recent hijackings tend to 'demonstrate a

[64] Hodgson, quoted in: F. Foley, *Countering Terrorism in Britain and France: Institutions, Norms and the Shadow of the Past* (Cambridge, 2013), p. 103.

[65] Gatto and Thoenig, quoted in: Anderson, *In Thrall to Political Change*, pp. 214–15.

[66] Anderson, *In Thrall to Politial Change*, p. 197.

[67] J. Bowyer Bell, *The Irish Troubles: A Generation of Violence 1967–1992* (Dublin, 1993, 1994), p. 213.

[68] N. L. Weiner, 'Policing in America' in D. W. Pope and N. L. Weiner (eds), *Modern Policing* (London, 1981), p. 77; 9/11 Commission, p. 72.

[69] 9/11 Commission Report, pp. 198, 213.

degree of confusion in Whitehall about responsibility as between departments'. Not entirely reassuringly, it then goes on to 'clarify' that if the hijacked aircraft is still in the air it is the problem of the Department of Trade, but as soon as it lands in the UK it will become the headache of the Home Office; while if it lands elsewhere the buck will stop with the Foreign and Commonwealth Office.[70] But even smaller scale crises are prone to suck in many official players: at the Columbine school shooting (20 April 1999), '35 law enforcement agencies were soon represented'.[71]

Thirdly, all the difficulties of inter-agency cooperation are likely to be multiplied and amplified when applied to the international level. While the history of such cooperation between both police and intelligence services is a long and persistent one that dates back to the late nineteenth century anarchist scare, the pitfalls are predictably numerous. Bi-lateral counter-terrorist cooperation between West Germany and France in the early 1980s, for instance, was badly hampered by the fact that the French had no central computerized collection and analysis agency.[72]

Decades later, and within the much more integrated arena of the European Union (EU), the picture remains Kafkaesque: a 'coordination nightmare'.[73] For its part, the European Commission 'has the reputation for being notoriously bad at coordination. For a start, the administrative structuring of the organisation in self-contained Directorate-Generals naturally leads to internal divisions'. Conversely, the summitry format of the European Council is 'more suited to grand bargains and strategic decisions than to the small details of internal coordination'.[74] In addition, '"Brusselisation", or transfer of decision-making authority to Brussels in counter-terrorism matters, has produced a plethora of committees, expert groups, agencies, and other bodies'.[75] Appropriately, the search for 'consistency'—at all levels, and running in all directions—is the overarching theme of the major academic study of the EU's counter-terrorist efforts.[76] And as Brexit debates have more recently highlighted, it is clear that such efforts remain potentially highly vulnerable to external political crosswinds as well.[77]

Such complexities resonate in multiple ways. In essence, they mean that campaigns of terror will tend to appear, and survive, in bureaucratic interstices and blind spots. 'No one was looking for a foreign threat to domestic targets' the 9/11 Commission concluded simply of the 2001 atrocities.[78]

[70] NA, FCO 871/946. [71] D. Cullen, *Columbine* (New York, 2009, 2016), p. 56.

[72] P. Wilkinson, 'Taking on Terrorism: An Interview with Professor Paul Wilkinson', *Violence, Aggression and Terrorism*, 3 (3), 1989, p. 211.

[73] J. Argomaniz, 'A "coordination nightmare"?' in C. Kaunert et al. (eds), *European Homeland Security: A European Strategy in the Making?* (London, 2012), pp. 72–94.

[74] Argomaniz, 'A "coordination nightmare"?', pp. 74, 89.

[75] Argomaniz, 'A "coordination nightmare"?', p. 85.

[76] J. Argomaniz, *The EU and Counter-Terrorism: Politics, Polity and Policies after 9/11* (London, 2012).

[77] *Guardian*, 20 June 2018 ['GCHQ chief warns Europe of need for Brexit security deal'].

[78] 9/11 Commission Report, p. 263.

Rivalries between police forces and agencies in devolved or federal administrations—and the resulting information gaps—have similarly been blamed for allowing terror campaigns to gain an early momentum that might otherwise have been denied them. David Laufer's assessment of the labyrinthine dysfunctionality of Belgian law and order in the mid-1980s is worth quoting at some length:

> Manpower is not the problem: on a *per capita* basis, Belgium is the most highly policed country in the EEC.... The *gendarmerie* is a national force organised over five regions. It is part of the armed forces and is responsible to the Minister of National Defence on military matters, to the Minister of Justice on matters of judiciary police work and internal security, and to the Minister of the Interior on matters of general police work.... Then there is the judicial police (PJ), which is organised into 27 precincts and reports to the Minister of Justice via the Procurator General. It is a centralised force composed of civil servants who carry out criminal investigations. Finally, there are the communal police forces which are usually under the control of municipal authorities and whose jurisdiction does not extend beyond communal boundaries. Belgium is composed of 589 communities. Coordinating a national investigation, therefore, becomes a nightmare, and is only exacerbated by linguistic problems and intercommunal rivalry.[79]

In addition, at the upper levels of the police hierarchy there were also no fewer than five anti-terrorist agencies in Belgium. A more hospitable institutional seedbed for the *Cellules Communistes Combattantes* (Communist Combatant Cells, or CCC) would have been hard to find. Despite having a grand total membership of just four, the CCC managed to conduct no fewer than twenty-six bombings between 1984 and December 1985.[80] Comparable points have been made about the operating environment for ISIS-inspired groups in Catalonia thirty years later.[81]

Paradoxically, some dim, but general, public awareness of the power of the state means that successful terror attacks are all too easily interpreted in truly catastrophic terms. Europe's troubled summer of 2017 furnished numerous examples: a firecracker was set off in Turin during the Champions League Final (3 June 2017); the crowd thought there had been a bomb and panicked: one person died and 1,527 were injured in the stampede. A week later an overhead conversation on an easyjet flight from Ljubljana to London Stansted was (wrongly) interpreted by the crew as evidence of an imminent terrorist attack. The flight was diverted to Cologne for an emergency landing, and nine passengers needed medical treatment for injuries sustained during evacuation. A car striking pedestrians at an Eid festival celebration in Newcastle-upon-Tyne (25 June 2017) prompted swift official clarification that this was an accident, not an attack. Local police clearly felt such apprehensions needed calming, and quickly.[82]

[79] D. Laufer, 'The Evolution of Belgian Terrorism' in J. Lodge (ed.), *The Threat of Terrorism* (Brighton, 1988), p. 201.

[80] Y. Alexander and D. Pluchinsky, *Europe's Red Terrorists: The Fighting Communist Organizations* (Abingdon, 1992, 2005), p. 148.

[81] Laufer, 'The Evolution of Belgian Terrorism', p. 201; *Economist*, 26 August 2017.

[82] *Guardian*, 4 June 2017 ('More than 1,500 Juventus fans in Turin injured after stampede'); *iweekend*, 17–18 June 2017 ('Careless talk costs time and money'); *Guardian*, 26 June 2017 ('Six injured after car hits crowd celebrating Eid in Newcastle').

Governments, for their part, flirted conspicuously with a doctrine of inverted Rooseveltianism: the only thing to fear was not fearing enough. Above all, they seemed to feel they must show their citizens that they are not complacent about terrorism. Since October 2015 the presidency of France, Europol, and Britain's twin intelligence services (MI5 and MI6) *all* independently described the terrorist threat as—a favourite word—'unprecedented'. Angela Merkel's New Year message for 2017 spoke of terrorism as constituting 'the biggest challenge facing Germany'.[83] Such claims are dramatic enough to warrant serious consideration. I turn now to evaluating them.

III

> Terrorism has been on the international agenda for a long time but until fairly recently it was relegated to a lowly place. From time to time, following some spectacular attack, terrorism would figure prominently in the media for a few days. There would be deliberations on the highest level of government, committees would be appointed and resolutions passed. But when calm returned the issue would be forgotten, for there seemed to be no particular urgency to deal with it. There were always some very important domestic and foreign issues that would take precedence, and in any case terrorism never threatened all countries in an equal measure. This has now changed, and terrorism is bound to remain high on the list of our priorities.
>
> – Walter Laqueur[84]

> Governments of the Industrial World, you weary giants of flesh and steel, I come from Cyberspace, the home of Mind. On behalf of the future I ask you of the past to leave us alone. You are not welcome among us. You have no sovereignty where we gather.
>
> – John Perry Barlow, Electronic Frontier Foundation[85]

In the immediate aftermath of the Cold War, Susan Strange argued bluntly that the power of the nation state was in headlong (or headless) retreat: 'today [1996] it seems that the heads of governments may be the last to recognize that they and their ministers have lost the authority over national societies and economies that they used to have.'[86] Such claims gained credence in the early twenty-first century: with statist power apparently in retreat before the forces of 'globalization'—loosely, if broadly, understood here as the exponentially increasing circulation of information, capital, and people accelerating in volumes that—allegedly—overwhelm the

[83] T. K. Wilson, 'Terrorism and Resilience: An Historical Perspective' in D. Muro (ed.), *Resilient Cities. Countering Violent Extremism at the Local Level* (Barcelona, 2017), p. 105.

[84] W. Laqueur, *No End to War: Terrorism in the Twenty-First Century* (New York, 2003), p. 7.

[85] Quoted in: A. Nagle, *Kill All Normies; Online Culture Wars From 4Chan and Tumblr to Trump and the Alt-Right* (Winchester, 2017), p. 25.

[86] S. Strange, *The Retreat of the State: The Diffusion of Power in the World Economy* (Cambridge, 1996, 1998), p. 3.

basic ability of governments to monitor, and hence, control what happens within their borders. Such changes resonate through the vector of the 'network society' that has emerged over recent decades through the transformation of electronic communications.

Such claims also frame an important challenge to a major argument of this book: that between the late eighteenth and twentieth centuries, western governments consolidated and sedimented their infrastructural power to the point where they became impregnable to turmoil generated from below. Most generally, has the long and slow process of growing state domination abruptly reversed in recent decades? And more specifically, what do recent changes mean for the present (and future) trajectory of political violence?

Certainly, the rise of the network society has introduced, or boosted, some new and powerful drivers of instability: and these are worth reviewing briefly here insofar as they impact upon the ability of states to maintain order. First, although 'control of information and entertainment, and through them, of opinions and images has historically been the anchoring tool of state power', such cables were decisively severed at the end of the twentieth century.[87] In its place, the rise of mass person-to-person communication has introduced historically novel dynamics. As Manuel Castells shrewdly notes 'the characteristics of the political message in the mass communication context induces the personalization of politics': as a result, the 'most potent political weapon is the discrediting of the opponent's persona': and, in general, the reinforcement of scandal politics as a key vector of power transitions. A more general consequence is to make the entire political class contemptible: 'the large majority of citizens around the world despise their representatives and do not trust their political institutions'.[88] Simultaneously, mass person-to-person communication creates cultures of on-line elitism: a looking-glass world of knowing references, in-jokes, and exclusive jargon. Out of such hazes of impenetrable irony, genuine killers can emerge.[89]

Secondly, the rise of the network society is changing societies in ways that can provoke very sudden crises of public order: a sinkhole effect that exposes the eroded foundations of state legitimacy. Sinkholes emerge when long-standing problems are revealed to a wider audience by a dramatic crisis that the authorities struggle to master swiftly. They are thus hybrid crises since both long- and short-term factors need to coincide. Sinkholes are an inherently local phenomenon: but they can imply a wider crisis, since there are always more places like them. As is well recognized, the network society boosts connections between key nodes, but at the price of creating widespread 'landscapes of despair' between them.[90] What such 'peripheral spaces, ex-industrial areas and provincial regions share are strong local bonds of community at risk from loss of the old ways of life'.[91]

[87] Castells, *The Information Age*, Vol. I, p. 316.

[88] M. Castells, *The Power of Identity*, Vol. II, *The Network Society* (Chichester, 1997, 2010), pp. xxxii–xxxiii.

[89] Nagle, *Kill All Normies*, pp. 98–100.

[90] Quoted in: Castells, *The Information Age*, Vol. I, p. xxxvi.

[91] J. Rutherford, 'Towards a new left conservatism', *New Statesman*, 28 June–4 July 2019, p. 35.

What does such a sinkhole crisis look like? Chemnitz (the former 'Karl-Marx Stadt') in Germany recently offered a rich case study. Located in the ex-industrial 'rustbelt' of Saxony, it has a well-established right-wing extremist scene with roots that go back to before the collapse of the Communist regime in 1989.[92] A festival organized to boost the city's profile for its 875th anniversary succeeded spectacularly—but for all the wrong reasons. In the very early hours of 26 August 2018, a 35-year-old German-Cuban carpenter was stabbed to death after a town festival, allegedly by two Arab asylum seekers. Within hours, 800 demonstrators were marching, overwhelming police and—it seems—roughing up those they considered sympathetic to refugees. By the evening of the same day a crowd of 6,000 Neo-nazis and far-right sympathizers had gathered, some summoned via the football hooligan scene.[93] A patently-inadequate force of police, just 591 strong, struggled to keep them apart from a smaller counter-demonstration of 1,500 people.[94] Information emerged from within the interior ministry to show that one of the suspects should have been deported weeks earlier.[95] The keynote of the crisis was the disarray of all constituted authority at all levels. Grassroots networks and individuals set the pace of mobilization by social media: and at every turn, police, officialdom, and elected politicians at municipal, state, and federal levels, struggled to keep up. Eventually, the head of Germany's intelligence services, Hans-Georg Maassen was forced to resign for downplaying the seriousness of the unrest.[96]

Thirdly, while individual contemporary terror campaigns seem to lack the stamina, sophistication, and organizational resilience of, say, the Provisional IRA, this is itself a rather mixed blessing. More diffuse and unpredictable threats may often seem harder to manage since closing down individual cells may bring only marginal gains, if much larger resistance networks can easily rebuild or re-route their activities. To borrow from a handful of recent British examples it is this dynamic that seems to be behind the repeated public statements of the security agencies that 'terrorism has increased, and it moves faster, and it is harder to detect' (Sir Mark Rowley, 2019); or that it is 'at the highest tempo I have seen in my career' (Andrew Parker, 2017); and that 'Britain's spy network has been stretched to breaking point by a barrage of new deadly threats...'(Ben Wallace, 2019).[97] Even allowing for the usual jockeying for budgets that often lies behind such headlines, these are stark claims.

Lastly, there is a contextual point worth making—not a direct consequence of the emergence of the network society as such, but very much a part of the general

[92] H. Betz, 'What's the Matter with Saxony' in W. Allchorn (ed.), *Tracking the Rise of the Radical Right Globally* (Stuttgart, 2019), pp. 161–4; B. Manthe, 'Scenes of "Civil War"? Radical Right Narratives on Chemnitz', in Allchorn (ed.), *Tracking the Rise of the Radical Right Globally*, pp. 169–73.

[93] *Der Spiegel*, Nr. 36/1 September 2018, pp. 10–20 ('Wer das Sagen hat').

[94] *Die Zeit*, 30 August 2018 ('Sechs Lehren aus Chemnitz').

[95] *Der Spiegel*, Nr. 36/1 September 2018, pp. 12–13 ('Wer das Sagen hat').

[96] *Guardian*, 6 November 2018 ('Ex-spy Chief "retired" for new claim of media fakery').

[97] *Guardian*, 17 October 2017 ('UK facing most severe terror threat ever' warns MI5 Chief'); M. Rowley, 'The Increase of Terrorism', *Terrorism Frequency Report* (Pool Re, March 2019), p. 12; *The Scottish Mail on Sunday*, 2 June 2019 ('MI5 Spies facing historic assault, warns Minister Whitehall boss's plea for cash to fight threats').

environment that has facilitated its rise. That point is peace—*for* the West, although certainly not *by* the West. The 1990s onwards has seen numerous military interventions globally, for better or worse. But it is hard to overstate the cultural effect of the lifting of the prospect of nuclear Armageddon from whole societies. Back in the 1970s terror attacks tended not to be discussed as an *existential* threat to civilization—if only because any reflective person could see that blowing drinkers to bits in Birmingham and Guildford pubs did not represent the same type of generalized threat as a nuclear exchange with the Soviet Union. By the end of that decade, 'people around the world had lived with the prospect of nuclear holocaust for 30 years'.[98] A shared cultural assumption lurked in the background that far worse, and more total, horrors were fully possible.

That perspective simply melted away in the 1990s. As early as 1997 Conor Gearty saw the way the wind was blowing: 'without any great war or massive insurgency to distract us, we have been able to indulge our anxieties about the terrorists' sporadic violence'.[99] But such reflections became increasingly rare. Certainly any such awareness often appeared muted after 2001.[100] At moments of high tension in the early twenty-first century, Western governments have often seemed primarily motivated by a desire to show their citizens that they are not complacent about terror. Inevitably, the result is a general acute pressure from government, media, and publics on the security services to stop each and every attack: an utterly unrealistic demand.

It is instructive here to compare two vignettes from London, very nearly a century apart. On 2 January 1911, the Metropolitan Police called at 100 Sydney Street in Stepney, east London, where they had been tipped off that anti-Tsarist revolutionaries were hiding out. Since this gang had recently killed three policemen during a botched robbery attempt, this was clearly going to be a highly dangerous assignment:

> The police now had a problem. If they went into the house they could not, according to law, open fire until they had been fired on first; this would put them at an impossible disadvantage. In addition, the staircase was narrow (3½ feet wide), with a bend at the top, which would make the operation extremely hazardous.[101]

In the event, Detective Sergeant Leeson was obliged to knock first at the door—and be shot (and severely wounded)—before an armed siege could officially commence.[102]

On 23 July 2005, Metropolitan police accosted a suspected suicide bomber. Suicide bombings had slaughtered 52 people just 16 days before; and another (failed) attempt to repeat these scenes had occurred just the day before. London

[98] T. Downing, *1983: Reagan, Andropov and A World on the Brink* (New York, 2018), p. 14.

[99] C. Gearty, *Terrorism* (London, 1997), p. 14.

[100] J. Mueller *Overblown: How Politicians and the Terrorism Industry Inflate National Security Threats and Why We Believe Them* (New York, 2006), pp. 13–14, 29–48.

[101] D. Rumbelow, *The Houndsditch Murders and the Siege of Sidney Street* (London, 1973, 1990), p. 128.

[102] *Gloucester Citizen*, 4 January 1911; *Newcastle Daily Journal*, 7 January 1911; Rumbelow, *The Houndsditch Murders and the Siege of Sidney Street*, pp. 128, 130.

was on edge. Rules of engagement were now highly permissive. So the police opted to shoot first, and asked questions afterwards. And when the questions were finally asked, it was found they had blown out the brains of an entirely innocent man: a Brazilian engineer named Jean Charles de Menezes.[103]

IV

Arguably, though, reports of the death of the Western state have been much exaggerated. We should not forget that Louis Beam started advocating a strategy of 'leaderless resistance' in the early 1990s as a strategy of *last* resort: in effect, an unwilling tribute to the power of the state at the dawn of the internet age.[104] Nor do attempts to rival the state's bureaucratic capacity offer sure results. One major academic study has concluded that terror campaigns need their own bureaucracy to aspire to any level of sustained and credible impact: but it is this very 'mundane side of terrorism; the bookkeeping requirements, disciplinary procedures, and recruiting dilemmas' that in turn presents such rich evidence trails for counter-terrorist investigators to follow. This is the true 'terrorist's dilemma'.[105]

As study after study has demonstrated, Western governments remain strikingly immune to overthrow or extortion from below: and well able to ride out sporadic campaigns of bombings, shootings, and hostage-takings.[106] Michael Henning, a survivor of the 7 July 2005 atrocity in London, saw this with great clarity: 'the terrorists think they are getting back at the state, but they're not, they have ripped apart the people—the state is unscathed. That's what makes it so cowardly.'[107]

In general terms, it is not obvious that the power of states are in irrevocable decline. 'State functions have shifted' concludes Michael Mann 'but not declined overall.'[108] This seems a judicious assessment. Decline may sometimes be more apparent than real: at least as far as the means of controlling system-destabilizing violence go. Looking back over the past century, Western governments have proved remarkably successful in keeping weapons of mass destruction—whether chemical, biological, or atomic—under tight control. Referring back to the 1920–21 period, the IRA's Director of Chemicals, Seamus O'Donovan, 'claimed to have considered the use of biological warfare including the spread of botulism among

[103] Foley, *Countering Terrorism*, pp. 259, 263.

[104] P. Gill, *Lone Actor Terrorists: A Behavioural Analysis* (Abingdon, 2015), p. 4.

[105] J. N. Shapiro, *The Terrorist's Dilemma: Managing Violent Covert Organizations* (Princeton, 2013), p. 2. See, too, the remark of one journalist on the IRA that their 'fondness for paper work often amazed me': T. P. Coogan, *The I.R.A.* (London, 1970, 1971), p. 69.

[106] M. Abrahms, 'Why Terrorism Does Not Work', *International Security*, 31, Fall 2006, pp. 42–78; M. Abrahms, 'The Political Effectiveness of Terrorism Revisited', *Comparative Political Studies*, 45, March 2012; D. Muro (ed.) *When Does Terrorism Work?* (London, 2019); English, *Does Terrorism Work?*; English, *Terrorism: How to Respond*, pp. 109–10.

[107] *Evening Standard*, 6 July 2018.

[108] M. Mann, *The Sources of Social Power*, Vol. IV, *Globalizations, 1945–2011* (Cambridge, 2013), p. 419.

British army cavalry horses, but this was never acted on'.[109] Similarly, in 1937 the Cagoulards' germ warfare expert Rodiot tried, but failed, 'in his attempts to get botulism samples from the Institut Pasteur'.[110] Such consistent failure has remained very much the pattern for the next eight decades (and counting). As periodic flurries of public concern indicate, this is an area where one serious lapse could prove genuinely catastrophic.[111] But to date Western governments have kept the more diabolical capacities of state violence under tight lock and key, with the exception of the 2001 anthrax attacks in the USA.[112] Given statist incontinence with more conventional arms supplies, this is a remarkable achievement.

More specifically, governments can also look ahead with some confidence. Since governments are themselves an integral part of the network age, we should not overlook the emergence of counter-trends that strengthen their authority. Since the early 1990s, 'we have witnessed an exponential growth in the ability of states, to track, monitor and store communications (evidenced by the Edward Snowden leaks)'.[113] Dispersal of power into electronic networks does not necessarily weaken the state, for instance. It may, indeed, help protect it—which, after all, was a key ambition of the early military sponsors of the designers of the internet.[114] No less a prophet of extreme transformation than Zygmunt Bauman recognized this clearly:

> If the time of systemic revolutions has passed, it is because there are no buildings where the control desks of the system are lodged and which could be stormed and captured by the revolutionaries.... One should be hardly taken aback or puzzled by the evident shortage of would-be revolutionaries: of the kind of people who articulate the desire to change their individual plights as a project of changing the order of society.[115]

Such observations apply to coups, too.[116] Some threats to stability have simply become obsolete.

Secondly, the surveillance opportunities of states (and, indeed, supermarkets) have been transformed in recent decades. Daily living spews out electronic evidence trails in all directions. The New Left memoirs make clear how hard living

[109] J. McGuire and J. Quinn (eds), *Dictionary of Irish Biography* (Cambridge, 2009), Vol. VII, p. 417.

[110] D. L. L. Parry, 'Counter Revolution By Conspiracy, 1935–1937', in N. Atkin and F. Tallett (eds.), *The Right in France: From Revolution to Le Pen* (London, 2003), p. 165.

[111] Laqueur, *No End to War*, pp. 226–8.

[112] A. Martin, *Rules of Security: Staying Safe in a Risky World* (Oxford, 2019), pp. 2, 34, 167. For close calls: B. Hoffman, *Inside Terrorism* (New York, 2006, 2017), pp. 285–92 [for Al-Qaeda's experiments]; M. Coleman, 'O'Donovan, James Laurence ("Jim", "Seamus")' in J. McGuire and J. Quinn (eds), *Dictionary of Irish Biography* (Royal Irish Academy, Cambridge, 2009), p. 417 [1920s IRA consider experiments with botulism]; J. Witcover, *Sabotage at Black Tom: Imperial Germany's Secret War in America, 1914–1917* (Chapel Hill, 1989), pp. 126–7, 136–7 [German glanders and anthrax plots in the First World War]. Also: W. Seth Carus, 'Bioterrorism and Biocrimes: the Illicit use of Biological Agents Since 1900', Working Paper (1998, 2001), Center for Counterproliferation Research, National Defense University, Washington, D.C; Dolnik, *Understanding Terrorist Innovation*, p. 34.

[113] Gill, *Lone Actor Terrorists*, p. 9.

[114] Castells, *The Information Age*, Vol. I, p. 59.

[115] Z. Bauman, *Liquid Modernity* (Cambridge, 2000, 2012), p. 5.

[116] D. Runciman, *How Democracy Ends* (London, 2018), pp. 26–81.

underground already was in the 1970s, and this in an age before bank cards and digital money transfer. Jonathan Lerner has thus wondered 'whether we could have built a clandestine organization and successfully maintained it for as long as we did, while the authorities never stopped trying to find us, if we had been living under the surveillance and security conditions in place today'.[117] It is a good question—and one that at least half-answers itself. The aftermath of the Chemnitz riots in the autumn of 2018 is equally thought-provoking. When a handful of neo-Nazis attempted to plan a bombing campaign, the security services had them rounded up very swiftly indeed. 'Revolution Chemnitz' and its fantasies of provoking civil war was stopped right in its tracks.[118]

So, frustratingly for analysts, risk managers and prophets, the early twenty-first century looks set to remain open-ended. In any longer-term perspective, the domestic strength of Western governments remains massively impressive. Their coercive capabilities and bureaucratic information-processing capacities remain intact, if they have not actually been enhanced by the information-processing revolutions. States may not be intrinsically much weaker than they were before the 1990s. And the conspiracies they face remain, if anything, more primitive. But public moods are certainly more febrile: more alarmist, more confused, and more embittered. And the times have never been better for the amateur propagandists of mayhem. 'With political parties fading away, it is the time of saviours', writes Manuel Castells: 'this introduces systemic unpredictability'.[119] Morbid symptoms abound.

[117] Lerner, *Swords in the Hands of Children*p. 75.

[118] 'Bürgerkrieg im Chat geplant', 2 October 2018, *Tageschau.de* Available at: https://www.tagesschau.de/inland/chatprotokoll-chemnitz-101.html

[119] Castells, *The Power of Identity*, Vol. II, p. 414.

PART II

SOCIETY AND TECHNOLOGY

INTRODUCTORY REMARKS

One does not advertise ideas as though they were laxatives or toothpaste.

– Karl Habsburg, last emperor of Austria-Hungary[1]

So far the focus of analysis has been top-down: on the myriad ways in which the evolution of the Western state has, in turn, shaped the behaviour of its violent challengers. Broadly, the emphasis has been placed largely upon the negative forces of constraint: upon the ways in which the infrastructure of modern states has caged or constrained unofficial or rebel violence in specific directions. As Siniša Malešević has put it, 'as human beings grow ever more dependent on the social organisations, the organisations themselves become more powerful and continue to increase their coercive reach and depth'.[2] In this latter tendency lies the potential 'barbarism of civilization'.[3]

In this second half of the book, this polarity is broadly reversed. Now the focus is upon counter-trends: the pull factors that have encouraged violence to take historically novel and disturbing forms. 'Many histories of terrorism studies', observes Mikkel Thorup 'portray terrorism as something abstracted from the rest of society's processes'.[4] Here a long-term perspective can help illuminate the wider role of social processes in determining what forms violence may take. Only this kind of historical survey is likely to reveal the intrinsic 'modernity' at the heart of contemporary political violence.

Rural societies of 'mechanical solidarity'—to return to Durkheim's terminology—tend to exert tight regimes of social control over the members. A village priest will likely know far more about each individual than any distant state bureaucrat, however diligent. By contrast, the anonymous and mobile societies of 'organic solidarity' can allow far more individual or group experimentation; including in violence. Indeed, the anonymity of the modern metropolis lends itself to use

[1] Quoted in: L. Hughes-Hallett, *The Pike: Gabriele D'Annunzio. Poet, Seducer and Preacher of War* (London, 2013), p. 382.

[2] S. Malešević, *The Sociology of War and Violence* (Cambridge, 2010), p. 7.

[3] Giambattista Vico, quoted in: L. Mumford, *The City in History* (Harmondsworth, 1961), p. 130.

[4] M. Thorup, *An Intellectual History of Terror: War, Violence and the State* (Abingdon, 2010), p. 3.

as a giant laboratory for depersonalized atrocity far more readily than the village. Simply put, there is far more opportunity for maverick killers—whether their motivations are conventionally political, or not. Societies that actively celebrate individualism can expect to tolerate a more or less permanent fringe phenomenon of violent individualism as well.

Here a general word on regime types is in order. That totalitarian regimes have often been far more successful in suppressing small-group terroristic violence is obvious. Conversely, the relative vulnerability of liberal democracies in this regard has also long been recognized. Usually, it has been explained in straightforward terms as an unfortunate by-product of freedom of movement and information.[5]

Seen in a much longer-term perspective, though, such vulnerabilities look more structurally embedded. Before the industrial revolution, society's outcasts—that is, casual labourers who enjoyed no access to trade or land—were fated to be a non-reproducing class: their fate was early death rather than marriage. Under contemporary conditions, those radically alienated from society are far less likely to fade away. The liberal state allows them to survive: and, by extension, their grievances to fester. A minority may then turn to terroristic violence. Liberal states are geared towards the suppression of mass coercion from below: but also create a permissive environment for the production of violent free-lancers.[6]

If communication is 'a—perhaps *the*—fundamental process of society', then the most significant long-term background change here has been its relentless acceleration.[7] The diary of James Woodforde, a clergyman based in a Norfolk village allows us to glimpse how far and fast the shock waves of the political turbulence of the late eighteenth century travelled. In 1789, it took a full ten days for Woodforde to hear of the storming of the Bastille. In January 1793, the news of the execution of King Louis XVI arrived rather quicker: within five days.[8] By contrast: 99.8 per cent of the American public had heard of the shooting of President Kennedy on 22 November 1963 within five and a half hours.[9] By March 2019 Brenton Tarrant could slaughter forty-two worshippers at the Al Noor mosque in Christchurch, New Zealand: and conveniently stream the entire massacre on Facebook.[10] Here, indeed, was the black apotheosis of the 'society of the spectacle': mass atrocity as live global entertainment.[11]

[5] J. Bowyer Bell, *A Time of Terror: How Democratic Societies Respond to Revolutionary Violence* (New York, 1978), pp. ix–x; P. Wilkinson, *Terrorism and the Liberal State* (London, 1977, 1979), pp. 19, 188–93; B. Posen, 'The Struggle Against Terrorism: Grand Strategy, Strategy, and Tactics', *International Security*, 26 (3) Winter 2001/02, p. 41.

[6] I am indebted to Marc Mulholland for this line of argumentation.

[7] W. Schramm, 'Communication in Crisis' in B. S. Greenberg and E. B. Parker (eds.), *The Kennedy Assassination and the American Public: Social Communication in Crisis* (Stanford, 1965), p. 1.

[8] J. Woodforde, *The Diary of a Country Parson, 1758–1802* (Oxford, 1929, 19679), pp. 355, 430–1.

[9] P. B. Sheatsley and J. J. Feldman, 'A National Survey on Public Reactions and Behavior' in B. S. Greenberg and E. B. Parker (eds.), *The Kennedy Assassination and the American Public: Social Communication in Crisis* (Stanford, 1965), p. 153.

[10] BBC, 30 March 2019 ('Facebook to consider live video restrictions after NZ attacks').

[11] G. Debord, *Society of the Spectacle* (London, 1992).

Acceleration of communication—and in more recent decades, its mutual thickening through the rise of the 'many-to-many' messaging that characterizes the network age—exerts a kind of 'Doppler effect' here upon the fundamental nature of social processes. They do not *just* speed up: or rather, in speeding up, they also become fundamentally different in quality and form. It is hardly to be expected that political violence, itself a form of communication, could remain immune from such wrenching transformations. And yet in practice such evolution remains relatively underexplored: at least before the dawn of the satellite TV age at the end of the 1960s.

Some broad linkage has indeed long been acknowledged by historians between the communications revolutions of the later nineteenth century onwards and the emergence of new forms of political violence (such as demonstrative assassination and dynamite attacks).[12] Yet the effects of a publicity culture on political violence are often assumed to be obvious. Here I address a few brief remarks on this subject, seeking to situate the emergence of new practices of political violence against wider trends in publicity in the late nineteenth century.

It is worth noting that the last decades of this century saw the emergence of recognizably modern mass advertising. In 1869 the Ayer and Son advertising agency was founded in Philadelphia. The De La Mar agency followed in the Netherlands in 1880.[13] But the same period also saw the emergence of sustained political campaigning: President Johnson's 'swing around the circle' of the north American cities (August 1866) and William Gladstone's 'Mid-Lothian Campaign' of 1879–80.[14] As its historian notes, this latter episode 'represented the flowering of a new style of politics, long in germination. As politics became more bureaucratized, extra-parliamentary speech-making provided the means for the Liberal intelligentsia to preserve its influence in British political life, and in doing so it linked the intellectual force of Liberal politics to a particular form of media-presentation'.[15]

What was becoming apparent was that an ability to pull the tides of mass attention back and forth itself constituted a new form of power. As observers in Paris had already noticed by 1860, 'life threatens to become public... the newspaper has killed the salon, and publicity has taken the place formerly occupied by society'.[16] Out of this brave new world arose what might, following media theorists, be termed 'pseudo-events': that is events that existed only to be publicized. In the television age, press conferences and ribbon-cutting ceremonies are pre-eminent examples.[17] But the deeper roots are in the nineteenth century: after all, the 'real

[12] M. Burleigh, *Blood and Rage: A Cultural History of Terrorism* (London, 2008, 2009), p. 79; M. Carr, *The Infernal Machine* (New York, 2006), pp. 50–1; D. Rapoport, 'The Four Waves of Rebel Terror and September 11' in C. W. Kegley (ed.), *The New Global Terrorism: Characteristics, Causes, Controls* (New Jersey, 2003), p. 38.

[13] S. Pincas and M. Loiseau, *A History of Advertising* (Cologne, 2008), pp. 32–3.

[14] E. Foner, *Reconstruction: America's Unfinished Revolution, 1863–1877* (New York, 1988, 2014), p. 264; H. C. G. Matthew, *Gladstone, 1875–1898* (Oxford, 1995), pp. 47–51.

[15] Matthew, *Gladstone*, pp. 49–50.

[16] S. Kracauer, *Offenbach and the Paris of His Times* (London, 1937), p. 243.

[17] See the fascinating discussion at: www.tiara.org/papers/roflcon_talk.txt

audience' of Gladstone's protracted series of Midlothian speeches was the newspaper-reading public.[18]

Seeing acts of modern political violence as 'pseudo-events' helps focus attention on their underlying 'production values' that help guarantee maximum attention. It has long been intuitively realized that—at least in the most spectacular cases—'terrorist acts are . . . easily transformed into major international media events—precisely because they are often staged specifically with this goal in mind.[19] But the deeper roots of this tendency have been less well recognized. Several points are worth sketching here to offer a brief overview of this process in terms of its historical background.

First, the urban bombing campaigns of the last decades of the nineteenth century emerged upon metropolitan stages that were themselves becoming impressively monumental. At very much this point, 'growing international competitiveness was mirrored in the large-scale rebuilding of capital cities, as the great powers bolstered their self-esteem in the most visible, ostentatious manner'.[20] Since 'monuments always speak a language of order, inheritance and shelter', they themselves became obvious targets to agents of destabilization.[21] In London, for instance, it was no accident that the Fenian bombers of 1883–5 targeted Whitehall, 'the imperial state's ceremonial and bureaucratic heart'.[22] Governmental grandeur had become a target in its own right.[23]

Secondly, a concomitant feature of this drive to create order through monumentalism was the growth of *synecdoche* as a common currency of mass communication. Thus, a mere handful of dramatic structures or locations came to be accepted as symbols of much wider entities: the Golden Gage Bridge for San Francisco (and so on). So familiar are these icons that their violation arouses strikingly strong popular reactions. After a failed communist bomb attack at the Victory Column in March 1921, the journalist Joseph Roth remarked that previously Berliners had entirely ignored it as part of the city's monumental furniture: but that now it had 'attained the level of popularity that only failed assassinations may confer'.[24] And when a B-25 bomber (accidentally) flew into the 79th floor of the Empire State Building on 28 July 1945 it knocked news of the continuing war against Japan off the front pages.[25] Such famous landmarks embody political stability at some mass visceral level: they are indeed 'signature structures' and—by extension—obvious targets.[26] As early as 1900, fiction writers could envisage anarchist attempts to blow up the Eiffel Tower.[27] Real-life attempts were, admittedly, slower to appear. But from the

[18] Matthew, *Gladstone*, p. 47. [19] B. Hoffman, *Inside Terrorism* (New York, 2006), p. 194.

[20] D. Cannadine, 'The Context, Performance and Meaning of Ritual: The British Monarchy and the "Invention of Tradition", c. 1820–1977', in E. Hobsbawm and T. Ranger (eds), *The Invention of Tradition* (Cambridge, 1983), p. 126.

[21] R. Hughes, *Barcelona* (London, 1992, 1996), p. 465.

[22] J. Vernon, *Distant Strangers: How Britain Became Modern* (Berkeley, 2014), p. 72.

[23] Hughes, *Barcelona*, p. 373.

[24] J. Roth, *What I Saw: Reports from Berlin 1920–33* (London, 1996, 2004), p. 179.

[25] A. Weingarten, *The Sky is Falling* (London, 1977), preface (no page number).

[26] 9/11 Commission Report, p. 1. [27] *Chichester Observer*, 18 July 1900.

mid-twentieth century onwards the attempts came thicker and faster. By the second decade of the twenty-first century they—briefly—became a blizzard.[28]

Thirdly, there are fashions in atrocity as in everything else. Attack forms that have recently gained significant attention are likely to be repeated more than others—until sudden saturation points are reached as if by some invisible consensus. Here many—though not all—forms of spectacular political violence are no different from other public events that 'seem to appear from nowhere; soon they will return to whence they came—they will fade into non-existence'.[29] Recent rising and falling in the incidence of vehicle ramming attacks illustrates the point. Much of this violence is supremely faddish in form. It occurs in waves—but these are not the forty-year long giant swells envisaged by David Rapoport in his schematic account of ideological motivations.[30] Rather, they are intensely short and choppy breakers. They reflect sudden mimetic flurries of activity, often with a promiscuous borrowing across ideological divides. Surging fast, they fall away; and are gone.

To describe contemporary political atrocities as 'pseudo events' is in no way to downplay their visceral and material horror. Clearly, the devastation they wreak is real, immediate, and lasting in its effects. But it is to identify their nature as fundamentally modern: and belonging firmly to our own age and civilization. It is time to bring the processes of its emergence into sharper focus.

[28] For attacks and plots directed against the Eiffel Tower: L. Collins and D. Lapierre, *Is Paris Burning?* (London, 1965, 1991), p. 230 [August 1944 Nazi plan]; A. Horne, *A Savage War of Peace: Algeria 1954–1962* (New York, 1977, 2006), pp. 318 [Front Liberation National bomb, 1958], 503 [January 1961 plot by the Organisation Armée Secrète]; *Guardian*, 6 February 1986 [militant Shia leaves bomb on 3rd level]; F. Foley, *Countering Terrorism in Britain and France* (Cambridge, 2013), pp. 25, 293 [December 1994 plot by GIA]; *The Independent*, 18 November 2015 [Eiffel Tower shut 'in new scare']; *The Sun*, 18 October 2018 [ISIS plot].

[29] Z. Bauman, 'Soil, blood and identity', *The Sociological Review*, 1992, p. 695.

[30] Rapoport, 'The Four Waves of Rebel Terror and September 11'.

4

The Hazards of Social Rank

Long may she be spared to roam
Among the bonnie Highland floral
And spend many a happy day
In the palace of Balmoral.

– William McGonagall, 'Attempted Assassination of the Queen'[1]

In any longer-term consideration of the evolution of political violence, it is tempting to start at the very top: with the killing of leaders. Assassination, however, is a more slippery concept than it appears at first glance. For Havens, Leiden, and Schmitt, assassination is a subset of murder: 'the deliberate, extralegal killing of an individual for political purposes'.[2] In a classic study, Franklin Ford offered a similar understanding, albeit with the caveat that motives of 'political' assassination often turn out to be far less clear-cut than they initially appear.[3] For Bowyer-Bell, assassination was simply the treacherous killing of the prominent or distinguished.[4] Such categorizations naturally tend to leave open the question of how politically significant a victim has to be before their murder counts as an assassination. Here I follow the general convention of treating assassination as the slaying of truly elite figures: the rulers. Next I broaden the discussion from killing to hostage-taking: another violent practice that in the more distant past tended to be directed exclusively at political elites. Finally, and very briefly, I note the general historical trend towards a 'democratization' of target-widening from the (upper) classes to the wider masses; preparing the way for a subsequent discussion of the specific ways and means by which the threat of political violence has come to be diffused more equitably throughout society.[5]

I

What in social scientific terms has proven to be the most controversial feature of Alex Schmid's 1988 definition of terrorism—that is, its general exclusion of

[1] W. McGonagall, *Poetic Gems: William McGonagall, Poet and Tragedian* (London, 1975), pp. 66–7.
[2] M. C. Havens, C. Leiden, and K. M. Schmitt, *The Politics of Assassination* (Englewood Cliffs, NJ, 1970), p. 4.
[3] F. L. Ford, *Political Murder: From Tyrannicide to Terrorism* (Harvard, 1985), p. 3.
[4] J. Bowyer Bell, *Assassin: Theory and Practice of Political Violence* (New Brunswick, 1979, 2005), pp. 22–3.
[5] For a thought-provoking set of reflections on this theme: E. J. Hobsbawm, *Globalisation, Democracy and Terrorism* (London, 2007, 2010), pp. 121–37.

assassination (of elite figures)—is thus, for the historian, a distinct analytical advantage in so far as it draws attention to different genealogies of political violence.[6] Put simply, so long as political elites remained tiny, political killing also remained a highly limited affair. Franklin Ford, for instance, has usefully drawn attention to the sheer rarity of assassination attempts against the kings of late seventeenth- and eighteenth-century Europe.[7]

Doubtless, assassination was discouraged by many factors. But it seems hard to downplay the enduring role of class deference as a force for elite preservation. 'Nothing much separated the mob, whether friendly or otherwise, from the powerful' observes Paul Johnson of the early nineteenth century: 'the amount of protection afforded the mighty of the earth was astonishingly little'.[8] Government remained an intimate matter. When King Frederick William of Prussia visited London in 1814 on what was supposed to be a joyous triumphal tour to celebrate the defeat of Napoleon, he was said to be as 'sulky as a bear' from the constant jostling of the crowds.[9] Sheer social distance, and not mere physical remoteness, protected him with surprising effectiveness.

This latter point is hard to over-state in importance. The rise of iconic assassination as a social rallying call ('propaganda of the deed') depended upon a prior social diffusion of new ways of thinking about what leaders stood for and why they mattered. Back in the 1850s the peasants of the Ariège 'imagined the Louvre to be a fantastic, fairytale palace, and the members of the imperial family to be some sort of storybook characters'.[10] This changed, but only gradually. Once leaders came to be seen in more abstract terms—as symbolic capstones of complete social orders—then a potential space began to open up to present their violent removal as a bold act of social engineering, rather than a mere act of defensive tyrannicide. Nor, indeed, were such hopes entirely delusional. After all, the 'decapitation' of Napoleon III—albeit through defeat on the battlefield, rather than through assassination—did indeed trigger a social revolution in Paris in 1870–1.[11]

Once more, it is important to stress the role of a burgeoning mass media in fostering contagion effects. Even before 1850 this effect had appeared in Britain. No less than three of the eight attempts to kill or threaten Queen Victoria with guns clustered within the years 1840–2.[12] But internationally, the crucial watershed for imitation came later: 'soon after the first shots were fired at Alexander II

[6] A. Schmid (ed.), *The Routledge Handbook of Terrorism Research* (New York, 2011, 2013), pp. 62–4.

[7] Ford, *Political Murder*, p. 180.

[8] P. Johnson, *The Birth of the Modern: World Society, 1815–1830* (London, 1991, 1992), p. 387.

[9] Johnson, *The Birth of the Modern*, p. 97.

[10] E. Weber, *Peasants into Frenchmen: The Modernization of Rural France, 1870–1914* (Stanford, 1976), p. 8.

[11] Correspondence with Marc Mulholland, 29 August 2019.

[12] B. Charles, *Kill the Queen! The Eight Assassination Attempts on Queen Victoria* (Stroud, 2012), pp. 5–54; P. T. Murphy, *Shooting Victoria! Madness, Mayhem and the Modernisation of the Monarchy* (London, 2012), pp. 53–235.

[of Russia] in May 1878, five attempts—an unprecedented number—were made to assassinate crowned heads of Europe'.[13]

Even after this point, though, assassination opportunities still remained limited by the relative lack of access of lowly-born killers to their social 'betters'. Rulers and ruled rarely interacted directly. Courts were closed worlds to outsiders. Even into the early twentieth century, it is striking just how many pre-1914 assassination attempts occurred during trips to the opera or theatre: occasions on which the movements of elite figures could be anticipated with some degree of accuracy.[14] George III of England survived two attempts on his life during trips to the theatre (1778, 1800).[15] No less than three such plots were hatched against Napoleon Bonaparte within the compass of a single year (1800).[16] Less fortunate was the Duc de Berry who was stabbed to death as he left the Paris opera (1820).[17] Like his uncle, Napoleon III survived a truly spectacular bomb attack on his way to the theatre (1858).[18] Abraham Lincoln was clinically shot in the back of the head as he watched a performance in Ford's theatre, Washington (1865).[19] More opportunistically, Carnot was stabbed to death on his way to the Grand Théâtrein Lyon (1894).[20] Later examples include the attack on King Alfonso XIII of Spain as he returned from the opera in Paris (1905); and the successful killing of the Russian Prime Minister, Stolypin, at the Kiev theatre house (1911).[21]

Sketched broadly, the peak age of European assassination attempts in the later nineteenth century falls in a transitional period for traditional authority. As has been shrewdly noted,

> The fact that more Europeans were ready to assassinate members of their royal families was not necessarily a sign of their decline in authority; on the contrary, it could equally be interpreted as a sign of affirmation that these old rulers continued to embody a political order, albeit one whose decline many considered overdue.[22]

And yet the demands of the new mass media were pushing monarchs into being figures of more or less constant public display (and hence of sharply increased vulnerability). Conversely, the caste pride of monarchies—and indeed, aristocracies in general—dictated that public courage must be demonstrated unflinchingly.

Such contradictory pressures required rulers, in effect, to run a public gauntlet. From the mid-nineteenth century, a banal but striking feature of assassination

[13] J. H. Billington, *Fire in the Minds of Men: Origins of the Revolutionary Faith* (Abingdon, 1980, 2017), p. 414.

[14] Gustav III of Sweden was killed at a masked ball at an opera house in 1792: but this was an elite conspiracy. See: Ford, *Political Murder*, p. 205.

[15] J. Black, *George III: America's Last King* (London, 2006), pp. 115, 172.

[16] J. North, *Killing Napoleon: The Plot to Blow Up Bonaparte* (Amberley, 2019), pp. 84, 108, 128.

[17] F. Harcourt (ed.), *Memoirs of Madame de la Tour de la Pin* (London, 1969, 1985), p. 449 n2.

[18] *The Times*, 16 January 1858. Also: Kracauer, *Offenbach and the Paris of His Time*, pp. 160, 172.

[19] R. Hofstadter and M. Wallace (eds), *American Violence: A Documentary History* (New York, 1971), pp. 409–11. E. Steers, *Lincoln's Assassination* (Carbondale, IL, 2014), pp. 53–5.

[20] E. A. Vizetelly, *The Anarchists: Their Faith and Their Record Including Sidelights on the Royal and Other Personages Who Have Been Assassinated* (London, 1911), pp. 178–81.

[21] *Lancashire Evening Post*, 1 June 1905; Laqueur, *The Age of Terrorism*, p. 16.

[22] D. Gusejnova, *European Elites and Ideas of Empire, 1917–1957* (Cambridge, 2016), p. 8.

attempts was how often they took place while monarchs were riding in open-topped carriages. Elevated, displayed, and trapped, they presented superb targets. Five of the eight attempts to threaten Queen Victoria took place when she was travelling in this manner.[23] Within a single summer (1878), Kaiser Wilhelm I was shot at twice whilst exposed in an open carriage: and in the second attack, seriously wounded with pellets fired down from a balcony.[24] A potshot was taken at the Prince of Württemberg on his way to church in 1889.[25] President Carnot of France was stabbed to death in an open carriage (1894).[26] Less seriously, Kaiser Wilhelm II had an axe thrown at him in Breslau (1900) and was actually caught below the eye by a buckle thrown at him as he was conveyed through Bremen (1901).[27] King Umberto of Italy was caught in a stabbing attempt (1897) and a shooting (1900) while effectively immobilized in open carriages—on the latter occasion fatally.[28] Similarly, King Carlos of Portugal and his heir were shot dead as literally sitting targets in an open carriage (1908).[29]

Such vulnerabilities carried over smoothly into the age of motor transport. In 1912, Count Cuvaj, the Hungarian Governor of Croatia, was shot at in an open car in Zagreb.[30] Even the nervous and hesitant Gavrilo Princip could not fail to miss Archduke Ferdinand and his wife Sophie when they stopped right in front of him (1914).[31] Walther Rathenau similarly stood no chance whatsoever when caught in a drive by shooting and bombing (1922).[32] Neither did King Alexander I of Yugoslavia and the French Foreign Minister Louis Barthou when attacked in Marseilles (1934).[33] Both Mussolini (1926) and Franklin D. Roosevelt (1933) were luckier here in surviving more amateur shooting attempts when trapped in open cars.[34]

Nazi attitudes to such exposed travelling were deeply schizophrenic. One school of thought insisted that imperiousness was its own best defence. 'Hitler drove into Eger next day', recalled one journalist of the annexation of the Sudetenland in 1938: 'Anyone could have shot him if anyone had thought of assassination. He stood up

[23] Murphy, *Shooting Victoria*, pp. 54, 172, 182, 212–13, 268, 316, 368, 385, 453–4. See also illustrations after pp. 176, 368.

[24] A. R. Carlson, *Anarchism in Germany*, Vol. I, *The Early Movement* (Metuchen, New Jersey, 1972), pp. 115, 139–40.

[25] F. L. Müller, 'Swabian Loyalty and the Uses of Gefühlspolitik', http://heirstothethrone-project

[26] N. Pernicone and F. M. Ottanelli, *Assassins Against the Old Order: Italian Anarchist Violence in Fin de Siècle Europe* (Champaign, IL, 2018), p. 66.

[27] *Le Petit Journal*, 24 March 1901; J. Röhl, *Wilhelm II: Into the Abyss of War and Exile, 1900–1941* (Cambridge, 2014), p. 133.

[28] Pernicone and Ottanelli, *Assassins Against the Old Order*, pp. 90–1 [22 April 1897]; R. Bach Jensen, *The Battle Against Anarchist Terrorism* (Cambridge, 2014), p. 199 [29 July 1900].

[29] *Sheffield Daily Independent*, 3 February 1908.

[30] Ford, *Political Murder*, p. 247.

[31] C. Clark, *The Sleepwalkers: How Europe Went to War in 1914* (London, 2012, 2013), pp. 374–5.

[32] M. Sabrow, *Der Rathenaumord* (Oldenbourg, 1994), pp. 82–3.

[33] Havens (et al., eds), *Politics of Assassination*, pp. 85–90. For vivid footage, see the original Universal Newsreel clip embedded in the Wikipedia page: 'Alexander I of Yugoslavia'.

[34] J. Bowyer Bell, *Assassin: Theory and Practice of Political Violence* (New Jersey, 1979, 2005), pp. 232 [Mussolini]; *New York Times*, 17 February 1933 ['How Roosevelt Saw It'].

in the open German army motor-car, saluting the packed crowds that chanted deliriously.'[35] In an after-dinner monologue on 3 May 1942 Hitler himself declared to his acolytes that he stood up in his open-topped car because 'the world belongs to the brave'.[36] Yet just weeks later—on 27 May—his plenipotentiary Reinhold Heydrich was mortally wounded in a bomb and gun attack as his Mercedes convertible slowed on a hairpin bend on his way into Prague.[37] Hitler then blamed him for not having been security-conscious enough.[38] In fact, it is clear that after Georg Elser's assassination attempt Hitler took travelling security very seriously indeed—and the fate of Rathenau seems to have lingered in his memory.[39]

Such exposed travelling seems to have generally fallen away by the mid-twentieth century: the assassination of President Kennedy in 1963 notwithstanding. It has survived only in special cases. British royal weddings with their self-conscious celebration of anachronism are one such exception; so, too, are Papal visits despite concerns 'about the Pope standing with little protection in an open vehicle'.[40] The Pope is, indeed, possibly the last world leader professionally obliged to rely primarily on convictions of divine protection. A series of various 'Pope Mobiles'—essentially see-through armoured cars—have nevertheless been designed to alleviate what had, by the late twentieth century, come to be seen as a major security headache.

Such a dramatic demise of open-topped carriages and cars serves as a useful illustration of wider security trends. Richard Bach Jensen has identified a first 'revolution in protection' in the early twentieth century that substantially modified how ruling elites have conducted their business: this has only accelerated, and deepened, throughout the following century.[41] As Franklin Ford points out, the leaders of the First World War appear to have been relatively little troubled by questions of personal security: their successors during the Second World War could not afford the same luxury.[42] In 1938 Elliot Paul witnessed the arrival of the Nazi Foreign Minister Von Ribbentrop in Paris:

> I had thought, until that day, that in the course of my years as a newspaperman I had seen police precautions. I was very wrong. The Place de la Concorde, the Quai d'Orsay, and all the streets leading in or out or around were packed with soldiers and police, shoulder to shoulder, and there were thousands of plain-clothes men to form a solid circle around the soldiers. The peace envoy's train had been shunted from the Gare de Lyon, where trains from Germany came in, to the Gare des Invalides, only a stone's throw from the Foreign Office.... Ribbentrop was kept at all times out of sight or

35 S. Morrell, *I Saw the Crucifixion* (London, 1938), p. 300.

36 H. Trevor-Roper (ed.), *Hitler's Table Talk: Hitler's Conversations recorded by Martin Bormann* (Oxford, 1988), p. 453 (3 May 1942).

37 R. Gerwarth, *Hitler's Hangman* (London, 2011, 2012), pp. 2, 7, 10–11.

38 Trevor-Roper, *Hitler's Table Talk*, p. 512.

39 Trevor-Roper, *Hitler's Table Talk*, pp. 453–4. Also: E. Kempka, *I Was Hitler's Chauffeur* (Frontline, 2010, 2012), p. 24.

40 P. Henze, *The Plot to Kill the Pope* (London, 1984), p. 3.

41 Bach Jensen, *The Battle Against Anarchist Terrorism*, pp. 203–14. For precursor moves in late nineteenth-century Germany see: M. Mühlnikel, *Fürst, Sind Sie Unverletzt? Attentate im Kaiserreich 1871–1914* (Paderborn, 2014), pp. 191–201. For Britain: B. Porter, *The Origins of the Vigilant State: the London Metropolitan Police Special Branch Before the First World War* (London, 1987).

42 Ford, *Political Murder*, p. 273.

> reach of the Paris population. There was not a cheer or a hearty sound of any kind as his bullet-proof limousine rolled two hundred yards between the station and the grey stone building which had been decked with French and German flags, the tricolour and the swastika so lovingly entwined.[43]

Later in the century such security precautions were to become more or less standard. Democratic leaders began to live like dictators. Indeed, in the 1970s, the West German Chancellor Helmut Schmidt was protected by a personal security detail that was three times as large as that of Adolf Hitler in 1935 (60 men to 20, respectively).[44] Meanwhile, 'Bonn, the federal village, became an armed camp. Barbed wire was laid around ministries where for years it had been possible to wander in with scarcely a check'.[45]

In general, over the course of the twentieth century leaders of all regime types and ideological convictions retreated from their own people: or, at least, from uncontrolled and unchoreographed appearances before them. The 'walk about' during election campaigns became important for its very rarity. Social distance was replaced by physical distance. Deference was replaced by governmental self-fortification. After the shooting of Robert Kennedy (4 June 1968), US Secret Service protection was extended to presidential candidates, and not just presidential nominees. Barak Obama thus began receiving protection 18 months before the 2008 election.[46] Nonetheless, Michelle Obama records the shock of seeing the full presidential security cavalcade for the first time: 'a snaking, vehicular army' at least twenty vehicles long.[47]

These were truly momentous changes: and ones with far-reaching consequences for the general respect in which political representatives would be held. If the top-level of governments were never better protected than in the early twenty-first century, the lower and mid-levels of political representation—Members of Parliament, mayors, councillors, and so on—have found themselves ever more exposed. And as the innate dynamics of social media fuels an age of character assassination, the threat of actual assassination looms much larger here, too. Back in 1970, one study had found that one in four US presidents had been targeted by assassins, but only one in 1,000 congressmen.[48] In the early twenty-first century, as the political class as a whole has become more and more popularly despised, this may well change.

[43] E. Paul, *The Last Time I Saw Paris* (London, 1942, 2011), p. 311.

[44] T. Gerraghty, *Bullet Catchers: The Bodyguards and the World of Close Protection* (London, 1988, 1989), p. 169; P. Hoffmann, 'Hitler's Personal Security', *Journal of Contemporary History*, 8 (2) April 1973, p. 28.

[45] J. Carr, *Helmut Schmidt: Helmsman of Germany* (London, 1985), p. 116.

[46] P. Mullen (et al.), 'The Role of Psychotic Illnesses in Attacks on Public Figures' in J. Reid Meloy (et al., eds), *Stalking, Threatening and Attacking Public Figures* (Oxford, 2008), p. 154.

[47] M. Obama, *Becoming* (New York, 2018), pp. 287–8.

[48] Havens (et al.), *The Politics of Assassination*, p. 31.

II

On 26 October 1941, in the privacy of a secret diary kept during the Nazi occupation of Paris, Jean Guéhemo reflected that 'the hostages in past wars were noble or bourgeois, "notables". This time it's usually just unimportant people who run the risk of being shot'.[49] A year later, in Amsterdam a young Anne Frank similarly reflected on the rise of mass hostage taking ('Can you imagine anything so dreadful?').[50] Such grassroots observations from the depths of the Second World War suggest some intuitive wider awareness that an abrupt step change in the general evolution of hostage-taking was underway. Since hostage-taking remains an almost entirely neglected historical subject, the wider effects of this change are hard to trace.[51] Relationships between hostage-taking in war and political hostage-taking in peacetime remain highly elusive, in particular. It is also worth stressing in this context that hostage-taking remains a minority terroristic technique in the recent history of political violence—Adam Dolnik estimated it has constituted 20 per cent of global 'terrorism incidents' between 1970 and 2007.[52] And yet these include truly spectacular set-piece dramas such as the Munich Olympics (1972).

It is worth establishing at the outset a basic conceptual distinction between hostage-taking that is a form of *deterrence* (to stop something happening: usually resistance) and hostage-taking that is a form of *blackmail* (to gain something). As a form of deterrence, particularly in contexts of war or revolution, hostage-taking is indeed truly venerable. It has often been a tactic of occupying powers, but has also been adopted by insecure revolutionary regimes such as the Paris Commune of 1871. Likewise, the Soviet Republic at Munich indulged in hostage-taking in 1918–19.[53] Soon the children were playing a new game of 'Reds and Whites' in which 'at the end the losers were arrested and locked in cellars and garden-sheds. These losers were dubbed "hostages"'.[54] The main point to note about such tactics is their broadening scope and brutality over time. Put simply, they ensnared more and more victims, and reached further down the social scale. German hostage-taking (and subsequent executions) in northern France in 1914 shocked contemporaries: but were as nothing compared to those inflicted in 1941 and after.[55] As a tool of governance and occupation control, hostage-taking became a shameful tactic after 1945.

[49] J. Guéhemo, *Diary of the Dark Years, 1940–1944* (Oxford, 1947, 2016), p. 123.

[50] A. Frank, *The Diary of Anne Frank* (London, 1947, 1972), p. 43.

[51] J. C. Griffiths, *Hostage: The History, Facts and Reasoning behind Hostage Taking* (London, 2003).

[52] A. Dolnik, *Understanding Terrorist Innovation* (Abingdon, 2007), p. 28.

[53] K. Marx, *The Civil War in France* (Moscow, 1948, 1977), p. 75; A. Horne, *The Terrible Year: The Paris Commune, 1871* (London, 1971), pp. 159, 161; M. Jones, *Founding Weimar: Violence and the German Revolution of 1918–1919* (Cambridge, 2016), pp. 286–7, 296, 299–309.

[54] R. Grunberger, *Red Rising in Bavaria* (London, 1973), p. 137.

[55] For the leading account: J. Horne and A. Kramer, *German Atrocities 1914* (London, 2001), pp. 15, 17, 50, 56, 61–2, 94, 162, 300, 311.

By contrast, hostage-taking as political blackmail has largely flourished *since* 1968.[56] Yet there are some semi-precursors which are worth exploring. Here it is useful to follow Dolnik's basic typology of terroristic hostage-taking incidents. His tri-partite schema divides hostage taking into: kidnappings (where the location of the victims is hidden); barricade situations (where the victims are corralled); and hijackings that use a mobile platform (and which, potentially at least, can be seen as a partial combination of the first two techniques).[57] Each requires its own brief discussion.

Kidnappings in the bandit tradition have traditionally been for ransom. In the 50 years before 1914 the Mediterranean region became the arena for a series of high-profile abductions that sucked in the attention of major Western powers.[58] In 1865, three aristocratic English travellers were captured in Greece.[59] In April 1870, Lord Muncaster, Frederick Vyner, and their Piedmontese companion, Count Alberto de Boÿl, were kidnapped on a sight-seeing trip north of Athens.[60] An American missionary, Miss Ellen Stone, was captured and held in Macedonia over the winter of 1901–02.[61] In 1904, the elderly Mr Ion Perdicaris was kidnapped from his villa just outside Tangier in Morocco: an abduction that distracted the American press from the Russo-Japanese War then raging: 'a rich old gentleman held to ransom by a cruel but romantic brigand, the American Navy steaming to the rescue—here was personal drama more immediate than the complicated rattle of unpronounceable generals battling over unintelligible terrain'.[62]

Several general points are worth making here. All of these cases became major international incidents: but the abductions were not generally driven by political demands. Only Stone was abducted by the self-styled revolutionaries of IMRO (the Macedonian Revolutionary Organisation): and even they were still primarily interested in financial extortion. In the end, IMRO were content with $66,000.[63] Secondly, the harming of hostages was the exception, not the general rule. True, Vyner and de Boÿl were killed—but this was during the exceptional circumstances of a botched rescue attempt.[64] Severing body parts to demonstrate determination was indeed a known technique, but one rarely practised.[65] Bandits generally did not feel they had to demonstrate their credentials as technicians of violence.

[56] M. Rasmussen, 'Terrorist Learning: A Look at the Adoption of Political Kidnappings in Six Countries, 1968–1990', *Studies in Conflict and Terrorism*, 40 (7), 2017.

[57] Dolnik, *Understanding Terrorist Innovation*, pp. 28–9.

[58] For a helpful overview: M. Blinkhorn, 'Avoiding the Ultimate Act of Violence: Mediterranean Bandits and Kidnapping for Ransom, 1815–1914' in S. Carroll (ed.), *Cultures of Violence: Interpersonal Violence in Historical Perspective* (Basingstoke, 2007), pp. 192–211.

[59] R. Jenkins, *The Dilessi Murders: Greek Brigands and English Hostages* (London, 1961, 1998), p. 15.

[60] Jenkins, *The Dilessi Murders*, pp. 25–34.

[61] R. B. Woods, 'Terrorism in the Age of Roosevelt: the Miss Stone Affair, 1901–1902', *American Quarterly*, 31 (4) Autumn 1979, p. 479.

[62] B. Tuchman, 'Perdicaris Alive or Raisuli Dead' in B. Tuchman, *Practising History* (London, 1981), pp. 104, 108.

[63] Woods, 'Terrorism in the Age of Roosevelt, p. 493.

[64] Jenkins, *The Dilessi Murders*, p. 81.

[65] Blinkhorn, 'Avoiding the Ultimate Act of Violence', p. 199.

Kidnappings as an explicit tool of political leverage to back up specific demands have a more chequered history. The concept itself emerged relatively early. At the fringes, nineteenth-century Irish radical politics was much haunted by such schemes: all of them delusional. In August 1849, Young Ireland activists planned to abduct Queen Victoria to the Wicklow Mountains: and use her as a bargaining counter to force the release of their captured leader, William Smith O'Brien.[66] Other plots in 1867 and 1874 assigned the Prince of Wales the role of lead hostage to force a more general release of Fenian prisoners.[67] In 1872, the decidedly optimistic Arthur O'Connor hoped to hold Queen Victoria hostage at gunpoint until she agreed on the spot to release them all.[68] As far we can reconstruct his intentions, O'Connor seems to have envisaged delivering his ultimatum in heroic slow-motion: whilst the full panoply of British power remained frozen at his sheer audacity. General possibilities for failure, or indeed the mere likelihood of interruption, seems not to have crossed his mind.[69] A couple of observations are worth offering here in passing. First, these Fenian dreams and schemes generally centred on trying to force mass prisoner release from a far more powerful state adversary: closely foreshadowing the specific form that hostage-taking was to take in the 1970s. Secondly though, and in contrast to the future of political hostage-taking, they only ever envisaged taking elite figures—indeed, members of the Royal family—prisoner. Lastly, they were invariably wildly impractical in the closely-administered territories of the United Kingdom: even in an age of minimal security precautions, the logistics were clearly near-impossible.

Other hostage-taking dreams of the age were, perhaps, even more ambitious in their demands. From the other side of the great divide of late nineteenth century Irish politics, the eccentric Colonel Crawford apparently proposed to kidnap the Liberal Prime Minister William Gladstone to derail Home Rule: a suggestion that earned him some ridicule from fellow loyalists (and the nickname 'Guy Fawkes').[70] Even more ambitiously, the original plan of William Booth in 1865 had been to abduct Abraham Lincoln, not shoot him: his ransom demand would be the recognition of the independence of the Confederacy.[71] Neither of these plans seems to have come to much.

Neither did the twentieth-century bring much change here. The Suffragette movement may have flirted with the idea of hostage-taking: but not, it seems, too seriously.[72] On 2 July 1915 Erich Muenter both planted a bomb in the US Capitol and attempted to take the family of the banker J. P. Morgan hostage in his one-man campaign to bring the world war to an end—but he was overpowered in the

66 Murphy, *Shooting Victoria*, p. 290.

67 *Downpatrick Recorder*, 16 November 1867; Murphy, *Shooting Victoria*, p. 367. Also: S. Kenna, *War in the Shadows: the Irish-American Fenians Who Bombed Victorian Britain* (Sallins, 2014), p. xxiii (Clan na Gael plot to kidnap Prince Arthur of Connaught).

68 Murphy, *Shooting Victoria*, pp. 380–1.

69 Murphy, *Shooting Victoria*, pp. 380–1.

70 A. Jackson, *Judging Redmond and Carson: Comparative Irish Lives* (Dublin, 2018), p. 161.

71 Hofstadter and Wallace, *American Violence*, p. 409; Steers, *Lincoln's Assassination*, p. 2.

72 B. Harrison, 'The Act of Militancy: Violence and the Suffragettes, 1904–1914' in M. Bentley and J. Stevenson (eds), *Peaceable Kingdom: Stability and Change in Modern Britain* (Oxford, 1982), p. 56.

latter attempt. He had found hostage-taking more demanding than expected.[73] So, too, did the IRA when—in objectively far more fortuitous circumstances—they captured Brigadier General Lucas during a fishing trip on the River Blackwater in County Cork on 26 June 1920. They had hoped to swap him for a high-level IRA prisoner, Michael Fitzgerald. Yet the logistics of maintaining Lucas in roving captivity were so daunting that in the end led to their giving him a deliberate chance to escape on 30 July. He took it.[74]

When elite kidnapping revived in the last three decades of the twentieth century, it was as a speciality of the New Left. Certainly, nationalist groups such as ETA and the Provisional IRA also turned to kidnapping for fund-raising. Local businessmen were their preferred targets.[75] But this was essentially a limited strategy for limited ends. In the 'golden age' of hijack and hostage dramas, the Provisional IRA's most famous abduction was of a race-horse.[76]

To the New Left, the supposed efficacy and élan of Latin American examples seems to have been a key inspiration: particularly the Tupamaros (of Uruguay) and the Montoneros (of Argentina).[77] Realities were less romantic. Across both north America and Western Europe, the peak age of elite kidnappings was short: about eight years or so, from 1970 to 1978. Despite a few tactical successes, as a strategy to support domestic insurrection, kidnapping was a strategy doomed to long-term failure, since if it approached any prospect of success—that is, if a truly important individual was abducted—governments would mobilize such resources that any option for repetition or escalation was comprehensively quashed. They might not be able to find and rescue the kidnapped in time—as the fates of Pierre Laporte, Hanns Martin Schleyer, and Aldo Moro all demonstrated. But they could ensure such adventures were unlikely ever to be repeated. As was well recognized at the time, such crises tended to have an intrinsically 'high noon' quality to them.[78] In the words of one German TV commentator, 'people will look back and divide the history of our country into the period before the Schleyer kidnapping and the period after it'.[79]

Yet what is striking is how rarely hostage-takers have been able to strike directly at the very apex of state power. Aldo Moro was indeed a truly front-rank figure in Italian politics: twice Prime Minister, a chief fixer and mediator for the Christian Democrats, and a key force behind the 'historic compromise', a grand coalition to bring the Communist Party within the fold of potential governing parties. But amongst the damned he was very much the exception. Only Hanns Martin

[73] B. Gage, *The Day Wall Street Exploded* (Oxford, 2009), pp. 21–3.

[74] A. Carroll and T. Toomey, 'The Capture of Brigadier General Lucas' in J. Crowley (et al., eds), *Atlas of the Irish Revolution* (Cork, 2017), pp. 416–19.

[75] J. Bowyer Bell, *The Irish Troubles: A Generation of Violence 1967–1992* (Dublin, 1993, 1994), p. 674; J. Zulaika, *Basque Violence: Metaphor and Sacrament* (Reno, Nevada, 1988), p. 87.

[76] C. Turner, *In Search of Shergar* (London, 1984).

[77] Carr, *The Infernal Machine*, pp. 117–18, 122–3; Rasmussen, 'Terrorist Learning': p. 543.

[78] G. Pridham, 'Terrorism and the State in West Germany during the 1970s: A Threat to Stability or a Case of Political Over-reaction' in J. Lodge (ed.), *Terrorism: A Challenge to the State* (Oxford, 1981), p. 32.

[79] Carr, *Helmut Schmidt*, p. 119.

Schleyer (President of both the Confederation of German Employers' Associations and the Federation of German Industries) came anywhere close to his public profile. By contrast, James Cross (UK Senior Trade Commissioner, Montreal), Pierre Laporte (Minister of Labour in the Quebec government), Patricia Hearst (granddaughter of a publishing magnate), Peter Lorenz (Christian Democrat candidate for the Mayoralty of West Berlin) would all surely be largely unknown today if they had not been abducted.[80]

Concentrating large number of hostages in one place—the so-called barricade situation—has a more chequered history. On 26 August 1896—in 'probably the first act of its kind in the history of political terrorism'—Armenian militants occupied the Ottoman Bank in Constantinople, the key nerve centre of Western finance.[81] Thus they made clear their protest was 'against the Powers of Europe, who had abandoned the Armenians. They had chosen the bank because it was the most suitable place for such a demonstration'.[82] Having heavily mined the building, they threatened to blow it up if entrance was forced.[83] With revolvers in hand, they then negotiated their own escape through an open window with the bank's governor, Sir Edgar Vincent, reminding him as 'the Governor of the Ottoman Bank that they held two of his directors and a number of his *employés* [sic] as hostages'.[84] Meanwhile, in the words of one of the hostage-takers, 'about a hundred and fifty of the personnel—most of them European—were trembling like mice in front of us. They dared not take a step without permission'.[85]

Several features of the 1896 hostage-taking in Constantinople mark it out as ahead of its time. First, there is the breadth of the political horizons of its architects: and the sophistication of their political calculations. Their central demand was improved security of Armenian populations throughout the Ottoman Empire. Yet their route to achieving this was to choose a target of such international prestige that—they hoped—the European powers would then pressurize the Sultan in their turn. Secondly, there is the sheer refinement of technique. Mass hostage-taking at an internationally iconic location (and involving several nationalities), accompanied by both the forced publication of a list of demands, and finally, safe escape for the perpetrators: here was a complete template, born fully-formed.

And yet the example of the 1896 publicity coup went unrepeated. It is hard not to believe that the *immediate* consequence of the bank occupation—a three-day pogrom of the Armenian community in the city—served to discourage attempts at any repetition. When barricade hostage situations re-emerged towards the end of

80 Carr, *The Infernal Machine*, pp. 153–7.

81 J. Salt, 'Britain, The Armenian Question and the Cause of Ottoman Reform: 1894–96', *Middle Eastern Studies*, 26 (3) July 1990, p. 322.

82 *The Times*, 29 August 1896.

83 *New York Times*, 29 August 1896. See also: *Scotsman*, 29 September 1896; G. Chaliand, *Terrorism: From Popular Struggle to Media Spectacle* (London, 1985, 1987), p. 79.

84 *The Times*, 29 August 1896. Emphasis in original.

85 This eye-witness account is given at the (admittedly hostile) website: 'The Raid on the Ottoman Bank' at www.tallarmeniantale.com/ottoman-bank.htm//news. My use of the primary sources here should not be taken as an endorsement of the spirit of genocide denial that appears to inform this website.

the next century, less vulnerable locations tended to be chosen. But still the extent to which the 1896 Ottoman Bank takeover accurately pointed to the shape of a distant future is hard to overstate. It is hard to find any mass hostage incidents at all before the late twentieth century that bear any degree of close comparison.

Hostages were indeed taken at the Chancellery in Vienna in July 1934; but this was the improvised aftermath of a failed Nazi coup attempt, not a planned action.[86] On 22 January 1961, a liner, *Santa Maria*, was hijacked by left-wing Portuguese rebels seeking to destabilize the regime in Lisbon. Strikingly, though, its architect, Henrique Galvao saw the hijacked as a logistical challenge to be managed and not as a resource to be exploited:

> True, there would be the problem of the passengers—but their situation would be like that of any individuals, whether citizens or foreigners, in a territory surprised by an armed political rebellion.
>
> Certainly they would be somewhat inconvenienced, but no less certainly their property and their persons would be much safer than in a city during an insurrection, for we proposed to treat them with great consideration and courtesy.[87]

In summary, although proto-types exist, the mass hostage drama as a consolidated tradition essentially belongs to the post-1968 period: and may fairly be seen as a spin-off from aircraft hijackings, a phenomenon to be discussed in more detail below. Its emergence at much the same time as the advent of satellite TV seems more than coincidental. As a closely choreographed spectacle of heightened theatricality it depends for its political importance on the ability of the late twentieth-century's media to make very many people to think about the fate of just a few: and to bypass usual governmental mechanisms of quarantining difficult problems to gain the undivided attention of the powerful. As a close observer of Presidents Carter (during the 1979 hostage crisis) and Reagan (during the 1985 TWA hijacking), Gary Sick comments on their intrinsically harrowing nature: 'If it is true that decision making in foreign policy is by its nature nonbureaucratic, then decision making in a hostage situation is the antithesis of the bureaucratic ideal of impersonal rules unemotionally applied'.[88]

III

In summary, both in political killing and hostage-taking the long-term trend has clearly been towards an expansion of the universe of deliberately-inflicted suffering. Indeed, what is perhaps most remarkable historically about contemporary violence is its social reach. Prime targets today are no longer the captains and kings.

[86] Anonymous, The *Death of Dolfuss: An Official History of the Revolt of July, 1934, in Austria* (London, 1935), pp. 135, 140, 142.

[87] H. Galvao, *Santa Maria: My Crusade for Portugal* (Cleveland, 1961), p. 108.

[88] G. Sick, 'Taking Vows: The Domestication of Policy-Making in Hostage Incidents' in W. Reich, *Origins of Terrorism: Psychologies, Ideologies, Theologies, States of Mind* (Washington, 1990, 1998), p. 243.

Quite deliberately, they are now the 'little people': those (formerly) of no account. Of course, as shall be seen, powerful individuals still remain the targets of violence. But they are not now the only, or even the main, targets of political killing. This is a huge shift.

One of the key features of the modern political cosmos, then, is that the threat of assassination has democratized radically: and in doing so become impersonal. Like modern bureaucracy, it too operates 'without regard for persons'. Unlike bureaucracy, it does so arbitrarily and without warning. Individual victims are selected for their exchange value in gaining attention. In Robert Louis Stevenson's novel, *The Dynamiter* (1885), the chief bomb-maker expresses his interest in targeting the humble housemaid to gain the attention of multiple audiences: 'her position between classes, parents in one, employers in another; the probability that she will have at least one sweetheart, whose feelings we shall address: yes, I have a leaning—call it, if you will, a weakness—for the housemaid'.[89]

Every major city centre becomes a potential shooting gallery; and every metro system a potential bomb alley. Democratic universalism is the hallmark of contemporary terroristic threats. Everyone and anyone may find themselves in the blast wave. As the popular saying puts it—with its striking presumption of perpetual motion—victims are simply 'in the wrong place, at the wrong time'.

The next chapters focus on the technological changes that have helped facilitate this banalization of barbarization. As far back as 1974 Paul Wilkinson noted that 'a surprising lacuna in strategic studies of revolutionary terrorism is the absence of a full treatment of weapon availability and supply and of the implications of new weapon technology for terrorism'.[90] Surprisingly, over four decades later, that observation still retains some currency. And although the following sections of this book cannot provide a comprehensive historical account, they may at least help to chart the size of the deficit in our understanding of the processes by which impersonal violence has become both technically feasible and—ultimately—culturally expected. And here the technology of violence is clearly crucial since although technology does not determine society, it does embody it.[91] No account of modern political violence would be complete without paying some attention to the means of destruction.

[89] R. L. Stevenson and F. Van De Grift Stevenson, *The Dynamiter* (London, 1885, 1914), pp. 168–9.

[90] P. Wilkinson, *Political Terrorism* (London, 1974), p. 135.

[91] M. Castells, *The Information Age*, Vol. 1, The Rise of the Network Society (Chichester, 1996, 2010), p. 5, footnote 3.

5

The Means of Destruction

In this chapter I disaggregate political violence not by cause or group, but by basic technique. However impressionistically, I attempt to identify the key means that underpin violent repertoires: and attempt to trace their evolution in conjunction with some reference to other major social and technological changes. At heart, this is a structural approach that leans towards identifying emerging opportunities for violence. Yet, paradoxically, such a structuralist approach can also help to highlight the key roles of agency and contingency. Again and again, new and shocking trends in political violence turn out to be exploiting ideas that are not fundamentally new, although they may indeed be adapted or transformed in importantly novel ways. Likewise, violent techniques may be practised in a very limited way—and then very suddenly achieve widespread imitation. In short, contagion patterns here can be very dramatic.

Unsurprisingly, perhaps, I devote considerable attention to the advent of modern explosives. The sudden emergence of dynamite towards the end of the nineteenth century as *the* archetypal weapon of militant protest is well referenced: but tends to be treated as a self-evident development. I believe it merits deeper exploration.[1] Even more puzzling, indeed, the use of explosives has retained its radical élan for 150 years or so (and counting). I then turn to consider firearms: whose destructive potential has also clearly accelerated the potential opportunities for impersonal and anonymous violence. But I try at the same time to devote some space to more primitive technologies of destruction as well: the petrol bomb and the knife.

I

> A simple reference to statistics will show that the use of firearms for play is productive of incomparably more accidents than this substance [i.e. dynamite], which is a great and valuable agent for the development of our mineral wealth.
>
> – Alfred Nobel[2]

[1] D. Rapoport, 'The Four Waves of Rebel Terror and September 11' in C. W. Kegley (ed.), *The New Global Terrorism: Characteristics, Causes, Controls* (New Jersey, 2003), pp.36–7; M. M. Carr, *The Infernal Machine* (New York, 2006), pp. 50–1. On the role of technology in society: J. Ellis, *The Social History of the Machine Gun* (London, 1975, 1987), p. 9. For an excellent new study that finally goes a long way towards filling this gap: A. K. Cronin, *Power to the People: How Open Technological Innovation is Arming Tomorrow's Terrorists* (Oxford, 2020), pp. 13, 61–125.

[2] E. Bergengren, *Alfred Nobel* (London, 1962), p. 173.

> 'Let's go to bed,' said Sam. He was jollier than he had been in weeks.
>
> We smoked half a joint and made love. Was it our first sex since I slept with Pat? Certainly it was the most tender and passionate in a long time. Sam had been invigorated by his success. He kissed me good-night and dropped off to sleep. I closed my eyes, but too many thoughts were speeding through my brain. As dawn came through the window, I saw the outlines of buildings along the East River beginning to become clear beyond the gutted tenements and smoke-stacks. Our refrigerator was full of dynamite, neat as the tubular chimes of an orchestra, waiting to be struck. How had I gotten here? What was the point after which I couldn't turn back? I would have given a great deal to know.
>
> – Jane Alpert[3]

In any general historical account of modern political violence, it is almost impossible to overstate the transformative importance wrought by explosives.[4] If explosions are defined broadly—that is, to include bombs, car-bombs, and firebombs—they comprise over half (55.1 per cent) of the incidents recorded in the TWEED database of terrorist incidents that occurred across Western Europe between 1950 and 1995.[5] Estimates for terrorist attacks in the United States between 1970 and 2011 yield very similar results (52.09 per cent).[6] Other global studies have found broadly comparable results: according to the US State Department's estimate for 1990, bombings had accounted for 63 per cent 'of all international terrorist incidents' in that year.[7] Bombs are by far the most important weapon in terrorist violence, concludes Adam Dolnik in summary.[8] Such an extraordinary degree of tactical dominance demands far more consideration than it tends to receive. Where does it come from historically?

Longer genealogies are here frustratingly hard to trace. Although vulnerable to damp, the spectacularly destructive potential of gunpowder was fully evident by the sixteenth century.[9] Its power entirely transformed the entire science of fortification.[10] An accidental explosion at Dublin in 1597 levelled much of the harbour area, killing perhaps 126 people.[11] Even more impressively, the invention of gunlocks allowed the development of what would now be called 'Improvised Explosive Devices', or IEDs. Sixteeenth-century IEDs already utilized sophisticated

[3] J. Alpert, *Growing Up Underground* (New York, 1981), p. 193.

[4] Cronin, *Power to the People*, pp. 61–125.

[5] J. O. Engene, *Terrorism in Western Europe: Explaining the Trends Since 1950* (Cheltenham, 2004), p. 60. However, there were missing data for 21.1% of incidents.

[6] M. Becker, 'Explaining Lone Wolf Target Selection in the United States', *Studies in Conflict and Terrorism*, 37 (11), 2014, p. 970.

[7] K. G. Moore, *Airport, Aircraft and Airline Security* (Boston, 1991), p. 177.

[8] A. Dolnik, *Understanding Terrorist Innovation* (Abingdon, 2007), p. 41. See also: B. Hoffman, 'Low Tech Terrorism', *The National Interest*, 130, March/April 2014, p. 66.

[9] I. Jones, *Malice Aforethought: A History of Booby Traps from World War One to Vietnam* (Barnsley, 2004, 2016), p. 17.

[10] G. Parker, *The Military Revolution: Military Innovation and the Rise of the West, 1500–1800* (Cambridge, 1988), pp. 9–16.

[11] C. Lennon, 'Dublin's Great Explosion of 1597', *History Ireland*, 3 (3) Autumn 1995.

clockwork timing devices. They could also be truly massive when combined with naval technology. In 1585, the floating 'Hellburners of Antwerp' blew up a pontoon bridge, killing possibly 1,000 Spanish soldiers who were besieging the city.[12] In April 1588, Dutch rebels also used similar technology against the Spanish forces. Such tactics have, indeed, recurred periodically ever since. Hence Al-Qaeda's attack on the USS Cole in October 2000 stands in a very long tradition.[13]

And yet such gunpowder-based IEDs appear to have remained, predominantly, a feature of naval warfare. A gunpowder explosion did accompany the assassination of the Earl of Darnley (by strangulation) outside Edinburgh, in February 1567.[14] It totally demolished the substantial building at Kirk O'Field, and presumably woke up much of the town ('the blast was fearfull to all about and many rose from their beds at the noise').[15] An attempt to blow up the Prince of Orange in 1584 similarly failed.[16] Rather more famously, the Gunpowder Plot of 1605 planned a radical decapitation of the entire English political elite along with its new Scottish king at the state opening of parliament.[17] Two salient features stand out from a close comparison of these plots. First, they both depended on elaborate and time-consuming preparations. Huge quantities of gunpowder had to be concealed in cellars in all three cases. Secondly, gunpowder was still unreliable. The 1567 detonation was botched, and apparently did not explode in time: hence the need to strangle Darnley.[18] The 1605 plot depended on the recruitment of Guy Fawkes as the explosives expert: the other conspirators were, presumably, not confident of handling gunpowder without him.[19] Such novelty of means may help explain why it is his name that has remained so stubbornly attached to the plot's conception.

These—admittedly basic—observations may go some way towards explaining why such conspiracies were not more common in early modern Europe. What is harder to explain is why they then remained absent for so long. Such an ambitious use of explosives seems to return only in the early nineteenth century. Here the assassination attempt against Napoleon Bonaparte (on Christmas Eve, 1800), and the Cato Street Conspiracy (of 1820) are the obvious exemplars.[20] This 200-year 'gap' thus overlaps with 'The Early Modern Interlude' that the historian Franklin

[12] J. Revill, *Improvised Explosive Devices* (London, 2016), pp. 5–6.

[13] R. Davies, 'April 6, 1588—A Dutch ship-borne IED' (1 September, 2014); 'USS Intrepid—Another ship-borne massive IED' (26 May 2014); 'Operation Lucid—to singe Mr Hitler's Moustache' (6 May, 2013); 'Big IEDs in Ships' (2 October, 2012); 'US made "Trojan Horse" IED used against the British in 1813' (20 June, 2012). Available at: http://www.standingwellback.com

[14] A. Fraser, *Mary Queen of Scots* (London, 1970, 1978), pp. 339–65.

[15] Fraser, *Mary Queen of Scots*, pp. 362–3.

[16] Revill, *Improvised Explosive Devices*, p. 5.

[17] F. L. Ford, *Political Murder: From Tyrannicide to Terrorism* (Harvard, 1985), p. 164–5.

[18] Fraser, *Mary Queen of Scots*, p. 363.

[19] M. Nicholls, 'Strategy and Motivation in the Gunpowder Plot', *The Historical Journal*, 50 (4) 2007, pp. 789–90; Revill, *Improvised Explosive Devices*, pp. 4–5. As Revill notes here, later attempts to assassinate Oliver Cromwell by similar means also proved failures.

[20] J. North, *Killing Napoleon: The Plot to Blow Up Bonaparte* (Stroud, 2019), p. 18; E. Royle, *Revolutionary Britannia? Reflections on the Threat of Revolution in Britain, 1789–1848* (Manchester, 2000), pp. 54–5.

Ford has identified: a pronounced slump in both the rate and volume of European assassinations that lasted from *c.* 1650 to *c.* 1790.[21]

Walter Laqueur has suggested that it was the successful advances in the miniaturization of explosives towards the end of the nineteenth century that constitutes *the* key technological development in modern political violence.[22] This is a helpful insight. But it still does not in itself explain why this development had not occurred earlier than it in fact did: or, to put the problem more precisely, to explain why use of miniaturized explosives had not become more commonplace earlier. Some miniaturization of explosives had been technically possible since the sixteenth century. Samuel Zimmerman of Augsburg depicts a shrapnel-laden device—more precisely, a booby-trapped purse left lying in the street—in his manual of 1573: as does another handbook from 1630. Nor was such knowledge purely theoretical. In 1581 a hand-delivered exploding chest was used at the siege of Psków to target the leadership of the defence.[23]

Why such attacks were not more common, or at least more recorded, must remain a tantalizingly open question. Insofar as one can hazard an explanation of an absence, it may simply be that specialist expertise in handling explosives long remained confined to military circles. In other words, the key retarding factors may well have been as much social as technological. Artillery schools in the sixteenth and seventeenth centuries were a speciality of European war-making—the Chinese and Indian theatres lacked equivalent institutions—and their dominance may have discouraged more freelance experiments.[24] 'Closed military technological innovation' is typically slow to diffuse.[25]

That said, Laqueur is surely correct to emphasize mid-nineteenth century improvements in precision engineering as a truly decisive development. Such advances facilitated the manufacture of the so-called Orsini bombs, designed by an Austro-Hungarian military engineer but manufactured in Birmingham. These caused dramatic scenes of carnage when used in an assassination attempt against Napoleon III in 1858.[26] Again, though, Orsini bombs remained highly clandestine products: albeit ones circulating swiftly in a highly permissive international environment.

Global markets finally and decisively introduced high explosive into the repertoire of militant politics in 1867. It has remained firmly there ever since. In other words, it was the *commercial* patenting of 'Guhr dynamite' by Alfred Nobel that marked the really key moment for the technological transformation of political violence.[27] The bombing tradition is thus a step-child of the late nineteenth-century's

[21] Ford, *Political Murder*, p. 180.

[22] W. Laqueur, *Terrorism* (London, 1977, 1980), p. 117.

[23] Jones, *Malice Aforethought*, pp. 11–12.

[24] F. Braudel, *Civilization and Capitalism: 15th to 18th Centuries*, Vol. 1, *The Structures of Everyday Life: The Limits of the Possible* (London, 1983), p. 396.

[25] Cronin, *Power to the People*, p. 12.

[26] *The Times*, 16 January 1858.

[27] Bergengren, *Alfred Nobel*, p. 68; Cronin, *Power to the People*, p. 99.

business world, not its wars. Nobel himself was appalled at the early adoption of dynamite by Prussian sappers against French fortifications in 1870.[28]

In summary, explosives did not leak into civilian life from the military sphere: rather they were triumphantly made ubiquitous via the world of civil engineering. Such a dramatic advance in the technology of destruction was widely celebrated across all levels of society, high and low. Looking back on her Scottish adolescence of the early 1880s, Margot Asquith recalled a storm that 'had destroyed half a wood on a hill in front of the library-windows and we wanted to see the roots of the trees blown up by dynamite'.[29] Dynamite constituted a breakthrough technology—quite literally so. Without it, the Central Pacific Railroad could not have been driven across the Sierra Nevada, nor the St Gotthard line in Switzerland put '9.3 miles through granite'.[30] And now the relentless dynamism of late nineteenth-century capitalism spread its fame, and its commercial availability, far and wide. Before long, indeed, this wonder stuff that moved mountains had become 'common as soap and cheap as sugar'.[31]

Criminal uses of dynamite pre-dated its adoption as a political weapon. Alfred Nobel would soon come to regret that his explosives 'have sunk to the infamous instruments of murder'.[32] But such a development was surely inevitable. In 1875, a premature dynamite explosion on the quayside at Bremerhaven in Germany killed 80 people. Strange to tell, this catastrophe had averted an even worse alternative. A conman had planned an 'insurance job' with a dynamite time-bomb that would remove his unwanted wife in the mid-Atlantic, neatly and with no trace.[33] An entire ship's complement of passengers and crew were to be the collateral damage of this act of domestic rearrangement. In an eerie presaging of the mid-twentieth-century wave of aircraft destructions, here was an early advertisement of the catastrophic potential of new technology to amplify the consequences of individual human depravity.

Right from the outset, then, it was clear that dynamite potentially lent itself to spectacular mass murder (and this was indeed to become one of its political uses: albeit a minority one). Similarly, it seemed to some enthusiasts that dynamite might lend itself to spectacular physical destruction: 'this dynamite war will go on til Ireland is free, or til London is laid in ashes', *Ireland's Liberation* had declared portentously in 1883.[34] In practice, damage turned out to be far less sweeping than this.[35] In the hands of trained professionals, dynamite could indeed move mountains. But when

[28] Bergengren, *Alfred Nobel*, p. 65.

[29] M. Asquith, *The Autobiography of Margot Asquith*, Vol. I (London, 1920, 1936), p. 37.

[30] Bergengren, *Alfred Nobel*, pp. 31, 68.

[31] N. Whelehan, '"Cheap as Soap and Common as Sugar": The Fenians, Dynamite and Scientific Warfare' in F. McGarry and J. McConnel (eds), *The Black Hand of Republicanism* (Dublin, 2009), p. 106.

[32] Bergengren, *Alfred Nobel*, p. 174.

[33] Whelehan, '"Cheap as Soap and Common as Sugar"', p. 110; A. Larabee, *The Dynamite Fiend* (Halifax, 2005).

[34] K.R.M. Short, *The Dynamite War* (Dublin, 1979), pp. 227–8.

[35] Whelehan, '"Cheap as Soap and Common as Sugar"', p. 119.

adopted by political militants, the levelling of cities proved impossibly ambitious: especially if explosions had to be calibrated to minimize civilian casualties.

Yet its use as a weapon endured. Indeed, dynamite spread: and spread quickly across, and between, political movements that had otherwise quite different agendas and ideological sympathies. Before 1900 numerous anarchists, the Russian *Narodnya Volna*, the Irish American *Clan na Gael*, and Armenian *Dashnaks* (amongst others) had all become enthusiastic dynamitards.[36] A brand new repertoire of action was emerging: one that would serve very different causes, but which was always firmly associated with radical protest. Even shocking acts soon develop their own codes. Use of explosives quickly became an unambiguous way in which militant social movements could clearly signal a desire for escalation. Because the effects of explosions will typically be sudden and dramatic—and to a degree, unpredictable—their use communicates resolve. As Emmeline Pankhurst was asked in 1909: 'if stone throwing failed, would she resort to bombs?'[37] It is a question still asked nervously of militants today.[38]

In summary, what I call 'the terroristic bombing campaign' has been a lasting nineteenth-century contribution to contemporary world civilization. A template pioneered by Irish-American bombers across British cities in 1881–5 has since spread around the globe.[39] With hindsight, initial beginnings seem rather modest. London saw around thirteen bomb attacks between 1881 and 1885.[40] Paris saw just eleven dynamite explosions between March 1892 and June 1894.[41] But the key point here is a simple one. In 1880 such campaigns were totally unknown. By 1980, they were (almost) everywhere. Like the traffic jam and air pollution, such bombings have come to represent an ineluctable hazard of modern urban living.

Such bombing campaigns are also complex social phenomena in their own right: and a reflection of a complex wider society. They are terroristic in the broad sense that the destruction they cause is intended to have some kind of percussive effect throughout society. It is violence designed to resonate disturbingly. Bombings shock; that, in large part, is their point. But the perceived need for sustained repetition suggests bombers sensibly assume that popular attention spans are short. A general sense of fear may easily evaporate, and so on. Such awareness is the hallmark of a society in which information and entertainment are plentiful. In such societies, attention becomes the scarce political resource to be cultivated. In effect, the bombing campaign coexists with, and must compete with, all other types of mass advertising and entertainment.[42] That is why it takes the form of a regular series of reminders of the constant possibility of public atrocity. Such a complex

[36] Laqueur, *Terrorism*, pp. 23–24; *New York Times*, 31 August 1896.

[37] A. Raeburn, *The Militant Suffragettes* (London, 1973), p. 114.

[38] See concerns of the German security services that far-rightists were plotting 'improvised explosives attacks' in the wake of the Chemnitz disturbances: *The Times*, 29 April 2019.

[39] Context hopefully clarifies here that I am not discussing aerial bombings. Although they, too, can be seen as a Western contribution to world civilization.

[40] My own estimate. See: Short, *The Dynamite War*, pp. 259–60; O. McGee, 'The Irish Republican Brotherhood' in J. Crowley (et al., eds), *Atlas of the Irish Revolution* (Cork, 2017), p. 131.

[41] D. Caute, *The Left in Europe since 1789* (London, 1966), p. 104.

[42] E. Gellner, *Nations and Nationalism* (Oxford, 1983, 1993), p. 25.

backdrop helps explain how the terroristic bombing campaign comes to take its distinctive modern form: a repetitious sequence of explosions staged 'from below' to achieve wider political effect.

Right from the outset, bombing campaigns tended to bifurcate into two broad types. Confronted by Fenian bombings, the British authorities concluded that this novel phenomenon was intended 'to murder and to blow up public buildings'.[43] In practice, though, these tended to become two relatively distinct strategies. They might indeed appear to overlap, especially when the inevitable reckless 'accidents' occurred. But more often they tended to pull in different directions.

Blowing up public buildings is perhaps best viewed as epic vandalism of the cityscape. The late nineteenth century was an age of monumental urbanism: an era of metropolitan gigantism. It also saw the emergence of the civic 'make over'—those temporary, but determined, efforts to 'clean up' major cities for some set-piece occasion that would attract international attention. The 1889 Universal Exhibition in Paris furnishes an early example of this type of social cleansing 'to remove from the streets itinerant traders, bogus doormen, menders of broken crockery, beggars, vagabonds, and sundry others'.[44] Such determined civic efforts to present vistas of perfect order inevitably invited counter efforts at subversion. If capital cities were to be judged by their spectacular appearance, then this in turn presented new targets to vitiate. Such bombings followed the simple logic of synecdoche that a dawning age of global publicity imposed. An age of mass literacy and mass newspaper circulation was thus the first era in which a spectacular bombing of an iconic public building could be staged in the confident expectation that it would be universally understood as an assault on a wider regime or society.[45] Despite its novelty, such symbolic logic was apparently so intuitively obvious that it attracted strikingly little overt comment.

By contrast, bombings to cause public carnage defied any easy interpretations. They were also a highly uneven phenomenon: and general ideological categorizations only dimly illuminate divergent local patterns here. After an early wave of crowd bombings in 1878 in Italy, attempts at mass murder then disappeared from that country: but later became a prominent feature of anarchist violence in both Spain and France.[46] Anarchist sympathizers inevitably tended to blame such attempts at mass murder on agents provocateurs: the government's professional slaughterers and scare-mongerers. By definition, this is a murky area to investigate. Without arbitrating on specific controversies, it is important to note that the prospect of escalation into mass carnage was always latent even in the most restrained of campaigns that conspicuously aimed at 'targeting stone and stucco rather than flesh and bone'.[47]

[43] S. Kenna, *War in the Shadows: the Irish-American Fenians Who Bombed Victorian Britain* (Sallins, 2014), p. 117.

[44] M. Anderson, *In Thrall to Political Change: Police and Gendarmerie in France* (Oxford, 2011), p. 151.

[45] J. Vernon, *Distant Strangers: How Britain Became Modern* (Berkeley, 2014), p. 72.

[46] N. Pernicone and F. M. Ottanelli, *Assassins Against the Old Order: Italian Anarchist Violence in Fin de Siècle Europe* (Champaign Illinois, 2018), pp. 51–5, 106.

[47] Pernicone and Ottanelli, *Assassins Against the Old Order*, p. 56.

By the 1880s, such bombing campaigns had come to stay: a full three decades before the aerial bombing of civilian populations commenced. Such precocity invites reflection on the relationship of the political use of explosives to the wider history of modern warfare. In general, this relationship seems rather loose and tangential: perhaps unsurprisingly, since the terroristic bombing campaign first emerged in peacetime and from a civilian background. Its fluctuations were largely moulded by *non-military* factors up until 1914: 'a close analysis of nearly 1,300 bombing incidents throughout the world during this first wave of violence shows that the number of attacks was directly related to a key set of economic and legal factors: fluctuations in the price of dynamite, regulations on transporting nitroglycerine products by rail, local trust activities, and whether or not there were strict factory export controls.'[48]

Still, the question repays some closer examination. One effect of the Great War was to revive a 'cult of the bomb' as one of the more unexpected spin-offs of the drift into trench warfare from late 1914.[49] Prior to the war grenades had been practically obsolete in European armies. But the raiding party tactics that emerged out of the relatively static confrontations of the Western Front and Gallipoli soon changed all that:

> In total, the belligerent nations developed roughly 100 models of grenade in the course of the war. As a weapon, it was one of the war's most interesting retro-innovations, its name inspired in the 15th century by the pomegranate and its cluster of seeds. Like the helmet, it had fallen into disuse prior to the conflict, and in 1914 was a marginal weapon; by 1918, it was ubiquitous.[50]

The British Expeditionary Force in France in 1914 had only a few hundred such bombs available at first. By 1918 it had 7.2 million.[51] Such was the demand for small bombs that could be thrown at short range that, if necessary, armies improvised: churning out thousands of home-made 'jam-tin bombs'.[52] In effect, trench warfare mass produced mass cadres of amateur bomb-makers.

What seems striking here is the limited transfer of such technology and tactics into post-war political violence.[53] In an obscure incident, a homemade shrapnel bomb thrown into a New Year's Eve concert at Dunkelsbuehl, Bavaria injured fifty.[54] Matthias Erzberger survived a hand grenade attempt on his life at an election meeting in May 1920.[55] More professionally, grenades were used in the clinical

[48] Cronin, *Power to the People*, p. 116.

[49] S. Bull, *Trench Warfare* (London, 2003), p. 75. See also: R. G. L. Waite, *Vanguard of Nazism: The Free Corps Movement in Postwar Germany, 1918–1923* (New York, 1952, 1969), pp. 23–4.

[50] F. Guelton, 'Technology and Armaments' in J. Winter (ed.), *The Cambridge History of the First World War*, Vol. II, *The State* (Cambridge, 2014), p. 253.

[51] Bull, *Trench Warfare*, p. 75.

[52] B. Gammage, *An Australian in the Great War* (Cambridge, 1976), p. 18; Bull, *Trench Warfare*, p. 64.

[53] For exceptions: IRA bomb factory; *Kattowitzer Zeitung*, 17 December 1920 [Polish chemist's hand grenade factory].

[54] *Sheffield Daily Telegraph*, 3 January 1922.

[55] M. Sabrow, *Der Rathenaumord: Rekonstruktion einer Verschwörung gegen die Republik von Weimar* (Oldenbourg, 1994), pp. 7–8.

assassination of the German Foreign Minister Walther Rathenau in June 1922.[56] More sporadically, the Nazi SA also used them: most notably, in the summer of 1932.[57] Grenades also added an escalatory dynamic to Belfast's sectarian confrontations. Some of the most locally notorious incidents of the 1922 Troubles included the throwing of grenades. Crowds, including playing children, were deliberately targeted, as well as homes.[58]

Yet such incidents seem to have remained relatively rare. Much more common in ethnically divided societies was the use of minor explosions—either from grenades or dynamite—to project mere menace or hostility. Such behaviour occurred repeatedly in Upper Silesia until the mid-1920s. Often a clear political 'message' is hard to discern.[59] Social or even sexual tensions often seem more plausible: at Rossberg in May 1921, for instance, Polish insurgents threw hand grenades at the houses of young women who wouldn't entertain them.[60] However unpleasantly intimidating, this seems a long way from any serious intention to cause mass carnage.[61] Compared to, say, later use of grenades against cafes in Algiers (in the later 1950s) or crowded airport concourses during the 1970s, such restraint seems rather striking.[62] Advice for German Communists in 1931 suggested a rich promiscuity of weapons and tactics. 'Knives, brass knuckles, oil-soaked rags, axes, bricks, boiling water to pour on the police-beasts raging in the streets of the workers' quarters, simple hand-grenades made of dynamite' were all advocated: in effect, everything and anything.[63] In general, though, it seems that weapons specifically developed for the battlefield were largely left there after 1918.

This point seems to hold true more generally, if the focus is shifted to more ambitious use of larger explosives. All armies in the First World War developed specialist expertise in handling IEDs 'the devil's eggs' as Ernst Jünger called them.[64]

[56] M. Sabrow, *Der Rathenaumord: Rekonstruktion einer Verschwörung gegen die Republik von Weimar* (Oldenbourg, 1994), pp. 86–7.

[57] R. Bessel, *Political Violence and the Rise of Nazism: The Stormtroopers in Eastern Germany 1925–1934* (Yale, 1984), pp. 89–91; *Yorkshire Post and Leeds Intelligencer*, 9 August 1932.

[58] G. B. Kenna, *Facts and Figures: Belfast Pogrom, 1920–1922* (Dublin, 1922), pp. 69 [Weaver Street: six children killed], 75 [13 March 1922 bombing of crowd: 12 injured]; P. J. Gannon, 'In the Catacombs of Belfast', *Studies: An Irish Quarterly Review of Letters, Philosophy and Science*, XI, 1922, p. 284; T. Wilson, '"The Most Terrible Assassination that Has Yet Stained the Name of Belfast": The McMahon Murders in Context', *Irish Historical Studies*, XXXVII (145) May 2010, p. 92 [bombing of house in Thompson Street].

[59] T. K. Wilson, *Frontiers of Violence: Conflict and Identity in Ulster and Upper Silesia, 1918–1922* (Oxford, 2010), pp. 189, 192; *Kattowitzer Zeitung*, 21 June 1922.

[60] *Oberschlesische Wanderer*, 27 May 1921.

[61] *Kattowitzer Zeitung*, 17 December 1920 [Polish chemist's handgrenade factory]; 29 December 1920 [grenades/dynamite being thrown around for New Year]; P. Chmiel, 'Zur Nationalitätenfrage in Ostoberschlesien im Spiegel der "Kattowitzer Zeitung" under des "Oberschlesischen Kuriers"', *Oberschlesisches Jahrbuch*, 2, 1986, pp. 62, 65–6, 75, 76–8 [1925 bomb attacks against German businesses and the *Kattowitzer Zeitung* newspaper].

[62] For a sample of the frequency of such grenade attacks on cafes in Algeria, see: *L'Écho d'Alger*, 1, 2, 3, 26 January, 19 February, 2, 5, 8, 9, 10–11 March 1957. For the fear they evoked: F. Dessaigne, *Journal d'une mère de famille pied-noir* (Paris, 1962), p. 46.

[63] E. Rosenhaft, *Beating the Fascists? The German Communists and Political Violence, 1929–1933* (Cambridge, 1983), p. 40.

[64] E. Jünger, *Storm of Steel* (London, 1920, 2004), p. 128; Jones, *Malice Aforethought*, pp. 36–78.

In the spring of 1917, the Germans in France fell back 20 miles along a 60-mile front to the pre-prepared Hindenburg line. The territory they abandoned was meticulously booby-trapped and mined, so the advancing British troops had to turn to their own mining engineers for expertise in the 'black art' of Explosive Ordnance Disposal (EOD). As a result, British soldiers came 'to think that all Tunnellers were anarchists, experts in bombs and delay-action mines'.[65] Such a lingering popular correlation between explosives and anarchists seems striking in the midst of much larger horrors.

Once again, though, the practical correlation between this mass experience of encountering explosives in a context of industrialized warfare, and the actual post-war tactics of political militants, seem rather faint. The Great War left huge quantities of explosives behind. During the Cagoulard scare of 1937, police searches for hidden arms proliferated across Paris. Grenades and bombs then turned up in litter bins as veterans scrambled to dump 'souvenirs' of the war.[66] Yet unlike Palestine during the troubled 1936–9 period, all this knowledge and hardware was not much recycled.[67] An expert booby-trap bomb that killed fifteen French soldiers in Upper Silesia on 9 April 1922 was very much the exception here.[68] More typical, perhaps, was the botched attempt by Nazi stormtroopers to assassinate a left-wing newspaper editor in Reichenbach by recycling an old artillery shell as an IED: the device exploded prematurely.[69]

An idea of scale of damage that could potentially have been effected much more widely is demonstrated by the strange case of the twin railway bombings that occurred in the late summer of 1931. Their (apparently sole) author was Sylvestre Matuschka who had served as a demolitions expert in the Austro-Hungarian army during the Great War. On 9 August, the international express from Basle was derailed 40 miles from Berlin: eighteen passengers were injured in all.[70] On 12 September an express train was blown off an 80-foot high viaduct near Budapest.[71] Early reports interpreted these bombings as Communist atrocities, on the basis of political placards that had supposedly been found near the scenes. Later reports emphasized very different—although, strictly speaking, not incompatible—motivations. Matuschka was said to be a sexual pervert who orgasmed at the sight of catastrophe.[72] Less gratifying was the experience for his mangled victims: ten were seriously injured in the first bombing; twenty-five were killed in the second.[73]

65 Jones, *Malice Aforethought*, p. 59.

66 *Hull Daily Mail*, 24 September 1937 [bombs found in gutter]; *Northern Whig*, 23 November 1937; *Yorkshire Evening Post*, 24 November 1937 [four bombs found in dustbins near Palais Royal]; 29 November 1937—doc 38.

67 T. K. Wilson, 'Turbulent Stasis: Comparative Reflections upon Intercommunal Violence and Territoriality in the Israel/Palestine Conflict', *Nationalism and Ethnic Politics*, 19 (1) 2013, pp. 60–61.

68 GSA, Rep 171/144/Band 4, p. 158.

69 Laqueur, *Terrorism*, p. 133.

70 *The Times*, 10, 12, 13 August, 1931.

71 *The Times*, 15, 16 September 1931; *Larne Times*, 19 September 1931. See also: 'Sylvestre Matuschka', http://Muderpedia.org

72 E. Leyton, *Hunting Humans* (London, 2001), p. 265.

73 *The Times*, 10 August, 1931; *Larne Times*, 19 September 1931.

Generally, though, time bombs were not a prominent feature of European radical politics in the interwar period: at least not to cause deliberate mass carnage. Here the Galleanists blazed the way in the USA, with a distinctly variant approach to the low level sabotage bombings of the radical labour movement. Rather they represented a more professional renewal of pre-war European anarchist traditions of demonstrative slaughter which shall be discussed shortly. The only group that came close to achieving similarly spectacular results were the Irgun in Palestine between 1937 and 1939.[74]

Since the Second World War was a war of movement, it was a war in which IEDs, time-bombs and mines were used on a truly industrial scale in an attempt to slow down enemy advances By 1944, indeed, factories in the German Reich were producing seven million detonators (or 'switches') a month.[75] Yet, again, this left little direct legacy for violent political campaigns after the war. Around the periphery of Europe it was a different story: terroristic bombing campaigns geared to generating mass civilian carnage erupted in Palestine (1947–8) Algeria (1956–7), and Lebanon (1958).[76] In the first two of these conflicts at least, there seems to have been a rather direct knowledge transfer from veterans of the Second World War.[77] By contrast, as shall be seen, European nationalists remained largely fixated to a highly limited use of explosives (to facilitate sabotage) for a full two decades after 1945.

American bombing traditions seem to have been little influenced by the country's participation in the Second World War. Instead, they followed their own traditions: albeit with some adaption, as necessary. In the South, white racism was deeply resilient: but the confidence of its most militant elements, less so. No organized mass movement committed to violence in defence of southern apartheid ever arose. 'Massive Resistance' turned out to have little appetite for self-sacrifice.[78] But a plethora of militant groups did emerge, often taking the classic cellular form of 'six to eight members'.[79] A defining feature of white supremacist violence in the era of Civil Rights thus became its heavy reliance on the use of explosives for hit-and-run attacks: a pattern that emerged as early as 1951. Reconstruction terror of the 1870s had not used dynamite bombings much (if at all): 'its favourite [weapon]

[74] Wilson, 'Turbulent Stasis', pp. 67–8; B. Hoffman, *Anonymous Soldiers: The Struggle for Israel, 1917–1947* (New York, 2015), pp. 76, 80–5.

[75] Jones, *Malice Aforethought*, p. 83.

[76] For Algeria: J. Massu, *La vraie battaile d'Alger* (Paris, 1971), pp. 35, 38–40, 202; A. Horne, *A Savage War of Peace* (New York, 1977, 2006), pp. 185, 192, 209, 317, 352; M. Hutchinson, *Revolutionary Terrorism: The FLN in Algeria, 1954–1962* (Stanford, 1978), pp. 14, 69–70, 89–90; M. Evans, *Algeria: France's Undeclared War* (Oxford, 2012, 2013), pp. 182, 203, 206–7, 218–19. For Lebanon: *Le Jour*, 23 May [bicycle bomb in souk]; 24 May [café bombed]; 27 May [tram bombed]; 6 June [sporadic explosions]; 10 June [shops bombed]; 22 June 1958 [three explosions].

[77] For Palestine: Y. Bauer, 'From Cooperation to Resistance: The Haganah 1938–1946' *Middle Eastern Studies*, 2 (3) 1966, p. 193; J. Bowyer Bell, *Terror out of Zion: Irgun Zvai Leumi, LEHI, and the Palestine Underground, 1929–1949* (New York, 1977), pp. 53–5, 178, 180; Hoffman, *Anonymous Soldiers*, p. 319; Jones, *Malice Aforethought*, pp. 220–3; L. Collins and D. Lapierre, *O Jerusalem!* (London, 1982), pp. 159–61.

[78] S. J. Whitfield, *A Death in the Delta: The Story of Emmet Till* (New York, 1988), p. 103. For an overview: C. Hewitt, *Understanding Terrorism in America: From the Klan to Al Qaeda* (London, 2003), pp. 25–29.

[79] Bull Connor, quoted in: M. F. Greene, *The Temple Bombing* (London, 1996), p. 227.

was the bullwhip'.[80] Now such bombings became *the* signature tactic of extremist resistance to change.

Their earliest epicentre was Florida (where local 'Klansmen had two specialities: anti-Semitism and dynamite').[81] Dynamite was readily available here (from the offshore drilling industry).[82] A campaign of eighteen bombings set the basic pattern for the future here: a handful of targeted assassinations against 'uppity' activist members of the black community, against a more general assault of intimidation bombings—usually at night—against black homes and churches, Catholic churches, and Jewish synagogues.[83] Such campaigns caused significant damage—the bombing of the Carver Village Housing Project for Negroes in Miami, a sixteen-unit apartment block, shattered windows to a distance of fifty blocks and used 200 pounds of dynamite.[84] Between 1 January 1956 and 1 June 1963, 138 dynamite bombings were broadly attributed to the Klan across the south: generally to small 'inner groups' so that official involvement could be denied.

Such attacks generally stopped short of mass carnage: but there were exceptions. Notoriously, the bombing of the 16th Street Baptist Church in Birmingham on 15 September 1963 that killed four children seemed to herald just such an escalation. 'We knew the rules had changed' writes Carolyn Maull McKinstry of this, and the subsequent bombings: 'Birmingham residents had once believed Klan bombs were meant only to intimidate people, not kill people. The shrapnel bomb changed all that'.[85] Overall, though, warnings also remained common: while explosions were often timed for the middle of the night, and showed some degree of discrimination (usually against key local leaders and activists).[86] The targeted themselves recognized that some attacks did not seem to have been calculated to kill or maim.[87] As a practical judgement—and not a moral defence—the white supremacist bombers were relatively restrained technicians of terror: promising, but never quite delivering on, an all-out racial war.[88]

In this, they were of their time: and—broadly—in step with wider trends. In the second half of the twentieth century in Europe (1950–95), only 10 per cent of bombs killed *anyone* at all.[89] And in the USA of the early 1970s, less than 1 per cent of bombings did so.[90] Even allowing for incompetence, these seem strikingly

[80] R. Zuczek (ed.), *Encylopedia of the Reconstruction Era*, Vol. II (London, 2006), p. 689.

[81] W. Craig Wade, *The Fiery Cross: The Ku Klux Klan in America* (London, 1987), pp. 294–5.

[82] In fairness, Wade does also add: 'There were also many veterans in the State who had been trained in demolition stints in the navy and marines'. See: Craig Wade, *The Fiery Cross*, pp. 294–5.

[83] Craig Wade, *The Fiery Cross*, pp. 294–5. Also: S. Kennedy, *I rode with the Ku Klux Klan* (London, 1954), pp. 219, 230–1.

[84] Kennedy, *I rode with the Ku Klux Klan*, pp. 219.

[85] C. M. McKinstry, *While the World Watched* (Carol Stream, IL, 2011), p. 171; Greene, *The Temple Bombing*, pp. 268–9.

[86] For night time bombings: Greene, *The Temple Bombing*, pp. 1–2.

[87] McKinstry, *While the World Watched* p. 234.

[88] J. George and L. Wilcos, *American Extremists: Militias, Supremacists, Klansmen, Communists, and Others* (New York, 1996), pp. 362–6; McKinstry, *While the World Watched*, pp. 57, 171.

[89] Engene, *Terrorism in Western Europe*, p. 66.

[90] B. Burrough, *Days of Rage: America's Political Underground, the FBI, and the Forgotten Age of Revolutionary Violence* (New York, 2015, 2016), p. 5.

low proportions: they suggest that in many of these cases significant physical destruction or loss of life had never been the primary aim. Indeed, we can be reasonably confident, primarily from contextual clues such (as timings), but also through the explicit confirmations of the New Left memorialists, that bombers often punch 'below their weight' quite deliberately. The rise of the ritualistic warning by telephone further confirms this impression of restraint. In June 1940, for instance, officials at the New York World's Fair had received several bomb threats—and on 4 July a bomb that had been left at the British pavilion did duly explode, killing two bomb disposal officers.[91] By the mid-twentieth century such anonymous warnings seem to have become standard: and, indeed, half-expected.[92] Such an obvious degree of restraint may be intended to signal that the bombers are 'reasonable' political actors: although it is also worth noting they are highly unlikely to be politically rewarded for this in the short term.[93] Or restraint may on occasion have been chosen to leave headroom for subsequent escalation. A night time explosion at St Patrick's Cathedral in New York in October 1962 was considered newsworthy simply for not having been preceded by any bomb threat.[94] Historically, then, 'bombing lite' or 'responsible terrorism' strategies have probably been the norm.[95]

Yet it is important not to downplay the sub-theme of mass casualty bombing. Such events, though rarer, naturally tend to cause higher social impact. How did they evolve? What, if any, are the longer-term patterns here? It is worth drawing a conceptual distinction here between different types of mass casualty bombing. Those whose primary aim is to project a sense of mass terror may be usefully delineated from—to adapt a phrase from Albert Camus—those of 'unfastidious' assassins: that is, killers who were prepared to slaughter many just to be sure of getting their victim.[96] Both may cause wanton carnage: but their basic logic is divergent. Here I deal with the first type.

A word of methodological caution also needs to be entered early on. Reading back intentions from the vagaries of outcomes is dangerous. Since the blast effects of amateur bombs in complex social settings are notoriously difficult to predict, consequences often lie very far from what was intended. Despite the notoriety of his bomb attack at the Café Terminus (on 12 February 1894), the French anarchist Emile Henry was disappointed to have killed only one customer: he had hoped for fifteen dead.[97] Conversely, the bombing of the *Los Angeles Times* on 1 October 1910 was meant to administer a mere warning against the paper's reporting of ongoing

[91] B. Whalen and J. Whalen, *The NYPD's First Fifty Years* (Lincoln, NE, 2014), pp. 202–3.

[92] For examples of bombs preceded by telephone warnings: *Liverpool Echo*, 27 January 1959 ['Found by Girl After Anonymous Phone Call'];

[93] J. H. Fowler, *Bombs and Their Reverberations* (London, 1939), p. 9; BBC News, 26 July 2005 ('IRA are not al-Qaeda says Blair').

[94] *Liverpool Echo*, 6 October 1962.

[95] M. Rudd, *Underground: My Life with SDS and the Weathermen* (New York, 2009, 2010), p. 215; Burrough, *Days of Rage*, p. 122.

[96] A. Camus (transl. A. Bower), *The Fastidious Assassins* (London, 1949, 2008), pp. 60–1.

[97] B. Tuchman, *The Proud Tower: A Portrait of the World Before the War, 1890–1914* (London, 1966, 1997), p. 93; J. Merriman, *The Dynamite Club: How a Bombing in Fin-de-Siècle Paris Ignited the Age of Modern Terror* (London, 2009), pp. 1–3, 153. See also: *The Times*, 17 February 1894.

disputes in the construction industry (which had themselves been accompanied by a long-running series of non-lethal dynamite attacks). Yet on this occasion perhaps as many as tweny-one died in the resulting inferno.[98]

Caveats aside, it is still possible to offer an impressionistic history of mass casualty bombing. Contextual clues, if taken together, can still be highly indicative here: 'it may be taken as a general rule that where any explosive device incorporates features which indicate that it is designed to project fragments over a large solid angle, then it is probably intended for anti-personnel use'.[99] A deliberate targeting of crowds; a preference for targeting enclosed 'crowd containers' (such as metro stations or concert halls); any absence of prior warning; devices packed with shrapnel—all these point (roughly) in the direction of a determination to cause indiscriminate carnage.[100] All of these points apply even more strongly when the attack is committed by a suicide bomber. Regardless of whether the resulting carnage does actually reach some arbitrary threshold of 'mass' victimhood—above five? ten? dead or injured—it still seems worth trying to trace a tradition of such attempts. The keynote is the intention to maximize physical harm.

Here it is clear that the dubious 'honour' of pioneering such mass casualty bombings belongs to elements within the wider European anarchist tradition of the late nineteenth century. It is true that Irish Republicans had already invented the terroristic bombing campaign. But as more sober observers at the time recognized, their bombs were largely timed to avoid mass slaughter. Writing to Queen Victoria on 29 February 1884, the Home Secretary Sir William Harcourt argued that 'the one mitigating feature in these horrors is that *at present* at least the aim of these villains appears rather to alarm by attacks on property than direct attacks on life, though of that too they are reckless enough'.[101]

Anarchist violence was more complex: and needs careful dissection. Its leading historian, Richard Bach Jensen, has argued that 'while the number of assassinated heads of state and government, and of monarchs of major countries was unprecedented, the anarchists outside of Spain, killed relatively few people'.[102] As a general observation this is fair enough—but it arguably risks downplaying within the wider universe of anarchist attacks a minority sub-set of attacks that were very much focused upon hurting and killing as many people as possible. Many were either total, or relative, failures. But such failures in turn further underline the general persistence of the trend.

[98] J. A. Clymer, *America's Culture of Terrorism* (Chapel Hill, NC, 2003), p. 171. B. Gage, *The Day Wall Street Exploded* (Oxford, 2009), pp. 90.

[99] H. J. Yallop, *Explosive Investigation* (Edinburgh, 1980), pp. 65–6.

[100] 'Rough' because bomb-making may still be approached with jaw-dropping casualness and lack of thought about likely consequences. See: C. Wilkerson, *Flying Close to the Sun: My Life and Times as a Weatherman* (New York, 2007, 2011), p. 343. For 'crowd containers' see: L. Mumford, *The City in History* (Harmondsworth, 1961), between pp. 160–1.

[101] G. Buckle (ed.), *Letters of Queen Victoria*, 2nd Series, Vol. III (London, 1926), pp. 480–2. Emphasis in original.

[102] R. Bach Jensen, 'Daggers, Rifles and Dynamite: Anarchist Terrorism in Nineteenth Century Europe', *Terrorism and Political Violence*, 2004, p. 116.

A handful of examples will suffice. As is well recognized, Santiago Salvador's bombing of the Barcelona Opera House on 7 November 1893 was the key turning point here. Thrown from above, Salvador's first bomb hit Row 14 in the stalls during a performance of *Wilhelm Tell* killing twenty-two, and wounding thirty. Underlining the vagaries of such attack methods, his second bomb failed to explode at all. Landing on a large and already prostrate victim, its impact was cushioned by rolls of bourgeois fat.[103] Yet that hardly mattered. Salvador had successfully set a new standard for anarchist atrocity: in one attack, he had created more victims than all the turmoil of the 1880s combined.[104] And in doing so, he had also radically revised the parameters of the thinkable.

A month later, August Vaillant had attacked the French Chamber of Deputies from the public gallery (9 December 1893): essentially, identical tactics to Salavador's. Vaillant subsequently downplayed his intention to cause mass carnage—but he did in fact cause widespread injury.[105] Weeks later, also in Paris, Emile Henry committed his bombing (12 February 1894). His failure to deliver carnage on the scale of Barcelona was incidental; and not for want of trying. Even allowing for forced improvisation, Henry's debt to Salvador's recent example seems clear enough. Forced away from a theatre, he deliberately searched for the most crowded venue he could find:

> His first idea, he says, was to throw the bomb in a theatre, and he went to one of the principal theatres, but was told there was no room. He next looked into cafes on the boulevards, but there were few people in them. He then strolled up to the St. Lazaire Station, and seeing the Café Terminus full of people he chose it for the bomb because he wished to kill as many people as possible.[106]

Even a summary overview suggests that attempts at mass casualty attacks in fact run throughout almost the entire period of anarchist attacks. On 7 June 1896, the Corpus Christi procession in Barcelona was bombed (killing twelve).[107] In contrast to the Irish Republican bombings on the London Underground on 30 October 1883—where devices had been thrown out of carriages—at Aldwych in 1897 the bomb exploded *inside* a First Class Carriage, killing two.[108] Just before Christmas 1902, a bomb was found near the doors inside St Peter's Cathedral in Geneva which appeared 'to have been filled with pieces of iron'.[109] In 1906, another unexploded nail bomb was found, this time in St Peter's Basilica, Rome.[110] Anarchists in America later took up this tradition, but with rather greater efficiency. As already seen, both of the set-piece 'spectaculars' that are usually attributed to the

[103] R. Hughes, *Barcelona* (London, 1992, 1993, 1996), pp. 419–21.

[104] Bach Jensen, 'Daggers, Rifles and Dynamite', p. 134.

[105] Oddly, historians have tended to take Vaillant's supposedly restrained intentions at face value. See: Merriman, *The Dynamite Club*, p. 138; Contemporary accounts paint a more sombre picture: *The Scotsman*, 11 December 1893.

[106] *The Times*, 17 February 1894.

[107] Hughes, *Barcelona*, pp. 421–2.

[108] *London Daily News*, 28 April, 12 October 1897; *Lloyds Weekly Newspaper*, 2 May 1897. Also: Short, *The Dynamite War*, pp. 160–2.

[109] *Morning Post*, 24 December 1902.

[110] *Belfast Weekly News*, 22 November 1906.

Galleanist movement—the bombing of the San Francisco Preparedness Day Parade (1916), and at Wall Street (1920)—were both technically well-executed attacks. On both occasions, powerful devices pre-set with reliable timers, and packed with shrapnel were left in high-profile, crowded locations.[111]

By contrast, and outside of Palestine, there were to be very few more such set-piece spectacular bombings against civilians after the First World War. One bizarre exception was the case of the Michigan farmer and school-board official, Andrew Kehoe: a sort of proto-Timothy McVeigh rebel figure, but with far more parochial political horizons. Convinced that his own financial difficulties were directly caused by local taxes levied to build the Bath Consolidated School in a nearby hamlet, he managed to get himself appointed as the school's handyman. He then used this position to mine the entire school with thousands of feet of wire linking 1,000 pounds of dynamite. On 17 May 1927, Kehoe murdered his wife; detonated the school; and then exploded a shrapnel-laden suicide car-bomb to kill the survivors. Besides himself, he killed another seven adults and no less than thirty-eight children; as well as causing severe injuries to forty-five more.[112]

As a long-running underground movement, the IRA provides an intriguing case study for the interwar period. We have a few glimpses into their internal discussions around whether to use mass casualty bombings against civilians at both the beginning and the end of this twenty-year period. Since the IRA had developed considerable expertise in using shrapnel-laden explosive devices against both the British Army and the Royal Irish Constabulary, this was no abstract debate.[113] Two general points seem clear in the 1919–21 period. First, the weight of senior opinion was against them: presumably because of calculations of the likely political fall-out. Secondly, although resisted, this 'terroristic temptation' was a recurrent one. Michael Collins explicitly had to rule out a proposal to bomb crowds leaving London theatres.[114] Meanwhile, unarmed devices were left in Belfast cinemas—apparently as an explicit warning of how IRA pressure could be sharply escalated.[115]

Under very the different circumstances of mid-1939, a rump IRA found it harder to resist the 'terroristic temptation'. It bears emphasis: the Sabotage

[111] M. Davis, *Buda's Wagon: A Brief History of the Car Bomb* (London, 2007), pp. 1–3 [Wall Street attack]; *Time*, 14 July 1930, Vol. XVI, No. 2 ('Crime: Mooney and Billings') [San Francisco attack]; Gage, *The Day Wall Street Exploded*, pp. 1, 31–6 [Wall Street, 1920] and 109–10 [San Francisco, 1916].

[112] For a fuller account: Davis, *Buda's Wagon*, pp. 14–16.

[113] E. T. Graham, 'Bombs found in Belfast', *Journal of the Royal Engineers*, October 1922, pp. 208–10. For an authoritative survey of IRA technological achievements in the 1919–22 period, see: R. Davies, 'IEDs in Belfast—1922' (30 April, 2018); 'Irish Republican Improvised Mortar Design—1920' (14 April, 2016); 'History Lessons' (11 July, 2015); 'Warflour, Paxo and Irish Cheddar' (2 January, 2015). All available at: http://www.standingwellback.com/

[114] M. Foy, 'Michael Collins and the Intelligence War' in J. Crowley (et al., eds), *Atlas of the Irish Revolution* (Cork, 2017), p. 425.

[115] Graham, 'Bombs found in Belfast', pp. 208–10. I am deeply grateful to Roger Davies for bringing this reference to my attention.

Plan—as the name proclaimed—was designed to avoid civilian carnage.[116] And at least in the early months, its apologists could argue with some justification that

> it should be clear to anyone that the IRA, far from disregarding human life, have taken extraordinary precautions to safeguard it. Only one life has been lost in over one hundred operations in densely populated areas.[117]

Under pressure of arrests and enhanced security, the IRA's campaign soon lost momentum. By the summer of 1939, bombing tactics evolved radically. Even by the most sympathetic assessment, the multiple bombings in London's West End (Saturday 24 June) were a reckless affair. In one case, a parcel bomb with a lit fuse was simply left in the middle of the pavement at Piccadilly Circus at about 10 pm: amidst the passing crowds. It is clear from the witness statements that passers-by varied greatly in how quickly they grasped they were in any danger in the seconds before the bomb exploded.[118]

Strangely, the self-serving claim that the bombing at Coventry on 25 August 1939 was the result of a panicked abandonment—and hence was not intended to be fatal—has received wider acceptance than it deserves.[119] Circumstantial evidence speaks powerfully against it: a time bomb was left in a bicycle basket on the High Street: and set to explode at 2.32 pm: peak shopping time.[120] Forty explosions had already occurred in the Coventry area: but this attack was unique by virtue of being left in a crowded location.[121] Moreover, we have the bomber's own explicit account that the bombs was deliberately intended to cause mass carnage: and that he was—or so he later claimed—ordered to carry out the attack despite his explicit protests ('leaving a bomb in a crowded street is nothing but cold-blooded murder').[122] In the event, it killed five and injured sixty: a publicity disaster for the IRA that knocked the bottom out of its campaign.[123]

Although largely obscured by the background mayhem of the Second World War, such 'amateur' mass casualty bombings against civilians did continue after 1939. On 18 May 1942 a bomb planted by Jewish Communists in Berlin at a Nazi propaganda exhibition in the Lustgarten injured eleven.[124] Likewise, French Resistance groups planned to bomb public lectures of the fascist *Parti Populaire Français* (PPF) in both Nîmes and Clermont-Ferrand in October 1943.[125] In July 1942 a bombing at Madrid South railway station killed four—but whether by

[116] L. Fairfield (ed.), *The Trial of Peter Barnes and Others* (London, 1953), pp. 155, 165.

[117] Fowler, *Bombs and Their Reverberations*, p. 9.

[118] NA, MEPO 3/1288. See in particular statements by: James Bastow; Henry White; Rene Riley; Abraham Snipper.

[119] T. I. Adams, *The Sabotage Plan: The IRA Bombing Campaign in England 1939–1940* (Titchfield, 2010), pp. 64, 71. Also: J. Bowyer Bell, *The Secret Army: The IRA 1916–1979* (Dublin, 1970, 1990), pp. 161–2.

[120] Fairfield, *The Trial of Peter Barnes and Others*, p. 21.

[121] Fairfield, *The Trial of Peter Barnes*, p. 21.

[122] *Sunday Times*, 6 July 1969.

[123] Fairfield, *The Trial of Peter Barnes*, p. 22.

[124] D. C. Large, *Berlin: A Modern History* (London, 2001), p. 342; W. Wippermann, *Die Berliner Gruppe Baum und der jüdische Widerstand* (Berlin, 1981, 2011), p. 7.

[125] J. S. Torrie, *German Soldiers and the Occupation of France, 1940–1944* (Cambridge, 2018), p. 189.

design or not is not clear.[126] Explosions at railway stations at bothNeuchâtel, Switzerland (July 1941) and Berlin (February 1943) are even more obscure.[127]

The aftermath of the Second World War presents a clearer picture. Mass casualty bombings largely disappear from America and Western Europe for a generation after 1945. French Algeria, of course, saw its fair share of horrors in this regard: but even here, the leakage of similar horrors back into metropolitan France was surprisingly limited. Indiscriminate murder in France at the time was the state's business: as the police slaughter of Algerians in Paris in 1961 demonstrated. With rare exceptions, Klan bombings in the Civil Rights era tried to avoid multiple fatalities.

Hence the shock of the neo-fascist bombing at the *Bianca Nazionale dell'Agricoltura* in the Piazza Fontana, Milan, on 12 December 1969. It killed seventeen; and wounded more than eighty. It also ushered in a renewed era of mass casualty bombing attempts across Europe that—with interruptions—has lasted down to the present.[128] The most significant change within this broad trend has been the advent of suicide bombing as a standard Islamist tactic in the early twenty-first century.

As is often the case, the main explanatory challenge here is not so much to explain the emergence of a new tactic, but to account for its delayed diffusion. Suicide bombing is old: and had, in principle, long been 'available'. Indeed, it might fairly be said to be a classic example of a tactic that 'lies around' until its time has come. Even leaving aside its specific use as an assassination tactic—which is usually dated back to Russia in 1881—what might loosely be termed 'private' suicide bombing has long predated the emergence of mass casualty bombings as a terroristic tactic.[129] Indeed, private suicide bombings have relentlessly pursued the spread of high explosive through first industry, and then wider society. In March 1893, a German miner named Boehme deliberately killed himself along with six others at a mine in the Harz mountains.[130] In a similar case, a mining foreman blew himself up (and injured ten others) at Susa, Piedmont, in 1926.[131]

Mid-twentieth-century America produced a particularly rich crop of human bombs. Such cases involved disgruntled men killing or wounding others in spectacular acts of self-immolation: and typically following some prior confrontation with an unyielding state bureaucracy.[132] In April 1949, for instance, Charles Hunter killed himself and injured three female clerks at the Los Angeles State Accident Commission offices.[133] On 15 September 1959—at a Houston primary

126 *Derby Daily Telegraph*, 24 July 1942.

127 *Newcastle Journal*, 11 July 1941 (Neuchâtel); *Evening Despatch*, 15 February 1943 (Friedrichstrasse, Berlin).

128 I. Sánchez-Cuenca, *The Historical Roots of Political Violence* (Cambridge, 2019), p. 64.

129 See: I. Overton, *The Price of Paradise: How the Suicide Bomber Shaped the Modern Age* (London, 2019), pp; 1–30; J. Bowyer Bell, *Assassin: Theory and Practice of Political Violence* (New Brunswick, 1979, 2005), p. 162 [Colonel Freiherr von Gersdorff plan to kill Hitler, March 1943].

130 *Western Morning News*, 20 March 1893.

131 *Belfast News Letter*, 5 July 1926.

132 Also: *Daily Mirror*, 13 January 1953 [man blows himself up at divorce lawyer's office]; *Coventry Evening Telegraph*, 5 January 1963 [65-year-old man blows himself and daughter-in-law through roof of the car in argument over money].

133 *Gloucester Citizen*, 8 April 1948.

school named after the Gothic horror writer, Edgar Allan Poe—a father who had failed to provide the correct paperwork to enrol his son, self-detonated in middle of the playground. Five adults and children were killed; and nineteen injured.[134] Such exploding patriarchs—and, significantly here, wounded masculinity seems to be a constant theme—may fairly be classified as amongst the 'primitive rebels' of late modernity.

It is impossible to gauge how much, if any, conscious learning there was between these cases. However, the fundamental point remains that suicide bombing suggested itself repeatedly to a small number of disturbed individuals well before this phenomenon became a general political and cultural preoccupation of the twenty-first century. No less a figure than President Truman warned against an assault on the USA by a holocaust of Korean suicide bombers in 1950, at an early peak of the Cold War.[135] Here it is useful to draw comparisons with the twenty-two murder-suicide plots that are known to have occurred between 1973 and 2001 that involved the deliberate crashing of planes.[136] Such horrors were both fully thinkable and realisable before 11 September 2001: indeed, they were discussed at the peak of the hijacking boom.[137] But they had not yet 'broken through' as a threat that was widely feared right across Western societies.

In short, the emergence of suicide bombing as the quintessential terroristic threat of the early twenty-first century is a highly complex phenomenon. Clearly, ideology matters. A growing Islamist death-cult was crucial to its diffusion; as were shortening 'feed-back' loops between Middle Eastern warzones and Europe. But Islamist suicide-bombing remains a very rare attack form in Europe: while, to date, the USA has been spared entirely. All in all, Islamist groups have found it hard to maintain the momentum of suicide attacks across Western countries: there simply has not been an endless supply of ardent self-destroyers to hand. Still, the ideal lingers because of its potential impact. Indeed, it is worth noting here in passing that even apolitical suicide cults have long sparked moral panics when they have threatened to develop international reach. Goethe's novel *The Sorrows of Young Werther* was alleged to have inspired a romantic fashion for young gentlemen blowing their brains out with pistols in the years after its publication in 1774. Similarly, both the 1930s Hungarian pop song *Gloomy Sunday* and the demonstrative self-destruction of Marilyn Monroe (1962) allegedly fuelled transnational spasms of self-destruction.[138]

134 *Los Angeles Times*, 16 September 1959.

135 M. S. Hamm and R. Spaaij, *The Age of Lone Wolf Terrorism* (New York, 2017), p. 238.

136 Dolnik, *Understanding Terrorist Innovation*, p. 38.

137 For instance: *The Times*, 16 September 1970.

138 M. Hulse, 'Introduction' in J. Von Goethe, *The Sorrows of Young Werther* (London, 1774, 1989), p. 12 For the supposed phenomenon of the 'Gloomy Sunday' suicides: *Hartlepool Daily Mail*, 6 April 1936 (13-year-old in Michigan); *Sunday Sun*, 19 April 1936 (ex-Tyneside businessman); *Belfast Telegraph*, 25 May 1936 (American student shoots himself); *Daily Herald*, 21 October 1937 (Brixton suicide). For the supposed contagion effects of the Marilyn Monroe suicide: Cronin, *Power to the People*, p. 53.

I wish now to shift attention to a much more neglected area of analysis: the emotional satisfactions of bombing. At least until the advent of suicide attacks, the social psychology of bombing remained largely neglected.[139] Yet in any general historical account that seeks to address the sheer longevity of bombing tactics, it surely demands some attention. And here there is no shortage of evidence hiding in plain sight. In particular, there are rich contextual clues to be garnered from the ways in which bombers, and their supporters, discuss their handicraft amongst themselves.

A first point to note is the consistency of playful language. Devices are referred to with the greatest flippancy. Letter bombs become the 'chemical parcels post'.[140] The time bomb—for Brendan Behan, at least—became a 'Sinn Fein conjuror's outfit'.[141] For both their Allied and Axis creators, the ubiquitous 'booby traps' of the Second World War were either 'toys' or else the tools of mockery.[142] The (very few) Irish Republican ballads that deal with mid-twentieth-century bombings treat them as a hilarious practical joke (*The Ould Alarm Clock, Up Went Nelson!*).[143] To summarize: a tone of ludic smugness is consistently used to describe improvised explosives across highly diverse contexts and by a widely variant array of actors, both unofficial and professional. This seems significant.

What seems to be being celebrated here are the secret satisfactions of surprise: a very private smugness. What explosives bestow is a sense of tactical superiority: and with it, some sense of control over future events (however illusory). Only the bomber knows where and when a device is set to explode. Even if only admitted indirectly through the medium of jest, this awareness commonly seems to afford deep satisfaction in itself. Even the mere possession of explosives can impart a strongly empowering effect.

As early as 1881 the *Irish World* had enthused about the unique power of dynamite to 'equalise the great and small'.[144] In literal terms, this was an ambitious claim—as the nugatory political effects of the Dynamite Wars (1881–7) were shortly afterwards to demonstrate convincingly. London was neither laid waste, nor Ireland set free. But in psychological terms the *Irish World* had perhaps been early to recognize something rather important: the elation of commanding a hidden

[139] With the exception of suicide bombings: see: M. Bloom, 'Dying to Kill: Motivations for Suicide Terrorism' in A. Pedhazur (ed.), *Root Causes of Suicide Terrorism: The Globalization of Martyrdom* (London, 2006, 2009), pp. 25–53; O. Roy, *Jihad and Death: The Global Appeal of Islamic State* (London, 2017), pp. 41–74.

[140] Speech by socialist agitator John Burns recorded in: *Observer*, 10 April 1887; preserved at: NA, HO 144/196/A46866B.

[141] B. Behan, *Borstal Boy* (London, 1958, 1990), p. 1.

[142] Quoted in: Jones, *Malice Aforethought*, p. 83. Likewise, the MD1 [Ministry of Defence 1] was known as 'Winston Churchill's Toy Shop': Ibid, p. 159.

[143] *The Ould Alarm Clock* commemorates the S-Plan Campaign of 1939; *Up Went Nelson!* the IRA's destruction of Nelson's Pillar in Dublin in 1966. See: T. K. Wilson, 'Review: IRA: The Bombs and the Bullets: a History of Deadly Ingenuity. By A. R. Oppenheimer. Pp 387. Dublin: Irish Academic Press. 2009. €60 hardback; €24.95 paperback; Years of Darkness: the Troubles remembered. By Gordon Gillespie. Pp 256. Dublin: Gill & Macmillan. 2008. €16.99 paperback', *Irish Historical Studies*, 36 (143), May 2009, pp. 474–6.

[144] Whelehan, '"Cheap as Soap and Common as Sugar"', p. 105.

means of destruction. Almost a century later, Jane Alpert experienced the acquisition of dynamite as a moment of both personal and group transformation:

> Action, almost any action that would give the appearance of bringing down the state, was what we longed for. At moments I caught Dana's eye or Ben's and felt we shared a magical secret: the dynamite.[145]

Wherein lies the magic? In part, the 'magical' or 'delicious' secret seems to lie simply in the relative ease with which such a means of tremendous destruction can be both concealed and moved.[146] Dynamite has long been celebrated as the 'pocket artillery' or the 'revolution in your pocket'.[147] It has long been feared for exactly the same reason: in an 1880s report to Congress, General Philip Sheridan warned of those who threatened the public buildings 'with means carried to perfect safety to themselves *in the pockets* of their clothing'.[148] Yet guns can also be easily concealed: and can also wreak huge destruction. The psychological attractions of using high explosive seem to lie deeper than this.

In the language of Randall Collins, bombing represents an inherently 'confrontation-minimizing tactic'. Collins has argued powerfully that paying close attention to the micro-dynamics of confrontation exposes a general (though certainly not universal) incompetence at violence. Most humans are simply not very good at it: violence is hard, in large part because prior confrontation is so deeply stressful.[149]

Hence techniques that bypass the confrontation stage successfully hold out the prospect of achieving more efficacious outcomes. In a provocative discussion of the place of bombings in wider social life, Collins goes on to comment:

> In an important sense, the history of terrorist attacks, since the first round of bombings in the 1880s, has depended upon the creation and diffusion of confrontation-minimizing techniques of attack. What has been adopted is not just the technology of how to make bombs and detonators but a micro-interactional technology. It is a social technology that has made it possible for ideologically motivated terrorism to be carried out by middle-class women and men without backgrounds in ordinary boisterous or criminal violence. As a generalization, the more clandestine and confrontation-avoiding the technique of violence, the more its practitioners are from the respectable middle class, and indeed from its non-boisterous, well-behaved sector. Terrorist bombing is, so to speak, the violence of the meek.[150]

This helpful categorization of bombings as a 'confrontation-minimizing' technique seems a key insight. It takes us closer to explaining the first appearance of the terroristic bombing campaign in the late nineteenth-century's 'society of strangers': and its periodic recurrence ever since.[151]

[145] Alpert, *Growing Up Underground*, p. 199.

[146] Alpert, *Growing Up Underground*, p. 188.

[147] Y. Levy, *Guerrilla Warfare* (Harmondsworth, 1941), p. 84; O' Donovan Rossa quoted in: Whelehan, '"Cheap as Soap and Common as Sugar"', p. 116.

[148] Quoted in: Clymer, *America's Culture of Terrorism*, pp. 6–7. Emphasis in original.

[149] R. Collins, *Violence: A Micro-Sociological Theory* (Princeton, 2008), pp. 10–19.

[150] Collins, *Violence: A Micro-Sociological Theory*, p. 446.

[151] Vernon, *Distant Strangers*, pp. 7–9.

Yet, as Collins's own tentative language of 'generalization' seems to indicate, this linkage with class cannot be pushed to extremes. Bombs have no exclusive class profile. Bombing campaigns by anarchists (1892–94), the IRA (1939–40;c. 1970-96) and the revived Klan (1951–64) have all been conducted primarily by working-class activists.[152] 'Dynamite Bob' Chambliss, the truck driver who directed the Birmingham bombings was authentically proletarian; as were his henchmen.[153] Bombing cannot be solely reduced to a bourgeois tactic.

Nor can it be reduced to an exclusively male tactic. 'Bomb-throwing was clearly considered a man's job' writes Walter Laqueur of the late nineteenth century: but this slowly changed in the following century.[154] On the cusp of Suffragette escalation in 1909, Emmeline Pankhurst portrayed 'bomb throwing, shooting and stone-throwing... [as] time-honoured masculine political arguments'.[155] Needless to say, this characterization did not preclude imitation: although the Suffragettes did stop short of public gunplay. However, there does seem some anecdotal evidence that it was male supporters of the Suffragettes who pioneered the use of bombs.[156] Lillian Lenton recalled that 'a few young men were very anxious to help us. But these young men only seemed to have one idea—and that was bombs'.[157]

In the American New Left, the twin drivers of female expertise in employing bombs seem to have been competition with fellow male activists, but also alarm at the latter's recklessness.[158] In a telling passage, Cathy Wilkerson describes a culture of insecure chauvinism in which the male bomb-maker was too under-confident to admit he did not understand the basic rules of handling explosives safely.[159] After the disastrous Townhouse explosion of 1970, it was female activists who pioneered the Weather Underground's very carefully calibrated use of explosives.[160] More banally, the resilience of traditionalist thinking about gender roles throughout the twentieth century should be stressed. A lingering assumption that women would be less vulnerable to early detection seems to have encouraged their repeated employment as bomb throwers or planters: a pattern seen in Paris (1921), Algiers (1956–57), Berlin (1969), New York (1969), Washington (1971), London (1972–3).[161]

[152] G. Woodcock, *Anarchism* (London, 1962, 1975), pp. 288–95; R. English, *Armed Struggle* (London, 2003, 2004), p. 136; Behan, *Borstal Boy*, pp. 1–4; J. W. Vander, 'The Klan Revival', *American Journal of Sociology*, 65, 1960, pp. 458, 460–62.

[153] B. J. Dierenfeld, *The Civil Rights Movement* (London, 2004), p. 90.

[154] Laqueur, *Terrorism*, p. 150.

[155] T. Wilson (ed.), *Political Diaries of C.P. Scott, 1911–1928* (London, 1970), p. 34.

[156] Such as Harold Laski: C. Bearman, 'An Examination of Suffragette Violence', *English Historical Review*, CXX (486) April 2005, p. 370.

[157] M. Arthur, *Lost Voices of The Edwardians* (London, 2006, 2007), p. 383.

[158] Alpert, *Growing Up Underground*, p. 208; Wilkerson, *Flying Close to the Sun* pp. 355.

[159] Wilkerson, *Flying Close to the Sun*, pp. 339, 343–4.

[160] Wilkerson, *Flying Close to the Sun*, pp. 355; Burrough, *Days of Rage*, pp. 122, 150.

[161] For Paris: *Irish News*, 24 October 1921 [waitress arrested]. For Algiers: Hutchinson, *Revolutionary Terrorism*, p. 118; *L'Écho d'Alger*, 13 February 1957. For Berlin: A. Rosenfeld, '"Anarchist Amazons": The Gendering of Radicalism in 1970s West Germany', *Contemporary European History*, 19 (4) November 2010, pp. 360–1. For American cities: Alpert, *Growing Up Underground*, pp. 212–14; Burrough, *Days of Rage*, p. 163. For London: B. Huntley, *Bomb Squad: My War Against the Terrorists* (London, 1977), pp. 1–33.

One final point bears emphasis. Regardless of ideology, in many militant circles the use of bombs continues to carry great prestige. The sheer effort expended in building them is evidence enough of that—especially when far more straightforward means of gaining attention are to hand. This is a recurrent pattern. Although they utterly failed to entirely master explosives, the Columbine school killers (20 April 1999) could not faulted for their lack of ambition:

> For investigators, the big bombs changed everything: the scale, the method, and the motive of the attack. Above all, it had been indiscriminate. Everyone was supposed to die. Columbine was fundamentally different from the other school shootings. It had not really been intended as a shooting at all. Primarily, it had been a bombing that failed.[162]

From the autumn of 2010 until the following summer Anders Breivik invested enormous money and time in building a truck bomb: he found it arduous, daunting, and worried constantly about detection. The end result killed far fewer people (eight) than his subsequent shooting-spree (sixty-nine).[163] Elements in the German far-right still periodically dream of an escalation into bombing.[164] Recently, Islamists have turned to vehicle attacks when it seems that bombings would have been their first choice. After all, it was the premature explosion of a bomb factory that led directly to the attack on Las Ramblas in Barcelona in 2017; while the use of (fake) suicide vests at both Cambrils (2017) and London (2017, 2019) also seems suggestive here.[165] Overall, Mathew Quinn has concluded from a survey of attacks in New York between 1975 and 2015 that the use of weapons was diversifying, but that explosives still remained the weapon of choice.[166] In summary, the bomb remains the defining means of destruction in modern political violence.

II

All the same, it is important not to overlook the bargain basement of rebel ordnance. Although often neglected analytically, the humble petrol bomb has proven to be a tactical weapon that—on occasion—has helped achieve significant political effect. From the ashes of the Paris Commune (1871) arose the idea of using petrol as a weapon of mass (property) destruction:

[162] D. Cullen, *Columbine* (New York, 2009, 2016), pp. 33–4, 44–5, 124.

[163] C. Hemmingby and T. Bjørgo, *The Dynamics of a Terrorist Targeting Process: Anders B. Breivik and the 22 July Attacks in Norway* (Basingstoke, 2016), pp. 52–8, 74.

[164] Revolution Chemnitz: *Times*, 29 April 2019. Also: I. Hasselbach, *Führer-Ex: Memoirs of a Former Neo-Nazi* (London, 1996), pp. 274–5.

[165] BBC News, 18 August 2017 ('Barcelona and Cambrils: "Bigger" Attacks were planned'); *Telegraph*, 11 June 2017 ('First Pictures of fake suicide belts worn by London Bridge attackers'); BBC News, 30 November 2019 ('London Bridge: Attacker had been convicted of terror offence'); *Guardian*, 30 November 2019 ('Usman Khan profile: terrorist who wanted to bomb London Stock Exchange').

[166] M. Quinn, 'A History of Violence: A Quantitative Analysis of the History of Terrorism in New York City', *Homeland Security Affairs*, 12, Article 4 (September 2016). Available: https://www.hsaj.org/articles/12153

> No legend was more widely believed than that of the *petroleuses*; fearful maenads from some infernal region who crept around the city, sometimes accompanied by their offspring, flinging fire-balls or bottles of petroleum into basement windows belonging to the bourgeoisie.[167]

Although much celebrated in anarchist song and story, in practice petrol remained effectively 'unweaponized' until well into the twentieth century.[168] The creation of the society of mass vehicle ownership was a prior condition for its dissemination as a weapon. As early as 1931, a German edition of a Comintern handbook advocated the use of 'oil-soaked rags'.[169] From the other end of the political spectrum, the rightist rioters trying to storm the National Assembly in Paris on 6 February 1934, threw 'flaming rags soaked in petrol'.[170] Yet such tactics were still far from ubiquitous. Neither British fascists not their opponents seem to have resorted to their use. They do not, for instance, seem to have featured at all at the Battle of Cable Street in October 1936.[171]

Undoubtedly, though, it was their military employment in first the Spanish Civil War (1936–9) and then the Soviet-Finnish Winter War (1939–40) that consolidated the basic design of a wick leading into a glass bottle only half-filled with petrol, thus letting the vapour ignite on impact.[172] In the desperate months following the fall of France, the Home Guard in England even promoted their semi-official manufacture in case of Nazi invasion. As a battlefield device, they remained very much a 'weapon of last resort': although they were pressed into action in Paris in August 1944.[173] As a tool of sabotage they had more utility: and were actively promoted in the Resistance manuals of the period.[174]

The post-1945 period saw the petrol bomb's political status secured.[175] It seems to have acquired its greatest prominence in situations of ethnic tension. In such situations it primarily served two tactical roles. First, it became a tool of racist intimidation—the firebombing of a home or shop sent a clear message that an individual was not welcome.[176] Secondly, they served as the 'artillery' of the great

[167] A. Horne, *The Fall of Paris: the Siege and the Commune*, 1870–1871 (London, 1965, 1968), pp. 522–3.

[168] E. A. Vizetelly, *The Anarchists: Their Faith and Their Record Including Sidelights on the Royal and Other Personages Who Have Been Assassinated* (London, 1911), pp. 42; Horne, *The Fall of Paris*, pp. 514–24.

[169] Rosenhaft, *Beating the Fascists?*, p. 40.

[170] B. Jenkins and C. Millington, *France and Fascism: February 1934 and the Dynamics of Political Crisis* (London, 2015, 2016), p. 79.

[171] N. Mosley, *Rules of the Game/Beyond the Pale: Memoirs of Sir Oswald Mosley and Family* (London, 1998), p. 377.

[172] T. Wintringham, 'Against Invasion—the Lessons of Spain', *Picture Post*, 15 June 1940, pp. 9–24. Also: G. L. Rottman, *World War II Allied Sabotage Devices and Booby Traps* (Oxford, 2010, 2014), p. 18.

[173] L. Collins and D. Lapierre, *Is Paris Burning?* (London, 1965, 1991), p. 195.

[174] Rottman, *World War II Allied Sabotage Devices*, p. 18.

[175] *Aberdeen Evening Express*, 8 November 1955 [Association of Former Partisans, Turin, targeted]; *Birmingham Daily Post*, 6 September 1958 [Hungarian Embassy in Paris].

[176] K. Thompson, *Under Siege: Racial Violence in Britain Today* (London, 1988), p. 13.

set-piece riots.[177] In England, the Notting Hill riots of 1958 showcased their widespread use.[178] Thus Lord Scarman was in error here in his report on the Brixton riots of 1981 that 'the Metropolitan Police faced in the petrol bomb a sinister and dangerous weapon, which had not previously been used on any substantial scale, if at all, in the United Kingdom outside Northern Ireland'.[179]

Petrol bombs also saw widespread use across north America. At the start of their campaign for the independence of Quebec, the FLQ briefly experimented with them as a sabotage weapon (1963).[180] In the USA, they appeared in rather more sustained fashion across the major ghetto riots of the mid-1960s: in Chicago (1964, 1966), Los Angeles (1965), and in Northern New Jersey, Plainfield, and Detroit (1967).[181] Television presumably spread general awareness of the technique, if not its mastery. Indeed, the chief of the fire department in Plainfield, New Jersey, was of the opinion that 'individuals making fire bombs did not know what they were doing, or they could have burned the city'.[182]

American students appear to have been less enthusiastic firebombers, although not for lack of instruction.[183] Richard Hofstadter specifically regretted that *The New York Review of Books* saw fit 'to feature on its cover a fully instructive diagram for making a Molotov cocktail'.[184] *Rat* magazine was similarly promotional as to their advantages ('yields at least one pig car in flames').[185] Even the horror movie *Night of the Living Dead* (1968) showcased their triumphant employment (albeit against zombies). Real-life experiments were, however, somewhat less inspiring. They do not seem to have been considered for use in the (far-from-spontaneous) 'Days of Rage' in Chicago in October 1969.[186] Later attempts to turn them up into timed devices led to disappointing results.[187]

In this hesitancy, the American New Left was broadly in step with their European counterparts. Employment of petrol bombs was distinctly uneven across the continent. Petrol bombs do not, for instance, seem to have featured in the student rioting in Rome (March 1968).[188] They were used in Paris in May 1968, but apparently more in the later stages of street confrontations.[189] In Berlin, though,

[177] L. Scarman, *The Scarman Report: The Brixton Disorders, 10–12 April 1981* (Harmondsworth, 1982), pp. 75–6.

[178] *Birmingham Daily Post*, 2 September 1958; *Newcastle Evening Chronicle*, 4 September 1958.

[179] Scarman, *The Scarman Report*, pp. 75–6.

[180] D. Jenish, *The Making of the October Crisis: Canada's Long Nightmare of Terrorism at the Hands of the FLQ* (Toronto, 2018), p. 18.

[181] U.S. Riot Commission, *Report of the National Advisory Commission on Civil Disorders* (New York, 1968), pp. 36–7 (Chicago), 37–8 (Los Angeles), 38–9 (Chicago), 71, 75 (Northern New Jersey), 78 (Plainfield), 91 (Detroit).

[182] U.S. Riot Commission, *Report of the National Advisory Commission*, p. 78.

[183] A. Hoffman, *Steal This Book* (New York, 1996, 2002), pp. 172–5.

[184] R. Hofstadter, 'Reflections on Violence in the United States' in R. Hofstadter and M. Wallace (eds), *American Violence: A Documentary History* (New York, 1971), p. 30.

[185] Alpert, *Growing Up Underground*, p. 193. See also: Hoffman, *Steal This Book*, pp. 172–5.

[186] B. Ayers, *Fugitive Days: A Memoir* (Boston, 2001), pp. 150–3, 167–72.

[187] Burrough, *Days of Rage*, p. 99; Wilkerson, *Flying Close to the Sun*, pp. 324–5, 336.

[188] *Birmingham Daily Post*, 2 March 1968 ('Student Riot Mob in Battle of Rome').

[189] D. Caute, *'68: The Year of the Barricades* (London, 1988), p. 211; Pathé report entitled 'France—Paris Riots (1968)' published on Youtube 13 April 2014; accessed 19 July 2019.

they were used frequently from 1969 onwards.[190] Holger Meins, the future Red Army Faction leader, even produced a short instruction film on how to manufacture them, before he moved onto more destructive explosives.[191]

However, the Molotov cocktail emerged as a weapon of some genuine significance during the early Northern Irish Troubles. In sporadic fashion, they had been used by Republicans in an earlier ill-fated Border Campaign.[192] By 26 July 1969, they were being used as a weapon of intimidation to enforce residential segregation in Belfast.[193] As early as 4 August 1969—that is, a full eight days before the Battle of the Bogside—a speaker in Derry could refer to 'the good old petrol bomb' as a weapon of choice in the event of future disturbances.[194] Nor was this any idle threat—when rioting did indeed break out, local dairies lost 43,000 milk bottles.[195] In Derry, use of the petrol bomb became well-refined: with an efficient (if highly gendered) division of labour; youthful supply teams and, above all, control of the commanding heights of Rossville Flats. Amidst choking clouds of tear gas, the journalist John Clare witnessed the operation close up:

> It was a ten-storey block lined by many teenagers, many girls. I counted eighteen milk crates, each containing twenty bottles half-full of petrol and with a piece of rag rammed down the neck. Girls aged 14 or 15 toiled up the stairs carrying crates of stones and bottles. After ten minutes I could hardly see with the tears running out of my eyes. In the courtyard behind the flats young people leant against the walls, weeping and choking. In a corner small boys aged 8 or 9 decanted petrol from a tin drum into milk bottles.[196]

Within this uniquely favourable constellation of local circumstances—elevation plus an almost limitless supply of petrol and glass bottles—the young people of the Bogside won a famous victory over the hated police, but also helped directly precipitate the arrival of the British Army on the streets: and, in turn, a full-scale constitutional crisis for Northern Ireland. Locally, though, the petrol bomb's status as an iconic weapon was secured ('Throw well, throw Shell!).[197]

A generation later, the Molotov cocktail dramatically re-emerged as *the* weapon of choice for xenophobic insurrection in the newly united Germany. It had the enormous advantage of flexibility—since it could be either a highly individualistic weapon deployed without warning by very small groups, or could be used as part of the larger set-piece riots, backed up by cheering crowds. Either way, it was petrol bombs that were directly responsible for the notorious atrocities that created a

190 Sánchez-Cuenca, *The Historical Roots of Political Violence*, p. 85.

191 *Wie baue ich einen Molotow-Cocktail?* Discussed at: D. de Bruyn, 'A German Youth Brings the Red Army Faction to the Melbourne International Film Festival: review', *The Conversation*, 3 August 2015.

192 *Londonderry Sentinel*, 14 May 1957; *Belfast Telegraph*, 31 May 1957.

193 L. Scarman, *Violence and Civil Disturbances in Northern Ireland in 1969*, Report of the Tribunal of Inquiry, Vol. I (Belfast, 1972), p. 31.

194 Scarman, *Violence and Civil Disturbances*, pp. 65–6.

195 J. Bardon, *A History of Ulster* (Belfast, 1992, 1994), p. 671.

196 Quoted in: Bardon, *A History of Ulster*, p. 668.

197 G. W. Target, *Unholy Smoke* (London, 1969), p. 111; E. McCann, *War and an Irish Town* (Harmondsworth, 1974), p. 59.

national sense of crisis around immigration.[198] Here Derry tactics were reversed: and apartment blocks attacked from the outside, potentially turning them into death traps. Dramatic TV footage of repeated petrol bomb attacks on a high-rise building inhabited by Vietnamese asylum seekers at Rostock sparked multiple imitations: its effect, writes Panikos Panayi 'was instant. On the weekend beginning on Friday evening 28 August [1992] as many as fifty incidents may have taken place, a significant percentage of them involving neo-Nazi youths attacking refugee hostels.'[199] In summary, the acceleration of these contagion patterns was particularly dramatic: indeed, annual totals for such arson attacks had been in single figures as recently as 1987.[200]

Following the death of three Turkish women in a fire-bomb attack at Mölln in Schleswig-Holstein on 23 November 1992, the *New York Times* quoted a local schoolgirl as declaring that

> this is exactly the way things began the last time, in Hitler's time. First you hear speeches full of hate, then come the firebombs, and then suddenly it's out of control.[201]

However noble these liberal sentiments, this was bad history. Indeed, it was the freelance use of petrol bombs that represented a key difference with the tactics of the highly regimented Brownshirts. In the years 1991–2, no less than 1,499 'extreme right-wing-motivated arson attacks were counted by the German authorities'.[202] Twenty years earlier such arson attacks had been running at a rate of about two a year (in West Germany). This was a crisis.[203]

Such attacks led to liberal revulsion, and a crack-down on neo-Nazi groups. Nonetheless, on 26 May 1993 the German Parliament voted to limit the number of asylum seekers entering the country: and it is hard not to draw the conclusion that the Molotov cocktail attacks were at least partially responsible.[204] Equally ominously, a template for future action had been established. Albeit at rather lower levels, during the refugee crisis created by the Syrian Civil War xenophobic arson attacks again peaked in Germany (2015–16).[205]

In summary, the petrol bomb remains a weapon whose cultural—and occasional political—significance is easily underestimated. Admittedly, it takes a special

[198] P. Panayi, 'Racial Violence in the New Germany, 1990–93', *Contemporary European History*, 3 (3) November 1994, pp. 265–87.

[199] Panayi, 'Racial Violence in the New Germany', p. 272. See also the dramatic footage from the documentary 'Pogrom Rostock' (1992) on Youtube under the title 'Brandanschläge auf Asylheime in Rostock 1992'. Accessed 27 July 2019.

[200] D. Koehler, *Right-Wing Terrorism in the 21st Century: The 'National Socialist Underground' and the History of Terror From the Far-Right in Germany* (Abingdon, 2017), p. 97.

[201] Quoted in: P. Merkl, 'Why Are They So Strong Now? Comparative Reflections on the Revival of the Radical Right in Europe' in P. Merkl and L. Weinberg (eds), *The Revival of Right-Wing Extremism in the Nineties* (London, 1997, 2005), p. 17.

[202] D. Koehler, 'Recent Trends in German Right-Wing Violence and Terrorism: What are the Contextual Factors behind "Hive Terrorism"?', *Perspectives on Terrorism*, 12 (6) December 2018, p. 76.

[203] Koehler, *Right-Wing Terrorism in the 21st Century*, p. 97.

[204] K. Hailbronner, 'Asylum Law Reform in the German Constitution', *American University International Law* Review, 9 (4) 1994, p. 159.

[205] Koehler, 'Recent Trends in German Right-Wing Violence and Terrorism', pp. 80–1.

set of facilitative circumstances for its true tactical potential to be shown—namely, in both Northern Ireland (1969) and (predominantly eastern) Germany (1991–3) widespread communal unrest and an overwhelmed (or indolent) police forces. But under these circumstances it can be a highly effective weapon: easily sourced and assembled, flexible in delivery, and highly telegenic in its effects.

III

By contrast, firearms have been a distinctly minority choice of weapon. Assassins apart, the frequency of their use has not tended to match their iconic status in rebel song and story. Only 18.5 per cent of terror incidents in Western Europe between 1950 and 1995 were what Jan Oskar Engene rather impressionistically calls 'armed attacks'—presumably with guns and knives.[206] Using global data, Adam Dolnik concluded that only 13 per cent of 'terrorist violence' had taken the form of shootings.[207] 'Armed struggle' has not tended to take the form of prolonged shooting wars.

Still, guns have been around for a very long time. To try to chart their longer use as political weapons is probably fairly unrewarding. As with gunpowder, it is hard to explain the variations in their use as tools of political violence in the deeper past. Firearms were employed as a tool for assassination in the sixteenth and seventeenth centuries—and with notable success against James Stewart, Earl of Morray (1570), and William the Silent (1584). Others who narrowly avoided the same fate included Elector Christian II of Saxony (1603) and Cardinal Klesl (1618).[208] But overall firearms remained of doubtful reliability: and held relatively limited attraction to would-be assassins. Stabbings were more dependable.

But experiments with assassinations by firearms did not disappear completely. In 1696 a bizarrely over-ambitious plot to assassinate King William III of England depended upon a 'musketoon', an early form of revolver that could fire up to six shots without reloading (and a supporting cast of no less than forty).[209] Much more elaborate self-firing devices were also developed soon afterwards. In 1712, for instance, a quick-thinking Jonathan Swift disarmed a device of pre-loaded pistols hidden in a hatbox that had been intended for the Earl of Oxford. In January 1764, a Colonel Poulsen in Denmark was indeed killed by a similar arrangement.[210]

Such incidents were presumably still rare in the eighteenth century. Indeed, it seems significant that Swift felt forced to publish his own account of the hatbox incident as an exercise in self-justification. There were, he conceded, still 'many

206 Engene, *Terrorism in Western Europe*, pp. 48, 60.

207 Dolnik, *Understanding Terrorist Innovation*, p. 25. From context, this seems to refer to estimates of 'terrorist violence' since 1945. See pp. 11–12.

208 C. Andrew, *The Secret World: A History of Intelligence* (London, 2018), pp. 163–4; Ford, *Political Murder*, p. 161; Wilson, *Europe's Tragedy*, pp. 219, 275.

209 J. Garrett, *The Triumphs of Providence: The Assassination Plot of 1696* (Cambridge, 1980), pp. 111, 120–1.

210 'Going Postal', *The Economist*, 6 November 2010.

doubting the truth of it, from the extravagancy and improbability of the design'.[211] By the nineteenth century, though, assassins in France had become decidedly more ambitious. Multi-barrelled 'infernal machines' capable of discharging barrages of bullets were later to feature in plots to kill both King Louis Philippe (1835) and Louis Napoleon (1851).[212]

For the present discussion, a far more important technical milestone in the history of political violence was the invention of the revolver in 1835.[213] As the mass product of industrial society, this portable, concealable, reliable, multi-shot weapon certainly made close-range killing technically much easier. Revolvers were to feature in six of the eight (or so) attempts to kill, or threaten, Queen Victoria in the course of her long reign.[214] By the time the revolver attained its modern form in the 1890s, it had become a standard assassination weapon: dynamite's only rival.

Such 'devilish inventions' were, in the judgement of one British imperial official, 'cheap, accurate, small and easy to smuggle'.[215] They were also durable. In 2018, the Christmas market at Strasbourg was shot up by a lone Islamist attacker. The main weapon used was a Lebel 1892 8mm revolver—standard issue for the French army in the First World War, a full century before.[216] Apparently, it still worked only too well.

Yet the cultural and political significance of revolvers went far beyond such practical advantages. Revolvers were highly individualistic weapons: they represented, in effect, 'a fistful of firepower'.[217] Here the revolver proved the ideal weapon for show-offs: as the steady litany of reports of accidental shootings showed.[218] A report from Posen, eastern Germany, in 1911 concluded that 'firearms, particularly at taverns and in disputes, are used not to fire at one another but to threaten and to fire shots in the air'.[219] As a classic firearms manual from 1910 noted, 'the

[211] J. Swift, *The Journal to Stella*, Letter LV, (15 November, 1712). Available here: https://www.gutenberg.org/files/4208/4208-h/4208-h.htm King Gustav III of Sweden was shot dead on 16 March 1792; while King George III of England was shot at in May 1800. See: Ford, *Political Murder*, pp. 205, 207.

[212] M. Mulholland, *The Murderer of Warren Street: The True Story of a 19th Century Revolutionary* (London, 2018), pp. 50, 169.

[213] E. J. Hobsbawm, *The Age of Revolution, 1789–1848* (New York, 1962), p. 214.

[214] P. T. Murphy, *Shooting Victoria! Madness, Mayhem and the Modernisation of the Monarchy* (London, 2012), pp. 55 [Oxford, 1840], 172 [Francis, 1842], 182 [Francis's 2nd attempt, 1842], 212–13 [Bean, 1842], 274 [Hamilton, 1849], 385 [O'Connor, 1872], 453–4 [Maclean, 1882]. The exceptions were the assault of Robert Pate's assault of Queen Victoria with his cane; and—possibly fictitious—'plot' by Irish dynamitards to assassinate the Queen during the Jubilee celebrations of 1887. See: Murphy, *Shooting Victoria*, pp. 316–17; B. Charles, *Kill the Queen! The Eight Assassination Attempts on Queen Victoria* (Stroud, 2012), pp. 136–46.

[215] Sir Mark Sykes, quoted in: S. Ball, 'The Assassination Culture of Imperial Britain, 1909–1979', *The Historical Journal*, 56 (1) March 2013, p. 232.

[216] N. Duquet et al., 'Armed To Kill: A Comprehensive Analysis of the Guns Used in Public Mass Shootings in Europe between 2009 and 2018', Flemish Peace Institute Report, 3 October 2019.

[217] P. Newark, *Firefight! The History of Personal Firepower* (London, 1989), p. 158.

[218] D. Ellerbrock, 'Gun Violence and Control in Germany 1880–1911: Scandalizing Gun Violence and Changing Perceptions as Preconditions for Firearm Control' in W. Heitmeyer (et al., eds), *Control of Violence: Historical and International Perspectives on Violence in Modern Societies* (New York, 2011), p. 198. Also: *Kattowitzer Zeitung*, 5 September, 14 November 1920. For Irish gun accidents: *Derry Journal*, 21 July 1920 and 9 February 1921.

[219] Ellerbrock, 'Gun Violence and Control in Germany 1880–1911', p. 197.

modern revolver is a weapon designed for quick work at close quarters and for use in one hand'.[220] Ominously, this tool for 'quick work' tended to short-circuit the socially recognized stages of escalation, and exit opportunities, that traditionally characterized confrontations with knives.

'Revolver heroes' (*Revolverhelden*) were thus to become the curse of the troubled frontier regions of Europe. This tendency was already evident by the late nineteenth century: but it became far more pronounced in the years after 1918.[221] In the Belfast Troubles of 1920–22, loyalist gunmen blasted away at Catholic districts in notably theatrical performances. 'We used to stand at a distance and see these fellows, usually with revolvers, firing across into Cullingtree Road' recalled one eyewitness: 'Sometimes, when they had the bravado, they would cross the road and fire straight into the Catholic streets. They made no attempt to cover their faces and the smoke was still coming from their weapons as they ran past us and into safe houses'.[222] Ten years later, a damning report for the Communist Party in Berlin also stressed the primacy of exhibitionism. It concluded that it had been a huge mistake to let their designated streetfighters take their guns home with them ('the result of this measure was that they played wild-west with them and blasted around quite senselessly in world history').[223]

In comparison with handguns, rifles remained fairly useless to determined opponents of the state under 'normal' conditions. In the Deep South during the Reconstruction period of the late 1860s, massed groups of Ku Klux Klan night-riders massively outgunned opponents with their 'Winchester rifles and six-shooters'.[224] 'They govern...by the pistol and rifle' commented a visitor to Louisiana as early as 1865.[225] In contrast, opponents typically had only 'the guns of poor folk, often single-shot shotguns loaded with cheap birdshot'.[226] But this situation was exceptional.

More generally, even for determined opponents of the modern state, rifles proved simply too cumbersome to conceal and transport in significant quantities. The sheer logistical challenges of gun-running proved a major vulnerability to Irish Republicanism: and the relentless cause of numerous arrests of highly talented organizers (including Michael Davitt in 1870).[227] Years later William O'Brien still recalled in vivid detail the sheer tension of smuggling even miniscule consignments

220 W. W. Greener, *The Gun and Its Development* (London, 1881, 1910), p. 535.

221 For a specific discussion of the use of revolvers in late nineteenth-century Ulster rioting: Londonderry Riot Inquiry Commission, *Report of a Commission Appointed to Inquire into Certain Disturbances Which Took Place in the City of Londonderry on the 1st November 1883* (Dublin, 1884), pp. viii–ix. For the post-war period: *Kattowitzer Zeitung*, 2 December 1920.

222 Quoted in: A. Parkinson, *Belfast's Unholy War: The Troubles of the 1920s* (Dublin, 2004), p. 281. For showing off with revolvers by 'Black and Tans': P. O'Shea, *Voices and the Sound of Drums: An Irish Autobiography* (Belfast, 1981), pp. 57–8. For Republican perspectives: J. McDermott, *Northern Divisions: The Old IRA and the Belfast Pogroms 1920–22* (Belfast, 2001), pp. 104, 152.

223 Rosenhaft, *Beating the Fascists?*, p. 105.

224 E. Foner, *Reconstruction: America's Unfinished Revolution, 1863–1877* (New York, 1988, 2014), p. 437.

225 Foner, *Reconstruction*, p. 119.

226 N. Johnson, *Negroes and the Gun: The Black Tradition of Arms* (New York, 2014), p. 91.

227 T. W. Moody, *Davitt and Irish Revolution 1846–82* (Oxford, 1981), pp. 70–9.

of arms into Cork. His rowing boat edged up 'until we were under the black hull of the Newport boat':

> Something wrapped in straw matting was protruded through the porthole, and then another, and another, until the whole consignment—I don't think it exceeded ten rifles all told—had been silently stowed away in the bottom of the yawl. To avoid suspicion on their travels, the stocks of the rifles were sawn in two under one of the rings of the barrel; how far they could ever be serviceable when pieced together again I have never been quite able to make out. As the last of the packing-cases was being slipped through there came a deep 'Hush!' from the seaman; and immediately the tramp of the police patrol on the deck resounded again.

All for naught: this entire consignment was discovered by the police within months.[228]

Even with more powerful resources and allies, Irish loyalists still faced major difficulties in trying to import rifles into Ireland during the Third Home Rule Crisis of 1912–14. By his own account, their chief gunrunner was a figure of fun to his peers who 'used to slap my pockets when I went into the Ulster Unionist Standing Committee and say "Well, Crawford, have you any rifles about your person?" '[229] Even his subsequent—and spectacularly successful—mass gun-running of April 1914 merely transformed the Ulster Volunteer Force from an essentially unarmed force into a badly-armed one. With good reason, local police complained that it was the political will to interdict the gun-running that had been lacking.[230] As it was, the successful landing, and subsequent distribution, of over 20,000 rifles in a single night was undoubtedly both a spectacular publicity coup and a giant step towards civil war in the north of Ireland.[231]

Availability of rifles in Belfast did then lead to the emergence of prolonged sniping battles during the Troubles of 1920–22: their sheer scale was a new development in the city's long history of sectarian confrontation. Sniper battles were frequently treated as a sort of spectator sport accompanied by large crowds lurking on the fringes.[232] Similar scenes were to recur in Belfast nearly fifty years later.[233] Broadly similar patterns were also seen in racial disturbances across North American cities in the troubled years after 1918.[234] Yet generally, for smaller insurrectionary groups, rifles have remained highly impractical weapons.

A general tightening of European laws in the first half of the twentieth century probably further reinforced the totemic significance of guns for underground

[228] W. O'Brien, 'Was Fenianism ever Formidable', *Contemporary Review*, 1897, pp. 689–90.

[229] K. Haines, *Fred Crawford: Carson's Gunrunner* (Donaghadee, 2009), p. 140.

[230] T. Bowman, *Carson's Army: The Ulster Volunteer Force, 1910–22* (Manchester, 2007), p. 142.

[231] Bardon, *A History of Ulster*, pp. 444–5; Bowman, *Carson's Army*, p. 144; T. Bowman, ' "Ulster Will Fight" ' in J. Crowley (et al., eds), *Atlas of the Irish Revolution* (Cork, 2017), pp. 157–8; A. T. Q. Stewart, *The Ulster Crisis* (London, 1967), pp. 176–85; Haines, *Fred Crawford: Carson's Gunrunner*, pp. 174–7.

[232] Kenna, *Facts and Figures: Belfast Pogroms*, p. 96; *Belfast Telegraph*, 23 July 1920 [photographs]; *Irish News*, 27 June, 3 July, 922.

[233] C. De Baroid, *Ballymurphy and the Irish War* (London, 1989, 2000), p. 42.

[234] D. F. Krugler, *1919: The Year of Racial Violence: How African Americans Fought Back* (Cambridge, 2015), p. 99–130.

movements. Eve Rosenhaft discusses the symbolic significance of firearms for Berlin Communists in the early 1930s. Around gun ownership clustered

> all the affects of popular mythology as well as of revolutionary legend. Since the possession of firearms was in itself unambiguously incriminating, the gun also had the quality of an entry-pass, if not into a secret society, then into a section of the Party and the community set apart from the rest by shared mysteries.[235]

This is not, of course, to suggest that the significance of these guns was *purely* symbolic. Communist activists did indeed use them sporadically—as a supplement to raids on Nazi bases, to aid escape and, indeed, to kill policemen.[236] But it is still important to point up their essentially limited use.

Such limits come into even sharper focus when compared to the wider social emergence of the handgun massacre from the late nineteenth century onwards. Despite an ineffectual anarchist attempt to shoot up the Paris Stock Exchange in 1886, politically-motivated mass shootings were to remain largely unknown for the next few decades.[237] Yet spree shooting had emerged in France as early as 1881.[238] Sacked for theft, a legal clerk named Morisset walked into a park at Tours and began shooting at random. He may have been suffering from paranoid tendencies—in one account, he seems to have assumed a small crowd singing a song were personally mocking him. Certainly, he was consumed by an acute sense of grievance against a society that had not recognized his own estimate of his talents: 'he had a soul above the lawyer's desk'.[239] Whatever the balance of Morisset's mind, the international press coverage was characterized by bewilderment: 'he deliberately shot an unoffending railway porter whom he had never seen in his life before, with whom he had no quarrel, and who was quietly dozing on a seat in one of the public promenades of Tours'.[240]

Where Morisset led, others soon followed. A school teacher named Ernst Wagner who was convinced he was about to be publicly shamed for a youthful act of bestiality, murdered his own family on the night of 4 September 1913: and then proceeded to set fire to four barns in the village of Mühlhausen, south west Germany. In the resulting confusion he shot dead nine people.[241] School shootings also appeared in Imperial Germany well before 1914.[242] What all these pre-1914 cases seem to have in common is the precarious social status of the petit bourgeois killers who seem to have feared public humiliation. Their killings represented a 'kind of primitive class war'.[243] Such spree killings continued to occur through the remainder of the twentieth century: with a particular concentration in the USA.[244]

235 Rosenhaft, *Beating the Fascists?*, p. 149.
236 Rosenhaft, *Beating the Fascists?*, pp. 112–14.
237 Bach Jensen, 'Daggers, Rifles and Dynamite', p. 131.
238 Or 1878, if an Indian case within a military context is considered: *Dundee Courier*, 27 June 1878 ('Wholesale Murder by a Sepoy').
239 *Belfast Telegraph*, 7 October 1881 ('An Interesting Murderer').
240 *Yorkshire Post and Leeds Intelligencer*, 23 September 1881.
241 Leyton, *Hunting Humans*, pp. 266–71; A. Cimino, *Spree Killers: The World's Most Notorious Gunmen and their Deadly Rampages* (London, 2010), pp. 8–11.
242 Ellerbrock, 'Gun Violence and Control in Germany', p. 198.
243 Leyton, *Hunting Humans*, p. 129.
244 Leyton, *Hunting Humans*, p. 284.

And yet it was not until the 1970s that spree shooting was adopted as a terroristic tactic. In the meantime, personal firepower had increased exponentially. The Thompson Gun enjoyed a very brief career with the IRA; and a longer one with Chicago gangsters and American entrepreneurs ('you can't run a mining company without a few tommy guns').[245] The Sten Gun, widely distributed throughout the Second World War, was still revered amongst some of the Italian far-left groups of the early 1970s.

And yet, as a political tactic, the demonstrative massacre—mass slaughter without any local build-up of prior confrontation—continued to be enacted through explosives not firearms. Such stubborn preferences endured regardless of ideological motivations. How far the shooting massacre remained unthinkable, and how far it was actively rejected as a tactic is, of course, impossible to say. Cathal Brugha, the IRA leader, planned to machine-gun London crowds as they left cinemas (*c.* 1920), but was overruled.[246] Some parts of the Weather Underground in 1969 apparently flirted with mass casualty bombings but, writes Jonathan Lerner, 'it never occurred to us to try something in the mode of terrorist attack more common today, such as walking into a target location and shooting the place up, even though acquiring guns would have been quite easy'.[247]

Whatever the reasons, restraints held. And when they finally gave way, it was in the Middle East. The Japanese Red Army's massacre at Lod, Israel, that killed twenty-six, established a new trend from 1972. Imitations soon followed across Europe.[248] By 1975, Provisional IRA active service units were driving through the West End of London bombing and machine-gunning restaurants where—they assumed—the ruling class dined.[249] Big picture trends captured by the Global Terrorism Database suggest a sharp rise in shooting incidents at the tail end of the twentieth century (Figure 5.1).

At first glance, the rarity of demonstrative shooting massacres seems surprising. Knowledge of how to use explosives has first to be learnt: a potentially arduous and daunting task for amateurs. Guns are factory-produced and come ready to use. They merely demand maintenance, not mastery. Furthermore, they have also become progressively much more destructive over time:

> The Lewis machine gun of World Wars One and Two, requiring two operators, weighing just 27 lb and firing 600 rounds per minute to 1,900 yd, gave firepower equivalent to fifty World War One riflemen. Today [1989], one infantryman can lay down the same firepower with a gun weighing barely a third as much.[250]

By the late twentieth century, indeed, a highly portable weapon such as the Armalite rifle could maintain the same rate of fire as a Maxim gun had done in 1884.[251]

245 Ellis, *The Social History of the Machine Gun*, p. 15.

246 F. McGarry, *Eoin O'Duffy: A Self-Made Hero* (Oxford, 2005), p. 369, n. 71.

247 J. Lerner, *Swords in the Hands of Children: Reflections of an American Revolutionary* (New York, 2017), pp. 165–6.

248 Moore, *Airport, Aircraft, and Airline Security*, p. 43.

249 G. McGladdery, *The Provisional IRA in England* (Dublin, 2006), pp. 102–3.

250 Newark, *Firefight!*, p. 6.

251 Dolnik, *Understanding Terrorist Innovation*, p. 25.

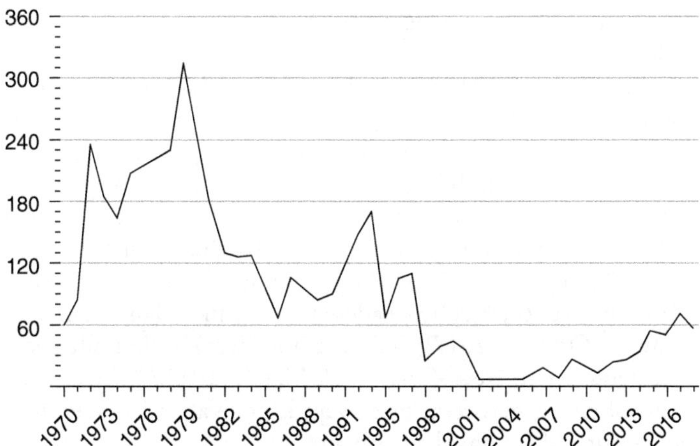

Figure 5.1. Attacks by firearm across North America and Western Europe, 1970–2018
Source: The Global Terrorism Database.

In that interim guns also became far more accurate over distance. On the battlefields of the twentieth century, killing distances therefore tended to expand widely. But the atrocities of peacetime typically take far more intimate forms. Adam Dolnik notes that the miniaturization of powerful firearms has tended to be more significant than the refinements of accuracy.[252] Most terroristic shooting tends to happen close up.

Such killing is not easy to initiate. Even Gavrilo Princip hesitated for a second before pulling the trigger.[253] Like knife attacks, this type of violence lies right at the opposite end of the spectrum to bombings, that archetypal form of confrontation-minimizing assault. As Ulrik Fredrik Malt the Professor of Psychiatry who examined Anders Breivik commented, 'it is one thing to set off a bomb. It is quite another to go ashore on an island and shoot young people and talk about it as if he had been picking cherries'.[254] Or as the anti-abortionist killer James Kopp put it:

> to pick up a gun and aim it at another human being, and to fire, it's not a human thing to do. It's not nice. It's not pleasant. It's gory, it's bloody. It overcomes every human instinct.[255]

Yet inhibitions can be overcome through learning: 'among lone wolf terrorists, there exists something akin to an institutional memory'.[256] Research has tended to downplay the role of the internet in 'radicalizing' perpetrators on its own: and often the bigoted go online to reinforce existing prejudices which themselves have emerged through face-to-face relationships.[257] But as a repository for learning *how*

[252] Dolnik, *Understanding Terrorist Innovation*, p. 26.
[253] D. J. Smith, *One Morning in Sarajevo: 28 June 1914* (London, 2008, 2009), p. 190.
[254] Å. Seirstad, *One of Us* (London, 2015), p. 472.
[255] Quoted in: P. Gill, *Lone Actor Terrorists: A Behavioural Analysis* (Abingdon, 2015), p. 170.
[256] Hamm and Spaaij, *The Age of Lone Wolf Terrorism*, p. 105.
[257] Gill, *Lone Actor Terrorists*, pp. 76–84.

massacre can be conducted, it seems hard to downplay the significance of the network society.

In any longer-term historical survey, it is hard not to be struck here by the emergence of spectacular set-piece shooting massacres as a contagion phenomenon of the early twenty-first century.[258] Lone shooters have begun to rack up death tolls to rival all but the largest bomb blasts. Although still highly exceptional events, a pattern of shooting massacres has emerged whose tally has approached, or exceeded, a new threshold of fifty deaths. Anders Breivk slaughtered sixty-nine on Utøya island, Norway (22 July 2011); Omar Mateen gunned down forty-nine in a Florida nightclub (12 June 2016); Stephen Paddock killed fifty-eight from a Las Vegas hotel window (1 October 2017); and Brenton Tarrant shot fifty-one in two mosques in Christchurch, New Zealand (15 March 2019).[259] By comparison, in the great wave of crowd massacres that swept Europe after 1918, entire machine gun companies often killed only half as many.

Of course, in part this trend must simply reflect the far greater firepower of assault weapons in the twenty-first century. But it also surely reflects a growing body of practical knowledge about how such things can 'best' be done to cause the maximum carnage possible: including the importance of first 'corralling' masses of victims into enclosed spaces.[260] It reflects the importance of dark social learning. Just as surely it reflects the wider social dissemination of media values where the highest death tolls command the greatest attention. After Seung-Hui Cho killed thirty-two (and then himself) at Virginia Tech, 'the press proclaimed it a new American record. They shuddered at the idea of turning school shootings into a competition, then awarded Cho the title'.[261]

IV

Finally, no discussion of changing repertoires of modern political violence would be complete without a brief discussion of the survival of a truly ancient weapon: the knife.

As a tool of assassination, the advantages of the easily-concealable knife are obvious enough: and it is of little wonder that its use can be traced unbroken from deep antiquity into modern times.[262] Indeed, Charlotte Corday's inspiration in choosing to stab Jean-Paul Marat seems to have been as much practical as classical in 1793.[263] Equally pragmatic was the knifing of the playwright August Von Kotzebue

[258] Gill, *Lone Actor Terrorists*, p. 59.

[259] For Breivik: Hemmingby and Bjørgo, *The Dynamics of a Terrorist Targeting Process*, p. 2. For Mateen: *Telegraph*, 15 June 2016 ('Orlando Victims: Everything We Know So Far About The 49 People Killed By Omar Mateen'). For Paddock: *Guardian*, 29 January 2019 ('FBI Investigation into Las Vegas Shooting Finds No Motive'). For Tarrant: BBC News, 14 June 2019 ('Christchurch Attack: Brenton Tarrant Pleads Not Guilty to All Charges').

[260] Hamm and Spaaij, *The Age of Lone Wolf Terrorism*, p. 43.

[261] Cullen, *Columbine*, p. 348.

[262] Ford, *From Tyrannicide to Terrorism*, pp. 64–7 [assassination of Caesar].

[263] S. Loomis, *Paris in the Terror* (Harmondsworth, 1964, 1970), pp. 105, 113.

by a German nationalist student, Carl Ludwig Sand (23 March 1819). Sand feinted with the knife to draw his victim's arms up in instinctive self-defence—at which point he stabbed him twice hard in the chest.[264] Assassination attempts by knife (or bayonet) were also a prominent feature of the Italian Risorgimento: they took the lives of both Count Pellegrino Rossi, chief minister to Pope Pius IX (15 November 1848) and Duke Charles III of Parma (26 March 1854).[265] Conducted skilfully, a knifing was devastatingly effective: as the swift demise of President François Sadi Carnot of France demonstrated (24 June 1894).[266]

But they were also hard to carry off successfully. The first strike had to be sure: and could easily go awry. Thus King Ferinando II of Naples survived a clumsy stabbing attempt (8 December 1856); while King Umberto of Italy saw off two similar attempts to knife him (17 November 1878; 22 April 1897)—although he did finally fall to an assassin's bullet (29 July 1900).[267] Likewise, the Conservative Prime Minister of Spain, Antonio Maura, survived a stabbing in Barcelona just a few years later (12 April 1904).[268]

Butchering humans was harder than it looked. Antonio Gallenga, the would-be assassin of King Carlo Alberto of Piedmont in 1834 prepared himself with a favourite lapis-handled dagger—but in the event found himself psychologically unable to go through with it.[269] By contrast, the Irish Invincibles displayed an unusual fixity of purpose in preparing their ambush of Lord Frederick Cavendish, Chief Secretary for Ireland, and the Under-Secretary, Thomas, Burke in Dublin's Phoenix Park in 1882. They procured long amputation knives especially from London; they wrapped cord around the handles for better grip; and they disdained to use their revolvers.[270] Even so, the long-planned killing turned out to be anything but surgical. Lord Cavendish's hand was nearly hacked off in the melee.[271]

Stabbings demanded guile, nerve, and strength. Yet for those very same reasons, they retained their shock quality. Although they would doubtless have been shocking enough events even if committed by other means, there was a particular quality of intimate savagery to both the Phoenix Park murders (6 May 1882) and the death of the Empress Elizabeth of Austria (10 September 1898) that seems to have impressed contemporaries deeply.[272] One of the lesser noticed side-effects in the revolution of personal security for elite figures that followed was that it largely rendered such stabbing attempts obsolete. Indeed, the Empress Elizabeth might

[264] Ford, *Political Murder*, p. 214.

[265] Pernicone and Ottanelli, *Assassins Against the Old Order*, p. 13.

[266] Pernicone and Ottanelli, *Assassins Against the Old Order*, p. 66.

[267] Pernicone and Ottanelli, *Assassins Against the Old Order*, pp. 13, 26–7, 66, 90–1.

[268] J. Romero Maura, 'Terrorism in Barcelona and Its Impact on Spanish Politics 1904–1909', *Past and Present*, 41 (December 1968), p. 136.

[269] Pernicone and Ottanelli, *Assassins Against the Old Order*, pp. 12–13.

[270] C. Townshend, 'Terror in Ireland: Observations on Tynan's The Irish Invincibles and their Times' in P. Wilkinson and A. M. Stewart, *Contemporary Research on Terrorism* (Aberdeen, 1987), pp. 181–2; T. Corfe, *The Phoenix Park Murders: Conflict, Compromise and Tragedy in Ireland, 1879–1882* (London, 1968), pp. 141–2, 188.

[271] Corfe, *The Phoenix Park Murders*, p. 188.

[272] Corfe, *The Phoenix Park Murders*, pp. 197–214; M. Twain, 'The Memorable Assassination', 1898. Available at: http://ebooks.adelaide.edu.au/t/twain/mark/what_is_man/chapter.5.html

well have survived if she had not explicitly refused to accept protection offered by local police.[273] The knife was destined to fade in the trajectory of twentieth-century assassinations at least at the very apex of politics. By the early twenty-first century, the knife was the tool of the unambitious assassin, content with targeting political representatives unimportant enough to merit close protection: Members of Parliament, mayors, and mayoral candidates.[274]

As a tool of mass terroristic violence, however, the knife has been of uncertain utility. Examples of their use are relatively rare: although there is an intriguing exception from Sicily, following its incorporation into Italy. On the evening of 1 October 1862, a coordinated series of thirteen stabbings took place in Palermo, the victims 'all of them inoffensive persons, and entire strangers to the political agitations of the hour'.[275] Sporadic stabbings continued into 1863.[276] At the time, conventional wisdom was that the attacks represented a plot by ex-Bourbon elements to destabilize the new regime.[277] More recently, the suggestion has been made that the violence originated from *within* the new regime: and represented an early prototype of later twentieth-century 'strategies of tension' that aim to bolster authoritarian government by the stoking of background fear.[278] Knives were also a central tool of the Ku Klux Klan during the counter-revolutionary terror of 1868–71 that restored a racial caste system in the Deep South of the USA.[279] Mutilated corpses of Republicans or 'uppity' freedmen left on public display served as advertisements for the reach and determination of the 'masked confederacy'.[280]

Although not conventionally included under the rubric of 'political' violence, it is worth noting here the massive impact of the 'Jack the Ripper' series of murders in East London in 1888–9: or, indeed, those of the Yorkshire Ripper between 1975–81.[281] On both occasions, it seems that a single knife-wielding killer succeeding in projecting an ambience of fear over both time and distance. Even if the goals of the killers were here apparently individual rather than social, there is something at least proto-political about such private projects of terror creation. A clear line of social stratification—gender—was reinforced using the most simple means of atrocity.

In general, though, for the more politically ambitious the disadvantages of bladed weapons as terroristic tools are clear enough. They can only dominate a relatively small field of threat. Using them effectively requires a confrontation maximizing approach. It is hardly surprising therefore that they remained prominent in two bounded social arenas which modern states long struggled to penetrate:

[273] Pernicone and Ottanelli, *Assassins Against the Old Order*, pp. 115–16.

[274] Respectively: R. Pantucci, *'We Love Death as You Love Life': Britain's Suburban Terrorists* (London, 2015), pp. 282–5 [attack on Stephen Timms, 14 May 2010]; Koehler, *Right-Wing Terrorism in the 21st Century*, p. 94 [stabbing of Henriette Reker, mayoral candidate for Cologne, 17 October 2015]; *Guardian*, 15 January 2019 [killing of Mayor of Gdańsk, Paweł Adamowicz].

[275] *Western Daily Mercury*, 20 October 1862.

[276] J. Dickie, *Cosa Nostra: A History of the Sicilian Mafia* (London, 2004, 2007), pp. 57–8.

[277] *North Devon Journal*, 5 October 1863.

[278] Dickie, *Cosa Nostra*, pp. 57–8.

[279] M. Fellman, *In the Name of God and Country* (New Haven, 2010), pp. 109, 116–17.

[280] P. Dray, *At the Hands of Persons Unknown* (New York, 2002), p. 45.

[281] J. Smith, *Misogynies* (London, 1989, 2013), pp. 163–202.

in both the aristocratic duel and the knife fights of 'under-class' neighbourhoods. Duelling represented an intensely rule-bound, micro-choreographed and highly predictable form of violence that was reserved for a tiny elite: 'the duel-exposed class'.[282] Its tyrannical conventions were designed to disguise its obvious resemblances to lower-class blood-letting (which was, in fact, equally driven by the obsessions of masculinized honour).

No modern government has ever quite managed to abolish the knife as a lower-class weapon entirely.[283] As Robert Muchembled has observed shrewdly, street culture may indeed give the impression of changing with bewildering speed 'but its internal codes have remained the same for centuries'.[284] But even in the latter case, this is the violence of local and marginalized sub-cultures, not the national stage: 'the members of inner-city gangs at the beginning of the 21st century are practising a concept of manly honour which has some echoes of that of the young men of earlier centuries, in that the destructive effects of their aggression are felt primarily by their peers'.[285]

Gangland knifings may indeed convey particular messages to chosen audiences, but those audiences, too, tend to be relatively intimate. Here the consistent use of knives by Cagoulard hit men against suspected informers in 1937–8 was exceptional: but does show some parallels with criminal underworlds.[286] It has recently been suggested that the most notorious of cases—that of Laetitia Toureaux who was found dying in a First-Class carriage on the Paris Métro on the night of 16 May 1937, a dagger still embedded in her neck—may have been the work of the Italian secret service rather than the Cagoule.[287] Whoever killed her, leaving the knife was apparently meant as some kind of calling card: a semi-private signalling to other potential informers, presumably.

In general, then, bladed weapons have generally lent themselves more to intimate, than impersonal, forms of violence. That said, they have acquired an entirely new prominence amongst Islamists in the early twenty-first century. The exact balance of forces driving this trend is hard to judge. Specifically, direct inspiration may have been taken from the advocacy of stabbings by Hamas in 2008.[288] More generally, the video communications revolution seems to facilitate overtly primitive techniques of violence whose visceral effects can now be captured and broadcast more effectively. Paul Gill holds up the butchery of Lee Rigby on a London street in May 2013 as a classic example of telegenic horror achieved by low-tech

[282] R. Hopton, *Pistols at Dawn: A History of Duelling* (London, 2007), p. 261.

[283] *Independent*, 6 July 2008 (J. Owen, '14,000 knife victims a year'); *Guardian*, 28 March 2017 (G. Younge, 'Beyond the Blade: the Truth about Knife Crime in Britain').

[284] R. Muchembled, *A History of Violence* (Cambridge, 2012), p. 296. See also pp. 286–95.

[285] Muchembled, *A History of Violence*, p. 22.

[286] G. K. Brunelle and A Finley-Croswhite, *Murder in the Metro: Laetitia Toureaux and the Cagoule in 1930s France* (Baton Rouge, 2010), pp. 26, 81, 86, 92, 94, 187.

[287] Brunelle and Finley-Croswhite, *Murder in the Métro*, p. 26.

[288] A search of the Global Terrorism Database (for Western Europe and North America only) records a first peak in what they term 'melee' attacks—which appears to incorporate knife attacks—as occurring around 1991 (at about 300); with a second peak in 2015 (of 550). See: https://www.start.umd.edu/data-tools/global-terrorism-database-gtd

means: 'television stations couldn't beam the images quick enough. Michael Adebolajo's blood-stained hands were an evocative image that will unfortunately live long in infamy'.[289]

Ambitiously, Islamist propaganda has promoted knife attacks along with vehicle ramming as constituting classic 'self-starter' techniques that almost anyone can adopt to launch 'the jihad of individuals'.[290] Lurking in the background also seems to be an Islamist aesthetic of kitsch medievalism: globally, beheading videos have become a notable specialist genre amongst the twenty-first-century's 'atrocity porn'.[291] Nonetheless, there seems something essentially faddish about these trends. It is hard to see knives consistently rivalling either bombs or firearms over the longer-term future.

[289] Gill, *Lone Actor Terrorists*, p. 181.

[290] BBC News, 3 May 2019 ('London Bridge Attack: What Happened'); *The Mail on Sunday*, 3 June 2018; *Sunday Herald*, 3 June 2018.

[291] *Daily Telegraph*, 9 May 2004 ('Daniel Pearl "refused to be sedated before his throat was cut"').

6

Violence, Sabotage, and the Mobile Society

'Every good urban guerrilla must be a driver'

– Carlos Marighella[1]

Dynamite's illicit political career is a useful reminder that new technology is often adopted, and adapted, in radically unforeseen ways. Likewise, the revolutions in transport that characterized the nineteenth and twentieth centuries have profoundly transformed the patterns and practice of political violence. Such transformations have been both active and passive. They have been active in that new means of transport—and the mobility they bring—have been used to facilitate radically new types of violence. And they have been passive in that means of transport have themselves recurrently become targets: indeed, the extent to which modern political violence has become fixated on complex transport networks is one of its most distinguishing features. In this chapter—and without entirely neglecting railways—I focus most heavily upon the rise of the motorized society and the arena of aviation: the new means of transport that distinguished the context of the twentieth century. Finally, I turn attention to deliberate tactics of forced immobilism—the attempts to use sabotage to attack the mobile society and its processes of production. Sabotage is a far broader phenomenon than attacks on transport, of course; but for reasons of analytical convenience I deal with it as an integrated subject area here.

I

As has been seen, the railway age benefited the forces of law and order far more readily than their opponents. It is true that railways allowed a rapid concentration of crowds that could potentially prove a local challenge to the state. The spread of the railways in Ireland led, for instance, to a definite spike in mass confrontations around Orange demonstrations.[2] In the southern USA, the emergence of lynchings before monster crowds of upwards of 10,000 in the 1890s was directly facilitated

[1] C. Marighella, *Mini-Manual of the Urban Guerrilla* (Montreal, 2002), p. 13.

[2] For examples: Lord Rossmore, *Things I can Tell* (London, 1912), p. 241 [on the Roslea Incident of October 1883]; Londonderry Riot Inquiry Commission, *Report of a Commission Appointed to Inquire into Certain Disturbances Which Took Place in the City of Londonderry on the 1st November 1883* (Dublin, 1884), pp. vi, viii, ix.

by special excursion trains.[3] Yet there was no equivalent in either the USA or Western Europe to the Russian experience of pogroms, where railways seemed to spread disorder faster than the state could cope with it (even if their forces had not been so entirely indifferent to the fate of the Jews). In Russia, the major railway lines turned out to be 'transmission mechanisms for public disorder'.[4]

The advent of the motor car was a different matter altogether. In general terms, mass car ownership has a fair claim to be *the* single most important twentieth-century invention that enabled sustained projections of violence beyond merely local settings. Even here, though, its *specific* roles have been highly variegated. A curiously classical use of motor vehicles (for instance) has been their use as chariots of triumph, dragging vanquished enemies behind them. As early as 1919, white racists hauled the body of a black veteran, Lucius McCarty, through the streets of Bogalusa, Louisiana.[5] At much the same time, Italian fascists were using identical tactics against Communist workers.[6]

More importantly, motor vehicles have allowed an unparalleled concentration of forces with both speed and flexibility: a potential that emerged with full clarity in the period immediately after the First World War. Here the motorized violence of peace had some parallels with the grander improvisations of conventional warfare. On 7 September 1914, the entire Paris reserve had been rushed to the front in taxis (five to a cab; and at a cost of the meter fare plus 27 per cent) to help turn the tide of the Battle of the Marne.[7] The Belgian army had already pioneered similar tactics: 'unarmoured touring cars—Excelsiors, Minervas and others—were pressed into service to carry sharpshooters equipped with rifles or machine-guns on lightning raids against the advancing Germans.'[8]

Two general features might be noted about the interwar boom in motorized raiding tactics. First, mass intimidation by motor quickly became a feature of both urban and rural confrontations. During the massive rioting at Tulsa, Oklahoma, in 1921, 'sixty or seventy motor cars filled with armed white men formed a circle around the negro section' of the city which they proceeded to torch.[9] Even more profoundly, it spread mass violence into the depths of the countryside. Secondly, it disproportionately benefited those with more access to motor vehicles: the Right. Those with easiest access to these—still expensive—means of transport were best placed to use them most effectively. Mobile terror heavily favoured the privileged. So long as motorized swarm tactics depended upon ready access to private car owners, the Right with its conservative friends remained disproportionately advantaged.

[3] P. Dray, *At the Hands of Persons Unknown* (New York, 2002, 2003), p. 78.

[4] N. Ferguson, *The War of the World: History's Age of Hatred* (London, 2006, 2007), pp. 66–7, 71.

[5] D. F. Krugler, *1919, The Year of Racial Violence* (Cambridge, 2015), p. 191.

[6] R. J. B. Bosworth, *Mussolini's Italy: Life Under the Fascist Dictatorship, 1915–1945* (London, 2005, 2007), p. 164.

[7] R. Humble, *Famous Land Battles: From Medieval to Modern Times* (London, 1979, 1980), p. 108; L. J. K. Setright, *Drive on! A Social History of the Motor Car* (London, 2002, 2004), p. 41.

[8] B. T. White, *Tanks and Other Armoured Fighting Vehicles, 1900–1918* (London, 1970), p. 117.

[9] R. Hofstadter and M. Wallace (eds), *American Violence: A Documentary History* (New York, 1970, 1971), p. 252.

The tactical advantages afforded by motor transport could be pronounced. While the Kapp Putsch was faltering in Berlin, rural intimidation proceeded more smoothly. On 18 March 1920, sixty men of the Freikorps Rossbach descended upon Mecklenburg village to break up a meeting of striking workers. Franz Slomski was singled out as a ringleader by the local land owner, Bachman: he was then abducted and shot.[10] Just a few months later—on the night of 21 February 1921—lorry loads of the Ulster Special Constabulary from Enniskillen swooped on the village of Roslea in County Fermanagh following an IRA attack that morning. Together with a local loyalist militia they attacked thirty-one houses occupied by Catholics: ten were burnt down.[11] Such enhanced response times were novel: and, for opponents, ominous.

Swarm manoeuvres of this sort were developed most fully by the Italian fascists across northern Italy: they 'adopted tactics of rapid incursions of squads who had arrived from other provinces, in this way making it impossible, or at least very difficult, to identify those responsible for the aggression'.[12] Fascists

> roared around the countryside, terrorising anyone who was, in their opinion, or might be, socialist. They did so with impunity. 'The *carabinieri* travel around with them in their lorries . . . sing their hymns and eat and drink with them,' reported a priest. A lot of these lorries were provided by the army, many high-ranking officers being kindly disposed towards the squads.[13]

Such tactics enabled major set-piece operations such as the sudden occupation by 1,000 squadrists of Grosseto 'the socialist stronghold of southern Tuscany and the capital of a province where until then the indigenous forces of reaction were virtually non-existent as an effective political force'. On the night of 29 June 1921 the major socialist headquarters and the homes of political opponents were sacked, 'leaving 55 people dead and 16 wounded': a ratio that speaks to the ferocity of the attack.[14]

Yet if Italy showcased such tactics at their most effective, by the early 1930s cavalcades of reaction became a pan-European phenomenon. In France, they were a speciality of the *Croix de Feu* whose 'penchant for motorised mobilisations, in which a motorcade of thousands of members would descend on a location kept secret until the last minute, raised suspicion that the league was preparing an attempt on power'.[15] In Germany, the Nazi storm troopers were very well organized in forming 'subsections that pooled militants who possessed motorcycles and

[10] E. J. Gumbel, *Vier Jahre Politischer Mord* (Berlin, 1922), p. 54. Also: https://nordwestmecklenburg.de

[11] See my own: T. K. Wilson, 'The Strange Death of Loyalist Monaghan, 1912–1921' in S. Pašeta (ed.), *Uncertain Futures: Essays About the Irish Past for Roy Foster* (Oxford, 2016), pp. 183–4.

[12] E. Gentile, 'Paramilitary Violence in Italy: The Rationale of Fascism and the Origins of Totalitarianism', in R. Gerwarth and J. Horne (eds), *War in Peace: Paramilitary Violence in Europe after the Great War* (Oxford, 2012, 2013), p. 97.

[13] L. Hughes-Hallett, *The Pike. Gabriele D'Annunzio: Poet, Seducer and Preacher of War* (London, 2013), p. 578. Also: Bosworth, *Mussolini's Italy*, pp. 127–8.

[14] F. M. Snowden, *The Fascist Revolution in Tuscany 1919–1922* (Cambridge, 1989), p. 201.

[15] B. Jenkins and C. Millington, *France and Fascism: February 1934 and the Dynamics of Political Crisis* (London, 2015, 2016), p. 153.

private cars'.[16] Above all, motor transport allowed the projection of an impression of strength (and menace) far wider than before:

> An element of SA tactics which created particular difficulties for the police was the use of motor transport. The advantages gained by the widespread use of motor vehicles were considerable in the eastern Prussian provinces, where distances were greater and the population more scattered than in western or central Germany. Faced with a sudden invasion of two or three hundred storm troopers, isolated groups of Social Democrats often could do little to protect their own meetings or confront the Nazis. Similarly, two or three police officers in an outlying village frequently found themselves unable to prevent the SA from disturbing the peace, ignoring bans on open-air demonstrations or the wearing of political uniforms, and terrorising their opponents.[17]

If motor transport allowed the rapid concentration of friendly forces, it also enabled a most convenient removal of opponents. The genealogy of such tactics is complex. It probably had no single source: though Weimar Germany perhaps can claim the dubious honour of leading the way here. On the night of 15–16 January 1919 Rosa Luxemburg and Karl Liebknecht were both separately abducted by car from the Eden Hotel in Berlin: and both separately murdered. The killings had an improvised, rather than ritualistic, quality.[18] By the autumn of 1920, though, the death squad operating out of the Bavarian Civil Guard had worked out a standard operating procedure: 'in several instances, vehicles traced to the Business Affairs Division were seen at times and in places where shots were heard or bodies were found'.[19] At exactly the same time, elements within the Royal Irish Constabulary were developing parallel tactics in Belfast. Their operating style was, however, notably more blatant:

> They always came at night, after curfew. They left plenty of witnesses alive. Above all, they took great care to ensure no ambiguity as to whether or not they were the police, so that there should be no doubt as to who was giving this message of terror; thus, they introduced themselves as 'police on duty'; they wore their uniforms; they mocked their victims by denying that they were the 'murder gang', by reassuring them that all would be well, and by returning afterwards to offer their families fake condolences.[20]

Such episodes probably had relatively little wider influence. Doubtless more influential—because more internationally notorious—was the example set by American gangsters. As early as the mid-1920s, the phrase to be 'taken for a ride' had entered American parlance. In November 1924, the Pennsylvania newspaper, *The Evening News* reported that 'another victim has been "taken for a ride". The body, bearing

[16] D. Siemens, *Stormtroopers: A New History of Hitler's Brownshirts* (New Haven, 2017), pp. 64–5.

[17] R. Bessel, *Political Violence and the Rise of Nazism: The Storm Troopers in Eastern Germany, 1925–1934* (New Haven, 1984), p. 82.

[18] M. Jones, *Founding Weimar: Violence and the German Revolution of 1918–1919* (Cambridge, 2016), pp. 233–8; K. Gietinger, *The Murder of Rosa Luxemburg* (London, 2008, 2019), pp. 33–42.

[19] A. D. Brenner, '*Feme* Murder: Paramilitary "Self-Justice" in Weimar Germany' in B. B. Campbell and A. D. Brenner (eds), *Death Squads in Global Perspective: Murder with Deniability* (New York, 2002), p. 65.

[20] T. K. Wilson, '"The Most Terrible Assassination that has yet stained the Name of Belfast": the McMahon Murders in Context', *Irish Historical Studies*, XXXVII (145), May 2010, p. 93.

three bullet wounds, was found slumped in an alley where, police believe it had been hurled from an automobile'.[21] Hymie Weiss, a Chicago gangster, has often been credited with the invention of the car as a private tumbril at around this time: 'his henchmen took kidnapped victims by car to open ground on the outskirts of Chicago, shot them en route or at arrival, and dumped the bodies'.[22] Reflected and refracted through the magic mirror of Hollywood, such tactics became both internationally known, and indeed, imitated.[23]

A notable variant here was pioneered by the right-wing Lapua movement in Finland. Generally—but not invariably—they preferred not to 'kill their opponents but kidnapped them, beat them up, and dropped them over the Russian border'.[24] A certain escalatory dynamic is nonetheless observable here. Early victims were typically small-fry opponents. But later targets included the two Communist members of the Constitutional Committee of Parliament (abducted in session) and the Liberal ex-President of Finland, K. J. Ståhlberg and his wife: 'all told, the balance of the wild "Lapua Summer" of 1930 was some 250 "rides" or attempts to that end'.[25] The Lapua's brief experiments in motorized abduction serve as a valuable reminder that in many circumstances terror can be administered in relatively small doses, and still make its impact.[26]

To put these developments in wider context: the emergence of the modern death squad is largely unthinkable without the prior emergence of a society of mass automobile ownership. Death squads began to appear after the First World War: and may fairly be taken as a symptom of its chaotic aftermath. But it is also worth noting that this is exactly the tipping point at which mass car ownership was becoming the norm. At end of 1913, there were already 500,000 model T-Ford cars on the roads of the USA.[27] This convergence of timing is in itself hardly surprising. Sudden arrival in the midst of the night; removal of the chosen victim; and the subsequent discovery of the body, typically on deserted wasteland or on the outskirts of the town—in short, the classic operating style of the death squad depends upon the availability of vehicles at every turn. It was common knowledge in Barcelona in 1936 that the Red Terror rode in the 'cars of fear and death'.[28] More than any other factor, indeed, it was access to motorized transport that have allowed death squads to maintain 'the paradox of being secretive and covert organizations that nevertheless often act in particularly public and gruesome fashion'.[29]

[21] Quoted in: htttps://.www.phrases.org.uk/meanings/taken-for-a-ride.html. Accessed: 12 July 2019.

[22] J. Ruiz, *The 'Red Terror' and The Spanish Civil War: Revolutionary Violence in Madrid* (Cambridge, 2012, 2014), pp. 136–7.

[23] Ruiz, *The 'Red Terror' and The Spanish Civil War*, pp. 135–8.

[24] W. Laqueur, *Terrorism* (London, 1977, 1980), p. 97.

[25] L. Karvonen, *From White to Blue-and-Black: Finnish Fascism in the Inter-War Era* (Helsinki, 1988), p. 20.

[26] S. Kalyvas, *The Logic of Violence in Civil War* (Cambridge, 2006), pp. 26–7.

[27] V. Cowles, *The Defiant Swansong* (London, 1967), p. 253.

[28] C. Ealham, *Anarchism and the City: Revolution and Counter-Revolution in Barcelona, 1898–1937* (Oakland, 2010), p. 185.

[29] B. B. Campbell, 'Death Squads: Definition, Problems, and Historical Context' in B. B. Campbell and A. D. Brenner (eds), *Death Squads in Global Perspective: Murder with Deniability* (New York, 2002), p. 5.

Death squads often abducted their victims from their homes: a symbolic removal from the community. But they were typically not taken too far away since they were meant to be found quickly.[30] In 1919–20, German killers thus deliberately left their corpses in public parks. Around Berlin these included the Tiergarten and the Tegeler Forst: in Munich, the Englischen Garten and the Forstenreider Wald.[31] In Belfast in 1921, the traditional area for the display of corpses killed by the police death squads were the lanes leading out of the west of the city into the hills.[32] Similarly, in Barcelona in the summer of 1936, it was the Arabassada Highway with its panoramic views over the city that was favoured for the jettisoning of bodies.[33] Madrid's killing grounds at the same time were a little more distant: but still no more than eight miles away.[34] Whatever the local variations, public display was always a requisite feature of such exemplary killings, fully intended to attract the curious 'like buzzing flies'.[35] Abandoned corpses projected the careful choreography of casual contempt.

In summary, an ability to appear, and disappear, suddenly lies at the heart of the phantasmagoric image that death squads aspire to project. It is worth noting in passing that those in the business of making nightmares often choose cartoonish-like names. In 1936, one of the communist death squads operating in the Western districts of Madrid called itself the 'Popeye Squad'.[36] The late twentieth century was to furnish further examples in the wider geo-political neighbourhood: the 'Ninjas' of Algeria (1993–4) and 'The Jokers' in the Croat-held areas of Bosnia: the latter a Batman reference, apparently.[37]

What, though, of the possibilities of individual rebellion? How did the flexibility of motor transport enhance these? They certainly paid rich psychological dividends. Both Irish Republicans and Catalan anarchists found the unwonted experience of commandeering automobiles a memorably invigorating experience.[38] Still, even before the First World War, France had seen the advent of the motor bandit: the Bonnot gang who professed anarchist principles although they

[30] Ruiz, *The 'Red Terror' and The Spanish Civil War*, pp. 134–5.

[31] R. G. L. Waite, *Vanguard of Nazism: The Free Corps Movement in Postwar Germany*, 1918–1923 (New York, 1952, 1969), p. 221; Gumbel, *Vier Jahre Politischer Mord*, pp. 14, 29, 64; Anonymous, 'Karl Liebknecht and Rosa Luxeburg [sic]: Last Hours', *The Communist Review*, January 1924, Vol. 4, No. 9. Available at: https://www.marxists.org/history/international/comintern/sections/britain/periodicals/communist_review/1924/09/last_hours.htm

Also: S. Delmer, *Weimar Germany: Democracy on Trial* (London, 1972), p. 37.

[32] T. P. Coogan, *The I.R.A.* (London, 1970, 1971), p. 209: J. McDermott, *Northern Divisions: The Old IRA and the Belfast Pogroms, 1920–1922* (Belfast, 2001), pp. 88–9.

[33] Ealham, *Anarchism and the City*, pp. 177–8. For brief details of some individual victims found there: https://catholicsaints.info (Maria Roqueta Serra; Teresa Subira Sanjaumo; Francisca Pons-Sarda). Accessed 15 July 2019.

[34] C. E. Lucas Phillips, *The Spanish Pimpernel* (London, 1960, 1962), p. 46.

[35] Coogan, *The I.R.A.*, p. 209: Ruiz, *The 'Red Terror' and The Spanish Civil War*, p. 135.

[36] Ruiz, *The 'Red Terror' and The Spanish Civil War*, p. 136.

[37] Ruiz, *The 'Red Terror' and The Spanish Civil War*, p. 136. J. Filiu, *From Deep State to Islamic State: the Arab Counter-Revolution and its Jihadi Legacy* (London, 2015), p. 97; *Washington Post*, 19 December 1997 ('Dutch troops capture two Croat War Crimes Suspects').

[38] F. Mac Bhloscaidh, 'Tyrone' in J. Crowley (et al., eds), *Atlas of the Irish Revolution* (Cork, 2017), p. 639 [ballad of Johnston's Motorcar']; Ealham, *Anarchism and the City*, pp. 175, 179.

'kept 90 per cent of the booty for personal use'.[39] Having pioneered 'the world's first getaway car', they proceeded to outrun the gendarmerie for a few heady months before coming to the bandit's traditional end in a hopeless siege.[40]

Strikingly, it was another two decades before their example was more widely imitated in Europe: here the reborn car bandit was a product of the Great Depression. In general, their political commitment was vestigial: although the Eierschlamm gang who carried out fifteen motorized robberies in the Greater Berlin area in 1931–2 do seem to have emerged from the Communist youth scene. They 'continued to meet in the Communist tavern in the Yorckstrasse and even to be politically active—to the extent of getting into fights with National Socialists—at the same time as they were carrying on their criminal career'.[41] Even this rather nugatory level of ideological commitment exceeded that of the Göthe brothers in 1936–7 who used the brand new autobahns of Nazi Germany to such good effect that they succeeded in getting several SS officers cashiered for cowardice in the face of the enemy.[42]

In the USA, car banditry simply emerged along with the society of mass car ownership. 'Seventy-five percent of all crimes now are perpetrated with the aid of the automobile' estimated one crime writer as early as 1924.[43] While the conditions of Great Depression indeed fuelled car crimes, 'the violence that catapulted men like John Dillinger to prominence in 1934 wasn't the beginning of a crime wave; it was the end of one'.[44] Ideological commitments for this new generation of motor bandits was nugatory in the extreme: at most 'the sensationalized run of characters like John Dillinger, whose robberies of banks and railroads played out like a populist fantasy of revenge on the big business interests behind the Great Depression, pushed some into supporting "the outlaw as social bandit"'.[45] For his part, 'Pretty Boy Floyd' made only the most formulaic pronouncements about targeting the rich rather than the poor. But they had a degree of recklessness that directly challenged federal authority.[46] A provocation such as the Kansas City Massacre, that killed four law enforcement officers (in June 1933), simply could not be ignored.[47] In challenging the federal state, such groups forced major governmental reorganization

[39] Laqueur, *Terrorism*, p. 128.

[40] L. Sante, *The Other Paris: An Illustrated Journey Through A City's Poor and Bohemian Past* (New York, 2015), p. 254. Also: M. Anderson, *In Thrall to Political Change: Police and Gendarmerie in France* (Oxford, 2011), pp. 81, 321.

[41] E. Rosenhaft, *Beating the Fascists? The German Communists and Political Violence, 1929–1933* (Cambridge, 1983), pp. 134, 136.

[42] H. H. Liang, *The Rise of the Modern Police and The European State System from Metternich to the Second World War* (Cambridge, 1992, 2002), p. 251, note 41.

[43] Quoted in: B. Burrough, *Public Enemies: America's Greatest Crime Wave and the Birth of the FBI, 1933–34* (New York, 2004), p. 17.

[44] Burrough, *Public Enemies*, p. 16.

[45] J. A. Densley, '"A Citadel of Crime": Saint Paul, Minnesota and the O'Connor System' in J. Windle, J. F. Morrison, A. Winter, and A. Silke (eds) *Historical Perspectives on Organized Crime and Terrorism* (Abingdon, 2018), p. 31.

[46] Burrough, *Public Enemies*, p. 21.

[47] Burrough, *Public Enemies*, pp. 48–9, 51–2. Also: https://www.kansascity.com/news/special-reports/kc-true-crime/article706028.html

before they were overcome—the modern FBI is their enduring monument.[48] Car radios also went a long way towards restoring the balance of advantage in favour of the police.[49]

Vehicles could be used not just as getaway vehicles but also to enhance attacks in their own right. The suggestion of using the car as a mobile firing platform seems to be very nearly as old as the car itself. Armoured cars were already distinguished exhibits at motor shows in both London and Paris as early as 1902.[50] Where military minds led, others were bound to follow. Against, this backdrop it is no great surprise that the drive-by shooting was an invention of the early twentieth century. It appears to have been first pioneered on 1 July 1917 during a race riot in East St Louis when 'a group of whites in a Ford drove through the black district, shooting into homes'.[51] Such tactics were further consolidated in the great riots that convulsed Chicago in 1919.[52]

Despite claims to the contrary, the drive-by shooting was therefore not actually 'established by predominantly Italian mobsters in New York and Chicago in the 1920s'.[53] That said, the psychopathic Hymie Weiss did offer a very public advertisement of its psychological impact on 20 September 1926:

> On that day a motorcade laid on by Weiss, Capone's chief rival at the time, slowly drove past his headquarters at the Hawthorne Inn, in Cicero, and as each car drove past its occupants methodically raked the building with machine-gun fire. The first man to fire had actually used blanks, hoping presumably to draw Capone outside. Luckily for the gang leader one of his men immediately pushed him to the floor, and during the entire shoot-out, in which one thousand rounds were fired, no one was hurt.[54]

By 1931, it would be firmly, if wrongly, 'remembered' that it was 'Hymie Weiss who invented murder by motor'.[55] Here, too, Hollywood doubtless had much to answer for. Even if technically erroneous, such origin myths still have their own social significance: they point to the resonant romance of gangsterdom.[56] And yet whether explicitly prompted by cinema's love affair with gangsters (or not), the same sort of possibilities could be adopted by various actors (more or less independently of each other).

In other words, the drive-by shooting was probably 'invented' many times over across different theatres. In Berlin, 'the Chicago on the Spree', neighbourhood struggles between Communists and Nazi Stormtroopers often centred upon control of key local bases: hence 'Schöneberg Communists arranged for two SA taverns to be fired on from a moving car' (in July 1932). Nonetheless, such experiments

[48] Burrough, *Public Enemies*, pp. 58–9.

[49] B. Whalen and J. Whalen, *The NYPD's First Fifty Years: Politicians, Police Commissioners, and Patrolmen* (Lincoln, Nebraska), pp. 191–2.

[50] White, *Tanks and Other Armoured Fighting Vehicles*, pp. 110–11.

[51] Hofstadter and Wallace, *American Violence*, p. 241.

[52] Krugler, *1919*, pp. 122, 128, 232.

[53] R. W. Novaco, 'Automobile Driving and Aggressive Behavior' in M. Wachs and M. Crawford (eds), *The Car and the City: The Automobile, The Built Environment, and Daily Urban Life* (University of Michigan, 1992), p. 243.

[54] J. Ellis, *The Social History of the Machine Gun* (London, 1975, 1987), p. 152–3.

[55] Ellis, *Social History of the Machine Gun*, p. 152.

[56] E. J. Hobsbawm, *Bandits* (London, 1969, 2001), pp. 186–7.

remained strongly discouraged by the party hierarchy.[57] In 1936, Falangists shot up the slums of Madrid as the country slid towards outright civil war.[58] Drive-by bombings were also briefly tried out by both Breton nationalists (in 1933) and by the IRA (in 1939).[59] Outside Europe, the Irgun was experimenting with both drive-by shootings and bombings across Arab areas of Palestine (in 1937–9).[60]

In general, drive-by shootings seem to have become most common as a tactic in ethnically divided societies where stark residential segregation creates dependable pools of victims from a rival community. It thus seems little coincidence that they have emerged at times of tension in urban arenas as diverse as: East St Louis (1917), Chicago (1919), and Belfast (1972–5): or—to look slightly further afield—across the Middle East in both Jerusalem (1937) and Algiers (1961–2). Such recurrence is striking and has been well recognized by affected populations. They learn to recognize the ominously low cruising speeds—about eight miles an hour—that typically precede such atrocities.[61] Since it is near impossible to shoot accurately from a speeding car, the drive-by shooting typically takes the slowed-down form of a nightmare.[62]

Across such segregated arenas, mobile terror transformed the sense of threat. It is a feature of cities with tense ethnic relations that trouble tends to cluster at the 'boundary areas' between different neighbourhoods. At times of tension, there is a generalized retreat into the safety of ghettoes: a collective response that tends to suppress more spontaneous opportunities for violence. Conversely, though, individuals who are forced to work in different areas of the city are left particularly exposed to attack. Streetcars and trolley-buses become the classic target of bombings and shootings since they transported a regular supply of trapped members of the 'wrong' ethnicity through hostile areas: in effect, a conveyer belt of potential victims. Such attack patterns were a recurrent feature of disturbances in both Chicago (1919) and Belfast (1921–2).[63] Oran and Algiers were similarly targeted

[57] Rosenhaft, *Beating the Fascists?*, pp. 127, 136.

[58] For Spain: P. Brendon, *The Dark Valley: A Panorama of the 1930s* (London, 2000), p. 317. Also: P. Preston, *The Spanish Holocaust: Inquisition and Extermination in Twentieth-Century Spain* (London, 2012, 2013), p. 74.

[59] *Leeds Mercury*, 8 August 1933 [bomb hurled from car at Hotel de Ville, Rennes]; NA, MEPO 3/1908 [bomb thrown from car on Edgeware Road]; *Birmingham Mail*, 1 April 1939. Bombs were also thrown from cars in Belfast as early as 1933—but contextual details are scanty: *Palestine Post*, 1 March 1933 ('Bombs in Belfast').

[60] For Palestine: B. Hoffman, *Anonymous Soldiers: The Struggle for Israel, 1917–1947* (New York, 2015), p. 95 [1939]; *The Times*, 18 March 1937, 8 July 1938.

[61] For fear of slow-moving cars: M. Feraoun, *Journal 1955–1962: Reflections on the French-Algerian War* (Lincoln, 1962, 2000), p. 311; E. O'Callaghan, *Belfast Days: A 1972 Teenage Diary* (Sallins, 2014), p. 155.

[62] For drive by shootings: East St Louis: Hofstadter and Wallace, *American Violence*, pp. 241, 249, 251. For drive by attacks in Palestine: *The Times*, 18 March 1937, 8 July 1938. For Algeria: M. Evans, *Algeria: France's Undeclared War* (Oxford, 2012, 2013), pp. 304–5; P. Henissart, *Wolves in the City* (London, 1973), pp. 154, 168, 287; R. P. De Laparre, *Journal d'un prêtre en Algérie: Oran 1961–1962* (no place of publication given, 1964), pp. 14, 17, 34, 45; F. Dessaigne, *Journal d'une mère de familie pied-noir* (Paris, 1962), p. 130; D. Prochaska, *Making Algeria French: Colonialism in Bône, 1870–1920* (Cambridge, 1990), p. 241. For Belfast in the 1970s: NA, CJ 4/829; O'Callaghan, *Belfast Days*, p. 156; A. Parkinson, *1972 and the Ulster Troubles* (Dublin, 2010), pp. 60, 196, 337–8.

[63] For Chicago: Krugler, *1919*, pp. 92, 109, 122, 187, 290; A. D. Grimshaw, 'Urban Racial Violence in the United States: Changing Ecological Considerations', *The American Journal of Sociology*, LXVI (2), September 1960, pp. 114, 117. For Belfast: McDermott, *Northern Divisions*, pp. 126, 128,

(1961–2).[64] Public transport became something to be avoided in these times and places, if at all possible.

By contrast, privatized transport allows killers to penetrate rival ghettoes at their own convenience. Mass car ownership has thus acted as a catalyst for both the fragmentation, and the ominous diffusion, of older patterns of confrontation. Such disembodied escalations of violence in turn help to create more generalizing effects of fear. Rioting is a transitory moment of mass mobilization. But a campaign of random assassination can be sustained more-or-less indefinitely. Rioting is an inherently local drama. It is strictly bounded. By contrast the drive-by shooting is, potentially at least, ubiquitous. Moreover, it can be performed by tiny groups. It does not require a supporting cast of thousands. Nor does it have to kill very many people to frighten many more.

However, as an 'attack platform' it is the development of the car bomb that has undoubtedly been of much wider political significance: 'the poor man's air force' as it has been called.[65] Although horse-drawn ancestors of the vehicle-bomb can indeed be traced back to the Wall Street bombing of September 1920 or the assassination attempt on Napoleon at Christmas 1800, the car-bomb is essentially a creation of the mid-twentieth century. Like so much else, it is primarily a product of that laboratory of terror tactics: the Holy Land.[66] Its successful use was mastered by the LEHI (*Lohamei Herut Israel*) in 1946–7, leading in turn to the full-scale tit-for-tat exchanges of spectacular vehicle bombs with the Arab Higher Committee that marked the dying months of the British Mandate.[67] Vehicle bombs efficiently prepared the ground for civil war in 1947–8.[68]

In the longer run, and against global horizons, the effects of this hybrid technology of the motorization of the major explosion have been no less profound. Here the assessment of the historian of the car-bomb is sobering:

> Between 1992 and 1999, 25 major vehicle bomb attacks in 22 different cities killed 1337 people and wounded nearly 12,000. More importantly from a geopolitical standpoint, the Provisional IRA and a Brooklyn cell of the Egyptian Islamist group, al-Gam'a al-Islamiyya, inflicted billions of dollars of damage on the two leading control-centers of the world economy—the City of London (1992, 1993, and 1996) and lower Manhattan (1993), respectively—and forced a reorganization of the global reinsurance industry.[69]

As 'the brutal hardware and quotidian workhorses of urban terrorism', vehicle bombs came fully of age in the last decades of the twentieth century. They are unlikely to disappear any time soon.

130; T. K. Wilson, *Frontiers of Violence: Conflict and Identity in Ulster and Upper Silesia, 1918–1922* (Oxford, 2010), pp. 177–8; *Irish News*, 13 February 1922; *Mid-Ulster Mail*, 18 February 1922.

[64] For Algiers and Oran: A. Horne, *A Savage War of Peace* (New York, 1977, 2006), p. 495; R. Delpard, *Ils ont vécu dans L'Algérie en guerre: Chronique d'un paradis perdu* (Montreal, 2012), pp. 138, 151, 158; Ferauon, *Journal*, p. 311; Dessaigne, *Journal d'une mère de familie pied-noir*, p. 124.

[65] M. Davis, *Buda's Wagon: A Brief History of the Car Bomb* (London, 2007), p. 4.

[66] Davis, *Buda's Wagon*, pp. 18–27. [67] Davis, *Buda's Wagon*, pp. 18–27.

[68] L. Collins and D. Lapierre, *O Jerusalem!* (London, 1982), pp. 159–61; Davis, *Buda's Wagon*, p. 28; T. K. Wilson, 'Turbulent Stasis: Comparative Reflections upon Intercommunal Violence and Territoriality in the Israel/Palestine Conflict', *Nationalism and Ethnic Politics*, 19 (1) 2013, p. 70.

[69] Davis, *Buda's Wagon*, p. 6.

And yet one of the many unpleasant surprises of the early twenty-first century has been the sudden emergence of vehicles as weapons in their own right. Ramming attacks have hardly been entirely unknown, of course, over the past 100 years. A combined vehicle-and-firearm attack killed a single European civilian in Oran, Algeria, in October 1961.[70] More spectacularly, on 10 July 1973, Olga Hepnarová rented a lorry in Prague and 'spent nearly half an hour circling a busy tram stop waiting for a satisfactory number of people to gather there. When some 25 people were present she drove the lorry straight into them at speed.' Eight died: and a further twelve were injured in what she described as an attack on society in general ('if the society destroys individuals, individuals can destroy society').[71]

Such incidents remained utterly exceptional events for over a century. In 2016–18, though, a spate of vehicle-ramming attacks by a variety of politically-motivated actors suddenly emerged. Of these by far the most lethal occurred on 14 July 2016 when Mohamed Lahouaiej-Bouhel killed eighty-six people by driving a lorry into a crowd on the seafront at Nice.[72] Other notable attacks in the aftermath included: a lorry attack on a Christmas market in Berlin (20 December 2016); Khalid Masood's car-and-knife assault at Westminster (22 March 2017); the Stockholm truck atrocity (7 April 2017); another combined vehicle and knife rampage in the London Bridge area (3 June 2017); Darren Osbourne's van attack outside Finsbury Park Mosque, north London (19 June 2017); James A. Fields's driving into a crowd at Charlottesville (12 August 2017); Salih Khater's botched vehicle attack at Westminster (14 August 2017); the Las Ramblas massacre in Barcelona (17 August 2017); Paul Moore's driving at pedestrians in Leicester (20 September 2017); Sayfullo Saipov's rampage on the Hudson River Park's bike path, New York (31 October 2017); a vehicle attack on a café in Kiepenkerl, Germany (8 April 2018); a rampage by a van driver, Alek Minassian, in Toronto that killed ten (23 April 2018).[73] More systematic attempts to chart the rise of this attack form confirm the abruptness of its diffusion (Figure 6.1).[74]

[70] Dessaigne, *Journal d'une mère de familie pied-noir*, p. 103.

[71] 'Olga Hepnarová—the last woman executed in Czechoslovakia'. Available at: http://.www.capitalpunishmentuk.org/hepnarova.html

[72] BBC News, 19 August 2016 ('Nice Attack: What We Know about the Bastille Day Killings').

[73] For Berlin: *i*, 20 December 2016 ('At Least Nine Dead As Truck Rams Christmas Market'). For Westminster: *Guardian*, 23 March 2017 ('Terror in Westminster'). For Stockholm: *Guardian*, 8 April 2017 ('Truck drives into Crowd in Stockholm, killing four people'). For London Bridge: *The Guardian*, 5 June 2017 ('Seven dead, 21 critically hurt: May says "enough is enough"'). For Finsbury Park Mosque, London: *The Daily Telegraph*, 20 June 2017 ('Terror Suspect "turned against Muslims" after London Attack'). For Charlottesville: *The Washington Post*, 29 November 2017 ('Man accused in death at Charlottesville rally was "filled with anger", prosecutor said'). For attempted repeat of Westminster attack: BBC News, 15 August 2017 ('Westminster Crash: Salih Khater named as Suspect'). For Barcelona: *Guardian*, 18 August 2017 ('Terror Strikes Barcelona'); For Leicester: *The Guardian*, 2 March 2018 ('Man convicted after running over Muslim Woman in Leicester'). For New York: BBC News, 2 November 2017 ('New York Truck Attack: Who is Suspect Sayfullo Saipov?'). For Kiepenkerl, Germany: *The Mail on Sunday*, 8 April 2018 ('Mown Down in the Marketplace'). For Toronto: *Guardian*, 27 September 2019 ('Toronto Van Attack Suspect Says he was "radicalized" online by "incels"'). For a fuller listing of incidents: V. Miller and K. J. Hayward, '"I Did My Bit": Terrorism, Tarde and the Vehicle Ramming Attack as an Imitative Event', *British Journal of Criminology*, 2018, pp. 7–8.

[74] Miller and Hayward, '"I Did My Bit"', p. 5.

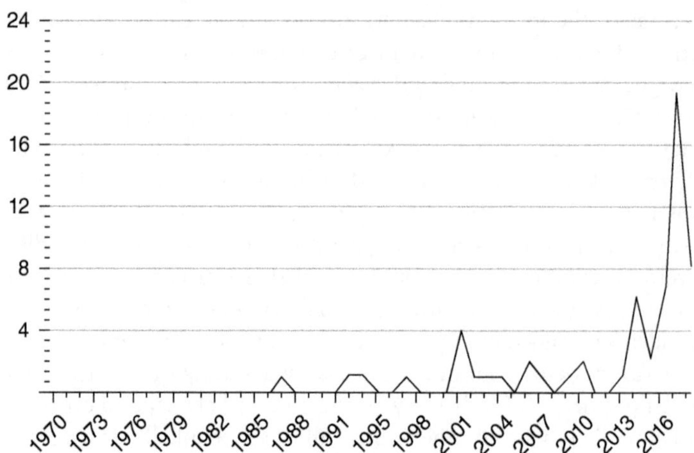

Figure 6.1. Vehicle ramming attacks across North America and Western Europe, 1970–2018
Source: The Global Terrorism Database.

However, the timing of this phenomenon remains very poorly understood. After all, when vehicle-ramming tactics spread, the drive-by shooting was very nearly 100 years old. Car-bombings were also already venerable: about seventy years old. Vehicle-ramming attacks had clearly been possible for all of that time. As Satya Savitsky remarks, 'there is a latent violence in speed, or acceleration': a potential notoriously celebrated by the Italian Futurists and also by Theodor Adorno ('which driver is not tempted, merely by the power of the engine, to wipe out the vermin of the streets, pedestrians, children and cyclists?').[75]

Vehicle accidents had also often demonstrated a clear potential for raising tensions. In Belfast in August 1969, Royal Ulster Constabulary vehicle tactics consisted in 'driving towards the crowds, on occasion mounting the pavements in an endeavour to frighten and disperse'.[76] The resulting injuries were deeply resented. On 3 July 1970, Charles O'Neill was killed by an armoured personnel carrier during the Falls Road Curfew, again severely fuelling local tensions.[77] In 1983, a confidential manual on public order (whose circulation was restricted to Chief Police Officers in England) conceded privately that 'Tactical Use of Vehicles' was 'an emotive subject'.[78] On 8 December 1987 the (accidental) killing of four Palestinian

[75] Quoted in: S. Savitsky, 'Killer Cars: The Violence of Automobility'. Available here: http://scrambledsystems.tumblr.com/ For the 1909 Futurist Manifesto: https://archive.compart.uni-bremen.de/2014/website/fileadmin/media/lernen/Futurist_Manifesto.pdf

[76] L. Scarman, *Violence and Civil Disturbances in Northern Ireland in 1969*, Report of the Tribunal of Inquiry, Vol. I (Belfast, 1972), pp. 61–2.

[77] D. McKittrick et al. (eds), *Lost Lives: The Stories of the Men, Women and Children Who died as a Result of the Northern Ireland Troubles* (Edinburgh, 1999, 2008), pp. 53–4.

[78] G. Northam, *Shooting in the Dark: Riot Police in Britain* (London, 1989), pp. 41–3, 103–4.

workers by an Israeli military tank transport vehicle in the Gaza Strip was locally interpreted as a deliberate attack: and sparked the First Intifada, or uprising.[79]

Attempts to explain why this spate of vehicle attacks emerged so dramatically in the early twenty-first century have broadly interpreted them as improvised primitivism.[80] In effect, vehicle attacks serve as an inverted tribute to the relative success of either 'target-hardening' (making classical terror tactics less easy or effective); or of the security services in foiling more complex plots (such as building bombs); or some combination of both. In this reading, the so-called 'weaponization of everyday life' is seen as a retro-turn that has been forced upon attackers. Ramming becomes widespread as staging car-bombs becomes too difficult, it is assumed. And ramming is a substitute tactic because it is—potentially, at least—a tactic of inferior signalling value. Ramming is often easily confused with 'normal' traffic accidents.

Certainly, this interpretation has much to recommend it. In general terms, the 'do-it-yourself' ethos of Islamist groups in the early twenty-fifst century bears a close resemblance to the Comintern's 'self-starting' advice. Both bear the hallmarks of improvisation under pressure: and of a cult of action, however amateur.[81] From 2010, Al-Qaeda's *Inspire* magazine sought to popularize vehicle-ramming tactics that had already begun to emerge in the laboratory of the Israel/Palestine conflict. Their exhortation was to turn heavy goods vehicles into 'Ultimate Mowing Machines' (a tasteless borrowing from advertising for the Ford F-Series 'Super Duty' pickup truck, dubbed the 'Ultimate Towing Machine'). Such tactics have also been explicitly recommended by ISIS.[82]

There is, in addition, rich anecdotal evidence that vehicle attacks have indeed been very much a second choice for many actors. Explosives remain the preferred option. The Stockholm truck attacker had a homemade bomb, although he apparently failed to detonate it fully.[83] When their bomb factory exploded prematurely, the ISIS cell in Barcelona turned to vehicle attacks. The fake suicide vests worn both at Cambrils and London Bridge that summer would seem to point in the same direction. Darren Osborne, the right-wing van attacker outside the Finsbury Park Mosque, had first dreamt of assassinating Jeremy Corbyn, the leader of the British Labour Party.[84] In all these cases, then, vehicles appear to have been adopted as weapons with some degree of resignation, or even reluctance.

In a valuable contribution, criminologists Vincent Miller and Keith Hayward have offered a searching critique of prevalent explanations for the vehicle ramming

[79] A. M. Lesch, 'Prelude to the Uprising in the Gaza Strip', *Journal of Palestine Studies*, 20 (1) Autumn, 1990, p. 1.

[80] D. A. Baird, 'Is Low-Tech Terrorism An Emerging Strategy in Western Europe? Analysing Patterns of Knife and Vehicle Attacks', University of St Andrews MA thesis, 2018; Y. Veilleux-Lepage, 'How and Why Vehicle Ramming Became the Attack of Choice for Terrorists', *The Conversation*, 29 March 2017.

[81] Rosenhaft, *Beating the Fascists?*, p. 40; M. R. D. Foot, *Resistance* (London, 1976, 1978), p. 55.

[82] Veilleux-Lepage, 'How and Why Vehicle Ramming Became the Attack of Choice for Terrorists'. Miller and Hayward, '"I Did My Bit"', pp. 9–10.

[83] *Independent*, 8 April 2017.

[84] *Guardian*, 30 January 2018 ('Finsbury Park attack accused "wanted to kill Jeremy Corbyn"').

phenomenon. They point out that there was a pronounced time-lag between ISIS calling for vehicle attacks and their frequency rising sharply: about four years. In addition, they point out that target-hardening has been a slow urban revolution that started decades ago.[85] (This latter point is perhaps rather narrowly framed: it does not allow for the possibility that bomb-making itself may recently have become easier to detect by the security services.) Miller and Hayward issue a call to take the study of contagion processes in their own right. Ultimately, they understand vehicle ramming as 'an imitative wave', very broadly comparable to other

> online events such as viral meme campaigns, memes and different forms of online activism/awareness-raising may not be as different as one might think. Both exhibit the same wave-like distribution or temporal clustering—a pattern of inactivity, a rapid increase in take-up, interest or diffusion (usually on a profoundly international scale) and finally a longer, but still rapid, drop-off in participation. For example, this typical pattern of wave-like temporal clustering was demonstrated when seventeen million people participated in the 'Ice bucket challenge', an imitative meme that captured global attention and participation for a brief period in 2014.[86]

This last point about the sudden—and, at the time of writing (2019), apparently final—falling off in vehicle attacks is very well taken.

Yet in a longer-term historical perspective, the question of the delayed emergence of vehicle ramming still lingers unanswered. Two basic points might be made here. The first is convergent with Miller and Hayward's emphasis upon communications networks. It is worth stressing here that the supposed primitivization of the vehicle-ramming phenomenon may be far more apparent than real. If the attack itself seems primitive, the process of its broadcasting is not. Any vehicle attack in the centre of any major city in the early twenty-first century is likely to occur in the presence of hundreds of camera phones. They will capture instant, and dramatic footage, before the emergency services arrive to help (and clean up). Such background conditions simply did not exist before: such an attack in, say, the 1970s would have likely generated poor visual footage. It is not necessarily the case that vehicle ramming attacks are therefore less 'cinematic': though they may tend to generate the 'art house' cinema of shaky, close-up mobile footage, rather than the 'Hollywood'-esque spectacle of 9/11.[87] Secondly, it is worth noting the intentionally self-destructive dimension to these vehicle attacks. In this respect, they belong authentically to the death cults of the twenty-first century. Attackers do not typically seem to make much, or any, provision for their own escape. On many occasions, Islamist attackers in particular seem to have anticipated, and welcomed, their own deaths. In this, such killers are very far removed from the phenomenon of hit-and-run drivers, whose callous determination to evade responsibility was recognized by psychiatrists as long ago as 1942.[88]

[85] Miller and Hayward, '"I Did My Bit"', pp. 9–10.
[86] Miller and Hayward, '"I Did My Bit"', p. 14.
[87] Miller and Hayward, '"I Did My Bit"', p. 10.
[88] L. S. Selling, 'The Feebleminded Motorist', *The American Journal of Insanity*, 98 (6) May 1942, pp. 834–8.

Facilitating roles of both new technology and new ideology thus need to be factored in to explain how vehicle-ramming tactics arose in the early twenty-first century, and not before. Their abrupt rise has been truly remarkable. Yet so, too, has been their decline. As an engine of direct destruction, the motor vehicle's career appears to have been both strikingly late to emerge and—apparently at least—strikingly short lived.

Summarizing all these changes, it seems hard to overstate the importance of the motor vehicle in transforming patterns of violent confrontation—whether as an attack platform (for drive-by shootings), a carriage for a major bombing ('the roving massacre' in the slang of Beirut) or, much more recently, a ramming weapon in its own right.[89] In what Ernest Gellner once called 'the hectically mobile society', it is the car above all that has helped political violence also become hectically mobile.[90]

Curiously, though, the actual infrastructure of the motorized society has not often proved an attractive target for either sabotage or mass casualty attacks. Since all major cities suffer from periodic traffic gridlock with rich attendant possibilities for multiplying mayhem further, this seems a rather striking omission. With some rare exceptions—such as the Provisional IRA's van bomb that blew a crater out of a major flyover junction at Staples Corner, London (11 April 1992)—road and port infrastructure seem to be rarely targeted.[91] It is this aspect that contrasts most pointedly with the world of aviation.

II

> I have always said that we don't hijack planes because we love Boeing 707s.
>
> – Ghassan Kannafani[92]

> By degrees, over the years, the airport experience has become an extreme example of a totalitarian regime at work, making you small and suspect, depriving you of control.... Younger travellers have no idea what has been lost.
>
> – Paul Theroux[93]

How did airports become such prestige stages for atrocity? How did airplanes become a terroristic target of choice—far more often, for instance, than cruise liners?[94] Such layered questions demand appropriately layered answers. So close is the cultural relationship between air travel and security in the twenty-first century,

89 *Iberian Daily Sun*, 18–19 December 1983. Cutting preserved in the Control Risks Archive, St Andrews: Lebanon, 1983 file.

90 E. Gellner, *Nationalism* (Oxford, 1983, 1993), p. 25.

91 A. R. Oppenheimer, *IRA: The Bombs and the Bullets* (Dublin, 2009), p. 125.

92 G. Kannafani, 'On the PLFP and the September Crisis', *New Left Review*, 1 (67) May/June 1971.

93 P. Theroux, *Deep South* (London, 2015, 2016), p. 19.

94 P. Lehr, '(No) Princes of the Sea: Reflections on Maritime Terrorism' in J. Krause and S. Bruns (eds), *Routledge Handbook of Naval Strategy and Security* (Abingdon, 2015), pp. 202–14.

that it bears emphasis that the historical intertwining of the repertoire of the tactics of political violence has actually been a rather long and complex process.

A striking cultural point is that the age of air terror was mentally anticipated long before it dawned in reality. Following the Nazi seizure of power in 1933, the great German airships were dogged by allegations of bombthreats. In 1934, rumours of a bomb plot against the *Graf Zeppelin* prompted an official denial.[95] In April 1937, a letter from Milwaukee was received in the German Embassy in Washington advising

> the Zeppelin company in Frankfurt-am-Main that they should open and search all mail before it is put on board prior to every flight of the Zeppelin *Hindenburg*. The Zeppelin is going to be destroyed by a time bomb during its flight to another country.[96]

The following month—6 May 1937—at an altitude of 260 feet, and a mere 700 feet away from the safety of the mooring mast at Lakehurst Naval Air Station, New Jersey, the *Hindenburg* was abruptly transformed into a *Titanic* of the skies: a fireball consumed it within just 34 seconds.[97] Although officially—and almost certainly correctly—denied, popular allegations of sabotage inevitably swirled around the charred skeleton of the giant airship.[98]

Thus a terroristic campaign of targeting air travel was widely thought fully possible, and plausible, as early 1937. At much the same time (1938), the tactical possibility of targeting civilian aviation was clearly implied in the IRA's S-Plan: although 'delay-action' devices were categorically ruled out.[99] In reality, the idea of time bombs to destroy an aircraft in flight had emerged as early as 1933.[100] With the exception of some experimentation during the Second World War, such tactics were to remain the preserve of insurance scamsters for the next forty years. In particular, the mid-twentieth century saw a mini-wave of such mass murder attempts.[101] And yet as a tactic of political atrocity, aircraft bombing did not really emerge until the very dawn of the 1970s.[102]

[95] *Yorkshire Post and Leeds Intelligencer*, 12 July 1934.

[96] R. Archbold and K. Marschall, *Hindenburg: An Illustrated History* (London, 1994), p. 172. Italics added.

[97] Archbold and Marschall, *Hindenburg*, pp. 190, 198.

[98] Archbold and Marschall, *Hindenburg*, pp. 196–204. Also: *Sheffield Independent*, 8 May 1937 ['Did Time-Bomb Cause Explosion of Hindenburg?']; *Western Morning News*, 8 May 1937 ['Did A Time-bomb Wreck Zeppelin?'].

[99] See: T. I. Adams, *The Sabotage Plan: The IRA Bombing Campaign in England, 1939–1940* (Titchfield, 2010), p. 112.

[100] P. Baum, *Violence in the Skies: A History of Aircraft Hijacking and Bombing* (Chichester, 2016), pp. 17–19.

[101] For the mid-twentieth=century wave of insurance-related aircraft destructions: *Aberdeen Press and Journal*, 24 September 1949 ['woman dynamited airliner']; *Daily Herald*, 25 February 1950 ['Bomb in Plane Charge']; *Belfast News Letter*, 15 November 1953 [time bomb kills mother and 43 others]; *Birmingham Daily Post*, 29 May 1962 [suicide pact?]; *Coventry Evening Telegraph*, 6 March 1963 [patent for a device to detect bombs following 1955 explosion]. Also: Baum, *Violence in the Skies*, p. 26 [1949 plot]; D. Gero, *Flights of Terror: Aerial Hijack and Sabotage Since 1930* (Sparkford, 1997), p. 13 [1950 plot].

[102] Baum, *Violence in the Skies*, pp. 63–5 [December 1969 plot at Heathrow; 21 February 1971 twin bombings by the Popular Front for the Liberation of Palestine—General Command (PFLP-GC).

Aircraft hijacking is effectively a quite separate tradition. Emerging in the mid-twentieth century primarily as a means of escape from Communist dictatorships, hijacking at first represented an opportunistic exploitation of the expansion of Soviet air capacity that the Second World War had created.[103] Such 'freedom flights' were not—at first—officially discouraged by Western governments.[104] In any case, they remained an essentially sporadic phenomenon: at least up until the late 1960s.[105]

The emergence of hijacking as a domestic American phenomenon was different: and spread very rapidly. Its diffusion was fuelled both by its inherently dramatic qualities and by recent revolutions in satellite communications. It thus exhibited all the classic features of 'wave-like' contagion:

> This 'virus' travelled via mass media, especially television newcasts; the networks' stately anchormen were forever narrating clips of hijacked planes and the tearful families of hostages. Rather than empathize with the victims, some viewers were titillated by the skyjackers' ability to create spectacles that held the whole country in thrall.[106]

Success fed success. It became clear to interested observers that determined hijackings usually succeeded. From basic research in a newspaper library in the spring 1969, Jane Alpert worked out that since the start of the year no fewer than nineteen out of twenty-one hijackings to Cuba had succeeded. She duly helped facilitate yet another—the successful escape of two members of the *Front de libération du Québec* (FLQ).[107] Others were probably more spontaneous—such as the 14-year-old from Cincinnati who improbably tried to hijack an airliner single-handed.[108] All in all, American hijacking acquired a gloss of rebel chic—whether it was ostensibly for purposes of escape or extortion. And since demands were relatively straightforward—and often met—a sense of menace was, as yet, relatively understated. Intimidation was still more implied than blatant.

This was to change. A slightly later development was the pioneering by the Popular Front for the Liberation of Palestine (PFLP) of the 'spectacle hijacking' in July 1968: namely, theatrical mass abductions as a tactic of coercive bargaining, often around demands for the release of prisoners.[109] In one pessimistic assessment:

> The developments in weapons mean that one man can now carry the fire power of a platoon and the development of the Jumbo jet has provided the terrorists with the ideal target. The Jumbo is totally under the control of the captain and a handful

For discussion of the barometric pressure mechanism: A. Dolnik, *Understanding Terrorist Innovation* (Abingdon, 2007), p. 83.

[103] Y. Veilleux-Lepage, *How Terror Evolves: The Emergence and Spread of Terrorist Technique* (Lanham, 2020). [Forthcoming].

[104] Baum, *Violence in the Skies*, p. 29. [105] Gero, *Flights of Terror*, pp. 11–21.

[106] B. I. Koerner, *The Skies Belong to Us: Love and Terror in the Golden Age of Hijacking* (New York, 2013), p. 8.

[107] J. Alpert, *Growing Up Underground* (New York, 1981), pp. 165–71.

[108] R. T. Holden, 'The Contagiousness of Aircraft Hijacking', *American Journal of Sociology*, 91 (4) January 1986, p. 881.

[109] B. Abu-Sharif and U. Mahnaimi, *Tried By Fire* (London, 1995, 1996), pp. 59–60. Also: Y. Sayigh, *Armed Struggle and the Search for State: The Palestinian National Movement, 1949–1993* (Oxford, 1997), p. 213; Dolnik, *Understanding Terrorist Innovation*, p. 31.

> of men on the flight deck and they are responsible for the lives of several hundred passengers confined within a vulnerable cell flying several miles high. Once terrorists achieve the position of being able to threaten the flight crew they have virtually achieved victory.[110]

In summary, the emergence of spectacle hijacking represented a momentous development. Bruce Hoffman writes simply that 'the advent of what is considered modern, international terrorism occurred on July 22, 1968' with the hijacking of an El Al flight from Rome to Tel Aviv by the Popular Front for the Liberation of Palestine (PFLP).[111] It was a moment when, in the words of one of the Palestinian architects of 'the hijacking carnival', 'the world had tilted slightly on its axis and it had tilted in our direction'.[112] Hijacking was claustrophobic drama projected big: it oozed 'human interest' for the media networks.[113] The 'flying prison' was simultaneously a world stage.[114] Hijackers could further increase their leverage and ratchet up the tension yet further by a creative use of deadlines.

Long-awaited executions had always proved a headache for governments to manage in controversial cases. In an age of mass media, the paradox was that the many could more easily come to identify with a doomed individual than with the fate of millions. Even in the age of radio, the anticipated executions of the anarchists Sacco and Vanzetti (1927), the IRA volunteer Tom Williams (1942), and the Communist spies, Julius and Ethel Rosenberg (1953), had all inspired clemency petitions that attracted hundreds of thousands of signatures.[115]

Now hijackers demonstrated how to harness mass fascination with the slow-burning drama of an anticipated execution for their own anti-state purposes. Although not absolutely novel in a global perspective—the Irgun had had much the same idea back in 1947—the scale and institutionalization of this technique was indeed revolutionary.[116] Between 1968 and 1972 there were no less than 326 hijack attempts on aircraft worldwide.[117]

Although certainly dramatic, this contagion pattern itself contains few intrinsic mysteries.[118] The spread of the 'skyjack virus' was a straightforward enough phenomenon: as, indeed, was its subsequent containment through the development of

[110] C. Dobson and R. Payne, *The Weapons of Terror: International Terrorism at Work* (London, 1979), p. 6.

[111] B. Hoffman, *Inside Terrorism* (New York, 2006), p. 63.

[112] Abu-Sharif and Mahnaimi, *Tried By Fire*, p. 60.

[113] A. P. Schmid, 'Terrorism and the Media: The Ethics of Publicity', *Terrorism and Political Violence*, 1, October 1989, p. 555.

[114] *The Times*, 9 January 1978 (P. Wilkinson, 'We have the means to beat the hijackers, all we need is the will').

[115] For Sacco and Vanzetti, see: P. Elliott, *The Last Time I saw Paris* (London, 1942, 2011), pp. 113, 119; J. P. T. Bury, *France*, p. 119; J. Gardner, *The Thirties: An Intimate History of Britain* (London, 2011), p. 719. For Williams: R. English, *Armed Struggle, The History of the IRA* (London, 2003, 2004), pp. 68–9; J. Bardon, *A History of Ulster* (Belfast, 1992, 1994), p. 582; Coogan, *The I.R.A.*, p. 232. For the Rosenbergs: J. S. Bowman (ed.), *The Cambridge Dictionary of American Biography* (Cambridge, 1995), pp. 628–9.

[116] Hoffman, *Anonymous Soldiers*, pp. 456–7.

[117] Holden, 'The Contagiousness of Aircraft Hijacking', p. 874.

[118] Holden, 'The Contagiousness of Aircraft Hijacking', pp. 875–7.

better airport security (and more professional counter-terrorist forces), as well as an emerging international consensus around non-negotiation.[119] 'By the end of 1972', writes Brendan Koerner, 'the skyjackers had become so reckless, so dismissive of human life, that the airlines and the federal government had no choice but to turn every airport into a miniature police state'.[120] Results were dramatic: 'in 1995 only three hostile acts against airlines were recorded throughout the world, compared to more than 80 such incidents in 1970'.[121]

A much more interesting question for the historian of violence is why this brief craze of hijacking aircraft has had such a long-lasting and general resonance. In effect, it established the status of the aviation industry as an ominously desirable target for demonstrative atrocity: and apparently permanently so. As mentioned, aircraft bombing had been a long-standing criminal, but not a terroristic, tactic before the 'hijacking carnival'.[122] Yet it became one afterwards. Likewise, airport buildings were not themselves scenes of massacre before enhanced security measures began to deter mass hijacking. Here the machine-gun attack at Lod Airport (31 May 1972) marked the specific juncture at which 'the point of confrontation... [moved] from the better protected aircraft to the more open terminal'.[123] Shortly afterwards, surface-to-air attacks were used against civil aircraft for the first time (at Rome airport in 1973).[124]

It is often implied that aviation disasters are somehow uniquely mesmerizing: and this explains their terroristic appeal. Philip Baum argues that 'it is the nature of aviation that when disaster strikes the whole world hears about it, while we pay little attention to the daily toll of lives which evaporate in motor vehicle accidents'.[125] There is clearly something to this—but it still seems insufficient reason on its own to account for the sheer effort invested both in trying to attack the aviation industry, and in its defence. After all, as Peter Lehr has shrewdly pointed out, cruise liners are also prestige targets whose sinking or hijacking would be hugely dramatic. Yet in practice, maritime transport seems to fall between two stools: more challenging to attack than classically 'soft targets' such as metro systems, yet not deemed as 'prestigious' as a successful attack on the aviation industry.[126]

Here both longer and wider-angled perspectives are valuable. A basic starting point here is that aviation began to be targeted for spectacle hijackings as international air travel first began to emerge as a mass social phenomenon: from the late 1960s.[127] Growing mass familiarity with aviation encouraged the watching many

119 Miller and Hayward, '"I Did My Bit"', p. 14.

120 Koerner, *The Skies Belong to Us*, p. 10.

121 Gero, *Flights of Terror*, p. 118.

122 Al-Hadaf quoted in: Sayigh, *Armed Struggle*, p. 257.

123 K. G. Moore, *Airport, Aircraft, and Airline Security* (Boston, 1991), p. 43. Twenty-five died; 76 were wounded.

124 M. Ashkenazi (et al., eds), 'Manpads: A Terrorist Threat to Civilian Aviation?', Brief 47, Bonn International Center for Conversion (Bonn, 2013), p. 8. For a listing of such attacks, see: ibid, pp. 12–16.

125 Baum, *Violence in the Skies*, p. 317. For a very similar view, K. James, *Heathrow Airport: An Illustrated History* (Stroud, 2016), p. 96.

126 Lehr, '(No) Princes of the Sea', pp. 202–14.

127 https://www.icao.int/sustainability/Pages/Facts-Figures_WorldEconomyData.aspx

to identify closely with the fate of the hijacked. Growing mass familiarity with aviation encouraged a maverick few to explore the possibilities for its catastrophic subversion. Hijacking thus first emerged at a propitious time for its rapid further diffusion. As the airport runway became the most 'important main street in any town', a new stage for publicity seekers also appeared.[128]

Secondly, it seems hard to overstate the cultural importance of aviation. Airports serve as symbolic junction points between different regions of the world. It is only in their 'iron-limbed halls pullulating with strangers, buildings that enabled a person to sense viscerally, rather than just grasp intellectually, the vastness and diversity of humanity'.[129] Here trust amongst strangers is most clearly at a premium. Here the sinews of late modernity's 'organic solidarity' are at their most exposed. 'Air travel reminds us who we are', concludes Don DeLillo simply: 'It's the means by which we recognize ourselves as modern'.[130]

And yet, as Alain de Botton notes in his ethnography of Heathrow Airport, deep anxieties still linger. A recurrent complaint he encountered concerned the prevalence of mall culture at the airport: 'the issue seemed to centre on an incongruity between shopping and flying, connected in some sense to the desire to maintain dignity in the face of death'.[131] He comments further:

> Despite the many achievements of aeronautical engineers over the last few decades, the period before boarding an aircraft is still statistically more likely to be the prelude to a catastrophe than a quiet day in front of the television at home. It therefore tends to raise questions about how we might best spend the last moments before our disintegration, in what frame of mind we might wish to fall back down to earth—and the extent to which we would like to meet eternity surrounded by an array of duty-free bags.[132]

In summary, the prospect of aviation terror works to amplify popular fears that are already very widely-shared. Over the last fifty years, the 'target-hardening' of the global aviation industry has served to enhance the prestige of successful attacks. So, too, of course did the maelstrom of 9/11: 'in a few days, the feeling of business euphoria, technological innovation, and personal freedom that characterized the first years of the information age in the wealthy countries and affluent classes, turned to an obsession with security, suspicion and control'.[133]

The 9/11 plot was in many ways very simple (if still hugely ambitious). But Al-Qaeda threats since have been remarkable both for their persistence and their repeated technical ingenuity.[134] While Islamist movements have generally encouraged a turn to primitive terror, they still have devoted truly enormous resources to overcoming aviation security: as the repeated bomb plots with soft drinks, printer

[128] Norm Crabtree, former aviation director, Ohio in: James, *Heathrow Airport*, p. 38.
[129] A. de Botton, *A Week at the Airport: A Heathrow Diary* (London, 2009), pp. 27–8.
[130] Quoted in: James, *Heathrow Airport*, p. 181.
[131] de Botton, *A Week at the Airport*, p. 61.
[132] de Botton, *A Week at the Airport*, 61.
[133] M. Castells, *The Power of Identity*, Vol. II, *The Network Society* (Chichester, 1997, 2010), p. 140.
[134] *Guardian*, 6 February 2010 (D. Gambetta, 'Why Does Al-Qaida target Planes?').

cartridges, shoes, and underpants all demonstrate.[135] As Ben Wallace, a Security Minister in the British government remarked in late 2018, 'aviation is still a blue riband event for these terrorists'.[136]

In the foreseeable future, this outlook does not look set to change. Global mobility depends upon the aviation industry: and by its very nature mass mobility generates fresh security vulnerabilities. And yet mobility itself can become a target. The final section of this chapter thus addresses attempts to frustrate mobility at source through sabotage. Sophisticated sabotage is the direct product of mobile societies with their networks of long-distance trade, production, and endlessly circulating human and financial capital. It therefore makes sense to deal with it next.

III

> Sabotage is the deliberate attempt to weaken or disable an economic or military system.
>
> – Thomas Rid, 2017[137]

> Today's city is the most vulnerable social structure ever conceived by man.
>
> – Martin Oppenheimer, 1969[138]

Despite the best efforts of E. P. Thompson to rescue the early nineteenth-century Luddites from the 'enormous condescension of posterity', few other historians have been inspired to follow his example of taking sabotage seriously.[139] Given that cyber-threats and 'critical infrastructural protection' are amongst the more prominent morbid symptoms of the early twenty-first century, this neglect by historians of the predecessors to the current anxiety of a looming 'terrorism of things' seems rather striking.[140] In an age where evaluating risk has become both a professional and academic industry in its own right, there is surely a case for taking longer-term views.

Yet general or integrated histories of sabotage hardly exist. This book can hardly hope to fill that gap alone. Nonetheless, it can (perhaps) make some contribution in highlighting a number of general outlines and trends of the development of sabotage broadly understood here as the wrecking tactics of industrialized society. Sophisticated sabotage depends upon an ability to analyse complex and interdependent systems to be able to disrupt them the better: it is dependent upon highly schematic and abstract thinking. 'All sabotage is predominantly *technical* in

135 Dolnik, *Understanding Terrorist Innovation.*

136 english.alarabiya.net, Sunday 23 December 2018 ('UK says Al-Qaeda is resurgent, plans to target airports and airliners').

137 T. Rid, *Cyber War Will Not Take Place* (London, 2013, 2017), p. 57.

138 M. Oppenheimer, *Urban Guerrilla* (Harmondsworth, 1969), p. 141.

139 E. P. Thompson, *The Making of the English Working Class* (Harmondsworth, 1963, 1991), pp. 13, 529, 541, 583, 593, 604–5, 611–12, 642.

140 Rid, *Cyber War Will Not Take Place*, pp. xiii–xvi; P. Martin, *The Rules of Security: Staying Safe in a Risky World* (Oxford, 2019).

nature', remarks Thomas Rid.[141] Gleaned from an overheard pub conversation, it was the insight that the British war effort in North America was ultimately dependent upon the smooth functioning of its Royal dockyards that launched James Aitken upon his solo arson campaign against them in the autumn of 1776.[142] But this early example is rather exceptional. In more general terms we might usefully distinguish here between two distinct bodies of nascent social knowledge that slowly emerged in parallel during the course of the nineteenth century.

The first came from labour unrest. Famously, the Luddites pioneered such tactics in the 1811–13 period.[143] Similarly, the silk weavers' strike at Lyon in 1834 saw workers using their sabots (wooden shoes) to smash machinery.[144] More ambitiously, at Barcelona in July 1854 workers attempted to burn down half a dozen factories.[145] How such repertoires of action spread—or how far they emerged in relative isolation from each other—must remain open questions. Such questions have evoked little curiosity then or since: in part, perhaps, because Friedrich Engels and the First International (1869) so decisively rejected machine-breaking as representing an inherently primitivist phase of resistance to capitalism.[146] At best, we may tentatively conclude that destruction tactics seem to have been a relatively sporadic, if still occasionally spectacular, feature of nineteenth century industrial disputes. During the Great Strike of 1877, for instance, citizens set fire to the Pittsburgh railroad yards, destroying over 100 locomotive and 2,000 railroad cars: 'a substantial portion' of the Pennsylvania Railroad's entire rolling stock. Yet this was a direct response to a militia massacre of twenty strikers rather than any kind of planned escalation.[147]

By comparison, it is worth noting in passing that arson had long been, and long remained, an entirely expected feature of rural unrest. Indeed, the invention of the Lucifer Match in 1827 was greeted with horror by farmers as a potential weapon of mass destruction that threatened all their barns and hayricks.[148] Outbreaks of incendiarism in both England and France around 1830 caused genuine panic amongst this class: and were long remembered.[149]

As a crime of darkness, arson spread rumour and fear far and wide. In July 1860 a widespread outbreak of arson across Texas was feared by slave-owners to portend

[141] Rid, *Cyber War Will Not Take Place*, p. 57. Emphasis in original.

[142] J. Warner, *John the Painter: The First Modern Terrorist* (London, 2004).

[143] Thompson, *The Making of the English Working Class*, pp. 529, 541, 583, 593, 604–5, 611–12.

[144] S. Salerno, 'Introduction' in S. Salerno (ed.), *Direct Action and Sabotage: Three Classic IWW Pamphlets from the 1910s* (Oakland, 2014), p. 7.

[145] See: R. Hughes, *Barcelona* (London, 1992, 1996), p. 275.

[146] Salerno, 'Introduction', pp. 4–5. See also V. Kiernan, 'Foreword' in F. Engels, *The Condition of the Working Class in England* (London, 1845, 1987), p. 19.

[147] E. Foner, *Reconstruction: America's Unfinished Revolution 1863–1877* (New York, 1988, 2002), p. 583.

[148] P. Johnson, *The Birth of the Modern: World Society, 1815–1830* (Phoenix, 1991, 1992), pp. 999–1000.

[149] E. J. Hobsbawm and G. Rudé, *Captain Swing* (London, 1969, 1993), p. 282. S. de Morsier (ed.), *Memoirs of the Comtesse de Boigne* (London, 1956), pp. 219–20; F. Engels, *The Condition of the Working Class in England* (London, 1845, 1987), pp. 267–8.

a general uprising against them.[150] August 1862 saw no less intense panic amongst peasants in the Dordogne region of southern France who feared pyrotechnic agents of the clerical party: 'there is frequent talk of a luxurious carriage said to be traveling mysteriously by night, without lights, allegedly in order to bring food and demolition devices to the arsonists'.[151]

By the first half of the nineteenth century, arson had also become a prominent feature of Irish rural unrest: as it was to remain long afterwards.[152] During the Irish Land War, for instance, there were 776 incendiary fires recorded between 1880 and 1882 alone.[153] Likewise, sustained 'campaigns of fire' backlit the later Irish Troubles of 1919–23.[154]

The second body of knowledge was military. With the advent of industrialized warfare, experiments in disruption flourished. While the failure of the Confederacy to turn to guerrilla warfare when facing defeat is perhaps one of the more surprising features of the American Civil War, its secret services did make some ambitious, if rather amateur, attempts to turn to sabotage tactics in the Union states. In the event, these efforts added up to little more than the burnings of nineteen hotels in Manhattan, and unfulfilled plans to poison a reservoir feeding New York.[155] Railway sabotage was to form a feature of both the Franco-Prussian War of 1870–71 and the Boer War of 1899–1902.[156]

It is worth noting here that when public debates in the United Kingdom swirled over the projected construction of a Channel Tunnel in 1883, security concerns focused almost solely on the possibility of a sneak invasion from France: that 'the tunnel might become to England what the wooden horse was to Troy'.[157] At most it was feared that Irish Republicans might try to seize the tunnel to enable their French allies to pour through: or else, in more general terms, that such a tunnel would prove an easy conduit for communist agitators to flood the United Kingdom.[158] Acts of sabotage were apparently not feared, nor even considered: a striking degree of complacency, perhaps, given the Irish Republican dynamite bombing campaigns that had begun in 1881 (and which were to continue sporadically until 1885).

[150] Hofstadter and Wallace, *American Violence*, pp. 201–3.

[151] A. Corbin, *The Village of Cannibals: Rage and Murder in France, 1870* (Harvard, 1992), pp. 15–16.

[152] G. Clark, 'Arson in Modern Ireland: Fire and Protest Before the Famine' in K. Hughes and D. M. Macraild (eds), *Crime, Violence and the Irish in the Nineteenth Century* (Liverpool, 2017), pp. 211–26.

[153] M. Mulholland, 'Land War Homicide' in S. Pašeta (ed.), *Uncertain Futures* (Oxford, 2016), p. 82.

[154] G. Clark, *Everyday Violence in the Irish Civil War* (Cambridge, 2014), pp. 54–97.

[155] E. Steers, *Lincoln's Assassination* (Carbondale, IL, 2014), p. 13.

[156] R. Davies, 'Attacking Railway Lines with IEDs -1870' (27 April, 2017); 'Attacking Railway Lines with IEDs using Firearm Initiation Systems' (16 May, 2017). Available at: http://www.standing-wellback.com/

[157] *The Manchester Examiner and Times*, 17April 1883 (page 106–7). Also: D. Abel, *Channel Underground* (London, 1961), pp. 18–19; J. Knowles (ed.), *The Channel Tunnel and Public Opinion* (London, 1883) p. 104.

[158] Knowles, *The Channel Tunnel and Public Opinion*, pp. 21, 109, 122–3, 124, 133. Also: *Spectator*, 14 February 1882; *Sunday Times*, 16 April 1882.

Sabotage seems to have become a more prominent feature of public debate around the turn of the twentieth century. It was in America that the first attempts to advance a theory of sabotage as effective class action appeared: a reflection, in part, of the peculiarly embittered labour relations of the New World that creatively combined a 'minimum of ideologically motivated class conflict [with]...a maximum of industrial violence'.[159] The deeply embittered Pullman Strike of 1894 saw widespread derailing and burning of freight cars. All traffic on all twenty-four railroads out of Chicago was halted.[160]

For the Industrial Workers of the World (founded 1905), keen to advance class struggle on highly unpromising terrain, the calculated 'withdrawal of efficiency' seemed to offer tempting prospects of acting as a force multiplier.[161] Between 1905 and 1911, eighty-six structural steel jobs were 'bombed or damaged in some way'.[162] Generally, this was a slow-burning, attritional struggle that caused relatively low-level damage: although the botched bombing of the *Los Angeles Times* killed over twenty of its employees.[163]

Appropriately (since the etymology of the term is French), it was the Old World that saw some of the most systematic attempts to use sabotage as the cutting edge of major strikes.[164] In particular, the great rail strike of 1910 was distinguished by apparent signs of 'a general sabotage organisation and plan to put the railways out of action'.[165] Signals were tampered with, wires cut, obstacles placed on lines, trains shot at and attempts made to bomb both bridges and tunnels.[166] In response, the French government hastily prepared an anti-strike bill which defined 'sabotage'—the British press clearly felt the need to introduce their readers to this still unfamiliar term—'as the wilful destruction, deterioration, or rendering useless, of instruments or other objects with a view to stopping or hampering work, industry or commerce'.[167]

General timing seems significant here. By the early twentieth century what was in effect a second industrial revolution had consolidated itself through 'the widespread use of electricity from the 1870s onwards [which] changed transportation, telegraphy, lighting, and, not least, factory work by diffusing power in the form of the electrical engine'.[168] In 1910, the American industrialist, Henry Ford, famously

[159] R. Hofstadter, 'Reflections on Violence in the United States' in R. Hofstadter and M. Wallace (eds), *American Violence: A Documentary History* (New York, 1971), p. 19.

[160] Hofstadter and allace, *American Violence: A Documentary History* (New York, 1970, 1971), pp. 151–6.

[161] E. Gurley Flynn, 'Sabotage: the conscious Withdrawal of the Workers' Industrial Efficiency' in S. Salerno (ed.), *Direct Action and Sabotage: Three Classic IWW Pamphlets From the 1910s* (Oakland, 2014), p. 93. For context: P. Renshaw, *The Wobblies: The Story of Syndicalism in the United States* (London, 1967).

[162] J. A. Clymer, *America's Culture of Terrorism* (Chapel Hill, North Carolina, 2003), p. 173.

[163] Hofstadter and Wallace, *American Violence*, pp. 425–9.

[164] F. F. Ridley, 'Syndicalism, Strikes and Revolutionary Action in France' in W. J. Mommsen and G. Hirschfeld (eds), *Social Protest, Violence and Terror in 19th and 20th Century Europe* (London, 1982), pp. 239–40; D. Caute, *The Left in Europe Since 1789* (London, 1966), pp. 145–51.

[165] *Leeds Mercury*, 18 October 1910.

[166] *Belfast Weekly News*, 20 October 1910.

[167] *London Daily News*, 30 November 1910.

[168] M. Castells, *The Information Age*, Vol. I, *The Rise of the Network Society* (Chichester, 1996, 2010), p. 37.

revolutionized automobile manufacture with the invention of the production line. Ford's achievement is remembered today as an exemplar of the wider phenomenon of 'scientific management' that had begun to emerge at the tail end of the nineteenth century 'by applying "scientific methods" not only to technology but to organization and calculation'.[169] At heart, theories such as Fordism (and the broadly equivalent phenomena of Taylorism and Fayolism) aimed to boost productivity by streamlining processes, making them routine and predictable, and ruthlessly eliminating bottlenecks.[170] Results were certainly dramatic: as the rise of the Model T Ford—the first car to be mass produced—demonstrated. Yet hegemonic systems potentially invite their own disruption. If routine becomes all governing, then routine itself becomes vulnerable.

Sabotage was, in effect, inverse Fordism: an attempt to maximize disorder, by causing cascades of disruption in tightly coupled systems.[171] Such tactics aimed to exploit key pinch points and bottlenecks to exert the maximum pressure possible: a finely calculated gearing of mayhem to totally disproportionate effect. But as a political tactic, it involved a radical broadening of the horizon of action from individual industrial disputes to take in the workings of society as a whole. As the Suffragette leader Emmeline Pankhurst put it in a 1913 speech (with more than a hint of menace), 'civilisation was so complicated that a very little thing could put everything out of working order'.[172] A 'scientific' management of disruption seemed to hold out almost infinite, and intoxicating, possibilities for political leverage.

And yet amateur sabotage turned out to be rather hard to make genuinely ubiquitous in its effects. General paralysis remained highly elusive. First, the very density of infrastructure in industrial societies often contains considerable 'redundancy': that is, extra-capacity for 'soaking up' disruption (or, at least, minimizing it massively). Over time it became clearer that 'the power of modern industry, transport and administration can be neutralised for a significant length of time only where it lies thin on the ground'.[173] Or to put it slightly differently, 'complexity in this sense contains its own saving remnant'.[174]

To use a technical term, mature industrial societies often turned out to be surprisingly well endowed with *passive resilience*: 'the ability to absorb disturbance, recover quickly from a setback, and return to normality'.[175] It takes highly specialist knowledge to unpick such strength in depth. The Suffragettes likely achieved an extraordinary amount of property damage that 'in 1913–1914 alone, cost the

[169] E. J. Hobsbawm, *The Age of Empire 1875–1914* (London, 1987), p. 53.

[170] *The Information Age*, Vol. I, p. 462; Hobsbawm, *The Age of Empire*, pp. 44–5; E. Weber, *The Hollow Years: France in the 1930s* (London, 1995), pp. 97–8.

[171] W. C. Smith, 'Sabotage: Its History, Philosophy and Function' in S. Salerno (ed.), *Direct Action and Sabotage: Three Classic IWW Pamphlets from the 1910s* (Oakland, 2014), p. 64.

[172] Quoted in: B. Harrison, 'The Act of Militancy: Violence and the Suffragettes, 1904–1914' in M. Bentley and J. Stevenson (eds), *Peaceable Kingdom: Stability and Change in Modern Britain* (Oxford, 1982), pp. 68–9.

[173] E. J. Hobsbawm, *Revolutionaries* (1977), p. 169.

[174] W. J. MacKenzie quoted in: L. Winner, 'Complexity and Human Understanding' in T. La Porte (ed.), *Organized Social Complexity: Challenge to Politics and Policy* (Princeton, 1975), p. 66.

[175] Martin, *The Rules of Security*, p. 76.

British economy between £1 and £2 million'. But they never managed to elevate their nuisance tactics into national paralysis.[176]

Rather less obviously, at a human level, enthusiasm for sabotage was often surprisingly hard to ignite. Put simply, it was psychologically difficult. Amongst slave labourers in Auschwitz in 1944, for instance, Primo Levi noted their—situationally incongruous—pride in a job well done. Even here, of all places, sabotage did not come instinctively or naturally.[177] Work is frequently a cornerstone of personal pride. Sabotage often cuts against the grain of that professional self-respect.

Amongst aristocracies of labour, in particular, opposition to sabotage could be very entrenched indeed. Across both the Old World and the New, the general resistance of skilled railway workers to sabotage was a sociological given.[178] 'No one believes that the railwaymen as a body approves of such methods', claimed one British journalist of the French Rail Strike in 1910.[179] In the Irish Civil War of 1922–3, the anti-Free State forces found locomotive drivers got extremely upset if their engines were wrecked ('they thought more of their old engines than of their wives').[180] French Resistance saboteurs encountered exactly the same phenomenon two decades later during their own railway war against the Nazis.[181] In summary, those skilled workers best placed to cause the most devastating damage were often the most reluctant to do so.

Unsurprisingly, then, the most ambitious and inventive saboteurs of the twentieth century frequently tended to be professional state agents. Germany led the way here. In the (admittedly uniquely benign) operating environment of the (still neutral) USA between 1914 and 1917, the German Embassy ran a sabotage operation whose achievements were nothing less than spectacular (though they failed in their ultimate goal of preventing the effective re-supply of the Allied war effort).[182] The detonation of the Black Tom munitions depot opposite Manhattan on 30 July 1916 destroyed eighty-seven railroad cars, thirteen warehouses, and six piers, causing in all $20 million of damage.[183] In the words of one eyewitness, 'the whole harbour was having a showerbath of shrapnel'.[184] The Statue of Liberty still bears the scars.[185] A later explosion at Kingsland, New Jersey, on 11 January 1917 destroyed 275,000 loaded shells, over one million unloaded shells, nearly half a million time fuses, 300,000 cartridge cases, 100,000 detonators, plus huge quantities

[176] C. Bearman, 'An Examination of Suffragette Violence', *English Historical Review*, CXX (486) April 2005, p. 369. For useful analyses of tactics, see: Harrison, 'The Act of Militancy', pp. 26–7, 51–9, 68–9, 71–2; R. Monaghan, '"Votes for Women": An Analysis of the Militant Campaign, *Terrorism and Political Violence*, 9 (2) 1997, pp. 65–78.

[177] P. Levi, *The Drowned and the Saved* (London, 1986, 1988), p. 98.

[178] Smith, 'Sabotage', p. 70.

[179] *Leeds Mercury*, 18 October 1910.

[180] B. Share, *In Time of Civil War* (Cork, 2006), pp. 15–16.

[181] L. Broch, *Ordinary Workers, Vichy and the Holocaust: French Railwaymen and the Second World War* (Cambridge, 2016), pp. 8, 26, 152, 154, 241.

[182] They were much less successful in the UK and Italy. See respectively: C. Andrew, *The Defence of the Realm: the Authorized History of MI5* (London, 2009, 2010), pp. 77–9; I. Jones, *Malice Aforethought: A History of Booby Traps From World War One to Vietnam* (Barnsley, 2004, 2016), p. 48.

[183] J. Witcover, *Sabotage at Black Tom: Imperial Germany's Secret War in America, 1914–1917* (Chapel Hill, 1989), p. 21.

[184] Witcover, *Sabotage at Black Tom*, p. 19.

[185] Witcover, *Sabotage at Black Tom*, p. 19.

of TNT explosive.[186] Less dramatic—indeed, rather amateur—efforts involved attempts to infect Europe-bound horses with glanders and anthrax bacilli.[187]

In the less hospitable conditions of Europe, the success of German sabotage efforts were distinctly uneven. Saboteurs were largely thwarted in both the UK and Italy: but German-trained sappers did manage to detonate a Russian munitions depot in northern Finland in 1916.[188] Some attempt also seems to have been made to spread anthrax and glanders amongst livestock destined for the Allied war effort across Norway, Romania, and Spain.[189] For its part, Imperial Germany took protection of its own critical infrastructure—or at least, its potential denial to the enemy—very seriously indeed. By the start of August 1914, steel mills and colliery towers in the border province of Upper Silesia were thoroughly primed for destruction against the threat of a Russian invasion that never came.[190] Wider awareness of sabotage tactics also seem to have percolated quickly through society. As a young boy, Sebastian Haffner had his summer holiday in Pomerania cut short abruptly by the outbreak of war. Returning by train to Berlin he found himself wondering if a spy had left a bomb beneath every railway bridge ('a pleasantly creepy sensation').[191]

An official German interest in state-sponsored sabotage lingered into the inter-war period, before being enthusiastically rejuvenated by the Nazis when they took power. During the Ruhr Occupation of 1923, 'passive resistance was not so passive as the government quite genuinely intended it to be'.[192] Underground 'demolition columns' succeeded in causing relatively widespread blocking of railways and canals.[193] A bombing of a Belgian troop train at Duisburg in June 1923 killed eleven.[194] Such activities were the speciality of the nationalist right-wing activists who enjoyed more-or-less ready access to supplies and support from sympathetic elements inside the state that doubtless increased their effectiveness.[195] There was also some continuity of key personnel: Kurt Jahnke, who had been one of the most

[186] Witcover, *Sabotage at Black Tom*, pp. 189, 193.

[187] Witcover, *Sabotage at Black Tom*, pp. 126–7, 136.

[188] German-trained saboteurs also blew up a Russian munitions depot at Kilpisjärvi in Lapland: J. Jalonen, 'From Underground Terrorism to State Terrorism and Beyond: The Question of Terrorism in the Finnish Jäger Movement during and after the First World War', *Terrorism and Political Violence*, 30 (5) September–October 2018, p. 817. For less successful German attempts in the UK and Italy, see: Andrew, *Defence of the Realm*, pp. 75–9; Jones, *Malice Aforethought*, p. 48 [German saboteurs discovered in Italian ammunition factories, May 1916].

[189] W. Barnaby, *The Plague Makers: The Secret World of Biological Warfare* (London, 1999), p. 121.

[190] K. Fuchs, 'Schlesien während des Ersten Weltkrieges', in C. Norbert and H. Brockmann (eds), *Deutsche Geschichte in Osten Europas: Schlesien* (Berlin, 1994), p. 608; W. J. Rose, *The Drama of Upper Silesia* (Vermont, 1935), p. 165; R. Vogel, *Deutsche Presse und Propaganda des Abstimmungskampfes in Oberschlesien* (Beuthen, 1931), pp. 25–6. The vulnerability of Germany's second most industrial area to Russian invasion, or even raids, remains oddly neglected in accounts of the First World War.

[191] S. Haffner, *Defying Hitler* (London, 2002, 2003).

[192] A. Ferguson, *When Money Dies: The Nightmare of the Weimar Hyperinflation* (London, 1975, 2010), p. 131.

[193] P. Ackerman and C. Kruegler, *Strategies of Nonviolent Conflict: The Dynamics of People Power in the Twentieth Century* (Westport, 1994), pp. 128–31.

[194] Ackerman and Kruegler, 'Strategies of Nonviolent Conflict', p. 131. Also: *Exeter and Plymouth Gazette*, 2, 4 July 1923; *Leeds Mercury*, 2 July 1923; *Northern Whig*, 4 July 1923 [two extra deaths]. An estimated death toll of eleven is taken from reading across these reports.

[195] Ferguson, *When Money Dies*, pp. 130–3.

accomplished German saboteurs in the USA, later turned up in the Ruhr campaigns of 1923.[196] Later destabilization campaigns that the Nazi regime waged in Austria in 1933–4 were notably professional in calibrating destruction to disable key infrastructure (such as hydro-electric dams and railway bridges), whilst avoiding the obloquy of mass carnage.[197]

By contrast, anti-state sabotage tended to remain distinctly amateur in both aim and execution. It barely advanced beyond rhetorical threats.[198] In general the post-war left remained attracted to the strike ('the open battle of the class struggle'), rather than to 'sabotage... [as] ... guerrilla warfare, the day-by-day warfare between two opposing classes'.[199] German communists, in particular, proved highly reluctant saboteurs: the *Manchester Guardian* correspondent thought they squandered ample opportunities to leverage destruction as a bargaining tactic during the bitter and bloody Ruhr confrontations of the spring of 1920: they kept saying 'that if they blew the mines they wouldn't have any places to work afterwards'.[200] During wildcat stoppages in Bergheim (in the British occupation zone) in 1923, threats to burn factories and smash machinery seem to have been similarly the stuff of desperation: and not any part of blueprints for definitive insurrection.[201]

For its part, the IRA's sabotage was distinctly uneven in results. In Ireland, their attacks on the railway network were sometimes devastatingly effective: the mining of a troop train in Armagh in June 1921 'killed four men, wounded another three, and caused the death of thirty cavalry horses'.[202] Indeed, this incident was 'probably the most successful attack by the IRA's 4th Northern division in the North'.[203] Yet in England the IRA's 1920 campaign remained notably more unfocused and amateur—with the exception of one spectacular episode of arson in Liverpool that destroyed nineteen buildings.[204] Equally ambitious plans for Manchester and London failed to materialize. Otherwise their diffuse and sporadic efforts were largely confined to cutting telegraph wires and farm-burnings: in effect, a rather literal and imitative attempt to bring the Irish 'war' home to the English public.[205] As with their adoption of hunger-striking at the same time, the brief flirtation with mass window-smashing may have owed much to the still redolent example of the

196 Witcover, *Sabotage at Black Tom*, pp. 81, 318; J. Wright, *Gustav Stresemann: Weimar's Greatest Statesman* (Oxford, 2002), p. 227. See also: R. Davies, 'Kurt Jahnke: the legendary German saboteur' (17 September, 2013). Available at: http://www.standingwellback.com/

197 Anonymous, *The Death of Dollfuss: An Official History of the Revolt of July, 1934, in Austria* (London, 1935), pp. 36–8.

198 *Guardian*, 6 April 1920.

199 Gurley Flynn, 'Sabotage', p. 93.

200 W. Duranty, *I Write As I Please* (London, 1935), pp. 94–5.

201 Ferguson, *When Money Dies*, p. 162.

202 P. Hart, *The I.R.A. at War, 1916–1923* (Oxford, 2003), p. 193; J. Crowley et al. (eds), *Atlas of the Irish Revolution* (Cork, 2017), pp. 688–90.

203 C. S. Day, 'Political Violence in the Newry/Armagh Area, 1912–1925', Queen's University, Belfast, PhD, 1999, p. 200.

204 Hart, *The I.R.A. at War*, p. 151.

205 Hart, *The I.R.A. at War*, pp. 144–77; Crowley et al., *Atlas of the Irish Revolution*, p. 524. G. Noonan, *The IRA in Britain, 1919–1923: 'In the Heart of Enemy Lines'* (Liverpool, 2014), pp. 135–85.

recent Suffragette campaign. Even here, though, some commentators at the time noted that 'the Suffragettes were far better at their job'.[206]

The IRA's next English campaign—the Sabotage (or S-) Plan of 1939–40—was a notably more impressive operation.[207] Since its architect, Seamus O'Donovan, had worked for the Irish government on the electrification of rural Ireland, this plan was distinguished by far sharper thinking about how to disable key infrastructure.[208] It achieved some notable tactical successes—including cutting off 25,000 people in north London from the electricity grid.[209] Rumours swirled of covert German assistance: a superficially plausible assumption, given the high-profile Nazi sabotage campaigns in both Austria and Czechoslovakia.[210]

In the longer run, though, the vertiginous ambitions of the S-Plan simply outran its very meagre resources. Shoddy materials—alarm clocks that failed were a recurrent weakness—inadequate training, utter inexperience, and a subsequent collapse of targeting focus all helped sap morale and impact.[211] Overall—in the words of a judicious assessment written a few years later—the S-Plan had provided an 'interesting warning of the vulnerability of a complex industrial civilization to sabotage, provided (and this is where the IRA failed) that there has been sufficient installation of the attacking party into the texture of the State'.[212]

On the eve of the Second World War, then, it had already become clear that such dark arts were best mastered with the aid of the state's insider knowledge of how key infrastructure actually worked. It is worth noting in passing here that there were close parallels with the emergent thinking of the precisionist theorists of air power that the aim of aerial bombing should be to cause 'the greatest disproportionality in the enemy's industrial system' or to target only 'the most vital centres'.[213]

[206] Noonan, *The IRA in Britain*, p. 182.

[207] A. Craig, 'Sabotage! The Origins, Development and Impact of the IRA's Infrastructural Bombing Campaigns, 1939–1997' *Intelligence and National Security*, 25 (3) 2010, pp. 309–26. We lack a proper study of the S-Plan. For useful overview accounts: Adams, *The Sabotage Plan*; English, *Armed Struggle*, pp. 61–2; J. Bowyer Bell, *The Secret Army: the IRA 1916–1979* (Dublin, 1970, 1990), pp. 142–67.

[208] M. Coleman, 'O'Donovan, James Laurence ("Jim", "Seamus")' in J. McGuire and J. Quinn (eds), *Dictionary of Irish Biography* (Royal Irish Academy, Cambridge, 2009), pp. 417–18.

[209] Andrew, *The Defence of the Realm*, p. 654.

[210] F. Owen, *The Eddie Chapman Story* (London, 1953), p. 77; Adams, *The Sabotage Plan*, p. 81; B. O'Connor, *Operation Lena and Hitler's Plots to Blow Up Britain* (Stroud, 2017), pp. 7, 16, 28, 32, 273.

[211] For the classic memoir of a (not very effective) teenage volunteer in the S-Plan see the opening pages of: B. Behan, *Borstal Boy* (London, 1958, 1990). For timing devices that failed to explode, see: *Palestine Post*, 19 January 1939 [Midlands pylon bomb found]; *Daily Record and Mail*, 4 March 1939 [Lancashire pylon bomb found].

[212] L. Fairfield, *The Trial of Peter Barnes and Others* (The I.R.A. Coventry Explosion of 1939) (London, 1953), p. 11.

[213] The British economist, John Jewks, in October 1939 quoted in: R. Overy, *The Bombing War* (London, 2013), p. 614. See also: T. Hippler, *Bombing the People* (Cambridge, 2013), pp. 109–10, 122; T. D. Biddle, 'Anglo-American Strategic Bombing, 1940–1945' in J. Ferris and E. Mawdsley (eds), *Fighting the War*, Vol. I (Cambridge, 2015), p. 490. I am grateful to Professor Phillips O'Brien for this last reference.

Under Nazi occupation from 1940, Western Europe became a giant laboratory for state-sponsored sabotage.[214] But early efforts remained distinctly amateur: with remote targets picked—presumably—for their opportunistic ease of access, rather than any strategic value. Authorities in France, for instance, realized early that it was emigrant wood cutters from Yugoslavia who were behind a sharp rise in cable sabotage after the Nazi invasion of the Balkans in the spring of 1941.[215] For amateur saboteurs, efforts at destruction often proved both hugely dangerous and hugely disappointing. Amongst the Italian partisans, Ada Gobetti's diary eloquently records the frustration at the slow learning needed to master the severing of railways and power lines.[216] Even as late as 1944, teenage resisters who blew up railway lines in the Lille–Calais–Dunkirk area were dismayed to find them fully restored within forty-eight hours.[217] Actually, this was slow: one 1941 manual on guerrilla warfare estimated that most train tracks could be repaired within just three to four hours.[218]

In general, though, sabotage became much more systematic, professional and better resourced as the tide of the wider war began to turn against the Third Reich.[219] Across northern Italy, railway lines were successfully brought to a halt on 800 separate occasions from late 1943.[220] Across France, there were 491 successful derailments just between December 1943 and February 1944.[221] In the week after D-Day alone, 960 acts of railway sabotage were carried out. Every train from Marseilles to Lyon was derailed at least once.[222] Compared to the titanic Soviet railway wars, though, the scale of these efforts still remained relatively modest.[223]

In Western Europe, then, sabotage remained an auxiliary, and firmly subordinate, tactic to more conventional warfare. Nonetheless, its association with the Resistance struggle seems to have boosted its prestige as the tactic of choice for separatist groups in the war's aftermath. For a full generation after 1945, extreme nationalists seem to have conceived of armed struggle as (more or less only) the business of toppling pylons and disrupting rail services.[224] For a while, it remained a feature of major industrial unrest as well: most notably in France in the great rail

[214] Foot, *Resistance*, pp. 43–9.

[215] H. Luther, *Der Französische Widerstand* (Tübingen, 1957), pp. 27–8.

[216] A. Gobetti, *Partisan Diary: A Woman's Life in the Italian Resistance* (Oxford, 1956, 2014), pp. 23, 30, 33, 47, 50, 76, 143.

[217] S. Grady, *Gardens of Stone: My Boyhood in the French Resistance* (London, 2013), pp. 297, 300–1.

[218] Y. Levy, *Guerrilla Warfare* (Harmondsworth, 1941), p. 68. Also, G. L. Rottman, *World War II Allied Sabotage Devices and Booby Traps* (Oxford, 2010), p. 27.

[219] G. Millar, *Maquis* (London, 1945, 1957), pp. 147, 165–74.

[220] T. Behan, *The Italian Resistance: Fascists, Guerrillas and Allies* (London, 2009), p. 3.

[221] Broch, *Ordinary Workers*, p. 155.

[222] J. Jackson, *France: The Dark Years, 1940–1944* (Oxford, 2001, 2003), p. 544.

[223] R. Davies, 'Ilya Starinov—the Godfather of Modern Insurgent IED Warfare' (29 May, 2019). Available at: http://www.standingwellback.com

[224] For South Tyrol: A. E. Alcock, 'Terrorism in South Tyrol' in P. Janke (ed.), *Terrorism and Democracy: Some Contemporary Cases* (London, 1992), pp. 8 [1956–1957 attacks], 1112 [1961 attacks]. For Scottish nationalist attacks on pylons: *Yorkshire Post*, 18 November 1953; *Dundee Courier*, 25 November 1953.

strikes of May–June 1947, and—on a more reduced scale—in 1953.[225] Despite the great wave of strikes in affluent countries between 1968 and 1971, sabotage seems to have fallen out of fashion. As Ignacio Sánchez-Cuenca comments: 'workers were emboldened to demand higher salaries and better working conditions. Their aspirations, however, were not revolutionary, except on the fringes of the labor movement.'[226]

In general, sabotage tactics almost completely faded away from the early 1970s onwards. This was not immediately apparent. Contemporary commentators frequently appear to assume that sabotage would remain a part of wider strategies of 'terrorism'. 'It is widely believed', wrote Walter Laqueur in 1977 'that with the growing vulnerability of modern technological society the prospects of urban terror are now greater than ever before.'[227] Richard Clutterbuck wrote in near-identical terms in the same year that 'the increasing vulnerability of modern society does attract terrorism'.[228] Yet in practice the cold science of destructionism held very limited appeal to the romantics of the New Left: Carlos Marighella's exhortation that 'factory workers acting as urban guerrillas are excellent saboteurs' did not resonate widely amongst largely student movements.[229] As avowed anti-technocrats they were generally poorly placed to fight 'technocratic totalitarianism' on its own terms.

Even in countries such as Italy—where militancy still had some foothold in the working-class, and where sabotage tactics had been an integral part of the Resistance struggle three decades earlier—the appeal of sabotage was fading fast. Even before his accidental death in 1972 (by his own bomb) the enthusiasm of Giangiacomo Feltrinelli for sabotage had bemused his fellow activists in the Red Brigades ('his idea of blowing up high-tension pylons in the mountains... struck us as rather eccentric').[230] Against the backdrop of protest against the reduction of public holidays in March 1977, the Prima Linea group blew up the power supply to the underground trains around Milan. But the social reaction was not what they had desired. Indeed 'the attempt to revive the legendary memory of similar acts of sabotage, carried out during the Resistance in March 1944 under Nazi occupation, in order to extend the strike which had broken out in a few Milanese factories, drew laughter and derision rather than set a new heroic precedent from which inspiration could be taken'.[231]

[225] For Belgium: *Sunderland Daily Echo and Shipping Gazette*, 25 July 1950 ['Sabotage Wave hits Belgium']. For France: Anderson, *In Thrall*, p. 120; *Hartlepool Northern Daily Mail*, 3 March 1949 [sabotage in French coalfields]; *Yorkshire Post and Leeds Intelligencer*, 24 August 1953 ['scattered sabotage' in French rail strike].

[226] I. Sánchez-Cuenca, *The Historical Roots of Political Violence* (Cambridge, 2019), p. 1.

[227] Laqueur, *Terrorism*, p. 105.

[228] R. Clutterbuck, *Guerrillas and Terrorists* (Ohio, 1977, 1980), p. 95.

[229] Marighella, *Mini-Manual of the Urban Guerrilla*, p. 29. Clutterbuck references a 'Trotskyist/Anarchist' pamphlet that describes itself as a 'compilation... of useful industrial techniques which, in our view, should be considered *more often* by militants' [my emphasis]. See: R. Clutterbuck, *Protest and the Urban Guerrilla* (New York, 1973, 1974), p. 184.

[230] Alberto Franceschini quoted in: P. Edwards, *More Work, Less Pay! Rebellion and Repression in Italy, 1972–7* (Manchester, 2009), p. 21.

[231] A. Jamieson, *The Heart Attacked: Terrorism and Conflict in the Italian State* (London, 1989), p. 251.

By 1977, then, it seems sabotage was out of ideological fashion. Doubtless, the pronounced decline of heavy industry across the western world contributed to its disappearance from labour disputes in the later twentieth century. So, most likely, did the rise of spectacular terror in an age of satellite TV: the 1970s, after all, was a time when it was first plausibly suggested that 'terrorism is theater'.[232] From an insurgent perspective, the downside of sabotage was that if it failed—however narrowly—it caused very little visible impact. That was now its principal drawback. Government ministers, state engineers and security services might indeed be badly shaken. But the panic of the experts is easily hidden. It would likely remain behind closed doors ('what cannot be measured are the attendant frustration and discontent lowering the enemy morale').[233] In a television age, such consolations were rarely sufficient to encourage perseverance.

The very long history of Irish Republican experiments in sabotage is suggestive here. On several occasions bombing teams did come very close to causing very major infrastructural dislocation. The Clan na Gael team came close to severing much of the water supply to Glasgow (1883), while, as seen, the S-Plan (1939) briefly held out real promise of causing widespread economic mayhem.[234] Later, the Provisional IRA almost cut the power to both Belfast (1971) and London (1996).[235] And yet they often seem to have remained entirely unaware of how close to success they had come.[236]

Taking the long view, indeed, what is striking is just how long it took the Provisional IRA to develop an intelligent strategy of locating the pressure points of British society and its economy. By targeting the City of London with weekend or night-time truck bombs, they hoped to drive insurance premiums up (and hence foreign banks out), whilst simultaneously avoiding mass fatalities. The explosion at the Baltic Exchange (10 April 1992) caused £800 million of damage. A year later the Bishopsgate bomb (24 April 1993) had the same explosive power as a small tactical nuclear weapon, caused greater 'ground waves' than an earthquake, and ultimately caused a possible £1.45 billion pounds worth of damage.[237] For the Republican movement here, finally, was a winning formula. But it was one that they had, apparently, stumbled over, rather than discerned by design.[238] To endorse the Provisionals' own estimate of their technical capabilities: they had indeed been (very) 'good electricians'.[239] But they had also been notably poor sociologists. Such spectacular bombings emerged only *after two decades* of prior attacks on London: an S-Plan for slow learners.

Sabotage has not revived notably with the rise of Islamist terror. To some extent, this seems highly surprising, given a notable preponderance of trained engineers in

[232] B. Jenkins, 'International Terrorism: A New Kind of Warfare', Rand Paper Series, 1974, p. 4.

[233] L. Bell, *Sabotage* (London, 1957, 1959), pp. 147–8.

[234] S. Kenna, War *in the Shadows the Irish-American Fenians Who Bombed Victorian Britain* (Sallins, 2014), pp. 86–8 [gasometer and aqueduct attacked, 20 January 1883]; G. McGladdery, *The Provisional IRA in England* (Dublin, 2006), pp. 33–45.

[235] Andrew, *The Defence of the Realm*, p. 796.

[236] Craig, 'Sabotage!', pp. 319–20.

[237] Oppenheimer, *IRA. The Bombs and the Bullets*, p. 126.

[238] Andrew, *The Defence of the Realm*, p. 855.

[239] Oppenheimer, *IRA. The Bombs and the Bullets*, p. 247.

their ranks.[240] But these are engineers who seem to be no longer very interested in engineering: beyond, perhaps, mastering the niche skills of bomb-making to further their adopted cause. 'There have been very few plans to target civilian infrastructure by new jihadis in Europe'—a pattern that broadly holds true for north America, too, with the exception of one plot to target fuel tanks at JFK airport.[241] Presumably this latter plot was designed more for visual effect than to cause systemic havoc. In general, the activists of Al-Qaeda and ISIS have been far better technicians of publicity than of infrastructural paralysis.

At the turn of the twenty-first century, then, it was striking how far sabotage tactics had become the preserve of niche pressure groups, usually with an environmentalist agenda.[242] If the overall incidence of such attacks is very low across Western Europe and North America, they can still deliver some spectacular results (Figure 6.2). Most notably, the Earth Liberation Front caused over $100 million of property damage between 1997 and 2006. Their arson attack on the ski resort at Vail, Colorado, caused no less than $26 million in damage.[243] Even allowing for recklessness and loose rhetoric, there has been a general strategy of avoiding, or minimizing, human casualties.

Any historical survey must consider this relationship of sabotage to tactics that have prioritized human fatality, or injury. Conceptually, a clear distinction has very

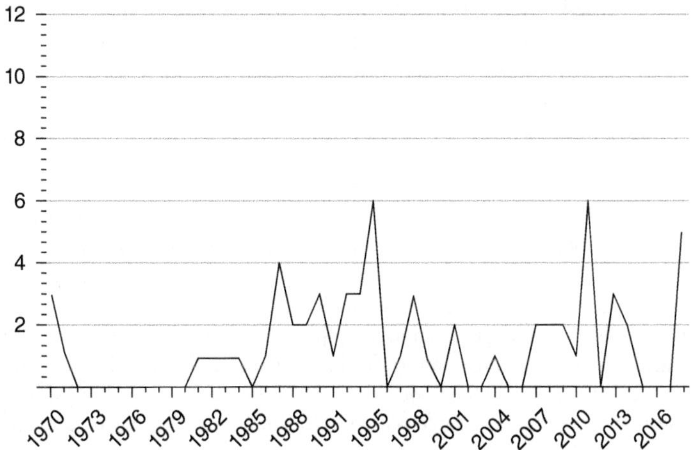

Figure 6.2. 'Sabotage equipment' attacks across North America and Western Europe, 1970–2018

Source: The Global Terrorism Database.

[240] D. Gambetta and S. Hertog, *Engineers of Jihad: The Curious Connection Between Violent Extremism and Education* (Princeton, 2016), pp. 6–14.

[241] P. Nesser, *Islamist Terrorism in Europe: A History* (London, 2015), p. 173; Jenkins, 'Would be Warriors', Rand Papers, 2010, p. 13.

[242] P. Joose, 'Leaderless Resistance and Ideological Inclusion: The Case of the Earth Liberation Front', *Terrorism and Political Violence*, 19 (3), 2007, pp. 351–68.

[243] D. R. Liddick, *Eco-Terrorism: Radical Environmental and Animal Liberation Movements* (Westport, 2006), pp. 4–5.

often been drawn between attacks on property and attacks on people. For the propagandists of the IWW at the dawn of the twentieth century, 'sabotage does not seek nor desire to take human life'.[244] The Suffragette leadership made similar points.[245] According to Che Guevara, 'sabotage has nothing to do with terrorism; terrorism and personal assaults are entirely different tactics'.[246] Ted Kaczinski in *The Unabomber Manifesto* also drew a clear distinction:

> By terrorism we mean actions motivated by a desire to influence the development of society and intended to cause injury or death to human beings. By sabotage we mean similarly motivated actions intended to destroy property without injuring human beings.[247]

Yet sabotage, if carried out ambitiously enough, also holds out the prospect of truly massive slaughter. Such incidents have historically been the exception, not the rule. But they are not entirely unknown. The massive explosion at a munitions plant at Eddystone, Pennsylvania, that killed 112 workers in April 1917 was probably the last shot of the German sabotage campaign.[248] The Provisional IRA's 1996 plot to knock out Greater London's electricity supply certainly had 'the potential to cause severe disruption, economic damage, and large-scale loss of life'.[249] The interesting implication is that the Provisionals may not have realized themselves the scale of the disaster they might precipitate. It certainly lay far outside any field of damage they had ever caused before. At a time of nominal ceasefire, it also lay outside their recent targeting praxis of trying to avoid mass casualties. At least in advance, projections of possible damage in such untried scenarios can tend to have an air of implausibility about them. But the plot was fully viable.

Such potential scenarios have, if anything, multiplied with the advent of the cyber-age. Thomas Rid comments:

> Successful attacks on industrial control systems that cause physical damage are very rare, but real. Sabotage, which dates back to industrial confrontations in the late nineteenth century, is again going industrial in the digitized twenty-first century: today's most formidable targets are industrial control systems.... Such systems are used in power plants, the electrical grid, refineries, pipelines, water and wastewater plants, the trains, underground transportation, traffic lights, heat and lighting in office buildings and hospitals, elevators, and many other physical processes.... Attacking an industrial control system is the most probable way for a computer attack to create physical damage and indirectly injure or kill people.[250]

And yet, as Rid points out, to date 'not a single human being has ever been killed or hurt as a result of a code-triggered cyber attack'.[251]

244 Smith, 'Sabotage', p. 60.

245 A. Raeburn, *The Militant Suffragettes* (London, 1973), p. 216.

246 Quoted in: M. Thorup, *An Intellectual History of Terror: War, Violence and the State* (Abingdon, 2010), p. 120.

247 Green Anarchist (ed.), *'Industrial Society and Its Future': The Unabomber Manifesto* (Camberley, 1995), p. 59.

248 Witcover, *Sabotage at Black Tom*, p. 231.

249 Martin, *The Rules of Security*, p. 45.

250 Rid, *Cyber War Will Not Take Place*, pp. 66–7.

251 Rid, *Cyber War Will Not Take Place*, p. 13.

Developing this point further, Rid argues that the general longer- term trend appears to have been for tactics of sabotage and physical violence to part ways, and develop separately.[252] Deep background matters here. Sabotage emerged directly from an industrial world in which life was very cheap. As a French government report put it in 1889, 'like a war, modern industry has its dead and wounded'.[253] In 1911, 28,000 employees were killed or injured on the British railways alone.[254] Industrial disputes could be no less bloody: a key propagandist argument for using sabotage was that it was more humane than alternatives. By contrast, most high-end cyber-attacks can disable 'an adversary's technical systems without *directly* physically harming the human operators and managers of such systems. Even more likely are scenarios of code-borne sabotage inflicting significant financial and reputational damage without causing any physical harm to hardware at all.'[255]

Despite the usual claims that sabotage 'dates back to the earliest days of human exploitation', sabotage is clearly modern.[256] It belongs firmly to an age of mature industrialization. Effective sabotage depends upon an ability to analyse complex processes of production or communication in the abstract: 'both avoiding excessive violence and avoiding identification may serve the ultimate goal of sabotage: impairing a technical system. Sabotage is therefore an indirect form of attack.'[257]

Against the confident predictions of Emmeline Pankhurst to the contrary, civilization was actually so complicated that it was extremely *hard* to know which 'very little thing could put everything out of working order'.[258] If one feature stands out from a general survey of modern sabotage, indeed, it is its hit-and-miss application. Certain aspects of modernity have been repeatedly targeted: others much less so. Railways have been a target of choice. So, too, have electricity supplies. The pylon has been described as the 'perfect modernist icon': but it was also—perhaps not coincidentally—the archetypal target of mid-twentieth-century European saboteurs as well.[259] But water supply—surely, 'critical' infrastructure by any definition—has been relatively rarely targeted. Especially in times of war or crisis, governments have invested heavily in protecting reservoirs.[260] Mass poisoning has often been threatened, but rarely attempted.[261] Bombing attacks on aqueducts have sometimes come close to causing major catastrophes in England, Scotland,

252 Rid, *Cyber War Will Not Take Place*, pp. 56–7.

253 Quoted in: Broch, *Ordinary Workers*, p. 27.

254 www.railwayaccidents.port.ac.uk

255 Rid, *Cyber War Will Not Take Place*, p. xiv. Emphases in original. See also: *Times*, 2 September 2018.

256 Smith, 'Sabotage', p. 61.

257 Rid, *Cyber War Will Not Take Place*, p. 57.

258 Quoted in: Harrison, 'The Act of Militancy', pp. 68–9.

259 Gardiner, *The Thirties*, p. 329.

260 J. E. Gumz, *The Resurrection and Collapse of Empire in Habsburg Serbia 1914–1918* (Cambridge, 2009), p. 42 [water reservoirs]; O' Connor, *Operation Lena and Hitler's Plots*, p. 151.

261 B. Burrough, *Days of Rage: America's Radical Underground, the FBI and the Forgotten Age of Revolutionary Violence* (New York, 2015, 2016), p. 152; B. Hoffman, 'Terrorist targeting: Tactics, trends, and potentialities', *Terrorism and Political Violence*, 5 (2), 1993, p. 17; J. K. Campbell, *Weapons of Mass Destruction Terrorism* (Seminole, Florida, 1997), p. 104.

and South Tyrol: but the attempts have not been repeated.[262] It may simply be that putting the lights out instantly is more appealing than interdicting water supplies. Still, this relative absence remains something of an explanatory puzzle. After all, in narrowly high political terms, the most consequential bombing attack of the entire Northern Irish Troubles was the 'false flag' attack on Belfast's water supply in 1969: in the words of the Northern Irish Prime Minister, Terence O'Neill, this 'quite literally blew me out of office'.[263]

Given geo-political sensitivity to any interruption in global oil and gas supplies, even more puzzling is how rarely energy has been targeted in the West. Relatively few pipelines and refineries supply whole continents: 'carbon comes into Europe through a couple of dozen pipes, ports and holes in the ground. It goes out through hundreds of millions of flues and exhaust pipes.'[264] On the eve of the Second World War, the cartoonist Hergé embarked on an entire Tintin adventure whose plot line concerned a general sabotage of oil supplies across Europe.[265] In general, though, in this area life has not followed art. During the S-Plan (1939), there were rumours that the IRA was trying to fire petrol dumps.[266] For their part, the British authorities increased their guard on oil depots: but these do not seem to have been a priority target for the IRA.[267] The Scottish Tartan Army in the 1970s did make some half-hearted attacks on oil infrastructure at Grangemouth.[268] For his part, Anders Breivik actively considered, but rejected, the prospect of attacking Norwegian oil or gas installations as inappropriate for the sort of sensational impact he wished to create.[269]

To conclude, the cleverly calculated sabotage of the few does indeed have the potential to upend wider society: a classic small-input/large-output phenomenon. That secret is hiding in plain sight. By the turn of the 1970s *Time* magazine feared that small groups already possessed 'a disproportionate power to render society immobile'.[270] In the observation of one Welsh nationalist in 1971

> Modern technological society needs very delicate social controls over its citizens, since its own organization is very delicate and vulnerable.... If the Welsh movements were to take a more violent turn, even quite a few people could cause vast disruption in the complicated web of public services and communications within such a densely populated country as Britain.[271]

262 Kenna, *War in the Shadows*, pp. 87–8; S. Webb, *The Suffragette Bombers: Britain's Forgotten Terrorists* (Barnsley, 2014), p. 126 [aqueduct]; Alcock, 'Terrorism in South Tyrol', p. 25.

263 Bardon, *A History of Ulster*, p. 664. I owe this sharp observation to Marc Mulholland.

264 Quoted in: M. Mann, *The Sources of Social Power*, Vol. 4, *Globalizations, 1945–2011* (Cambridge, 2013), p. 375.

265 H. Thompson, *Tintin: Hergé and His Creation* (London, 1991, 2011), p. 113–14.

266 MOA, 5406, Sunday 5 November 1939.

267 *Palestine Post*, 30 May 1939 [East Anglian oil depots being guarded].

268 A. Beckett, *When the Lights Went out: Britain in the Seventies* (London, 2009), p. 185.

269 C. Hemmingby and T. Bjørgo, *The Dynamics of A Terrorist Targeting Process: Anders B. Breivik and the 22 July Attacks in Norway* (Basingstoke, 2016), p. 21.

270 Quoted in: M. Carr, *The Infernal Machine* (New York, 2006), p. 111. Carr does not give an exact date here.

271 N. Thomas, *The Welsh Extremist: A Culture in Crisis* (London, 1971), p. 122.

At the height of the bombing campaign of the so-called 'Unabomber' in the United States in the 1990s, a senior official of the postal service reflected that it was 'almost unreal, the power of one person to affect an entire state'.[272] Such disproportionality of effect might indeed be expected to appeal widely to the disgruntled in the highly individualistic societies of the West.

And yet truly paralysing sabotage has remained a mercifully rare event, because it is hard to execute on a large scale: and all the more so for amateurs with finite resources and limited access to technical expertise. A sabotage strategy often promises very uncertain dividends for such groups: especially if instant publicity is a key aim. For advocates the uncertainty that often surrounds sabotage is often heralded as a key advantage. For W. C. Smith writing in 1913, 'sabotage is the smokeless powder of the social war. It scores a hit, whilst its source is seldom detected'.[273] The US government's 1944 *Simple Sabotage Field Manual* made the same point: 'it is carried out in such a way as to involve a minimum danger of injury, detection, and reprisal'.[274] But the downside is that most sabotage is not especially spectacular, or noteworthy. Often it is not actually clear whether sabotage has even occurred, or not: Josef Goebbels reflected in his diary on 14 November 1939 that there had been a 'serious railway accident in Silesia with almost 50 killed. There have been rather a lot of accidents lately. Could sabotage be involved?'[275] Anti-Nazi Germans hearing reports of a fire at a sawmill in Copenhagen in June 1941 were equally unsure what to make of the news.[276]

Such uncertainties may go some way towards explaining why some apparently obvious tactics (such as poisoning water reservoirs) seem, in practice, to have been rather rarely attempted.[277] Calibrating sabotage exactly is hard. Here the significant—and surely enduring—lesson of twentieth-century sabotage remains that it was states that have understood best how to dismember the public and economic life of other states. Even in—or perhaps especially in—an age replete with complex cyber-threats, the momentum of that older dynamic still invites sober reflection.[278]

[272] R. Graysmith, *Unabomber: A Desire to Kill* (Berkeley Books, 1997, 1998), p. 270.
[273] Smith, 'Sabotage', p. 71.
[274] Anonymous, *Simple Sabotage Field Manual* (Washington, 1944), p. 1. Available here: https://www.cia.gov/news-information/featured-story-archive/2012-featured-story-archive/CleanedUOSSSimpleSabotage_sm.pdf
[275] F. Taylor (ed.), *The Goebbels Diaries, 1939–1941* (London, 1982), p. 48.
[276] R. S. Kellner (ed.), *My Opposition: The Diary of Friedrich Kellner—A German Against the Third Reich* (Cambridge, 2018), p. 121.
[277] Brendon, *The Dark Valley*, p. 242 [Nazis allege reservoirs being poisoned, 1933]; O' Connor, *Operation Lena and Hitler's Plots*, p. 151 [Ministry of Health tightens security at reservoirs, 1942].
[278] Martin, *The Rules of Security*.

Conclusion

The Relationship to Modernity

Sweeping claims to the sheer antiquity of terrorism are commonplace. For Juliet Lodge, terrorism was as 'old as the hills'.[1] For Paul Wilkinson, it was simply 'one of the oldest forms of violence known to man'.[2] But such claims are of little help when the analytical focus is reduced in scope. If we simply ask *how* political violence has evolved over the past 250 years, it is harder not to be impressed both by the sheer degree of change; and, indeed, of abrupt discontinuity. Change on this scale in turn invites reflection as to its underlying drivers. Here I have approached political violence not just as mere mayhem, but as a mirror—however dim—of wider historical processes. Violence never stands wholly apart from its times.

What have those processes been? Across the West, the first has been the relentless centralization of state power and, with it, the 'monopolization' of all system-threatening violence by the state. How much 'other' violence the state is prepared to tolerate in society is largely a matter of culture; and, as such, shifts over time. Here the great dividing line run downs the Atlantic (and along the northern border of the USA). The USA has preserved—or even revived—older traditions that equate citizenship with the right to bear arms: a tacit admission, in effect, that private and ghetto violence can be securely ignored since it is never likely to endanger either the federal government nor the fundamental strength of the American state. Whatever the human cost, this has not been a crazy calculation historically—the state that until 1934 had lacked an effective federal police force could, just ten years later, direct and organize the D-Day invasions. By contrast, the Western European (and Canadian) tradition formally aspires to the suppression of all private violence altogether.

Of course, grassroots realities are always far messier than this. Any social conquests of violence are always partial, incomplete, and reversible. Some areas matter less than others. Local pockets of violent crime may indeed endure for decades: but so long as the violence of the ghetto remains in the ghetto and does not spill out, it may receive little sustained attention from the state or media. Some victims matter far less than others—here serial killers are well advised to concentrate on targeting prostitutes about whom no one, least of all the police, tend to care very much.[3]

[1] J. Lodge, *Threat of Terrorism* (Brighton, 1988), p. 1.

[2] P. Wilkinson, *The Lessons of Lockerbie* (London, 1989), p. 32.

[3] N. McKeganey and M. Barnard, *Sex Work on the Streets: Prostitutes and Their Clients* (Maidenhead, 1996, 1997), p. xii); R. Jarossi, *The Hunt for the '60s Ripper* (London, 2017), pp. 276–7; J. Smith,

Even after the achievement of the women's franchise across western democracies in the first half of the twentieth century, long dominant cultural assumptions simply continued to classify the bulk of violence against women as 'domestic': and hence both invisible and trivial. *The Hite Report on Male Sexuality* (1978) contains two accounts of psychiatrists recommending men rape their own wives.[4]

And yet, when all caveats have been duly entered, Weber's 'monopoly of violence' captures an extraordinary shift by which the modern state came to appropriate to itself the sole right to use, or license, public violence—and, by comparison with previous ages, to make that claim socially meaningful. In the first half of this book, I charted the processes by which the modern state in nineteenth-century Western Europe—and north America, albeit with a varied iteration of priorities—'squeezed' proto-political violence out of most public life, even across their remotest territories. The claims of local communities to administer their own judgments and punishments were relentlessly pegged back: the fading of traditions of 'rough music' and lynching was a slow, but ultimately irreversible, process. So, too, was the demise of banditry.

Behind this rise of the modern state lay an infrastructural revolution. In the end, the ability to project power evenly across the national territory depended upon control of the files. Seen from this perspective, the history of modern political violence has essentially been the story of residual tactics: the forms of violent resistance that are left when the state becomes too powerful to confront directly. In Europe, the survival of forms of essentially nineteenth-century revolutionary mobilization, such as barricade building, into the later twentieth century may be attributed to the greater crises of state stability engendered by the World Wars: in both 1918–19 and 1944–5 regimes collapsed right across Europe. Regime implosion under these exceptional circumstances rehabilitated 'archaic' street tactics that otherwise would likely have become obsolete earlier.[5] And in that sense, conversely, the post-1968 surge of terroristic violence may indeed be seen as a reversion to late nineteenth-century templates: another era of impregnable government.

Yet this sketch on its own is too reductionist. Western modernity has repeatedly facilitated the recasting of violence into new forms; and with new possibilities. Behind this tendency has lain the relentless force of industrial capitalism. Both the mass-produced revolver and dynamite—that between them transformed the revolutionary violence of the late nineteenth century—emerged from the commercial, and not the military, sectors. Such technological change mattered because it made new forms of destruction and harm possible—but, equally, in doing so, it helped change mentalities as well. New horrors became thinkable. Herein lay a crucial difference with earlier ages—the acute sense that the social conventions that had previously restrained unofficial violence were fast dissolving.[6]

Misogynies (London, 1989, 2013), pp. 188–9; P. Vronsky, *Sons of Cain: A History of Serial Killers From the Stone Age to the Present* (New York, 2018), p. 73.

[4] S. Hite, *The Hite Report on Male Sexuality* (London, 1978, 1981), p. 731.

[5] E. Hazan, *A History of the Barricade* (London, 2013, 2015), pp. 123–4.

[6] E. J. Hobsbawm, 'Political Violence and Political Murder: Comments on Franklin Ford's Essay' in W. J. Mommsen and G. Hirschfeld (eds), *Social Protest, Violence and Terror in Nineteenth- and Twentieth-Century Europe* (London, 1982), p. 16.

More accurately, a new repertoire of radical protest was emerging that was strikingly transnational: indeed, Jeremy Varon has asserted that 'modern political violence has a distinct grammar, arguably known to all its far-flung practitioners'.[7] In this new grammar of outrage it was the logic of synecdoche—the transfiguration of individual targets into wider symbols—that dominated. Its hallmark was sensationalism. In this it simply marched with the times: the late nineteenth century also saw the more or less simultaneous emergence of recognizably modern campaigns: of advertising, moral panics, and electioneering.[8] As a social phenomenon, the terroristic attack thus firmly belongs to the 'society of the spectacle'.[9] An observant teenage witness to the 1884–5 Fenian bombings in London noticed that everyone's first instinct when they heard an explosion was to glance at the clock ('there are continual scares about dynamite, and every time any one hears a loud noise they mark the time'). Such reactions perhaps derived, in part, from an awareness of the need to establish a common reference point for later conversations.[10] In the late nineteenth-century 'society of strangers', a dynamite attack represented a rare shared reference point. In this respect, the technicians of political violence increasingly aspired to create common talking points: what would by the twenty-first century be called 'water cooler' moments. Publicity values were coming to dominate: and, in turn, to define what constituted 'success', at least in the short term.

Close attention to such media values continue to dominate the most 'successful' (and notorious) attacks. Thus, they must target important people (though these are often dauntingly well protected); or else important places, or else simply achieve a scale that ensures they will not be ignored. Centres of 'world cities' are thus favourite locations: but so, too, are airports. Both offer prestigious and floodlit global stages. Suburban killers such as the Washington Sniper of 2002 may actually succeed in projecting a far more intense sense of general fear, albeit within a limited radius.[11] But the media are not likely to stay interested in such 'nowhere places' for very long. Finally, the media love league tables of atrocity according to what Paul Wilkinson back in 1977 called 'Gresham's Law of terrorism': 'they who spill the most blood get the biggest headlines'.[12] As Anders Breivik accurately noted, 'in order to get international press, there must be a large impact…one must exceed a certain limit'.[13] In sum, the presentational values of mass media led to the institutionalization of transgression: and helped structure the horrors of the modern age.

Seen from this perspective, terroristic attacks may fairly be judged to be extreme examples of what media scholars of press conferences, ribbon-cutting ceremonies (and so on) categorize as the 'pseudo-event'—that is, an event that is staged not for

[7] J. Varon, '"The Sound of a Thunder": Weatherman and the Music of Late-Life Regrets', *Los Angeles Review of Books* (1 September, 2017).

[8] A. N. Wilson, *The Victorians* (London, 2007), pp. 236–43.

[9] G. Debord, *Society of the Spectacle* (London, 1992).

[10] L. Linder (ed.), *The Journal of Beatrix Potter: from 1881 to 1897* (London, 1966), pp. 87, 123.

[11] C. A. Moose and C. Fleming, *Three Weeks in October: The Hunt for the Washington Sniper* (London, 2003, 2004).

[12] P. Wilkinson, *Terrorism and the Liberal State* (London 1977, 1979), p. 112.

[13] Quoted in: P. Gill, *Lone Actor Terrorists: A Behavioural Analysis* (Abingdon, 2015), p. 150.

its own sake, but merely so that it may be broadcast.[14] Not the act of destruction itself, but its publicity half-life, matters. And it is this logic, primarily, that distinguishes it from war which does remain, at heart, a 'material event': one where the weight of destruction matters in its own right.[15] Much of the reason for the declining popularity of sabotage from the late twentieth century probably lies in an innate recognition of these divergent realities.

I

All too often modern terror remains understood as a pseudo-military phenomenon. It is understood as the continuation of war by the *same* means—albeit means highly constrained by amateur military capability. It is, in Alex Schmid's famous phrase, 'the peacetime equivalent of war crimes'.[16] It is, so to speak, excessive battlefield violence that is somehow obscenely out of context.

And yet any close examination of the evolution of violent political actions suggests deep roots in civilian society. Direct relationships with modern twentieth-century warfare turn out to be far more opaque than might be assumed. Both the terroristic bombing campaign and the mass hostage-taking crisis, for instance, had already emerged well before 1914. Broadly speaking, total war has fundamentally acted as a general advertisement for the permissibility of impersonal slaughter, rather than as a detailed instruction manual in its own right. As Eric Hobsbawm put it in 1982, impersonal atrocity was 'not merely the signature of fringe groups. After all in modern mass war, certainly in the Second World War, a great deal of the strategy was deliberately aimed at the innocent, those who were not fighting rather than those who were fighting.'[17]

In similar fashion, George Mosse pointed to the First World War as a threshold in the 'brutalization' of European society—although many scholars have remained unpersuaded by a term that has been seen as nebulous and inherently inflationary.[18] Still, brutalization remains a usefully provocative concept: and, if employed in a more restricted sense, may still be used as a useful lens to trace the evolution of specific techniques of violence.

One might make a powerful argument that *as far as pro-state forces go*—particularly, their irregular formations, militias, and freelance supporters—there does indeed seem to have been some direct leakage from the battlefield to wider society in the chaotic post-1918 period. Two examples will have to suffice here. First, the use of headshots. Of course, it is hard to generalize confidently. But a standard

[14] C. Rojek, *Celebrity* (London, 2001), pp. 18, 198.

[15] S. Malešević, *The Sociology of War and Peace* (Cambridge, 2010), p. 68.

[16] A. Schmid, *The Definition of Terrorism. A Study in Compliance with CTL/9/91/2207 for the U.N. Crime Prevention and Criminal Justice Branch* (Leiden, Dec. 1992), pp. 8–9.

[17] Hobsbawm, 'Political Violence and Political Murder', p. 14.

[18] R. Gerwarth and J. Horne, 'Paramilitarism in Europe after the Great War: An Introduction' in R. Gerwarth and J. Horne (eds), *War in Peace: Paramilitary Violence in Europe after the Great War* (Oxford, 2012, 2013), pp. 2–3.

instinct of assassins in the 1881–1914 period seems to have been to aim for the chest. If anything, the clinical headshot was an American speciality: and a prerogative of Wild West killers.[19] After 1918, however, the practice of headshots seems to diffuse rather more widely. Weimar killers, in particular, stand out as notably more competent than their anarchist predecessors.[20]

Secondly, there is the rhetorical exculpation that prisoners had been 'shot whilst trying to escape'. Here both the wider cultural resonance, and direct imitation, of battlefield practices seems particularly easy to trace.[21] Again, this subterfuge had not been *entirely* unknown before 1914. Amongst prisoners, indeed, it was justifiably feared in Tsarist Russia after the failed 1905 revolution.[22] But it was not yet, apparently, a familiar ruse further afield—Sebastian Haffner writes that he first heard the phrase concerning Karl Liebknecht's death in January 1919: and people were still so naive that they took it literally.[23] Across the disturbed regions of Europe it quickly became the standard euphemism—liberally employed by both German Freikorps and the Black and Tans in Ireland, for instance.[24] By 1938, it was familiar enough to turn up as a plot device in Tintin's cartoon adventures.[25]

Equally striking, though, seems to be the *rather limited* transfer of other battlefield skills. As seen, neither sniping nor use of IEDs profoundly transformed the practice of political violence after the First World War. Albeit with a few spectacular exceptions, this was a period in which mass casualty bombing attempts seem to have declined. Similar absences become even more striking after the Second World War—which had, after all, been a war of movement in which IEDs and mass-produced mines played a major role. Certainly, there seems to have been a direct effect here—separatist groups in Europe after 1945 largely concentrating on using explosives for sabotage: a direct manifestation of the Resistance legacy. But both

[19] P. Newark, *Firefight! The History of Personal Firepower* (London, 1989), p. 77 [death of Wild Bill Hickok]; T. J. Stiles, *Jesse James: Last Rebel of the Civil War* (London, 1993, 2007), p. 375 [death of Jesse James]. Abraham Lincoln, too, had been killed by a shot to the head: E. Steers, *Lincoln's Assassination* (Carbondale, IL, 2014), p. 54.

[20] For Weimar Germany, see: S. Delmer, *Weimar Germany: Democracy on Trial* (London, 1972), p. 40 [death of Liebknecht]; K. Gietinger, *The Murder of Rosa Luxemburg* (London, 2018, 2019), p. 40 [death of Luxemburg]; A. E. Gurganus, *Kurt Eisner: A Modern Life* (New York, 2018), p. 424 [death of Eisner]; M. Jones, *Founding Weimar: Violence and the German Revolution of 1918–1919* (Cambridge, 2016), p. 307 [execution of the Munich hostages]; M. Sabrow, *Der Rathenaumord: Rekonstruktion einer Verschwörung gegen die Republik von Weimar* (Oldenbourg, 1994), pp. 18–19 [death of Erzberger]. See also: U. C. Hoffmann, 'Fememorde' [death of Wilhelm Hörnlein, 31 October 1921]. Available here: https://www.historisches-lexikon-bayerns.de/Lexikon/Fememorde For left-wing death squads in the Spanish Civil War: C. E. Lucas Phillips, *The Spanish Pimpernel* (London, 1960), p. 49.

[21] N. Ferguson, *The Pity of War* (London, 1998, 1999), p. 377.

[22] D. Rumbelow, *The Houndsditch Murders and the Siege of Sidney Street* (London, 1973, 1988, 1990), p. 35.

[23] S. Haffner, *Defying Hitler* (2002, 2003), p. 28.

[24] For Germany: G. Mosse, *Fallen Soldiers: Reshaping the Memory of the World Wars* (Oxford, 1990, 1991), p. 178; E. J. Gumbel, *Vier Jahre politischer Mord* (Berlin, 1922), pp. 10, 18, 26, 54, 55, 56, 57–8, 59, 60, 61, 62. For Ireland: J. Crowley (et al., eds) *Atlas of the Irish Revolution* (Cork, 2017), pp. 415, 878.

[25] Hergé, *King Ottokar's Sceptre* (London, 1958), pp. 31–2; H. Thompson, *Tintin: Hergé and His Creation* (London, 1991, 2011), pp. 103–10.

the USA and Europe were largely spared the mass casualty bombings that were such a conspicuous feature of other arenas in this period (such as Palestine and Algeria, in particular).

Here, presumably, we see the retarding influence of ideological restraints: since the widespread practical knowledge of handling explosives clearly existed to facilitate mass atrocity. At a lower level of destruction, the military conflicts of 1937–45 certainly established the Molotov Cocktail in the armoury of popular protest. And both this period and its successor confrontation, the Cold War, flooded the world with guns. According to one estimate five out of six American weapons used in Vietnam were lost.[26] Globally, there are perhaps between 70 and 100 million Kalashnikov assault rifles operational today: a direct legacy of previous Soviet promotion of this most robust and portable of killing machines.[27] Still, none of these weapons emerged easily or automatically on the streets of western cities. Molotov cocktails were relatively rarely used before the later 1960s: and it was not until the 1972 Olympics hostage-taking that Kalashnikovs became truly notorious.[28]

In summary, direct effects of world wars on post-war patterns of both political and anti-social violence across the West are not at all easy to discern. One 1970 study did detect clusters of elite assassination attempts during, or just after, major crises: after the First World War in 1919–23 (nine attempts), during the Great Depression in 1932–4 (seven), after the Second World War in 1946–51 (twelve) and again during the turmoil of 1963–6 (eleven).[29] Rather more broadly, suggestions have been made that the glut of serial killers in American society can be interpreted as a delayed legacy of the 1941–5 conflict: even though, in general, war and murder rates seem to be inversely related.[30]

Surely more impressive, then, has been the broadly *antonymic* relationship between modern war and peace. Although framed in global terms, the observation of Brian Jenkins in 1974 that 'perhaps only in times of relative peace in the world can world attention be attracted by lesser episodes of violence' largely holds true for the experience of Western Europe and North America over the last century.[31] Indeed, 'the fear of terrorism is often greatest in times of relative peace and stability, when violence appears to be a social anomaly'.[32] Indeed, with the exception of genuine (but brief) crises of state stability in Europe in 1918–23 and 1944–5, dividing lines between war and peace have remained stark.

[26] *Irish Times*, 13 October 1981.

[27] A. K. Cronin, *Power to the People: How Open Technological Innovation is Arming Tomorrow's Terrorists* (Oxford, 2020), p. 127.

[28] Cronin, Power to the People, p. 158.

[29] M. C. Havens, C. Leiden, and K. M. Schmitt, *The Politics of Assassination* (Englewood Cliffs, NJ, 1970), p. 28. It is these authors' choice to designate 1963–6 as a discrete period in its own right.

[30] Vronsky, *Sons of Cain*, pp. 310–38; For suggestions that both inter-personal violence and assassination tend to run counter-cyclical to major wars, see respectively: R. Muchembled (transl. J. Birrell), *A History of Violence* (Cambridge, 2012), p. 40; F. L. Ford, *Political Murder: From Tyrannicide to Terrorism* (Harvard, 1985), p. 239.

[31] B. Jenkins, *International Terrorism: A New Kind of Warfare*, The Rand Paper Series, June 1974, p. 9.

[32] M. Carr, *The Infernal Machine: A History of Terrorism from the Assassination of Tsar Alexander II to Al-Qaeda* (New York, 2006), p. 37.

So while the general notion of a 'brutalization' of Western societies following the World Wars may indeed have considerable explanatory power, it does little to explain why the terroristic atrocity of anti-state rebels first accelerated only after 1968; and then again during the 1990s. In my introduction I wrote of an intention to focus upon 'how' not 'why' questions. As a heuristic device, this simplifying approach certainly has its uses. But one use, ironically, is to highlight some of the family resemblances between 'how' and 'why' explanations. Viewed alongside each other, means and motives begin to look like 'eternal twins'.[33]

Without downplaying the significance of the particular ideological agendas at play pushing for atrocity, it is important here to draw attention to the wider facilitative environment of the communications revolutions that have repeatedly rewarded extreme, novel, and spectacular tactics. Mass hijacking and hostage-taking flourished at the dawn of satellite TV (1968–75); suicide-bombing as the internet age emerged (mid-1990s onwards); and more 'primitive' tactics of car ramming and knife attacks as camera phones became ubiquitous (*c.* 2016–18). None of these communication developments *caused* these atrocities, of course: but it would be impossible to explain their rapid diffusion as internationally recognized tactics without them. As the stage of global public attention became ever more crowded, it is not surprising that the competition for attention should become ever more frenetic. When information is plentiful, attention becomes the scarce resource: a key precondition for the emergence of 'new terrorisms'.

At the macro-level, improved communications tightened the feed-back loops between conflict zones as laboratories of creative new atrocities—here the Middle East stands out supreme—Western global interests and power projection; and the stability of Western heartlands themselves. Writing of Islamist terror in the early twenty-first century, Peter Nesser argues that it is 'this connection between Europe-based extremism and the conflict zones [that] plays a vital role in the emergence of terrorist cells in Europe today'.[34] Despite the early warning of the 1993 World Trade Center bombing, the USA was still entirely unprepared for this effect until the catastrophe of 11 September 2001. Yet, from a longer perspective, this side-effect of globalization is easy to trace. From this perspective, it is the 'Short Twentieth Century' (*c.* 1917–91) that appears as the aberration. In the 1990s, the same forces of accelerating capital and populations picked up again: and with it, broadly similar dynamics of transnational terror whose imitative reach suddenly expanded. In that respect, Al-Qaeda has been the true heir to the nineteenth-century anarchists' 'propaganda of the deed'.[35] That ageing example still resonates.

[33] Z. Ivianksy, 'Individual Terror: Concept and Typology', *Journal of Contemporary History*, 12 (1), 1977, p. 44.

[34] P. Nesser, *Islamist Terrorism in Europe: A History* (London, 2015), p. 2.

[35] M. Mann, *The Sources of Social Power*, Vol. 4, Globalizations, 1945–2011 (Cambridge, 2013), pp. 281–3, 293–310.

II

> The motion picture with its universal language, the aeroplane with its speed, and the wireless with its coming international programme—these will soon bring the world to a complete understanding.
>
> – Henry Ford, 1920[36]

What, then, of the future?

'All that is solid melts into air' wrote Karl Marx famously of the very nature of modernity: and prediction of its future shape is no exception.[37] All that can be sure about the future is that it will be a nest of surprises. And as far as the future of political violence goes, it is a betting certainty that some of those surprises will be highly unpleasant ones. Beyond that it is hard to say anything very definite. Futurology is bunk.

Should, then, the future of political violence be simply left to look after itself? That is a tempting response. But it seems too much of an intellectual abdication—historians should have something to say on the subject. After all, 'history cannot get away from the future, if only because there is no line which divides the two'.[38] Reading the likely forward momentum of ongoing tendencies that began in the past might therefore still prove a worthwhile exercise. Even some highly *indefinite* observations about more or less likely futures might be better than nothing.

Gilbert Ramsay has written perceptively that 'we forget that technology doesn't just help us get more of what we want. It changes what we want, and how we understand our very existence'.[39] That tendency has formed a major running theme of my account of the past 250 years. But looking ahead, it is already clear that in profound ways the social media revolution—the rise of many-to-many communication—allows dreamers to dream new dreams. Rather than an arduous process of joining some highly clandestine underground revolutionary cell, there are now free-wheeling radical movements with extensive penumbras of hangers-on, online sympathizers, and 'useful idiots'. And all too often the most extreme sub-cultures online are powered by the endlessly renewable energy of outrage and self-pity. They look set to run for the foreseeable future.

Contemporary society also seems to produce a steady, if numerically modest, supply of self-appointed avengers: violent individuals who step forward to combat 'injustice', however idiosyncratically understood. This, too, looks set to continue. It is important to stress that this phenomenon is not, in itself, entirely new. All of the classic behaviours associated with lone attackers were already present in the

36 Quoted in: D. Edgerton, *The Shock of the Old* (London, 2006, 2008), p. 114.

37 For a discussion of this classic passage: M. Berman, *All that is Solid Melts into Air: The Experience of Modernity* (London, 1982, 2010), p. 21.

38 E. J. Hobsbawm, *On History* (London, 1997, 2013), p. 50.

39 Quoted in: D. Holbrook, 'Social Media and Terrorism' in D. Muro and T. K. Wilson (eds) *Contemporary Terrorism Studies* (Oxford, 2021) [forthcoming].

eighteenth century.[40] And yet the scale of such attacks does seem to have swelled in the early twenty-first century: and shows no sign of subsiding. Again, it is also important to stress that this trend is global, and not just Western. But it does seem particularly concentrated in the historic heartlands of hyper-individualism: Western Europe and the USA.

Indeed, as a laboratory for individualistic violence the USA is truly unique. Mark Hamm and Ramon Spaaij calculated in a 2017 study that half of what they call thev 'world's lone wolf terrorism attacks' have occurred in the USA.[41] Research on serial killers has reached similar conclusions: 'If we were charged with the responsibility of designing a society in which all structural and cultural mechanisms leaned towards the creation of the killers of strangers, we could do no better than to present the purchaser with the shape of modern America'.[42] Nor does it seem a complete coincidence that the USA has become a major cradle of the so-called 'incel' ('involuntary celibate') killers—that monstrous regiment of misogynistic men who valorize mass murder over masturbation.[43] Elliot Rodger's exemplary rampage through Isla Vista, California in 2014 has much to answer for here.[44] A highly ominous precedent has been set.

We should not exaggerate this crisis of the West. Looking back offers some comfort. Despite present crises, far worse horrors lie in the background on both sides of the Atlantic: in the unspeakable carnage that convulsed the USA (between 1861–5) and, indeed, in the even greater horrors that the two-fold collapse of European civilization engendered (in 1914–18 and again in 1939–45). Moreover, any wide-angled survey of the evolution of political violence over the past 250 years should, indeed must, pay attention to the deep foundations of macro-stability in modern Western societies. And these are unlikely to collapse; or, at least, they are highly unlikely to do so overnight. Control of public violence, indeed, remains one of the great success stories of the Western state, achieved through a relentless exertion of infrastructural power. More than any other single factor, this has relentlessly squeezed the prospect of insurrectionist violence out of modern politics. Revolutions, coups, civil wars all appear to belong to the past. Basic state stability endures: despite the new challenges that the rise of the network society and the new populism throw up. What political violence is left does not seem any kind of existential threat. We would do well to worry far more about melting ice caps. Or pandemics.

But this is not the whole story. Backward glances prove unsettling as well. Above all: they show us how we have come to tolerate barbarities as entirely mundane that

[40] For preoccupation with her future fame and giveaway 'leakage' behaviour displayed by the assassin Charlotte Corday in 1793: S. Loomis, *Paris in the Terror* (Harmondsworth, 1964, 1970), pp. 105–6, 112. See also: J. Warner, *John the Painter: The First Modern Terrorist* (London, 2004), p. xii.

[41] M. S. Hamm and R. Spaaij, *The Age of Lone Wolf Terrorism* (New York, 2017), p. 261.

[42] E. Leyton, *Hunting Humans* (London, 2001), p. 284.

[43] *War on the Rocks*, 27 November 2019 (B. Hoffman and J. Ware, 'Are We Entering a New Era of Far-Right Terrorism?').

[44] Six died. See: BBC News, 28 April 2018 ('Elliot Rodger: How Misogynist Killer Became "Incel Hero"').

would have been quite incomprehensible to our ancestors. Before the revolutions of the late eighteenth century, indeed, violent threats to political elites remained highly limited and highly sporadic. And they remained narrowly focused against the very top of society, because that is where real power was located.

By the early twenty-first century, in contrast, danger has democratized. Attacks can now be against anyone; and for any cause. Resentments, myths, and pseudo-grievances bubble away merrily online. And within the giant magic lantern show of social media the shadows continue to grow longer and larger. Seen from this longer-term vantage point, the dark progress of western political violence has taken the form of a relentless and irresistible diffusion: from assassination to massacre: from hazard of social rank to rank social hazard; from the classes to the masses; from feud to fad—an ever widening gyre.

Bibliography

MANUSCRIPT AND ARCHIVAL SOURCES

Berlin
Geheimes Staatsarchiv, Preussischer Kulturbesitz, Dahlem (GSA)
GSA, Rep 171/144/Band 4

London
National Archives (NA)
NA, KV3/439. 15/11/1947
NA, CJ4/829
NA, MEPO 3/1288
NA, MEPO 3/1908
NA, HO 144/196/A46866B
NA, FCO 871/946

Brighton
Mass Observation Archive
MOA, 5406, Sunday 5 November 1939

NEWSPAPER ARCHIVES

American Newspapers and Periodicals
Crisis
Los Angeles Times
New York Times
Time
Washington Post

British Newspaper Archive
Many provincial newspapers carried syndicated news from around the world. The following nineteenth- and twentieth-century British (and Irish) newspapers were consulted via: british-newspaperarchive.co.uk
Aberdeen Evening Express
Aberdeen Journal
Aberdeen Press and Journal
Belfast News Letter
Belfast Telegraph
Belfast Weekly News
Berwick Advertiser
Berwickshire News and General Advertiser
Birmingham Daily Post
Birmingham Mail
Chichester Observer

Coventry Evening Telegraph
Daily Herald
Daily Mail
Daily Mirror
Daily Record
Daily Record and Mail
Daily Telegraph
Derby Daily Telegraph
Derry Journal
Downpatrick Recorder
Dundee Courier
Dundee Evening Telegraph
Exeter and Plymouth Gazette
Evening Despatch
Evening Standard
Gloucester Citizen
Gloucestershire Echo
Guardian
Hartlepool Daily Mail
Hartlepool Northern Daily Mail
Hull Daily Mail
Impartial Reporter
Irish News
Lancashire Evening Post
Larne Times
Leeds Mercury
Liverpool Daily Echo
Liverpool Echo
Lloyds Weekly Newspaper
London Daily News
Londonderry Sentinel
Mail on Sunday
Manchester Examiner and Times
Morning Post
Newcastle Daily Journal
Newcastle Evening Chronicle
Newcastle Journal
North Devon Journal
Northern Daily Mail
Northern Whig
Nottingham Journal
People
Scotsman
Sheffield Daily Independent
Sheffield Daily Telegraph
Sheffield Independent
Shields Daily News
Sunday Herald
Sunday Sun

Sunday Times
Western Daily Mercury
Western Daily Press
Western Morning News
Yorkshire Evening Post
Yorkshire Post and Leeds Intelligencer

Contemporary British Newspapers (*c.* 1989 onwards)
Daily Mail
Daily Telegraph
Economist
Guardian
i
Independent
Irish Times
New Statesman
Spectator
Sun
The Times

French Newspapers
Écho d'Alger [for Algiers]
Le Jour [for Beirut]
Le Petit Journal

Newspapers Relating to the Upper Silesian Conflict, 1918–1922
Kattowitzer Zeitung
Der Oberschlesische Arbeiterfreund
Die Obserschlesische Grenzzeitung
Der Oberschlesische Wanderer
Polak
Volkswille

Contemporary German Periodicals
Der Spiegel
Die Zeit

Control Risks Archive, University of St Andrews
Iberian Daily Sun, 18–19 December 1983. Cutting preserved in: Lebanon, 1983 file.

Miscellaneous
Palestine Post

ONLINE MEDIA

Al Arabiya.net
Bloomberg
BBC News
Tagesschau.de

FILM FOOTAGE

The following footage was viewed on Youtube:

'Brandanschläge auf Asylheime in Rostock 1992' [from the documentary 'Pogrom Rostock', 1992]

'France—Paris Riots (1968)' [Pathé report published on Youtube, 13 April 2014]

'Ministry of Silly Walks' [Monty Python sketch posted on Youtube, 6 December 2016]

Also:

'Alexander Murdered' (1934) [Universal Newsreel's report embedded in the Wikipedia page on 'Alexander I of Yugoslavia']

ONLINE RESEARCH RESOURCES

http://www.capitalpunishmentuk.org/hepnarova.html
https://catholicsaints.info
https://www.start.umd.edu/research-projects/global-terrorism-database-gtd
https://www.historisches-lexikon-bayerns.de/Lexikon/Fememorde
https://www.icao.int/sustainability/Pages/Facts-Figures_WorldEconomyData.aspx
https://www.kansascity.com/news/special-reports/kc-true-crime/article706028.html
http://www.Muderpedia.org
https://nordwestmecklenburg.de
https://www.pewresearch.org/
https://www.phrases.org.uk/meanings/taken-for-a-ride.html
www.railwayaccidents.port.ac.uk
http://www.standingwellback.com/
www.tallarmeniantale.com/ottoman-bank.htm//news
www.zbojnickiszlak.pl

ONLINE LIBRARIES

Marinetti, F. T., 'The Futurist Manifesto' (1909)

Available at: https://archive.compart.uni-bremen.de/2014/website/fileadmin/media/lernen/Futurist_Manifesto.pdf

Swift, J., *The Journal to Stella*, Letter LV, (15 November, 1712)

Available at: https://www.gutenberg.org/files/4208/4208-h/4208-h.htm

Twain, M., 'The Memorable Assassination', 1898

Available at: http://ebooks.adelaide.edu.au/t/twain/mark/what_is_man/chapter.5.html

The following items were consulted via: https://www.marxists.org

Anonymous, 'Karl Liebknecht and Rosa Luxeburg [sic]: Last Hours', *The Communist Review*, January 1924, 4 (9)

Trotsky, L., 'Terrorism and Communism: A Reply to Karl Kautsky' (1920)

Wintringham, T., 'Against Invasion—the Lessons of Spain', *Picture Post*, 15 June 1940

ONLINE COMMENTARY

Buckley, A., 'Fighting and Fun: Spectators and Stone-Throwers in Ulster Riots'.

Available at: http://www.anthonydbuckley.com/fighting-and-fun-stone-throwers-and-spectators-in-ulster-riots.html

Hoffman, B. and J. Ware, 'Are We Entering a New Era of Far-Right Terrorism?'

War on the Rocks, 27 November 2019

Available at: https://warontherocks.com/2019/11/are-we-entering-a-new-era-of-far-right-terrorism/

Müller, F. L., 'Swabian Loyalty and the Uses of Gefühlspolitik'.

Available at: http://heirstothethrone-project

Pool Re Terrorism Research and Analysis Centre, 'Post-Incident Report: Three Attacks in three Months—Westminster, Manchester and London Bridge', 7 June 2017

Available at: https://www.poolre.co.uk/wp-content/uploads/2019/09/Post-Incident-Report_V2_lo-res.pdf

Savitsky, S., 'Killer Cars: The Violence of Automobility'.

Available at: http://scrambledsystems.tumblr.com/

Varon, J., '"The Sound of a Thunder": Weatherman and the Music of Late-Life Regrets', *Los Angeles Review of Books* (1 September, 2017)

Available at: https://lareviewofbooks.org/article/sound-thunder-weatherman-music-late-life-regrets/

Veilleux-Lepage, Y., 'How and Why Vehicle Ramming Became the Attack of Choice for Terrorists', *The Conversation*, 29 March 2017

Available at: https://theconversation.com/how-and-why-vehicle-ramming-became-the-attack-of-choice-for-terrorists-75236

PRINTED PRIMARY SOURCES

Abu-Sharif, B. and U. Mahnaimi, *Tried By Fire* (London, 1995, 1996)

Albright, D. (ed.), *W. B. Yeats: The Poems* (London, 1990, 2001)

Allen, J. (et al.), *Without Sanctuary: Lynching Photography in America* (Sante Fe, Twin Palms, 2000)

Alpert, J., *Growing Up Underground* (New York, 1981)

Anonymous, *A Woman in Berlin* (London, 1954, 2011)

Anonymous, *Simple Sabotage Field Manual* (Washington, 1944)

Asquith, M., *The Autobiography of Margot Asquith*, Vol. I (London, 1920, 1936)

Ayers, B., *Fugitive Days: A Memoir* (Boston, 2001)

Ayers, J. (ed.), *Paupers and Pig Killers: The Diary of William Holland, A Somerset Parson, 1799–1818* (Gloucester, 1984)

Bakunin, M., *Statism and Anarchy* (Cambridge, 1990)

Baumann, B., *Wie alles anfing* (Berlin, 1991)

Beam, L., 'Leaderless Resistance', *The Seditionist*, No. 12, February 1992

Behan, B., *Borstal Boy* (London, 1958, 1990)

Braunthal, J., *In Search of the Millennium* (London, 1945)

Buckle, G. (ed.), *Letters of Queen Victoria*, 2nd Series, Vol. III, (London, 1926)

Buford, B. *Among the Thugs* (London, 1991, 1992)

Burke, E., *Reflections on the Revolution in France* (Harmondsworth, 1790, 1969)

Camus, A. (transl. A. Bower), *The Fastidious Assassins* (London, 1949, 2008)

Conrad, J., *The Secret Agent* (London, 1907, 2007)

Dąmbski, S., *Egzekutor* (Warsaw, 2010)

de Botton, A., *A Week at the Airport: A Heathrow Diary* (London, 2009)

de Commynes, P. (transl. M. Jones), *Memoirs: the Reign of Louis XI 1461–1483* (Harmondsworth, 1972)

de Laparre, R. P., *Journal d'un prêtre en Algérie: Oran 1961–1962* (no place of publication given, 1964)

de Morsier, S. (ed.), *Memoirs of the Comtesse de Boigne* (London, 1956)

Dessaigne, F., *Journal d'une mère de familie pied-noir* (Paris, 1962)
Dickens, C., *Little Dorrit* (London, 1857, 2003)
Duranty, W., *I Write As I Please* (London, 1935)
Dylan, B., *Writings and Drawings* (London, 1972, 1987)
Elliott, P., *The Last Time I saw Paris* (London, 1942, 2011)
Engels, F., *The Condition of the Working Class in England* (London, 1845, 1987)
Feraoun, M., *Journal 1955–1962* (Lincoln, Nebraska, 1962, 2000)
Footman, D., *Balkan Holiday* (London, 1935)
Frank, A., *The Diary of Anne Frank* (London, 1947, 1972)
Galvao, H., *Santa Maria: My Crusade for Portugal* (Cleveland, 1961)
Gannon, P. J., 'In the Catacombs of Belfast', *Studies: An Irish Quarterly Review of Letters, Philosophy and Science*, XI, 1922
'Giorgio', *Memoirs of an Italian Terrorist* (New York, 1981, 2003)
Glombowski, F., *Frontiers of Terror: The Fate of Schlageter and His Comrades* (London, 1934)
Gobetti, A. (transl. J. Alano), *Partisan Diary: A Woman's Life in the Italian Resistance* (Oxford, 1956, 2014)
Grady, S., *Gardens of Stone: My Boyhood in the French Resistance* (London, 2013)
Green Anarchist (ed.), *'Industrial Society and Its Future': The Unabomber Manifesto* (Camberley, 1995)
Griffin, J., *Black Like Me* (Boston, 1961)
Guéhemo, J., *Diary of the Dark Years, 1940–1944* (Oxford, 1947, 2016)
Gumbel, E. J., *Vier Jahre politischer Mord* (Berlin, 1922)
Haffner, S., *Defying Hitler* (London, 2002, 2003)
Harcourt, F. (ed.), *Memoirs of Madame de la Tour de la Pin* (London, 1969, 1985)
Hasselbach, I., *Führer-Ex: Memoirs of a Former Neo-Nazi* (London, 1996)
Hergé, *King Ottokar's Sceptre* (London, 1958)
Hitler, A. (transl. R. Manheim), *Mein Kampf* (London, 1969, 1992)
Hoelz, M., *Vom 'Weissen Kreuz' zur roten Fahne: Jugend-, Kampf- und Zuchthauserlebnisse* (Berlin, 1929, 2019)
Hoffman, A., *Steal This Book* (New York, 1996, 2002)
Huntley, B. (and H. Edgington), *Bomb Squad: My War Against the Terrorists* (London, 1977)
Jędruszak, T. and Z. Kolankowski (eds), *Żrodła do dziejów powstań Śląskich* (3 vols, Wrocław, 1963–1974), Vol. 2
Jünger, E. *Storm of Steel* (London, 1920, 2004)
Kellner, R. S. (ed.), *My Opposition: The Diary of Friedrich Kellner—A German Against the Third Reich* (Cambridge, 2018)
Kempka, E., *I Was Hitler's Chauffeur* (Barnsley, 2010, 2012)
Kennedy, S., *I rode with the Ku Klux Klan* (London, 1954)
Kessler, H., *Diaries of a Cosmopolitan, 1918–1937* (London, 1961, 1971)
King, M. L. Jnr, *Why We Can't Wait* (New York, 1963, 1964)
Knowles, J. (ed.), *The Channel Tunnel and Public Opinion* (London, 1883)
Lahr, J. (ed.), *The Diaries of Kenneth Tynan* (London, 2001)
Lerner, J., *Swords in the Hands of Children: Reflections of an American Revolutionary* (New York, 2017)
Levi, P., *The Drowned and the Saved* (London, 1986, 1988)
Linder, L. (ed.), *The Journal of Beatrix Potter: from 1881 to 1897* (London, 1966)
Londonderry Riot Inquiry Commission, *Report of a Commission Appointed to Inquire into Certain Disturbances Which Took Place in the City of Londonderry on the 1st November 1883* (Dublin, 1884)

McCann, E., *War and an Irish Town* (Harmondsworth, 1974)
McGonagall, W., *Poetic Gems: William McGonagall, Poet and Tragedian* (London, 1975)
Marighella, C., *Mini-Manual of the Urban Guerrilla* (Montreal, 2002)
Marx, K., *The Civil War in France* (Moscow, 1948, 1977)
Massu, J., *La vraie battaile d'Alger* (Paris, 1971)
Millar, G., *Maquis: Personal Record of Sabotage, Escape and Guerrilla Warfare in Occupied France* (London, 1945, 1956)
Morrell, S., *I Saw the Crucifixion* (London, 1938)
Mosley, N., *Rules of the Game/Beyond the Pale: Memoirs of Sir Oswald Mosley and Family* (London, 1998)
National Commission on Terrorist Attacks upon the United States, *9/11 Commission Report* (New York, 2004)
Nixon, R., *The Memoirs of Richard Nixon* (London, 1978)
Obama, M., *Becoming* (New York, 2018)
O'Brien, W., 'Was Fenianism ever formidable?', *Contemporary Review*, 1897
O'Callaghan, E., *Belfast Days: A 1972 Teenage Diary* (Sallins, 2014)
Orwell, G., *Homage to Catalonia* (London, 1938, 1989)
O'Shea, P., *Voices and the Sound of Drums: An Irish Autobiography* (Belfast, 1981)
Pankhurst, E., *Suffragette: My Own Story* (1914, 2016)
Paul, E., *The Last Time I Saw Paris* (London, 1942, 2011)
Pottle, F. (ed.), *Boswell's London Journal 1762–3* (London, 1950, 1966)
Reck-Malleczewen, F., *Diary of a Man in Despair* (London, 2000, 2001)
Lord Rossmore, *Things I can Tell* (London, 1912)
Roth, J., *What I Saw: Reports from Berlin 1920–33* (London, 1996, 2004)
Rudd, M., *Underground: My Life with SDS and the Weathermen* (New York, 2009, 2010)
Salerno, S. (ed.), *Direct Action and Sabotage: Three Classic IWW Pamphlets from the 1910s* (Oakland, 2014)
Scarman, L., *The Scarman Report: The Brixton Disorders 10–12 April 1981* (London, 1981, 1982)
Scarman, L., *Violence and Civil Disturbances in Northern Ireland in 1969*, Report of the Tribunal of Inquiry, Vol. I (Belfast, 1972)
Serge, V. (transl. P. Sedgwick and G. Paizis), *Memoirs of a Revolutionary* (New York, 1951, 2012)
Sorel, G., *Reflections on Violence* (Cambridge, 1999, 2012)
Smollet, T., *Travels Through France and Italy* (Oxford, 1979, 1992)
Stern, S., *With the Weathermen: the Personal Journey of a Revolutionary Woman* (Piscataway, NJ, 2007)
Stevenson, R. L. and F. Van De Grift Stevenson, *The Dynamiter* (London, 1885, 1914)
Stirling, A. M. W. (ed.), *The Richmond Papers* (London, 1926)
Styles, G., *Bombs Have No Pity: My War Against Terrorism* (London, 1975)
Taylor, F. (ed.), *The Goebbels Diaries, 1939–1941* (London, 1982)
Theroux, P., *Deep South* (London, 2015, 2016)
Trevor-Roper, H. (ed.), *Hitler's Table Talk: Hitler's Conversations recorded by Martin Bormann* (Oxford, 1988)
Trotsky, L., *1905* (Harmondsworth, 1971, 1973)
Turner, T., *The Diary of a Georgian Shopkeeper* (Oxford, 1925, 1979)
Twain, M., *The Innocents* (New York, 1869, 1966)
United States of America Congressional Record, *Proceedings and Debates on the 83rd Congress*, 2nd Session, Vol. 100, Part 2, Feb. 8, 1954 to March 8, 1954 (Washington, 1954)

U.S. Riot Commission Report, *Report of the National Advisory Commission on Civil Disorders* (New York, 1968)
Von Goethe, J., *The Sorrows of Young Werther* (London, 1774, 1989)
Werth, A., *The Last Days of Paris* (London, 1940)
Werth, L., *33 Days* (London, 1992, 2015)
Wilkerson, C., *Flying Close to the Sun: My Life and Times as a Weatherman* (New York, 2007, 2011)
Wilson, T. (ed.), *Political Diaries of C.P. Scott, 1911–1928* (London, 1970)
Wolf, M., *Memoirs of a Spymaster* (London, 1997, 1998)
Woodforde, J., *The Diary of a Country Parson, 1758–1802* (Oxford, 1929, 1978)

PRINTED SECONDARY WORKS

Abel, D., *Channel Underground* (London, 1961)
Abrahms, M., 'Why Terrorism Does Not Work', *International Security* 31 (Fall 2006)
Abrahms, M., 'The Political Effectiveness of Terrorism Revisited', *Comparative Political Studies*, 45 (March 2012)
Ackerman, P. and C. Kruegler, *Strategies of Nonviolent Conflict: The Dynamics of People Power in the Twentieth Century* (Westport, 1994)
Adams, T. I., *The Sabotage Plan: The IRA Bombing Campaign in England 1939–1940* (Titchfield, 2010)
Alcock, A. E., 'Terrorism in South Tyrol' in P. Janke (ed.), *Terrorism and Democracy: Some Contemporary Cases* (London, 1992)
Alexander, Y., 'Age of Terror' in W. P. Lineberry (ed.), *The Struggle Against Terrorism* (New York, 1977)
Alexander, Y. and D. Pluchinsky, *Europe's Red Terrorists: The Fighting Communist Organizations* (Abingdon, 1992, 2005)
Alexander, Y. and J. Sinai, *Terrorism: the PLO connection* (New York, 1989)
Allchorn, W. (ed.), *Tracking the Rise of the Radical Right Globally* (Stuttgart, 2019)
Anderson, M., *In Thrall to Political Change: Police and Gendarmerie in France* (Oxford, 2011)
Anderson, M. S., *War and Society in Europe of the Old Regime, 1618–1789* (Stroud, 1988, 1998)
Andrew, C., *The Defence of the Realm: the Authorized History of MI5* (London, 2009, 2010)
Andrew, C., *The Secret World: A History of Intelligence* (London, 2018)
Anemone, A. (ed.), *Just Assassins: The Culture of Terrorism in Russia* (Evanston, Illinois, 2010)
Anonymous (transl. J. Messinger), *The Death of Dollfuss: An Official History of the Revolt of July, 1934, in Austria* (London, 1935)
Archbold, R. and K. Marschall, *Hindenburg: An Illustrated History* (London, 1994)
Argomaniz, J., 'A "coordination nightmare"?' in C. Kaunert et al. (eds), *European Homeland Security: A European Strategy in the Making?* (London, 2012)
Argomaniz, J., *The EU and Counter-Terrorism: Politics, Polity and Policies after 9/11* (London, 2012)
Aron, R., *Histoire de L'Épuration* (Paris, 1967)
Arthur, M., *Lost Voices of The Edwardians* (London, 2006, 2007)
Ashkenazi, M. (et al., eds), 'Manpads: A Terrorist Threat to Civilian Aviation?', Brief 47, Bonn International Center for Conversion (Bonn, 2013)
Atkinson, D., *Rise up Women! The Remarkable Lives of the Suffragettes* (London, 2018)
Aust, S., *The Baader Meinhof Complex* (London, 2008)

Avrich, P., *The Haymarket Tragedy* (Princeton, 1984)
Bach Jensen, R., 'Daggers, Rifles and Dynamite: Anarchist Terrorism in Nineteenth Century Europe', *Terrorism and Political Violence*, Vol. 16, No. 1 (2004), 116–53
Bach Jensen, R., *The Battle Against Anarchist Terrorism: An International History, 1878–1934* (Cambridge, 2014)
Bach Jensen, R., 'Anarchist Terrorism in Europe/World' in R. Law (ed.), *The Routledge History of Terrorism* (Abingdon, 2015)
Baird, D. A., 'Is Low-Tech Terrorism an Emerging Strategy in Western Europe? Analysing Patterns of Knife and Vehicle Attacks', University of St Andrews MA thesis (2018)
Ball, S., 'The Assassination Culture of Imperial Britain, 1909–1979', *The Historical Journal*, Vol. 56, No. 1 (March 2013)
Bardon, J., *A History of Ulster* (Belfast, 1992, 1994)
Barnaby, W., *The Plague Makers: The Secret World of Biological Warfare* (London, 1999)
Batović, A., *The Croatian Spring: Nationalism, Repression and Foreign Policy under Tito* (London, 2017)
Bauer, Y., 'From Cooperation to Resistance: The Haganah 1938–1946,' *Middle Eastern Studies*, Vol. 2, No. 3 (1966)
Baum, P., *Violence in the Skies: A History of Aircraft Hijacking and Bombing* (Chichester, 2016)
Bauman, Z., *Modernity and the Holocaust* (Cambridge, 1991, 2006)
Bauman, Z., 'Soil, blood and identity', *The Sociological Review* (1992)
Bauman, Z., *Liquid Modernity* (Cambridge, 2000, 2012)
Bauman, Z., *The Individualized Society* (Cambridge, 2001, 2005)
Bearman, C. 'An Examination of Suffragette Violence', *English Historical Review*, Vol. CXX, No. 486 (April 2005)
Becker, J., *Hitler's Children: the Story of the Baader-Meinhof Gang* (London, 1978)
Becker, M., 'Explaining Lone Wolf Target Selection in the United States', *Studies in Conflict and Terrorism*, Vol. 37, No. 11 (2014)
Beckett, A., *When the Lights Went out: Britain in the Seventies* (London, 2009)
Behan, T., *The Italian Resistance: Fascists, Guerrillas and Allies* (London, 2009)
Bell, L., *Sabotage* (London, 1957, 1959)
Bentley, M., *Lord Salisbury's World: Conservative Environments in Late Victorian Britain* (Cambridge, 2001)
Bergengren, E., *Alfred Nobel* (London, 1962)
Berman, M., *All that is Solid Melts into Air: the Experience of Modernity* (London, 1982, 2010)
Bessel, R., *Political Violence and the Rise of Nazism: The Storm Troopers in Eastern Germany, 1925–1934* (New Haven, 1984)
Bessel, R., *Germany after the First World War* (Oxford, 1993, 2002)
Bessner, D. and M. Stauch, 'Karl Heinzen and the Intellectual Origins of Modern Terror', *Terrorism and Political Violence*, Vol. 22, No. 2 (April–June 2010)
Betz, H., 'What's the Matter with Saxony' in W. Allchorn (ed.), *Tracking the Rise of the Radical Right Globally* (Stuttgart, 2019)
Bew, P., *The Politics of Enmity 1789–2006* (Oxford, 2007)
Biały, F., *Niemieckie Ochotnicze formacje zbrojne na Śląsku, 1918–1923* (Katowice, 1976)
Biddle, T. D., 'Anglo-American Strategic Bombing, 1940–1945' in J. Ferris and E. Mawdsley (eds), *Fighting the War*, Vol. I (Cambridge, 2015)
Billington, J. H., *Fire in the Minds of Men: Origins of the Revolutionary Faith* (Abingdon, 1980, 2017)

Bjørgo, T. (ed.), *Terror from the Extreme Right* (London, 1995)

Black, J., *George III: America's Last King* (London, 2006)

Blackbourn, D., *The Fontana History of Germany 1780–1918: The Long Nineteenth Century* (London, 1997)

Blinkhorn, M., 'Avoiding the Ultimate Act of Violence: Mediterranean Bandits and Kidnapping for Ransom, 1815–1914' in S. Carroll (ed.), *Cultures of Violence: Interpersonal Violence in Historical Perspective* (Basingstoke, 2007)

Blok, A., *Honour and Violence* (Cambridge, 2001)

Bloom, C., *Riot City: Protest and Rebellion in the Capital* (Basingstoke, 2012)

Bloom, M., *Dying to Kill: The Allure of Suicide Terror* (New York, 2005)

Bloom, M., 'Dying to Kill: Motivations for Suicide Terrorism' in A. Pedhazur (ed.), *Root Causes of Suicide Terrorism: The Globalization of Martyrdom* (London, 2006, 2009)

Bloom, S. F.,'The "Withering Away" of the State', *Journal of the History of Ideas*, Vol. 7, No. 1 (January 1946)

Blumenau, B., *The United Nations and Terrorism: Germany, Multilateralism, and Antiterrorism Efforts in the 1970s* (London, 2014)

Blumenau, B., 'Unholy Alliance: The Connection between the East German Stasi and the Right-Wing Terrorist Odfried Hepp', *Studies in Conflict and Terrorism* (2018)

Bo Kaspersen, L. and J. Strandsbjerg (eds), *Does War Make States? Investigations of Charles Tilly's Historical Sociology* (Cambridge, 2017)

Bosworth, R. J. B., *Mussolini's Italy: Life Under the Fascist Dictatorship, 1915–1945* (London, 2005, 2006)

Botz, G., 'Political Violence, its Forms and Strategies in the First Austrian Republic' in J. Mommsen and G. Hirschfeld (eds), *Social Protest, Violence and Terror in 19th and 20th Century Europe* (London, 1982)

Boulton, D., *The Making of Tania Hearst* (London, 1975)

Bourdrel, P., *La Cagoule* (Paris, 1970)

Bower, T., *Klaus Barbie: Butcher of Lyons* (London, 1984, 1987)

Bowie, N. G. and A. P. Schmid, 'Databases in Terrorism' in: A. P. Schmid (ed.), *The Routledge Handbook of Terrorism Research* (New York, 2011, 2013)

Bowman, J. S., *The Cambridge Dictionary of American Biography* (Cambridge, 1995)

Bowman, T., *Carson's Army: The Ulster Volunteer Force, 1910–22* (Manchester, 2007)

Bowman, T., '"Ulster Will Fight"' in J. Crowley (et al., eds), *Atlas of the Irish Revolution* (Cork, 2017)

Bowyer Bell, J., *The Secret Army: The IRA 1916–1979* (Dublin, 1970, 1990)

Bowyer Bell, J., *Terror out of Zion: Irgun Avai Leumi, LEHI, and the Palestine Underground, 1929–1949* (New York, 1977)

Bowyer Bell, J., *A Time of Terror: How Democratic Societies Respond to Revolutionary Violence* (New York, 1978)

Bowyer Bell, J., *Assassin: Theory and Practice of Political Violence* (New Jersey, 1979, 2005)

Bowyer Bell, J., *The Irish Troubles: A Generation of Violence 1967–1992* (Dublin, 1993, 1994)

Boyd, D., *Voices from the Dark Years: The Truth About Occupied France 1940–1945* (Stroud, 2007)

Bradley, G. (with B. Feeney), *Insider: Gerry Bradley's Life in the IRA* (Dublin, 2009, 2011)

Braudel, F., *Civilization and Capitalism: 15th to 18th Centuries*, Vol. 1, *The Structures of Everyday Life: The Limits of the Possible* (London, 1983)

Brendon, P., *The Dark Valley: A Panorama of the 1930s* (London, 2000)

Brenner, A. D., '*Feme* Murder: Paramilitary "Self-Justice" in Weimar Germany' in B. B. Campbell and A. D. Brenner (eds), *Death Squads in Global Perspective: Murder with Deniability* (New York, 2002)

Broch, L., *Ordinary Workers, Vichy and the Holocaust: French Railwaymen and the Second World War* (Cambridge, 2016)

Broers, M., *Europe Under Napoleon 1799–1815* (London, 1996)

Broers, M., *Napoleon's Other War: Bandits, Rebels and their Pursuers in the Age of Revolutions* (Oxford, 2010)

Brooke, N., *Terrorism and Nationalism in the United Kingdom: The Absence of Noise* (London, 2018)

Brown, W., *Violence in Medieval Europe* (Harlow, 2011)

Brunelle, G. K. and A. Finley-Croswhite, *Murder in the Métro: Laetitia Toureaux and the Cagoule in 1930s France* (Baton Rouge, 2010)

Bryan, J., *This Soldier still at War* (New York, 1975)

Buckmaster, M., *They Fought Alone* (London, 1958, 2014)

Buckser, A. S., 'Lynching as Ritual in the American South', *Berkeley Journal of Sociology*, Vol. 37 (1992)

Bull, S., *Trench Warfare* (London, 2003)

Burleigh, M., *The Third Reich: A New History* (London, 2000)

Burleigh, M., *Blood and Rage: A Cultural History of Terrorism* (London, 2008, 2009)

Burrough, B., *Public Enemies: America's Greatest Crime Wave and the Birth of the FBI, 1933–34* (New York, 2004, 2005)

Burrough, B., *Days of Rage: America's Radical Underground, the FBI and the Forgotten Age of Revolutionary Violence* (London, 2015, 2016)

Burton, R., *Blood in the City: Violence and Revelation in Paris, 1789–1945* (Ithaca, 2001)

Byman, D., *Deadly Connections: States that Sponsor Terrorism* (Cambridge, 2005)

Calvocoressi, P. and G. Wint, *Total War: Causes and Courses of the Second World War* (Harmondsworth, 1972, 1974)

Campbell, B. B., 'Death Squads: Definition, Problems, and Historical Context' in B. B. Campbell and A. D. Brenner (eds), *Death Squads in Global Perspective: Murder with Deniability* (New York, 2002)

Campbell, B. B. and A. D. Brenner (eds), *Death Squads in Global Perspective: Murder with Deniability* (London, 2000, 2002)

Campbell, J. K., *Weapons of Mass Destruction Terrorism* (Seminole, FL, 1997)

Campbell, M. W. 'The Making of the "March Fallen": March 4, 1919 and the subversive potential of occupation', *Central European History*, Vol. 39, No. 1 (March 2006)

Cannadine, D., 'The Context, Performance and Meaning of Ritual: The British Monarchy and the "Invention of Tradition", c. 1820–1977', in E. Hobsbawm and T. Ranger (eds), *The Invention of Tradition* (Cambridge, 1983)

Carlson, A. R., *Anarchism in Germany*, Vol. I, *The Early Movement* (Metuchen, NJ, 1972)

Carlton, C., 'The Impact of the Fighting' in J. Morrill (ed.), *The Impact of the English Civil War* (London, 1991)

Carr, G., *The Angry Brigade: The Cause and the Case* (London, 1975)

Carr, J., *Helmut Schmidt: Helmsman of Germany* (London, 1985)

Carr, M., *The Infernal Machine: A History of Terrorism from the Assassination of Tsar Alexander II to Al-Qaeda* (New York, 2006)

Carroll, A. and T. Toomey, 'The Capture of Brigadier General Lucas' in J. Crowley (et al., eds), *Atlas of the Irish Revolution* (Cork, 2017)

Carroll, S. (ed.), *Cultures of Violence: Interpersonal Violence in Historical Perspective* (Basingstoke, 2007)

Carus, W. S., 'Bioterrorism and Biocrimes: the Illicit use of Biological Agents Since 1900', Working Paper (1998, 2001), Center for Counterproliferation Research, National Defense University, Washington, DC

Castells, M., *The Information Age*, Vol. I, *The Rise of the Network Society* (Chichester, 1996, 2010)

Castells, M., *The Power of Identity*, Vol. II, *The Network Society* (Chichester, 1996, 2010)

Castells, M., *End of Millenium*, Vol. III, *The Network Society* (Chichester, 1998, 2010)

Caute, D., *The Left in Europe Since 1789* (London, 1966)

Caute, D., *'68: The Year of the Barricades* (London, 1988)

Cavendish, R., 'The Amritsar Massacre', *History Today*, Vol. 59, No. 4 (April 2009)

Chaliand, G., *Terrorism: From Popular Struggle to Media Spectacle* (London, 1985, 1987)

Chaliand, G. and A. Blin, *The History of Terrorism: From Antiquity to Al-Qaeda* (Berkeley, 2007)

Chapman, R. D. and M. L. Chapman, *The Crimson Web of Terror* (Boulder, 1980)

Charles, B., *Kill the Queen! The Eight Assassination Attempts on Queen Victoria* (Stroud, 2012)

Chenoweth, E., R. English, A. Gofas, and S. Kalyvas (eds), *The Oxford Handbook of Terrorism* (Oxford, 2019)

Chickering, R. (et al., eds), *The Cambridge History of War*, Vol. IV, *War and the Modern World* (Cambridge, 2012)

Chmiel, P., 'Zur Nationalitätenfrage in Ostoberschlesien im Spiegel der "Kattowitzer Zeitung" under des "Oberschlesischen Kuriers" ', *Oberschlesisches Jahrbuch*, Vol. 2 (1986)

Cimino, A., *Spree Killers: The World's Most Notorious Gunmen and their Deadly Rampages* (London, 2010)

Clark, C., *The Sleepwalkers: How Europe Went to War in 1914* (London, 2012, 2013)

Clark, G., *Everyday Violence in the Irish Civil War* (Cambridge, 2014)

Clark, G., 'Arson in Modern Ireland: Fire and Protest Before the Famine' in K. Hughes and D. M. Macraild (eds), *Crime, Violence and the Irish in the Nineteenth Century* (Liverpool, 2017)

Clutterbuck, L., 'The Progenitors of Terrorism: Russian Revolutionaries or Extreme Irish Republicans?', *Terrorism and Political Violence*, Vol. 16, No. 1 (Spring 2004)

Clutterbuck, R., *Protest and the Urban Guerrilla* (New York, 1973, 1974)

Clutterbuck, R., *Guerrillas and Terrorists* (Ohio, 1977, 1980)

Clymer, J. A., *America's Culture of Terrorism* (Chapel Hill, NC, 2003)

Cobb, M., *The Resistance: The French Fight Against the Nazis* (London, 2009)

Cobb, R. C., *The Police and the People: French Popular Protest 1789–1820* (Oxford, 1970)

Cockburn, A., *Corruptions of Empire* (London, 1987, 1989)

Coleman, M., 'O'Donovan, James Laurence ("Jim", "Seamus")' in J. McGuire and J. Quinn (eds), *Dictionary of Irish Biography* (Royal Irish Academy, Cambridge, 2009)

Collins, L. and D. Lapierre, *Is Paris Burning?* (London, 1965, 1991)

Collins, L. and D. Lapierre, *O Jerusalem!* (London, 1982)

Collins, R., *Violence: A Micro-Sociological Theory* (Princeton, 2008)

Conway, M., *The Sorrows of Belgium: Liberation and Political Reconstruction, 1944–1947* (Oxford, 2012)

Coogan, T. P., *The IRA* (London, 1970, 1971)

Cook, R., *Sweet Land of Liberty? The African-American Struggle for Civil Rights in the Twentieth Century* (London, 1998)

Cooke, P., *The Legacy of the Italian Resistance* (Basingstoke, 2011)
Coolsaet, R., 'Anticipating the Post-Daesh Landscape', *Egmont Papers*, Vol. 97 (2017)
Corbin, A., *The Village of Cannibals: Rage and Murder in France, 1870* (Cambridge, MA, 1992)
Coren, R., *The Soviet Union and Terrorism* (London, 1984)
Corfe, T., *The Phoenix Park Murders: Conflict, Compromise and Tragedy in Ireland, 1879–1882* (London, 1968)
Cornils, I., '"The Struggle Continues": Rudi Dutschke's Long March' in G. J. DeGroot (ed.), *Student Protest: The Sixties and After* (London, 1998)
Cowles, V., *The Defiant Swansong* (London, 1967)
Craig, A., *Crisis of Confidence: Anglo-Irish Relations in the Early Troubles* (Dublin, 2010)
Craig, A., 'Sabotage! The Origins, Development and Impact of the IRA's Infrastructural Bombing Campaigns, 1939–1997' *Intelligence and National Security* Vol. 25, No. 3 (2010)
Craig Wade, W., *The Fiery Cross: The Ku Klux Klan in America* (London, 1987)
Crenshaw, M., 'The Causes of Terrorism' in M. Crenshaw, *Explaining Terrorism: Causes, Processes and Consequences* (Abingdon, 2011)
Crenshaw, M., *Explaining Terrorism: Causes, Processes and Consequences* (Abingdon, 2011)
Cronin, A. K., *Power to the People: How Open Technological Innovation is Arming Tomorrow's Terrorists* (Oxford, 2020)
Crowley, J. et al. (eds), *Atlas of the Irish Revolution* (Cork, 2017)
Cullen, D., *Columbine* (New York, 2009, 2016)
Dangerfield, G., *The Strange Death of Liberal England* (New York, 1935, 1961)
Davies, N., *God's Playground: A History of Poland*, Vol. II: *1795 to the Present* (Oxford, 1981)
Davis, M., *Buda's Wagon: A Brief History of the Car Bomb* (London, 2007)
Day, C. S., 'Political Violence in the Newry/Armagh Area, 1912–1925', Queen's University, Belfast, PhD (1999)
De Baroid, C., *Ballymurphy and the Irish War* (London, 1989, 2000)
Debord, G., *Society of the Spectacle* (London, 1992)
de Bruyn, D., 'A German Youth Brings the Red Army Faction to the Melbourne International Film Festival: review', *The Conversation*, 3 August 2015
DeGroot, G. J. (ed.), *Student Protest: the Sixties and After* (New York, 1998)
Delmer, S., *Weimar Germany* (London, 1972)
Delpard, R., *Ils ont vecu dans L'Algerie en guerre: Chronique d'un paradis perdu* (Montreal, 2012)
Densley, J. A., '"A Citadel of Crime": Saint Paul, Minnesota and the O'Connor System' in P. J. Windle (et al., eds) *Historical Perspectives on Organized Crime and Terrorism* (Abingdon, 2018)
Dickie, J., *Cosa Nostra: A History of the Sicilian Mafia* (London, 2004, 2007)
Diehl, J. M., *Paramilitary Politics in Weimar Germany* (Indiana, 1977)
Dierenfeld, B. J., *The Civil Rights Movement* (London, 2004)
Dobson, C. and R. Payne, *The Weapons of Terror: International Terrorism at Work* (London, 1979)
Doder, D., *The Yugoslavs* (New York, 1978, 1979)
Dolnik, A., *Understanding Terrorist Innovation* (London, 2007)
Downing, T., *1983: Reagan, Andropov and a World on the Brink* (New York, 2018)
Doyle, W., *The Oxford History of the French Revolution* (Oxford, 1989, 1991)
Doyle, W. (ed.), *Old Regime France 1648–1788* (Oxford, 2001)

Drake, C. J. M., *Terrorists' Target Selection* (Basingstoke, 1998)

Dray, P., *At the Hands of Persons Unknown: The Lynching of Black America* (New York, 2002, 2003)

Duncan, G. (et al., eds), *State Terrorism and Human Rights: International Responses Since the End of the Cold War* (Abingdon, 2013)

Duquet, N. et al., 'Armed to Kill: A Comprehensive Analysis of the Guns Used in Public Mass Shootings in Europe between 2009 and 2018', Flemish Peace Institute, 3 October 2019.

Ealham, C., *Anarchism and the City: Revolution and Counter-Revolution in Barcelona, 1898–1937* (Oakland, 2010)

Ebner, M. R., *Ordinary Violence in Mussolini's Italy* (Cambridge, 2011)

Edgerton, D., *The Shock of the Old* (London, 2006, 2008)

Edwards, P., *More Work, Less Pay! Rebellion and Repression in Italy, 1972–1977* (Manchester, 2009)

Eley, G., *Forging Democracy: A History of the Left in Europe, 1850–2000* (Oxford, 2002)

Ellerbrock, D., 'Gun Violence and Control in Germany 1880–1911: Scandalizing Gun Violence and Changing Perceptions as Preconditions for Firearm Control' in W. Heitmeyer (et al., eds), *Control of Violence: Historical and International Perspectives on Violence in Modern Societies* (New York, 2011)

Elliott, B. J., *Western Europe after Hitler* (London, 1984)

Ellis, J., *The Social History of the Machine Gun* (London, 1975, 1987)

Engene, J. O., *Terrorism in Western Europe: Explaining the Trends Since 1950* (Cheltenham, 2004)

English, R., *Armed Struggle: The History of the IRA* (London, 2003, 2004)

English, R., *Terrorism: How to Respond* (Oxford, 2009, 2010)

English, R., *Does Terrorism Work? A History* (Oxford, 2016)

Evans, M., *Algeria: France's Undeclared War* (Oxford, 2012, 2013)

Fairfield, L., *The Trial of Peter Barnes and Others (The I.R.A. Coventry Explosion of 1939)* (London, 1953)

Favretto, I., 'Rough Music and Factory Protest in Post-1945 Italy', *Past and Present,* Vol. 228, No. 1 (August 2015)

Fellman, M., *In the Name of God and Country: Reconsidering Terrorism in American History* (New Haven, 2010)

Ferguson, A., *When Money Dies: The Nightmare of the Weimar Hyperinflation* (London, 1975, 2010)

Ferguson, N., *Pity of War* (London, 1998, 1999)

Ferguson, N., *The War of the World: History's Age of Hatred* (London, 2006, 2007)

Figes, O., *A People's Tragedy: The Russian Revolution 1891–1924* (London, 1996, 1997)

Filiu, J., *From Deep State to Islamic State: the Arab Counter-Revolution and its Jihadi Legacy* (London, 2015)

Fitzhugh Brundage, W., *Lynching in the New South: Georgia and Virginia, 1880–1930* (Chicago, 1993)

Fitzhugh Brundage, W. (ed.), *Under Sentence of Death: Lynching in the South* (London, 1997)

Fleury, G., *Histoire secrete de l'O.A.S.* (Paris, 2002)

Foley, F., *Countering Terrorism in Britain and France: Institutions, Norms and the Shadow of the Past* (Cambridge, 2013)

Foner, E., *Reconstruction: America's Unfinished Revolution 1863–1877* (New York, 1988, 2014)

Foot, M. R. D., *Resistance* (London, 1976, 1978)

Ford, F. L., *Political Murder: From Tyrannicide to Terrorism* (Harvard, 1985)
Fowler, J. H., *Bombs and Their Reverberations* (London, 1939)
Foy, M., 'Michael Collins and the Intelligence War' in J. Crowley (et al., eds), *Atlas of the Irish Revolution* (Cork, 2017)
Fraser, A., *Mary Queen of Scots* (London, 1970, 1978)
Friday, N., *My Secret Garden: Women's Sexual Fantasies* (London, 1973, 1991)
Fuchs, K., 'Schlesien während des Ersten Weltkrieges', in C. Norbert and H. Brockmann (eds), *Deutsche Geschichte in Osten Europas: Schlesien* (Berlin, 1994)
Gaddis, J. L., *We Now Know: Rethinking Cold War History* (Oxford, 1997, 1998)
Gage, B., *The Day Wall Street Exploded: A Story of America in Its First Age of Terror* (Oxford, 2009, 2010)
Gall, S., *Afghanistan: Travels with the Mujahideen* (London, 1988, 1989)
Galtung, J., 'Violence, Peace, and Peace Research', *Journal of Peace Research*, Vol. 6, No. 3 (1969)
Gambetta, D., (ed.), *Making Sense of Suicide Missions* (Oxford, 2005, 2012)
Gambetta, D. and S. Hertog, *Engineers of Jihad: The Curious Connection Between Violent Extremism and Education* (Princeton, 2016)
Gammage, B., *An Australian in the Great War* (Cambridge, 1976)
Gardiner, J., *The Thirties: An Intimate History of Britain* (London, 2011)
Garrett, J., *The Triumphs of Providence: The Assassination Plot of 1696* (Cambridge, 1980)
Gearty, C., *Terrorism* (London, 1997)
Geifman, A., *Thou Shalt Kill: Revolutionary Terrorism in Russia, 1894–1917* (Princeton, 1993)
Geifman, A., *Death Orders: The Vanguard of Modern Terrorism in Revolutionary Russia* (Santa Barbara, 2010)
Gellner, E., *Nations and Nationalism* (Oxford, 1983, 1993)
Gellner, E., *Nationalism* (London, 1997, 1998)
Gelvin, J., 'Al-Qaeda and Anarchism: A Historian's Reply to Terrorology', *Terrorism and Political Violence*, Vol. 20, No. 4 (2008)
Gentile, E., 'Paramilitary Violence in Italy: The Rationale of Fascism and the Origins of Totalitarianism', in R. Gerwarth and J. Horne (eds), *War in Peace: Paramilitary Violence in Europe after the Great War* (Oxford, 2012, 2013)
George, J. and L. Wilcos, *American Extremists: Militias, Supremacists, Klansmen, Communists, and Others* (New York, 1996)
Gero, D., *Flights of Terror: Aerial Hijack and Sabotage Since 1930* (Sparkford, 1997)
Gerraghty, T., *Bullet Catchers: The Bodyguards and the World of Close Protection* (London, 1988, 1989)
Gerth, H. H. and C. Wright Mills (eds), *From Max Weber: Essays in Sociology* (London, 1948, 1977)
Gerwarth, R., *Hitler's Hangman* (London, 2011, 2012)
Gerwarth, R., *The Vanquished: Why the First World War Failed to End, 1917–1923* (London, 2016, 2017)
Gerwarth, R. and J. Horne, 'Paramilitarism in Europe after the Great War: An Introduction' in R. Gerwarth and J. Horne (eds), *War in Peace: Paramilitary Violence in Europe after the Great War* (Oxford, 2012, 2013)
Gerwarth, R. and J. Horne (eds), *War in Peace: Paramilitary Violence in Europe after the Great War* (Oxford, 2012, 2013)
Ghosh, D., *Gentlemanly Terrorists: Political Violence and the Colonial State in India, 1919–1947* (Cambridge, 2017)
Gietinger, K., *The Murder of Rosa Luxemburg* (London, 2008, 2019)

Gildea, R., *Barricades and Borders: Europe 1800–1914* (Oxford, 1986, 2002)

Gildea, R., *Fighters in the Shadows: A New History of the French Resistance* (London, 2015, 2016)

Gill, P., *Lone Actor Terrorists: A Behavioural Analysis* (Abingdon, 2015)

Gillespie, G., *Years of Darkness: The Troubles Remembered* (Dublin, 2008)

Gilpin, R. B., 'American Racial Terrorism' in Randall D. Law (ed.), *The Routledge History of Terrorism* (Abingdon, 2015)

Goebel, S., 'Cities' in J. Winter (ed.), *Cambridge History of The First World War* (Cambridge, 2014), Vol. II

Goldman, A., *The Lives of John Lennon* (London, 1988)

Goldstein, R. J., *Political Repression in 19th Century Europe* (London, 1983)

Graeber, D., *The Utopia of Rules* (London, 2015, 2016)

Graham, E. T., 'Bombs found in Belfast', *Journal of the Royal Engineers* (October 1922)

Graham, S., 'Cities as Strategic Sites: Place Annihilation and Urban Geopolitics' in S. Graham (ed.), *Cities, War and Terrorism: Towards an Urban Geopolitics* (Malden, 2004), p. 36

Graham, S. (ed.), *Cities, War and Terrorism: Towards an Urban Geopolitics* (Malden, 2004)

Graves, R. and A. Hodge, *The Long Weekend: A Social history of Great Britain, 1918–1939* (London, 1940, 1950)

Graysmith, R., *Unabomber: A Desire to Kill* (New York, 1997, 1998)

Greenburg, M. M., *The Mad Bomber of New York* (New York, 2011)

Greene, M. F., *The Temple Bombing* (London, 1996)

Greener, W. W., *The Gun and Its Development* (London, 1881, 1910)

Griffiths, J. C., *Hostage: The History, Facts and Reasoning behind Hostage Taking* (London, 2003)

Grimshaw, A. D., 'Urban Racial Violence in the United States: Changing Ecological Considerations', *The American Journal of Sociology*, Vol. LXVI, No. 2 (September 1960)

Grunberger, R., *Red Rising in Bavaria* (London, 1973)

Guelton, F., 'Technology and Armaments' in J. Winter (ed.), *The Cambridge History of the First World War*, Vol. II, *The State* (Cambridge, 2014)

Gumz, J. E., *The Resurrection and Collapse of Empire in Habsburg Serbia 1914–1918* (Cambridge, 2009)

Gurganus, A. E., *Kurt Eisner: A Modern Life* (New York, 2018)

Gurley Flynn, E., 'Sabotage: the conscious Withdrawal of the Workers' Industrial Efficiency' in S. Salerno (ed.), *Direct Action and Sabotage: Three Classic IWW Pamphlets From the 1910s* (Oakland, 2014)

Gusejnova, D., *European Elites and Ideas of Empire, 1917–1957* (Cambridge, 2016)

Häberlen, J. C., *The Emotional Politics of the Alternative Left: West Germany, 1968–1984* (Cambridge, 2018)

Hagenlücke, H., 'Germany and the Armistice' in H. Cecil and P. H. Liddle (eds), *At the Eleventh Hour: Reflections, Hopes and Anxieties at the Closing of the Great War, 1918* (Barnsley, 1998)

Hailbronner, K., 'Asylum Law Reform in the German Constitution', *American University International Law Review*, Vol. 9, No. 4 (1994)

Haines, K., *Fred Crawford: Carson's Gunrunner* (Donaghadee, 2009)

Hamm, M. S. and R. Spaaij, *The Age of Lone Wolf Terrorism* (New York, 2017)

Hampton, H. and S. Fayer (eds), *Voices of Freedom: An Oral History of the Civil Rights Movement from the 1950s through the 1980s* (London, 1990, 1995)

Hanley, B. and S. Millar, *The Lost Revolution: the Story of the Official IRA and the Workers' Party* (Dublin, 2009)

Hanser, R., *A Noble Treason* (New York, 1979)

Harrison, B., 'The Act of Militancy: Violence and the Suffragettes, 1904–1914' in M. Bentley and J. Stevenson (eds), *Peaceable Kingdom: Stability and Change in Modern Britain* (Oxford, 1982)

Hart, P., *The I.R.A. at War, 1916–1923* (Oxford, 2003, 2005)

Hart-Davis, D., *Hitler's Olympics: The 1936 Games* (London, 1986)

Hartnett, L., 'The Making of a Revolutionary Icon: Vera Nikolaevna Figner and the People's Will in the Wake of the Assassination of Tsar Alexandr II', *Canadian Slavonic Papers*, Vol. 43, No. 2/3 (June–September 2001)

Harvey, A. D., 'The Attempt to Assassinate the Bulgarian Cabinet, 16 April 1925', *Terrorism and Political Violence*, Vol. 4, No. 1 (Spring 1992)

Haupt, H. and K. Weinhauer, 'Terrorism and the State' in D. Bloxham and R. Gerwarth (eds), *Political Violence in Twentieth-Century Europe* (Cambridge, 2011)

Havens, M. C., C. Leiden, and K. M. Schmitt, *The Politics of Assassination* (Englewood Cliffs, NJ, 1970)

Hawranek, F. et al.(eds), *Encyklopedia powstań Śląskich* (Opole, 1982)

Haynor, A. L., 'Classical Sociological Theory' in K. O. Korgen, *The Cambridge Handbook of Sociology*, Vol. 1 *Core Areas in Sociology and the Development of the Discipline* (Cambridge 2017)

Hazan, E., *A History of the Barricade* (London, 2013, 2015)

Hemmingby, C. and T. Bjørgo, *The Dynamics of a Terrorist Targeting Process: Anders B. Breivik and the 22 July Attacks in Norway* (Basingstoke, 2016)

Henissart, P., *Wolves in the City* (London, 1973)

Henze, P., *The Plot to Kill the Pope* (London, 1984)

Hewitt, C., *Understanding Terrorism in America: From the Klan to Al Qaeda* (London, 2003)

Hibbert, C., *King Mob: The Story of Lord George Gordon and the Riots of 1780* (London, 1959)

Hibbert, C., *Benito Mussolini* (Harmondsworth, 1962, 1965)

Hippler, T., *Bombing the People* (Cambridge, 2013)

Hite, S., *The Hite Report on Male Sexuality* (London, 1978, 1981)

Hobsbawm, E., *The Age of Revolution 1789–1848* (New York, 1962)

Hobsbawm, E., *Age of Extremes: The Short Twentieth Century 1914–1991* (London, 1994, 1996)

Hobsbawm, E., *On the Edge of the New Century* (New York, 2000)

Hobsbawm, E. and G. Rudé, *Captain Swing* (London, 1969, 1993)

Hobsbawm, E. J., *Bandits* (London, 1969, 2001)

Hobsbawm, E. J., *Revolutionaries* (London, 1973, 1977)

Hobsbawm, E. J., 'Political Violence and Political Murder: Comments on Franklin Ford's Essay' in W. J. Mommsen and G. Hirschfeld (eds), *Social Protest, Violence and Terror in Nineteenth- and Twentieth-Century Europe* (London, 1982)

Hobsbawm, E. J., *The Age of Empire 1875–1914* (London, 1987)

Hobsbawm, E. J., *On History* (London, 1997, 2013)

Hobsbawm, E. J., *Globalisation, Democracy and Terrorism* (London, 2007, 2010)

Hoffman, B., 'The Contrasting Ethical Foundations of Terrorism in the 1980s', *Terrorism and Political Violence*, Vol. 1 (July 1989)

Hoffman B., 'Terrorist targeting: tactics, trends, and potentialities', *Terrorism and Political Violence*, Vol. 5, No. 2 (1993)
Hoffman, B., *Inside Terrorism* (New York, 2006)
Hoffman, B., 'Low Tech Terrorism', *The National Interest*, 130 (March/April 2014)
Hoffman, B., 'A First Draft of the History of the America's Ongoing Wars on Terrorism', *Studies in Conflict and Terrorism*, Vol. 38, No. 1 (2015)
Hoffman, B., *Anonymous Soldiers: The Struggle for Israel, 1917–1947* (New York, 2015)
Hoffman, B., *Inside Terrorism* (New York, 2017) Hoffmann, P., 'Hitler's Personal Security', *Journal of Contemporary History*, Vol. 8, No. 2 (April 1973)
Hofstadter, R., 'Reflections on Violence in the United States' in R. Hofstadter and M. Wallace (eds), *American Violence: A Documentary History* (New York, 1971)
Hofstadter, R. and M. Wallace (eds), *American Violence: A Documentary History* (New York, 1970, 1971)
Holbrook, D., 'Social Media and Terrorism' in D. Muro and T. K. Wilson (eds) *Contemporary Terrorism Studies* (Oxford, 2021) [forthcoming]
Holden, R. T., 'Contagiousness of Aircraft Hijacking', *American Journal of Sociology*, Vol. 91, No. 4 (January 1986)
Hopton, R., *Pistols at Dawn: A History of Duelling* (London, 2007)
Horne, A., *The Fall of Paris: the Siege and the Commune, 1870–1871* (London, 1965, 1968)
Horne, A., *The Terrible Year: The Paris Commune, 1871* (London, 1971)
Horne, A., *A Savage War of Peace: Algeria 1954–1962* (New York, 1977, 2006)
Horne, J. and A. Kramer, *German Atrocities 1914* (London, 2001)
Horowitz, D., *Deadly Ethnic Riot* (Berkeley, 2001, 2002)
House, J. and N. MacMaster, *Paris 1961: Algerians, State Terror, and Memory* (Oxford, 2006, 2009)
Hughes, R., *Barcelona* (London, 1992, 1996)
Hughes-Hallett, L., *The Pike: Gabriele D'Annunzio. Poet, Seducer and Preacher of War* (London, 2013)
Hulse, M., 'Introduction' in J. Von Goethe, *The Sorrows of Young Werther* (London, 1774, 1989)
Humble, R., *Famous Land Battles: From Medieval to Modern Times* (London, 1979, 1980)
Hutchinson, M., *Revolutionary Terrorism: The FLN in Algeria, 1954–1962* (Stanford, 1978)
Iviansky, Z., 'Individual Terror: Concept and Typology', *Journal of Contemporary History*, Vol. 12, No. 1 (1977)
Jackson, A., *Judging Redmond and Carson* (Dublin, 2018)
Jackson, J., *France: The Dark Years 1940–1944* (Oxford, 2001, 2003)
Jacobs, H. (ed.), *Weatherman* (Berkeley, 1970)
Jacobs, R., *The Way the Wind blew: a History of the Weather Underground* (New York, 1997)
Jalonen, J., 'From Underground Terrorism to State Terrorism and Beyond: The Question of Terrorism in the Finnish Jäger Movement during and after the First World War', *Terrorism and Political Violence*, Vol. 30, No. 5 (September–October 2018)
James, K., *Heathrow Airport: An Illustrated History* (Stroud, 2016)
Jamieson, A., *The Heart Attacked: Terrorism and Conflict in the Italian State* (London, 1989)
Janke, P. (ed.), *Terrorism and Democracy: Some Contemporary Cases* (London, 1991, 1992)
Jarossi, R., *The Hunt for the '60s Ripper* (London, 2017)
Jenish, D., *The Making of the October Crisis: Canada's Long Nightmare of Terrorism at the Hands of the FLQ* (Toronto, 2018)
Jenkins, B., 'International Terrorism: A New Kind of Warfare', The Rand Paper Series (June 1974)

Jenkins, B., 'Would-Be Warriors: Incidents of Jihadist Terrorist Radicalization in the United States Since September 11, 2001', Rand Occasional Paper (2010)

Jenkins, B. and C. Millington, *France and Fascism: February 1934 and the Dynamics of Political Crisis* (London, 2015, 2016)

Jenkins, R., *The Dilessi Murders: Greek Brigands and English Hostages* (London, 1961, 1998)

Johnson, N., *Negroes and the Gun: The Black Tradition of Arms* (New York, 2014)

Johnson, P., *The Birth of the Modern: World Society, 1815–1830* (London, 1991, 1992)

Johnston, J. A., 'Student Activism in the United States Before 1960: An Overview' in G. J. DeGroot (ed.), *Student Protest: the Sixties and After* (London, 1998)

Jones, I., *Malice Aforethought: A History of Booby Traps from World War One to Vietnam* (Barnsley, 2004, 2016)

Jones, M., *Founding Weimar: Violence and the German Revolution of 1918–1919* (Cambridge, 2016)

Jones, T., 'Anarchist Terrorism in the United States' in Randall D. Law (ed.), *The Routledge History of Terrorism* (Abingdon, 2015)

Joose, P., 'Leaderless Resistance and Ideological Inclusion: The Case of the Earth Liberation Front', *Terrorism and Political Violence*, Vol. 19, No. 3 (2007)

Julian, J., *France: The Dark Years, 1940–1944* (Oxford, 2001)

Kalyvas, S., *The Logic of Violence in Civil War* (Cambridge, 2006, 2008)

Kannafani, G., 'On the PLFP and the September Crisis', *New Left Review*, Vol. 1, No. 67 (May/June 1971)

Kaplan, J., 'Right Wing Violence in North America' in T. Bjørgo (ed.), *Terror from the Extreme Right* (London, 1995)

Kaplan, J., 'Leaderless Resistance', *Terrorism and Political Violence*, Vol. 9, No. 3 (1997)

Karch, B., *Nation and Loyalty in a German-Polish Borderland: Upper Silesia, 1848–1960* (Cambridge, 2018)

Karski, S., 'Das Deutsche Kattowitz von 1865 bis 1922' in H. Kostorz and S. Karski (eds), *Kattowitz: seine Geschichte under Gegenwart* (Dülmen, 1985)

Karvonen, L., *From White to Blue-and-Black: Finnish Fascism in the Inter-War Era* (Helsinki, 1988)

Kautsky, J. H., 'Centralization in the Marxist and in the Leninist Tradition', *Communist and Post-Communist Studies*, Vol. 30, No. 4. (1997)

Kelling, G. and J. Wilson, 'Broken Windows: the Police and Neighbourhood Safety', *The Atlantic* (March 1982)

Kelland, G., *Crime in London* (London, 1986, 1988)

Kenna, G. B., *Facts and Figures: Belfast Pogrom, 1920–1922* (Dublin, 1922)

Kenna, S., *War in the Shadows: the Irish-American Fenians Who Bombed Victorian Britain* (Sallins, 2014)

Kennedy, J. C., *A Concise History of the Netherlands* (Cambridge, 2017)

Kiernan, V., 'Foreword' in F. Engels, *The Condition of the Working Class in England* (London, 1845, 1987)

King, D., *Death in the City of Light* (London, 2011, 2012)

Koehler, D., *Right-Wing Terrorism in the 21st Century: The 'National Socialist Underground' and the History of Terror From the Far-Right in Germany* (Abingdon, 2017)

Koehler, D., 'Recent Trends in German Right-Wing Violence and Terrorism: What are the Contextual Factors behind "Hive Terrorism"?', *Perspectives on Terrorism*, Vol. 12, No. 6 (December 2018)

Koerner, B. I., *The Skies Belong to Us: Love and Terror in the Golden Age of Hijacking* (New York, 2013)

Kolinsky, E., 'Terrorism in West Germany' in J. Lodge (ed.), *The Threat of Terrorism* (Brighton, 1988)
Kopkind, A., 'The Radical Bombers' in H. James (ed.) *Weatherman* (Berkeley, 1970)
Korgen, K. O., *The Cambridge Handbook of Sociology*, Vol. 1, *Core Areas in Sociology and the Development of the Discipline* (Cambridge 2017)
Kracauer, S., *Offenbach and the Paris of His Times* (London, 1937)
Kramer, A., '"Law Abiding Germans"? Social Disintegration, Crime and the Re-imposition of Order in Postwar Western Germany, 1945–1949' in R. Evans (ed.), *The German Underworld: Deviation and Outcasts in German History* (Abingdon, 1988)
Kranzberg, M., *The Siege of Paris 1870–1871: A Political and Social History* (Ithaca, 1950)
Krugler, D. F., *1919: The Year of Racial Violence: How African Americans Fought Back* (Cambridge, 2015)
Kuromiya, H., *Freedom and Terror in the Donbass: A Ukrainian-Russian Borderland, 1870s–1990s* (Cambridge, 1998)
Lang, H. H., *The Berlin Police Force in the Weimar Republic* (University of California Press, 1970)
Laqueur, T., 'Festival of Punishment', *London Review of Books*, Vol. 22, No. 19 (5 October, 2000)
Laqueur, W., *Terrorism* (London, 1977, 1980)
Laqueur, W., *The Age of Terrorism* (London, 1987)
Laqueur, W., *No End to War: Terrorism in the Twenty-First Century* (New York, 2003)
Larabee, A., *The Dynamite Fiend* (Halifax, 2005)
Large, D. C., *Berlin: A Modern History* (London, 2001)
Laufer, D., 'The Evolution of Belgian Terrorism' in J. Lodge (ed.), *The Threat of Terrorism* (Brighton, 1988)
Law, R., *Terrorism: A History* (Cambridge, 2009)
Law, R. D. (ed.), *The Routledge History of Terrorism* (Abingdon, 2015)
Lawlor, D., 'Political Priests: the Parnell Split in Meath', *History Ireland*, Vol. 18, No. 2 (March/April, 2010)
Le Carré, J., 'Introduction' in *The Observer, Siege: Six Days at the Iranian Embassy* (London, 1980)
Lehr, P., '(No) Princes of the Sea: Reflections on Maritime Terrorism' in J. Krause and S. Bruns (eds), *Routledge Handbook of Naval Strategy and Security* (Abingdon, 2015)
Lehr, P., *Counter-Terrorism Technologies: A Critical Assessment* (Cham, Switzerland, 2019)
Leiken, R. S., *Europe's Angry Muslims: The Revolt of the Second Generation* (Oxford, 2012)
Leitch, D., 'Explosion at the King David Hotel' in M. Sissons and P. French (eds), *Age of Austerity, 1945–1951* (Harmondsworth, 1963, 1964)
Lennon, C., 'Dublin's Great Explosion of 1597', *History Ireland*, Vol. 3, Issue 3 (Autumn 1995)
Lesch, A. M., 'Prelude to the Uprising in the Gaza Strip', *Journal of Palestine Studies*, Vol. 20, No. 1 (Autumn, 1990)
Lèvi- Valensi, J. (ed.), *Camus at Combat* (Princeton, 2007)
Levy, Y., *Guerrilla Warfare* (Harmondsworth, 1941)
Lewin, R., *Hitler's Mistakes* (London, 1984)
Lewis, G., *Massive Resistance: the White Response to the Civil Rights Movement* (Hodder Education, 2006)
Leyton, E., *Hunting Humans* (London, 2001)
Liang, H., *The Berlin Police Force in the Weimar Republic* (Berkeley, 1970)
Liang, H., *The Rise of the Modern Police and the European State System From Metternich to the Second World War* (Cambridge, 1992, 2002)

Liddick, D. R., *Eco-Terrorism: Radical Environmental and Animal Liberation Movements* (Westport, 2006)
Lieberman, B., 'Nationalist Narratives', *Journal of Genocide Research*, Vol. 8, No. 3 (2006)
Lineberry, W. P. (ed.), *The Struggle Against Terrorism* (New York, 1977)
Littlejohn, D., *The Patriotic Traitors: A History of Collaboration in German Occupied Europe 1940/1945* (London, 1972)
Lodge, J. (ed.), *The Threat of Terrorism* (Brighton, 1988)
Loomis, S., *Paris in the Terror* (Harmondsworth, 1964, 1970)
Lottman, H. R., *The People's Anger: Justice and Revenge in Post-Liberation France* (London, 1986)
Lowe, K., *Savage Continent: Europe in the Aftermath of World War II* (London, 2012, 2013)
Lucas, C., 'Themes in Southern Violence' in G. Lewis and C. Lucas (eds), *Beyond the Terror* (Cambridge, 1983)
Lucas Phillips, C. E., (London, 1960, 1962)Luther, H., *Der Französische Widerstand* (Tübingen, 1957)
Luttwak, E. N., *Coup d'État: A Practical Handbook* (Harvard, 1968, 2016)
Lutz, B. J. 'Historical Approaches to Terrorism' in E. Chenoweth (et al., eds), *The Oxford Handbook of Terrorism* (Oxford, 2019)
Mac Bhloscaidh, F., 'Tyrone' in J. Crowley (et al., eds), *Atlas of the Irish Revolution* (Cork, 2017)
MacBride, I., 'Provisional Truths' in S. Pašeta (ed.), *Uncertain Futures: Essays About the Irish Past for Roy Foster* (Oxford, 2016)
McCleery, M., 'Randall Collins' forward panic pathway to violence and the 1972 Bloody Sunday killings in Northern Ireland', *The British Journal of Politics and International Relations*, Vol. 18, No. 4 (2016)
McConaghy, K., *Terrorism and the State: Intra-State Dynamics and the Response to Non-State Political Violence* (London, 2017)
McDermott, J., *Northern Divisions: The Old IRA and the Belfast Pogroms, 1920–1922* (Belfast, 2001)
McFarlane, K. B., *England in the Fifteenth Century: Collected Essays* (London, 1981)
McGarry, F., *Eoin O'Duffy: A Self-Made Hero* (Oxford, 2005)
McGee, O., 'The Irish Republican Brotherhood' in J. Crowley (et al., eds), *Atlas of the Irish Revolution* (Cork, 2017)
McGladdery, G., *The Provisional IRA in England* (Dublin, 2006)
McGuire, J. and J. Quinn (eds), *Dictionary of Irish Biography* (Cambridge, 2009), Vol. VII
McKeganey, N. and M. Barnard, *Sex Work on the Streets: Prostitutes and Their Clients* (Maidenhead, 1996, 1997)
McKinstry, C. M. (with Denise George), *While the World Watched: A Birmingham Bombing Survivor Comes of Age during the Civil Rights Movement* (Carol Stream, IL, 2011)
McKittrick, D. et al. (eds), *Lost Lives: The Stories of the Men, Women and Children Who died as a Result of the Northern Ireland Troubles* (Edinburgh, 1999, 2008)
Malaparte, C. (transl. J. Bertrand), *Technique du Coup d'Etat* (Paris, 1931)
Malešević, S., *The Sociology of War and Violence* (Cambridge, 2010)
Mankowitz, Z. W., *Life Between Memory and Hope: The Survivors of the Holocaust in Occupied Germany* (Cambridge, 2002)
Mann, M., 'The Autonomous Power of the State: its Origins, Mechanisms and Results', *European Journal of Sociology*, Vol. 25, No. 2 (1984)
Mann, M., *Fascists* (Cambridge, 2004, 2006)
Mann, M., *The Dark Side of Democracy: Explaining Ethnic Cleansing* (Cambridge, 2005)
Mann, M., *The Sources of Social Power*, Vol. 4, *Globalizations, 1945–2011* (Cambridge, 2013)

Manthe, B., 'Scenes of "Civil War"? Radical Right Narratives on Chemnitz', in W. Allchorn (ed.), *Tracking the Rise of the Radical Right Globally*(Stuttgart, 2019)
Marshall, B., *The White Rabbit* (London, 1952, 1954)
Martin, P., *The Rules of Security* (Oxford, 2019)
Mathewson, W., 'Incident in Holland' in W. P. Lineberry (ed.), *The Struggle Against Terrorism* (New York, 1977)
Matthew, H. C. G., *Gladstone, 1875–1898* (Oxford, 1995)
Mayer, A. J., The *Furies: Violence and Terror in the French and Russian Revolutions* (Princeton, 2000, 2002)
Mazarr, M., *Unmodern Men in the Modern World* (Cambridge, 2007)
Mazower, M., *Dark Continent: Europe's Twentieth Century* (London, 1999)
Mazower, M., *Hitler's Empire: Nazi Rule in Occupied Europe* (London, 2008, 2009)
Medick, H. and P. Selwyn, 'Historical Event and Contemporary Experience: the Capture and Destruction of Magdeburg in 1631', *History Workshop Journal*, No. 52 (Autumn, 2001)
Mehnert, K., *The Twilight of the Young: the Radical Movement of the 1960s* (London, 1976)
Merari, A. and S. Elad, *The International Dimension of Palestinian Terrorism* (Abingdon, 1986, 2019)
Merkl, P., 'Why Are They So Strong Now? Comparative Reflections on the Revival of the Radical Right in Europe' in P. Merkl and L. Weinberg (eds), *The Revival of Right-Wing Extremism in the Nineties* (London, 1997, 2005)
Merriman, J., *The Dynamite Club; How a Bombing in Fin-de-Siècle Paris Ignited the Age of Modern Terror* (London, 2009)
Michel, H., *The Shadow War: Resistance in Europe, 1939–45* (London, 1970, 1972)
Mickolus, E. F. (et al., eds), *International Terrorism in the 1980s: A Chronology of Events*, Vol. 2: *1984–1987* (Iowa State University Press, 1989)
Miller, M., 'The Intellectual Origins of Modern Terrorism in Europe' in M. Crenshaw (ed.), *Terrorism in Context* (University Park, PA, 1995)
Miller, M., 'Ordinary Terrorism in Historical Perspective', *Journal for the Study of Radicalism*, Vol. 2, No. 1 (Spring 2008)
Miller, M., *Foundations of Modern Terrorism* (Cambridge, 2013)
Miller, R. M., 'Lynching in America: Some Context and a Few Comments', *Pennsylvania History: A Journal of Mid-Atlantic Studies*, Vol. 72, No. 3 (Summer 2005)
Miller, S. G. (ed. and transl.), *Disorientating Encounters. Travels of a Moroccan Scholar in France in 1845–1846* (Oxford, 1992)
Miller, V. and K. J. Hayward, '"I Did My Bit": Terrorism, Tarde and the Vehicle Ramming Attack as an Imitative Event', *British Journal of Criminology*, Vol. 59, No. 1 (2019)8
Mitchell, A., *Revolution in Bavaria, 1918–1919: the Eisner Regime and the Soviet Republic* (Princeton, 1965)
Monaghan, R., '"Votes for Women": An Analysis of the Militant Campaign', *Terrorism and Political Violence*, Vol. 9, No. 2 (1997)
Moody, T. W., *Davitt and Irish Revolution 1846–82* (Oxford, 1981)
Moore, K. G., *Airport, Aircraft and Airline Security* (Boston, 1991)
Moose, C. A. (and Charles Fleming), *Three Weeks in October: The Hunt for the Washington Sniper* (London, 2003)
Morrill, J. (ed.), *The Impact of the English Civil War* (London, 1991)
Morris, B., *Righteous Victims: A History of the Zionist-Arab Conflict, 1881–2001* (New York, 1999, 2001)
Morrissey, S. K., 'The "Apparel of Innocence": Toward a Moral Economy of Terrorism in Late Imperial Russia', *The Journal of Modern History*, Vol. 84, No. 3 (September 2012)

Mosse, G. L., *Fallen Soldiers: Reshaping the Memory of the World Wars* (Oxford, 1990, 1991)
Mowat, C. L. (ed.), *The New Cambridge Modern History* (Cambridge, 1960, 1968, 1988), Vol. 12
Muchembled, R. (transl. J. Birrell), *A History of Violence* (Cambridge, 2012)
Mueller, J., *Overblown: How Politicians and the Terrorism Industry Inflate National Security Threats, and Why We Believe Them* (New York, 2006)
Mühlnikel, M., *Fürst, Sind Sie Unverletzt? Attentate im Kaiserreich 1871–1914* (Paderborn, 2014)
Mulholland, M., *Bourgeois Liberty and the Politics of Fear: From Absolutism to Neo-Conservatism* (Oxford, 2012)
Mulholland, M., 'Inventing the Working Class', *Dublin Review of Books* (June 2013)
Mulholland, M., 'Land War Homicide' in S. Paseta (ed.), *Uncertain Futures* (Oxford, 2016)
Mulholland, M., *The Murderer of Warren Street: The True Story of a 19th Century Revolutionary* (London, 2018)
Mullen, P. (et al.), 'The Role of Psychotic Illnesses in Attacks on Public Figures' in J. Reid Meloy (et al., eds), *Stalking, Threatening and Attacking Public Figures* (Oxford, 2008)
Mumford, L., *The City in History* (Harmondsworth, 1961)
Muro, D. (ed.) *When Does Terrorism Work?* (London, 2019)
Muro, D. and T. K. Wilson (eds), *Contemporary Terrorism Studies* (Oxford, 2021)
Murphy, P. T., *Shooting Victoria! Madness, Mayhem and the Modernisation of the Monarchy* (London, 2012)
Mussolini, V., *Mussolini* (London, 1973, 1975)
Nagle, A., *Kill All Normies; Online Culture Wars From 4Chan and Tumblr to Trump and the Alt-Right* (Winchester, 2017)
Naimark, N. M., 'Terrorism and the Fall of Imperial Russia', *Terrorism and Political Violence*, Vol. 2, No. 2 (Summer 1990)
Neitzel, S. and H. Welzer, *Soldaten: On Fighting, Killing and Dying* (London, 2011, 2012)
Nesser, P., *Islamist Terrorism in Europe: A History* (London, 2015)
Newark, P., *Firefight! The History of Personal Firepower* (London, 1989)
Nic Dháibhéid, C., *Terrorist Histories: Individuals and Political Violence Since the 19th Century* (London, 2017, 2018)
Nicholls, M., 'Strategy and Motivation in the Gunpowder Plot', *The Historical Journal*, Vol. 50, No. 4 (2007)
Noonan, G., *The IRA in Britain, 1919–1923: 'In the Heart of Enemy Lines'* (Liverpool, 2014)
North, J., *Killing Napoleon: The Plot to Blow up Bonaparte* (Stroud, 2019)
Northam, G., *Shooting in the Dark: Riot Police in Britain* (London, 1989)
Novaco, R. W., 'Automobile Driving and Aggressive Behavior' in M. Wachs and M. Crawford (eds), *The Car and the City: The Automobile, The Built Environment, and Daily Urban Life* (Ann Arbor, 1992)
Obert, J., *The Six-Shooter State* (Cambridge, 2018)
O'Connor, B., *Operation Lena and Hitler's Plots to Blow Up Britain* (Stroud, 2017)
Ofer, Y., *Operation Thunder: The Entebbe Raid. The Israelis' Own Story* (Harmondsworth, 1976)
Offord, D., *The Russian Revolutionary Movement in the 1880s* (Cambridge, 1986)
Oppenheimer, A., *IRA. The Bombs and the Bullets: A History of Deadly Ingenuity* (Dublin, 2009)
Oppenheimer, M., *Urban Guerrilla* (Harmondsworth, 1969)
Ousby, I., *Occupation: The Ordeal of France 1940–1944* (London, 1997, 1999)

Overton, I., *The Price of Paradise: How the Suicide Bomber shaped the Modern Age* (London, 2019)
Overy, R., *The Bombing War* (London, 2013)
Overy, R. J., *The Interwar Crisis, 1919–39* (London, 1994, 1995)
Owen, F., *The Eddie Chapman Story* (London, 1953)
Panayi, P., 'Racial Violence in the New Germany, 1990–93', *Contemporary European History*, Vol. 3, No. 3 (November 1994)
Pantucci, R., *'We Love Death as You Love Life': Britain's Suburban Terrorists* (London, 2015)
Pape, R., *Dying to Win: The Strategic Logic of Suicide Terrorism* (New York, 2005)
Parker, G., *The Military Revolution: Military Innovation and the Rise of the West, 1500–1800* (Cambridge, 1988)
Parker, G. and A. Parker, *European Soldiers 1550–1650* (Cambridge, 1977)
Parkinson, A., *Belfast's Unholy War: The Troubles of the 1920s* (Dublin, 2004)
Parkinson, A., *1972 and the Ulster Troubles* (Dublin, 2010)
Parry, D. L. L. 'Counter Revolution in Conspiracy, 1935–37' in N. Atkin and F. Tallett (eds), *The Right in France: From Revolution to Le Pen* (London, 2003)
Pavone, C., *A Civil War: A History of the Italian Resistance* (London, 2013, 2014)
Pedhazur, A. (ed.), *Root Causes of Suicide Terrorism: The Globalization of Martyrdom* (London, 2006, 2009)
Pernicone, N. and F. M. Ottanelli, *Assassins against the Old Order: Italian Anarchist Violence in Fin de Siècle Europe* (Champaign, Illinois, 2018)
Persico, J. E., *11th Month, 11th Day, 11th Hour: Armistice Day 1918: World War One and Its Violent Climax* (London, 2004)
Pfeifer, M. J., *Rough Justice: Lynching and American Society 1874–1947* (Chicago, 2004)
Phillips, D., *Skyjack: The Story of Air Piracy* (London, 1973)
Pincas, S. and M. Loiseau, *A History of Advertising* (Cologne, 2008)
Pinfari, M., 'The Orsini Attentat and Terrorist Assassinations', *Terrorism and Political Violence*, Vol. 21, No. 4 (October–December 2009)
Pinker, S., *The Better Angels of Our Nature* (London, 2011, 2012)
Pope, D. W. and N. L. Weiner (eds), *Modern Policing* (London, 1981)
Porter, B., *The Origins of the Vigilant State: the London Metropolitan Police Special Branch Before the First World War* (London, 1987)
Posen, B., 'The Struggle Against Terrorism: Grand Strategy, Strategy, and Tactics', *International Security*, Vol. 26, No. 3 (Winter 2001/02)
Pospieszalski, K. M., 'The Bomb Attack at Tarnów and Other Nazi Provocations Before and After the Outbreak of the 1939 War. Did Hitler Want the German Minority to Suffer Losses?', *Polish Western Affairs*, No. 2, 1986
Postgate, R., *How to Make a Revolution* (Yardley, 1934, 2018)
Preston, P., *The Triumph of Democracy in Spain* (London, 1986)
Preston, P., *The Spanish Holocaust: Inquisition and Extermination in Twentieth-Century Spain* (London, 2012, 2013)
Pridham, G., 'Terrorism and the State in West Germany during the 1970s: A Threat to Stability or a Case of Political Over-Reaction?' in J. Lodge (ed.), *Terrorism: A Challenge to the State* (Oxford, 1981)
Prochaska, D., *Making Algeria French: Colonialism in Bône, 1870–1920* (Cambridge, 1990)
Quinn, M., 'A History of Violence: A Quantitative Analysis of the History of Terrorism in New York City', *Homeland Security Affairs*, 12, Article 4 (September 2016)
Raeburn, A., *The Militant Suffragettes* (London, 1973)

Rapoport, D. C., 'The Four Waves of Rebel Terror and September 11' in C. W. Kegley (ed.), *The New Global Terrorism: Characteristics, Causes, Controls* (New Jersey, 2003)
Rasmussen, M., 'Terrorist Learning: A Look at the Adoption of Political Kidnappings in Six Countries, 1968–1990', *Studies in Conflict and Terrorism*, Vol. 40, No. 7 (2017)
Read, A. and D. Fisher, *The Fall of Berlin* (London, 1992, 1993)
Read, A. and D. Fisher, *Berlin: The Biography of a City* (London, 1994)
Rees, L., *The Nazis: A Warning from History* (London, 1997, 1998)
Renshaw, P., *The Wobblies: The Story of Syndicalism in the United States* (London, 1967)
Revill, J., *Improvised Explosive Devices* (London, 2016)
Richards, M., *After the Civil War: Making Memory and Remaking Spain since 1936* (Cambridge, 2013)
Richardson, L., *What Terrorists Want: Understanding the Terrorist Threat* (London, 2006)
Richie, A., *Faust's Metropolis: A History of Berlin* (London, 1999)
Rid, T., *Cyber War Will Not Take Place* (London, 2013, 2017)
Ridley, F. F., 'Syndicalism, Strikes and Revolutionary Action in France' in W. J. Mommsen and G. Hirschfeld (eds), *Social Protest, Violence and Terror in 19th and 20th Century Europe* (London, 1982)
Robbins, M., *The Railway Age* (Harmondsworth, 1962, 1970)
Robert, J., 'Paris, London and Berlin on the eve of the war' in J. Winter and J. Robert (eds), *Capital Cities at War: Paris, London, Berlin 1914–1919* (Cambridge, 2007)
Rodgers, D. T., *Age of Fracture* (Harvard, 2011)
Röhl, J., *Wilhelm II: Into the Abyss of War and Exile, 1900–1941* (Cambridge, 2014)
Rojek, C., *Celebrity* (London, 2001)
Romero Maura, J., 'Terrorism in Barcelona and its Impact on Spanish Politics 1904–1909,' *Past and Present* (Dec. 1968)
Rose, W. J., *The Drama of Upper Silesia* (Vermont, 1935)
Rosenberg, W. G., 'Paramilitary Violence in Russia's Civil Wars 1918–1920' in R. Gerwarth and A. Horne (eds), *War in Peace: Paramilitary Violence in Europe after the Great War* (Oxford, 2012)
Rosenfeld, A., '"Anarchist Amazons": The Gendering of Radicalism in 1970s West Germany', *Contemporary European History*, Vol. 19, No. 4 (November 2010)
Rosenhaft, E., 'The KPD in the Weimar Republic and the Problem of Terror during the "Third Period", 1929–33', in W. J. Mommsen and G. Hirschfeld (eds), *Social Protest, Violence and Terror in 19th and 20th Century Europe* (London, 1982)
Rosenhaft, E., *Beating the Fascists? The German Communists and Political Violence, 1929–1933* (Cambridge, 1983)
Rothschild, J., *East Central Europe between the Two World Wars* (Seattle and London, 1974, 1990)
Rottman, G. L., *World War II Allied Sabotage Devices and Booby Traps* (Oxford, 2010, 2014)
Roy, O., *Jihad and Death: The Global Appeal of Islamic State* (London, 2017)
Royle, E., *Revolutionary Britannia? Reflections on the Threat of Revolution in Britain, 1789–1848* (Manchester, 2000)
Rubin, B., *Revolution until Victory? The Politics and History of the PLO* (London, 1994)
Rudé, G., *The Crowd in the French Revolution* (Oxford, 1972)
Rudé, G., *The Crowd in History: A Study of Popular Disturbances in France and England, 1730–1848* (London, 1995)
Ruiz, J., *The 'Red Terror' and The Spanish Civil War: Revolutionary Violence in Madrid* (Cambridge, 2012, 2014)

Rumbelow, D., *The Houndsditch Murders and the Siege of Sidney Street* (London, 1973, 1988, 1990)

Runciman, D., *How Democracy Ends* (London, 2018)

Ruruep, R. (ed.), *Berlin 1945* (Arenhoevel, 1995)

Rutherford, J., 'Towards a new left conservatism', *New Statesman*, 28 June–4 July 2019

Sabrow, M., *Der Rathenaumord: Rekonstruktion einer Verschwörung gegen die Republik von Weimar* (Oldenbourg, 1994)

Sadkovich, J. J., 'Terrorism in Croatia, 1929–1934', *East European Quarterly*, Vol. XXII, No. 1 (March 1988)

Salt, J., 'Britain, The Armenian Question and the Cause of Ottoman Reform: 1894–96', *Middle Eastern Studies*, Vol. 26, No. 3 (July 1990)

Sánchez-Cuenca, I., *The Historical Roots of Political Violence* (Cambridge, 2019)

Sante, L., *The Other Paris: An Illustrated Journey through a City's Poor and Bohemian Past* (London, 2015)

Sayigh, Y., *Armed Struggle and the Search for State: The Palestinian National Movement, 1949–1993* (Oxford, 1997)

Schmid, A., 'Terrorism and the Media: The Ethics of Publicity', *Terrorism and Political Violence*, Vol. 1 (October 1989)

Schmid, A., *The Definition of Terrorism. A Study in Compliance with CTL/9/91/2207 for the U.N. Crime Prevention and Criminal Justice Branch* (Leiden, December 1992)

Schmid, A. (ed.), *The Routledge Handbook of Terrorism Research* (Abingdon, 2011, 2013)

Schramm, W., 'Communication in Crisis' in B. S. Greenberg and E. B. Parker (eds), *The Kennedy Assassination and the American Public: Social Communication in Crisis* (Stanford, 1965)

Seale, P. and M. McConville, *French Revolution 1968* (Harmondsworth, 1968)

Seirstad, Å., *One of Us* (London, 2015)

Selling, L. S., 'The Feebleminded Motorist', *The American Journal of Insanity*, Vol. 98, No. 6 (May 1942)

Seton-Watson, R., 'King Alexander I's Assassination: Its Background and Effects', *International Affairs*, Vol. 14, No. 1 (January–February 1935)

Setright, L. J. K., *Drive on! A Social History of the Motor Car* (London, 2002, 2004)

Shapiro, J. N., *The Terrorists' Dilemma: Managing Violent Covert Organizations* (Princeton, 2013)

Share, B., *In Time of Civil War* (Cork, 2006)

Sheatsley, P. B. and J. J. Feldman, 'A National Survey on Public Reactions and Behavior' in B. S. Greenberg and E. B. Parker (eds), *The Kennedy Assassination and the American Public: Social Communication in Crisis* (Stanford, 1965)

Shepherd, B. and J. Pattinson (eds), *War in a Twilight World: Partisan and Anti-Partisan Warfare in Eastern Europe, 1939–45* (Basingstoke, 2010)

Short, K. R. M., *The Dynamite War: Irish American Bombers in Victorian Britain* (Dublin, 1979)

Sick, G., 'Taking Vows: The Domestication of Policy-Making in Hostage Incidents' in W. Reich, *Origins of Terrorism: Psychologies, Ideologies, Theologies, States of Mind* (Washington, 1990, 1998)

Siemens, D., *Stormtroopers: A New History of Hitler's Brownshirts* (New Haven, 2017)

Singer, D., *Prelude to Revolution: France in May 1968* (London, 1970)

Singh, R., *Hamas and Suicide Terrorism: Multi-Causal and Multi-level Approaches* (London, 2011)

Singh, R., 'Suicide Terrorism' in E. Chenoweth, R. English, A. Gofas, and S. Kalyvas (eds), *The Oxford Handbook of Terrorism* (Oxford, 2019)
Skolnick, J. H., *The Politics of Protest* (New York, 1969)
Smith, D. J., *One Morning in Sarajevo: 28 June 1914* (London, 2008, 2009)
Smith, J., *Misogynies* (London, 1989, 2013)
Smith, W. C., 'Sabotage: Its History, Philosophy and Function' in S. Salerno (ed.), *Direct Action and Sabotage: Three Classic IWW Pamphlets from the 1910s* (Oakland, 2014)
Snowden, F. M., *The Fascist Revolution in Tuscany 1919–1922* (Cambridge, 1989)
Sperber, J., *The European Revolutions, 1848–1851* (Cambridge, 1994)
Steers, E., *Lincoln's Assassination* (Carbondale, IL, 2014)
Stern, J. P., *Hitler: The Führer and the People* (Glasgow, 1975)
Stevenson, J., *Popular Disturbances in England, 1700–1870* (London, 1979)
Stevenson, W., *90 Minutes at Entebbe* (New York, 1976)
Stewart, A. T. Q, *The Ulster Crisis* (London, 1967)
Stiles, T. J., *Jesse James: Last Rebel of the Civil War* (London, 1993, 2007)
Strange, S., *The Retreat of the State: The Diffusion of Power in the World Economy* (Cambridge, 1996, 1998)
Swaroop Sharma, V., 'War, Conflict and the State Reconsidered' in L. Bo Kaspersen and J. Strandsbjerg (eds), *Does War Make States? Investigations of Charles Tilly's Historical Sociology* (Cambridge, 2017)
Takagamli, S., 'The Fenian Rising in Dublin 1867', *Irish Historical Studies*, Vol. 39, No. 15 (May 1995)
Target, G. W., *Unholy Smoke* (London, 1969)
Thatcher, M., 'Foreword' in S. Gall, *Afghanistan: Travels with the Mujahideen* (London, 1988, 1989)
Thomas, N., *The Welsh Extremist: A Culture in Crisis* (London, 1971)
Thomas, T., 'The Second Battle of Chicago 1969' in H. Jacobs (ed.), *Weatherman* (Berkeley, 1970)
Thompson, E. P., *The Making of the English Working Class* (London, 1963, 1991)
Thompson, E. P., 'The Moral Economy of the English Crowd in the Eighteenth Century', *Past and Present*, Vol. 50, No. 1 (1971)
Thompson, E. P., 'Rough Music Reconsidered', *Folklore*, Vol. 103, No. I (1992)
Thompson, H., *Tintin: Hergé and His Creation* (London, 1991, 2011)
Thompson, K., *Under Siege: Racial Violence in Britain Today* (London, 1988)
Thorup, M., *An Intellectual History of Terror: War, Violence and the State* (Abingdon, 2010)
Tilly, C., *Coercion, Capital, and European States, AD 990–1992* (Malden, 1990, 1992)
Tilly, C., L. Tilly, and R. Tilly, *The Rebellious Century 1830–1930* (Harvard, 1975)
Tindall, G., *Célestine: Voices From a French Village* (London, 1995, 1996)
Tolnay, S. E. and E. M. Beck, *A Festival of Violence: An Analysis of Southern Lynchings, 1882–1930* (Chicago, 1993)
Tolnay, S. E., G. Deane, and E. M. Beck, 'Vicarious Violence: Spatial Effects on Southern Lynchings, 1890–1919', *American Journal of Sociology*, Vol. 102, No. 3 (November 1996)
Toobin, J., *American Heiress: The Kidnapping, Crimes and Trial of Patty Hearst* (London, 2016)
Torpey, J. C., *The Invention of the Passport: Surveillance, Citizenship and the State* (Cambridge, 2000, 2018)

Torrie, J. S., *German Soldiers and the Occupation of France, 1940–1944* (Cambridge, 2018)
Townshend, C., 'Terror in Ireland: Observations on Tynan's The Irish Invincibles and their Times' in P. Wilkinson and A. M. Stewart (eds.), *Contemporary Research on Terrorism* (Aberdeen, 1987)
Townshend, C., *The Republic: The Fight for Irish Independence, 1918–1923* (London, 2013, 2014)
Townshend, C., *Easter 1916: The Easter Rebellion* (London, 2015, 2016)
Trampe, G. (ed.), *Die Stunde Null: Erinnerungen an Kriegsende und Neuanfang* (Stuttgart, 1995)
Traugott, M., *The Insurgent Barricade* (Berkeley, 2010)
Tuchman, B., *The Proud Tower: A Portrait of the World Before the War, 1890–1914* (London, 1966, 1997)
Tuchman, B., 'Perdicaris Alive or Raisuli Dead' in B. Tuchman, *Practising History* (London, 1981, 1989)
Tucker, D., 'What is New About the New Terrorism and How Dangerous is it?', *Terrorism and Political Violence*, Vol. 13, No. 3 (2001)
Turner, C., *In Search of Shergar* (London, 1984)
Vander, J. W., 'The Klan Revival', *American Journal of Sociology*, Vol. 65, 1960
Van Ginneken, J., *Crowds, Psychology and Politics, 1871–1899* (Cambridge, 1992)
Varon, J., *Bringing the War Home: The Weather Underground, The Red Army Faction, And Revolutionary Violence in the Sixties and Seventies* (London, 2004)
Veilleux-Lepage, Y., *How Terror Evolves: The Emergence and Spread of Terrorist Technique* (Lanham, 2020)
Vernon, J., *Distant Strangers: How Britain Became Modern* (Berkeley, 2014)
Vizetelly, E. A., *The Anarchists: Their Faith and Record Including Sidelights on the Royal and Other Personages Who Have Been Assassinated* (London, 1911)
Vogel, R., *Deutsche Presse und Propaganda des Abstimmungskampfes in Oberschlesien* (Beuthen, 1931)
Vronsky, P., *Sons of Cain: A History of Serial Killers from the Stone Age to the Present* (New York, 2018)
Waddington, P. A. J., 'Swatting Police Paramilitarism: A Comment on Kraska and Paulsen', *Policing and Society*, Vol. 9 (1999)
Waite, R. G. L., *Vanguard of Nazism: The Free Corps Movement in Postwar Germany 1918–1923* (New York,1952, 1969)
Walker, T. and A. Gowers, *Arafat: The Biography* (London, 2003)
Wambaugh, S., *Plebiscites Since the World War: With a Collection of Official Documents*, Vol. I (Washington, 1933)
Warner, J., *John the Painter: The First Modern Terrorist* (London, 2004)
Warring, A., 'Intimate and Sexual Relations' in R. Gildea, O. Wieviorka, and A. Warring (eds), *Surviving Hitler and Mussolini: Daily Life in Occupied Europe* (Oxford, 2006)
Wasserstein, B., *The Secret Lives of Trebitsch Lincoln* (London, 1988, 1989)
Wawro, G., *The Franco-Prussian War* (Cambridge, 2003)
Webb, S., *The Suffragette Bombers: Britain's Forgotten Terrorists* (Barnsley, 2014)
Weber, E., *Action Française: Royalism and Reaction in Twentieth-Century France* (Stanford, 1962)
Weber, E., *Peasants into Frenchmen: The Modernization of Rural France, 1870–1914* (Stanford, 1976)
Weber, E., *The Hollow Years: France in the 1930s* (London, 1995)

Weiner, N. L., 'Policing in America' in D. W. Pope and N. L. Weiner (eds), *Modern Policing* (London, 1981)

Weingarten, A., *The Sky is Falling* (London, 1977)

Wexler, L., *Fire in a Canebrake: the Last Mass Lynching in America* (New York, 2003)

Whalen, B. and J. Whalen, *The NYPD's First Fifty Years: Politicians, Police Commissioners, and Patrolmen* (Lincoln, NE, 2014)

Whelehan, N., '"Cheap as Soap and Common as Sugar": The Fenians, Dynamite and Scientific Warfare' in F. McGarry and J. McConnel (eds), *The Black Hand of Republicanism* (Dublin, 2009)

Whelehan, N., *The Dynamiters: Irish Nationalism and Political Violence in the Wider World, 1867–1900* (Cambridge, 2012)

White, B. T., *Tanks and Other Armoured Fighting Vehicles, 1900–1918* (London, 1970)

Whitfield, S. J., *A Death in the Delta: The Story of Emmet Till* (New York, 1988)

Wilkinson, P., *Political Terrorism* (London, 1974)

Wilkinson, P., *Terrorism and the Liberal State* (London, 1977, 1979)

Wilkinson, P., *The Lessons of Lockerbie* (London, 1989)

Wilkinson, P., 'Taking on Terrorism: An Interview with Professor Paul Wilkinson', *Violence, Aggression and Terrorism*, Vol. 3, No. 3 (1989)

Wilson, A. N., *The Victorians* (London, 2007)

Wilson, P., *Women in 20th Century Italy* (London, 2010)

Wilson, P. H., *Europe's Tragedy: A New History of the Thirty Years War* (London, 2009, 2010)

Wilson, T. K., 'Why was women's suffrage so delayed?' Essay in author's possession (unpublished, 1993)

Wilson, T. K., 'Review: *IRA: The Bombs and the Bullets: A History of Deadly Ingenuity.* By A. R. Oppenheimer. Pp 387. Dublin: Irish Academic Press. 2009. €60 hardback; €24.95 paperback; *Years of Darkness: the Troubles Remembered.* By Gordon Gillespie. Pp 256. Dublin: Gill & Macmillan. 2008. €16.99 paperback', *Irish Historical Studies*, Vol. 36, No. 143 (May 2009)

Wilson, T. K., *Frontiers of Violence: Conflict and Identity in Ulster and Upper Silesia, 1918–1922* (Oxford, 2010)

Wilson, T. K., '"The Most Terrible Assassination that Has Yet Stained the Name of Belfast": The McMahon Murders in Context', *Irish Historical Studies*, Vol. XXXVII, No. 145 (May 2010)

Wilson, T. K., 'State Terrorism: An Historical Overview' in G. Duncan (et al., eds), *State Terrorism and Human Rights: International Responses Since the End of the Cold War* (Abingdon, 2013)

Wilson, T. K., 'Turbulent Stasis: Comparative Reflections upon Intercommunal Violence and Territoriality in the Israel/Palestine Conflict', *Nationalism and Ethnic Politics*, Vol. 19, No. 1 (2013)

Wilson, T. K., 'The Strange Death of Loyalist Monaghan, 1912–1921' in S. Pašeta (ed.), *Uncertain Futures: Essays About the Irish Past for Roy Foster* (Oxford, 2016)

Wilson, T. K., 'Terrorism and Resilience: An Historical Perspective' in D. Muro (ed.), *Resilient Cities. Countering Violent Extremism at the Local Level* (Barcelona, 2017)

Winner, L., 'Complexity and Human Understanding' in T. La Porte (ed.), *Organized Social Complexity: Challenge to Politics and Policy* (Princeton, 1975)

Wippermann, W., *Die Berliner Gruppe Baum und der jüdische Widerstand* (1981, 2011)

Witcover, J., *Sabotage at Black Tom: Imperial Germany's Secret War in America, 1914–1917* (Chapel Hill, 1989)

Wood, A. L., *Lynching and Spectacle: Witnessing Racial Violence in America, 1890–1940* (Chapel Hill, NC, 2009)

Woodcock, G., *Anarchism* (Harmondsworth, 1963, 1975)

Woods, R. B., 'Terrorism in the Age of Roosevelt: the Miss Stone Affair, 1901–1902', *American Quarterly*, Vol. 31, No. 4 (Autumn 1979)

World Committee for the Victims of German Fascism, *Das Braune Netz: wie Hiters Agenten im Auslande arbeiten und den Krieg vorbereiten* (Paris, 1935)

Wright, J., *Gustav Stresemann: Weimar's Greatest Statesman* (Oxford, 2002)

Yallop, H. J., *Explosive Investigation* (Edinburgh, 1980)

Ziglar, W. L., 'The Decline of Lynching in America', *International Social Science Review*, Vol. 63, No. 1 (Winter 1988)

Zuczek, R. (ed.), *Encylopedia of the Reconstruction Era*, Vol. II (London, 2006)

Zulaika, J., *Basque Violence: Metaphor and Sacrament* (Reno, NV, 1988)

Index

Note: Figures are indicated by an italic "*f*", respectively, following the page number.

For the benefit of digital users, indexed terms that span two pages (e.g., 52–53) may, on occasion, appear on only one of those pages.